THE GROUP IN DEPTH

THE GROUP
IN
DEPTH

Helen E. Durkin, Ph.D.

INTERNATIONAL UNIVERSITIES PRESS, INC.

New York

Contents

PART II: Group Psychotherapy

To my husband with love and
appreciation of his patient impatience

Preface

Group psychology has caught the interest not only of therapists and of practitioners who deal with human relations in a number of other fields such as education, social work, and industrial psychology, but of academicians engaged in teaching and research. It has also enormously aroused the curiosity of the intelligent layman. The peak of this interest seems to lie in group psychotherapy. Because of its multidisciplinary origins and mushroom growth, diversity of opinion and misunderstanding still becloud the fundamental issues in this relatively new discipline. It seemed timely to describe what I considered the three basic approaches to group psychotherapy. I tried to do so both in broad outline and in concrete detail. The material itself forced me to examine the relationship between group psychotherapy and the theories of group psychology. My intent is to give the average group therapist an overview of the whole field because I know very well that it is difficult to acquire a clear view of exactly what group therapists of different persuasions than our own are doing and, more especially, why they are doing it.

Besides acquainting the general reader with some of the difficulties and problems that group therapists have had to face and are still facing, I hope my survey will serve several practical purposes: (1) to give the inexperienced group therapist a sound basis for choosing the method best suited to his training, his personality, and the needs of his prospective patients; (2) to provide the more seasoned but busy practitioner with knowledge of theories and techniques other than his own; (3) and to offer the trail blazer a reasonably clear-cut base of theory and operations from which to take his departure so that he may pursue his visions free from the blur of misconception.

I hope, too, that this summary of the fairly established though still emerging principles of group therapy and group psychology will provide a source through which certain new and urgent needs in our expanding field may be met. Our decade is marked by a growing demand for ways of adapting the standard procedures of group psychotherapy to border areas. While intensive analytic psychotherapy may be the method of choice for adult neurotics and character problems, different levels of group therapy are urgently needed for other populations such as delinquents, hospitalized psychotics and so on. Public mental health programs with partly educational and partly therapeutic goals require other kinds of adaptations. The same holds true for the school management of certain not too neurotically involved learning problems, for the improved understanding of human relations in industry and in community problems. I believe, with Harris Peck (1961), that it is possible to work out some "viable hybrids" between group psychotherapy and training groups.

There is no question of the need and no point in arguing about whether to call these adaptations therapy or not. The needs of each group must be assessed, the appropriate group techniques delineated, and the requirements for training and practice established. If my work makes a modest contribution toward the development of such a program, I shall be satisfied.

Acknowledgments

There is no doubt in my mind that all my colleagues and my patients have contributed substantially to the thinking that has gone into the preparation of this book. It would be impossible to give credit to everyone who influenced it. However, some special appreciation is in order. The willingness of the supervisory staff of the Postgraduate Center for Mental Health to examine all points of view and to encourage independence of thought provided a stimulating atmosphere in which to develop my own thinking. Special mention is due to the broad vision of its Medical Director, Dr. Robert Lewis Wolberg, and to Asya Kadis who initially stimulated my interest in group dynamics.

My colleagues Jeanette Hirsch, Henriette Glatzer, and Edrita Fried have been unfailing in their readiness to exchange ideas and to offer warm support and counsel in puzzling situations. The latter two were generous enough to read and criticize parts of the manuscript.

I became convinced, as I tried to report on the methods of other therapists in the spirit in which they have worked, that such a project is full of pitfalls, and I am therefore most grateful to Drs. Hugh Mullan, Thomas Hora, and Milton Berger for their meticulous review of what I wrote about existential group psychotherapy. And my thanks go to Dr. Donald Jackson for providing me with so much of the literature on family therapy from the communications point of view, and for reading that chapter.

In gathering and evaluating the material on group dynamics, much of which had not yet been published, I received heartwarming support and stimulation from the many social scientists whom I came to know. Here, again, a few stand out. Professor Warren Bennis whose creative thinking, penetrating suggestions, and welcome enthusiasm meant much to me; Drs. Dorothy Stock and William C. Schutz whose brilliant research inspired me and whose generosity with their material and critical comment proved invaluable to my project. Drs. William F. Hill, Jack Gibb and many others contributed materially. I want to extend my warmest thanks to Drs. Lee Bradford and Chris Argyris for so cordially inviting me to join the training groups at Bethel and making it possible for me to participate in their theoretical discussions.

There is a fourth group of people for whose constant understanding and help I am very grateful. Geraldine Mindell's desire to make a contribution to group therapy was expressed by her devoted nurture of the manuscript through its many stages of development. Harriet Mason's persistent editorial efforts often challenged me to make explicit ideas which were not clearly enough expressed. She also coped in friendly tenacity with an author's stubbornness. And finally, Margaret Gordon who took all responsibilities off my hands while I was immersed in production, and who cheerfully handled many difficult situations with efficiency and diplomacy.

PART I

Group Psychology

Introduction

When I undertook to describe the major methodological approaches to group psychotherapy, I hoped also to clarify some of the misunderstandings among the different schools of thought in an attempt to dispel the conceptual confusion prevalent in the field and to pave the way, if possible, for the development of a generally acceptable group theory. The first serious problem arose in trying to decide just what was to be included under the heading of group dynamic therapy. The works of Foulkes and Bion and their colleagues were clear-enough examples, but that of the American social scientists, called group dynamicists, raised many questions. Were they really engaging in group dynamic group therapy? It was apparent that many analytic group therapists thought that they were claiming to do so, for they raised their voices in protest. When I set out to determine the facts, I found that some group counseling had been done on group dynamics principles and that leadership and human relations training groups, the purpose of which was not therapy but improvement of group competence, had become popular and were often confused by outsiders with group therapy, although the training leaders themselves were meticulous in making the distinction. Finally, a good deal of research was being done by the social psychologists in a group therapy context. This research resembled but did not purport to be a group therapy method.

3

In spite of the general impression to the contrary, there was almost no therapy actually being conducted on solely group dynamics principles by group dynamicists. From private correspondence with some of the leading social scientists, I learned that they did not acknowledge group dynamics therapy as an identifiable approach and that they were meticulous in distinguishing between their work and group therapy. Most of them remained primarily interested in research and those who became group therapists combined group dynamics with other therapeutic methods. Dr. Morton Deutsch stated in a public meeting at the Postgraduate Center for Psychotherapy that the two fields should not be confused and that group dynamics should not be substituted for therapeutic techniques.

The following excerpts from some of my correspondence will serve to reinforce the point.

Dorothy Stock, Assistant Professor of Psychology at the University of Chicago, wrote in a letter to me: "... in so far as I know there is no group in this country, certainly no coherent school of persons, who conduct what could be called 'American group dynamics group therapy.' There are, of course, a number of persons who are conducting group therapy, who are acquainted with the experimental and theoretical literature in group dynamics, and who recognize the existence and relevance of 'group dynamics' in therapy groups. But speaking from my own experience, I would guess that anyone who actually conducts group therapy does not and cannot restrict his interventions to group level phenomena but must also offer interpersonal and individual interpretations to the group." Stock goes on to indicate her own approach, which will be described in Chapter IV.

John R. P. French, Jr., of the Institute for Social Research, Ann Arbor, Michigan, wrote me: "I don't know of any 'group dynamics principles' which are based on solid research in group psychotherapy, so I cannot conceive of basing a therapeutic process on them alone. Principles based on research with other types of groups are often applicable but hardly adequate.... Such principles are more adequate for designing a program of human relations training, but even for this purpose they must be supplemented by a great deal of intuitive knowledge based on experience rather than on research. I do not know anybody doing therapy, training, or any other applied work with groups who thinks that all of his procedures are based on group dynamics research."

Further investigation proved that the social psychologists like the British psychoanalysts who engaged in group dynamic therapy were in every instance combining group dynamics with a reputed therapeutic process (usually a form of psychoanalysis). The significant distinction was this: they all considered the group forces as the primary source of group therapy. Group dynamics constituted, for them, the new and determining ingredient. This is what distinguishes dynamic therapy.

I Group Psychology and the Second Scientific Revolution

"We cannot escape our past: it continuously shapes our ideas and our actions."
Colin Cherry

The controversial issues of present-day group psychology and group psychotherapy reach back to Descartes' seventeenth century formulations.[1] His consistent emphasis on refining the methods for achieving abstract truth bore its best fruit in the empirical method. The widespread use of this fine instrument brought about a tremendous flowering of scientific knowledge, and enabled each branch of science to fill in many gaps in its information with proven concrete facts. The uniquely scientific values of each branch thus became established and was gradually freed from the restrictive hand of philosophy to whom they had thus far been handmaidens. One by one they began to set up their own separate departments in the universities. This was the first scientific revolution. It was three centuries later that discontent with the mechanistic philosophy that had been its unintentional result began to grow.

It was the physicists who flourished most in the age of mechanism, and it was they who laid the ground rules for the science of the era. The concrete data of physics lent themselves perfectly to the measurement, the quantification, and the experimental verifi-

[1] See also Chapter XVI.

6

cation which were the hallmarks of the new science. It was in order to do away with the lingering superstitious tendencies to anthropomorphize which had long interfered with the progress of knowledge, that they had ruled out the study of purpose and all subjects the facts of which could not be grasped by sensory perception. Only that which could be directly observed was considered "real" and therefore worthy of scientific investigation.

The social sciences, with their less tangible data and with goal-directed behavior to account for, were in a serious dilemma. They suffered from the new requirements for membership in the scientific fraternity. Sociology went its own way, but psychology self-consciously strove to follow the trend in order to be accepted. To do so they had to sacrifice the study of their most interesting and most uniquely human problems. The surface of human behavior could barely be scratched while there was a premium on quantification. The most intrinsic qualitative aspects of psychology were either ignored or pressed into an uncongenial mechanistic mold.

Nevertheless, in following the empirical trend, psychologists did lay the foundations for their science. British associationism gave us the great names of Locke, Hobbes, and Hartley, who developed the experimental method and the theory of associationism. According to the latter, the mind was a "tabula rasa" on which sensations could be registered and built up into patterns to account for all the phenomena of mental life. Associationism provided a framework for collecting and organizing knowledge. Its limitations did not show up for some time. In Germany empiricism brought forth an experimental physiology from which experimental psychology was born. Based on the distinguished work of Helmholtz, E. H. Weber, and Fechner, experimental psychology was systematized by Wundt and brought to America by Titchener. It seemed for a time to have provided the royal road to a bona fide scientific psychology.

Gradually the first high hopes for a quantitative scientific psychology subsided. The limitations enforced upon its subject matter by the mechanistic approach began to be keenly experienced. Most "academic psychologists" continued stubbornly on their course. They rejected Freud; but voices expressing dissatisfaction. criticism, and new ideas continued to be heard. One of the first came from Europe. Brentano began to shift the emphasis from structure to function, from substances to process. Külpe and his Würzburg School called attention to what the individual did "to or with" the sensations he passively experienced. Wertheimer, Köhler, and Koffka, with their gestalt psychology, built up the school that was perhaps the most influential in American psychology. From them also came Kurt Lewin's topological psychology.

But unfortunately American psychologists on the whole continued all too patiently to carry the bit of mechanism in their teeth. They waited for physics to lead the way. Fortunately the shortcomings of mechanism were also making themselves felt in other sciences including physics, and big changes were in the making which psychologists were eventually willing to follow.

By the second half of the nineteenth century the physical sciences had begun to show signs of failure to achieve their goal of systematic perfection. As physicists studied ever smaller and smaller units, they were swiftly carried to a point of no return. They soon found themselves dealing with submicroscopic units whose existence could not be grasped by direct perception even with the help of the microscope, but whose reality could nevertheless be proved mathematically and demonstrated by practical application of the new formulae. Increasing reliance on mathematics was the result.

Moreover the submicroscopic units sometimes failed to behave according to the established laws. A whole new principle for understanding the universe seemed to be needed. The old substantive hypotheses like those of ether and energy had to be replaced or revised. Certain paradoxes had presented themselves in terms of contradictory theories which served as a challenge to progress. For example Newton's corpuscular theory of energy and light had been challenged by Huygens, another seventeenth-century scientist. Huygens presented a wave theory of light which held that radiation or energy was absorbed or emitted in a continuous manner. For a hundred years longer Newton's theory remained the predominant one because it possessed that most important characteristic of a good theory, the ability to explain certain facts that Huygens could not. In the early nineteenth century Clerk Maxwell, working wholly by mathematical methods, came upon the distinction between invisible electromagnetic waves and visible light waves. According to his calculations they differed in length but traveled at the same speed. He inferred that light was also an electromagnetic phenomenon and thus refuted Newton's theory and backed up Huygens. Twenty years later Heinrich Hertz proved experimentally the existence of Maxwell's electromagnetic waves. From then on two opposing and seemingly contradictory theories of energy and radiation competed for acceptance. The newer one seemed to be the more conclusive and there was a tendency to discredit the corpuscular theory. The philosophers of science, however, contemplated the frustrating paradox with keen interest. It was Max Planck (1858-1917) who finally resolved it by proposing a basic principle, his quantum theory, which reconciled the two views. According to this, the energy of the body, as well as the radiation of light, were absorbed or emitted in infinitesimal but definite integral units called quanta. Thus the corpuscular unit theory and the continuous wave theory were reconciled, and the concept of the electromagnetic field made possible.

The formulation of field theory proved to be one of the most important concepts in physics since the time of Newton. It paved the way for quantum mechanics. Together with the discovery of a four-dimensional geometry, and the subsequent investigation of the problems of relationship between matter and field, and between mass and energy, it paved the way for relativity theory. They heralded a world-shaking revolution. Einstein took the crucial step by mathematically formulating the theory of relativity. This progression constituted the second scientific revolution. It incidentally provided a model for transcending the inevitable paradoxes of the group psychology of our day.

There was, of course, a vital repercussion in psychology and the social sciences which hinged first of all upon the change in perspective as to what was considered real. Just as the reality of the submicroscopic units of physics was confirmed, so was that of those larger, more complex social systems called groups. It no longer mattered that their existence could only be demonstrated by their results. Psychologists could, at last, also investigate with impunity the intangibles of human personality, including motivation. They could and did begin to accept Freud's depth psychology.

Moreover, the new physics soon provided psychologists with engineering models which proved more precise and illuminating than the older ones for the finer nuances of human behavior, i.e., Freud, as a pioneer in this movement, had to rely on the then current biological theories of instinct; while Lewin, coming later, could take advantage of the less controversial concept of needs and quasi-needs. Likewise, Freud had only the first law of thermodynamics (the law of the conservation of energy) with which to work out his theory of energy. Lewin selected as his model for a theory of energy the new physical concept of systems-in-tension. In translating field theory into psychological terms he was able to provide new methods suitable for analyzing the complexities of the data of group behavior, yet precise enough to win scientific approval. The discovery of the second law of thermodynamics provided other psychologists with a more modern and scientific, if less warmly human, theory of energy. According to this law, human beings could be perceived as subject to entropy (without the application of energy in the form of work, things tend toward chaos) and had at their command negative entropy, that is, the ability to use energy in the form of work to stem the chaos and maintain organization. The communications theorists, transaction psychologists, and a number of psychotherapists, like Ruesch and Bateson (1951), applied these concepts to their therapeutic work. This thinking was in line with growing belief in the reflexive nature of interaction. Altogether this new thinking was more congenial to Sullivanian phenomenological psychiatry than to Freudian concepts, which were made on a higher level of inference. Thus it happened that psychological science and psychotherapy moved so rapidly that while Freud's monumental contributions were still being increasingly accepted in the world of science during his own lifetime, he was already considered old-fashioned and even mechanistic! The fact that ego psychology has brought psychoanalysis up to date in many ways has not yet been fully appreciated by these critics.

Social psychology and sociology also responded rapidly to the revolutionary changes. Among the results was the intensive study of group behavior in which the group was defined as a system-in-tension. A whole new body of knowledge began taking shape. It covered a wide range of experiments and a variety of theoretical formulations which came to be known as group dynamics and was destined to have a strong impact on group psychology and group psychotherapy. (See Chapter XXI.) For almost two decades group dynamics as a discipline shared with group psychotherapy an interest in a common body of data, yet so dissimilar was their approach that they remained relatively indifferent to each other, traveling, it seemed, on different wave lengths. It was only when group dynamicists began to apply their learnings to the goal of changing individual behavior and were therefore impelled to investigate the role of personality dynamics in group formation that contact was made. Since then there has been a good deal of tension between them, and a number of new paradoxes challenge our investigation.

II What is Group Dynamics?

RESEARCH IN GROUP BEHAVIOR

For centuries sociologists had, in a philosophical vein, been pondering concepts about groups. In the eighteenth century[1] August Comte had foreshadowed a dynamic approach to groups with his concept of "telesis," according to which society was perceived as a self-directing whole. Emil Durkheim, at the close of the nineteenth century, had stressed the idea that the group, for which he used the term "collective representation," had an identity of its own which was more than a mere additive factor. Georg Simmel had, in the early twentieth century, emphasized the centrality of interaction (*Wechselwirkung*) in groups and written about the importance of group "belongingness" (*Gruppenzugehörigkeit*). Particularly meaningful for group therapy because it takes into account the concept of conflict was his application of the theory of "the relation of opposition between contraries." "Opposition," he wrote, "is a high tension state involving success or failure by a social group in

[1] This material is based, for the most part, on Bonner (1959) and Cartwright and Zander (1953, 1960).

12

transcending the barriers of its freedom of locomotion. When the conflict ends in the transcendence of the barriers, equilibrium is restored." Simmel's use of spatial concepts in describing group structure influenced Kurt Lewin to choose topological concepts in formalizing his system. Charles Cooley's writings in the first two decades of the twentieth century are often omitted from recent accounts of group dynamics—certainly they are rarely if ever mentioned by analytic group therapists—yet his ideas could be conceived as a bridge between group dynamics and Freudian group psychology, for Cooley pointed out that the origins of group structure are rooted in the family. It is in this group, he says, that the individual learns to feel vicariously the experiences of other persons, and to play the roles of others. In this process sympathy is developed, and persons closely identify themselves with one another so that what happens to one is the intimate concern of all members of the group. "It involves," he writes, "the sort of sympathy and mutual identification for which 'we' is the natural expression." Order is similarly achieved, in the small face-to-face groups investigated by social science, by role playing, by sympathetic perception of another's ideas and sentiments, and by consensus through collective problem solving (Bonner, 1959). Under the stimulus of the second scientific revolution, concepts such as these began to be formulated more exactly and put to the test of empirical research.

Social psychologists had also become increasingly concerned with the meaning of groups. It was they who contributed most in the area of methodology and theory building. A long period of deductive reasoning among them was followed by one of experimental investigation, in the course of which their standards became higher, their designs tighter, and their techniques more rigorous. The early laboratory studies, such as those by Triplett (1897),[2] comparing the performance of children working alone and working together with other children, and those of Moede (1920),[3] who studied experimentally the affects of having a number of people taking psychological examinations simultaneously, demonstrated that the influence of groups and individual behavior could be studied scientifically, and provided the first techniques, which were later developed and refined (Bonner, 1959).

[2] Referred to by Bonner (1959).
[3] *Ibid.*

One interesting controversy illuminates both the changing approach to the study of groups and the strangely recurrent fascination with their intangible supersummative aspects. In the twenties Allport (1924), on the basis of empirical studies, challenged the more theoretical conclusions of McDougall's (1921) "group mind" concept. Allport maintained that only individuals are real, while groups are abstractions from collections of individual organisms. But although he punctured the earlier vitalistic theories about groups, the concept of the group as an entity with a reality of its own persisted. The resulting paradox was transcended by the general acceptance of Lewin's statement that the group and the individual factors are merely different aspects of the same phenomena in constant interaction with one another. The group could now be understood scientifically as having a conceptual rather than a biological entity. Lewin's experimental work with the properties of groups did much to validate the concept.

Yet the more animistic notion of a group mind never died out completely. The organismic nature of the group continued to lend itself to speculation. The similarity of its organization to that of an individual led some group therapists to use such terms as group ego and group superego. They were immediately accused of animism. Recently the idea has had a revival. Schutz (1958b), a well-known group dynamicist, suggested that the individual be used as a model for the group, and that, in addition, the reverse would prove instructive. With tongue in cheek, he therefore entitled a recent paper "The Group Mind Revisited." In it he made an excellent case for the scientific practicability of his "model."

Reflecting the new attitude of the scientific revolution about the "reality of groups," and stimulated by the emerging techniques for their investigation, sociologists, anthropologists, and social psychologists in the United States began, in the late thirties, to collect a prodigious amount of empirical data on group behavior. Group dynamics was born. Each discipline which contributed to it followed its particular interests and goals, and developed its own methods and terminology. There were the field studies of the sociologists who were interested in a variety of institutions; the experimental investigation of artificial groups by the psychologists who wanted to find out what conditions affect group behavior; and the participant-observer techniques of the anthropoligsts who compared the behavior in groups living under a wide range of cultural conditions. Certain specific techniques played an appreciable role in establishing group dynamics as a science. One example consisted of the technical refinement of observational methods both by the child psychologists, who emphasized objectivity, and the anthropologists who insisted on participation. Objective behavioral categories were established and several trained observers employed so that the correlation between their judgments would be meaningful and their results could be verified by independent observers. Another technique consisted of the development of scientific rating scales both in simple forms (Likert, 1932), and in the highly complex forms of Thurstone (1928), who, on the basis of comprehensive study of its diverse problems, put psychological scaling on a scientific footing. Cattell's (1948) application of extremely sophisticated statistical procedures, such as factor analysis, is another example. Moreno's (1954) sociometric method measured "who likes whom" under a variety of conditions. It produced quantifiable data, which had the advantage of being translatable into diagrammatic form. Sometimes there was collaboration among these disciplines, more often not. But their common aim, which was the purposeful scientific investigation of group behavior and the formulation of the basic principles which governed it, provided a modicum of unity among them all.

Among the investigators there were a number of workers who insisted upon restricting themselves to completing their collection of empirical data before making any theoretical formulations whatever. Others preferred to conduct experimental investigations within a theoretical framework to prove or disprove the series of hypotheses which might be derived from that framework. Among the latter several over-all theoretical frameworks have been developed, for example, Bales' (1950) interaction process analysis; role theory, and cognitive theory, both described in *The Handbook of Social Psychology*, Volume I, and Cattell's (1948) syntality theory. Of them all, Kurt Lewin's was perhaps the most representative and widely used; and, since it is the one which is perhaps most compatible with psychoanalysis, we shall single it out for description in the following section.

Some Basic Initial Researches

The psychologist Sherif combined a systematic analysis of the current theories of the social norm with a presentation of a laboratory study of its development under experimental conditions. By setting up a variety of situations to study the "autokinetic effect" (if a subject looks at a point of light in a dark room he will see it as moving), Sherif proved that (1) each individual brings to the situation a "mental set" which will determine the range of movement he sees and (2) the individual is then influenced within his own range of judgments by the group norm (Sherif, 1936). Here was clear-cut empirical proof of the utmost significance for the new discipline. What had long been assumed about the influence of social norms (traditions, rules, culture, values, and standards) on individuals was now experimentally demonstrable. The supraindividual qualities that arise in the group situation could be manipulated. Hence they were "real."

In the late thirties Newcomb (1943) completed a different kind of project along sociological lines. He studied the effect of the culture from which an individual came upon his reactions in a new group and the later effect of the new group upon his earlier frame of reference. Unlike Sherif, Newcomb used natural groups. His subjects were students at Bennington College and he investigated the changes in their political attitudes from conservative to liberal that resulted from exposure to college studies and campus atmosphere. He controlled and checked his observations by means of attitude scales (questionnaires), interviews, and sociometric studies. Like Sherif, he brought sound empirical evidence to prove some of the armchair theories that had prevailed for so long in sociology.

Kurt Lewin was, of course, one of the pioneers in research on group phenomena. At the Child Welfare Research Station of the University of Iowa, together with Lippitt and White (1939), he studied the effect of "social climates" which were established by different types of leadership. In three groups of ten-year-old boys, one leader employed the principle of laissez faire, leaving the boys to their own devices and not himself participating voluntarily; one leader was democratic, participating in a "fact-minded" way, without directing or ordering them; and the third was authoritarian, determining policies and activities and making personal evaluations. The results clearly indicated that in the democratic group, initiative and productivity were greater than in the other two. There was less frustration and aggressiveness and more interest in participation. In this work the psychological field theory which Lewin had developed in the previous decades in Europe was put to the test. The specific findings concerning the effects of leadership and group atmosphere which proved useful to those interested in problems of management and education were however not in themselves as significant, from Lewin's point of view, as the fact that a new method had been found to which such questions might be subjected. At last science had been demonstrated to be of concrete service in solving social problems.

A Typical Theoretical Orientation

Lewin was among those who believed strongly in the value of theory. The field theoretical principles which he laid down for individuals were applicable to groups as well. This method was representative of the best group dynamics research, and he was the first to use the term group dynamics. For this, and for the reasons we have already mentioned, it seems appropriate that we become acquainted with his substantial contribution to dynamic group psychology. It will provide a basis for understanding its relationship to Freudian group psychology and will throw light on the even more complex relationship between group dynamic and analytic group psychotherapy. His first hypothesis took him beyond mechanistic associationism into field theory; and because the way in which he arrived at it illustrates the refinements of his methodological skill, we shall review his first experiments.

Lewin was a scientist of the higest order. His early work in Berlin as a student of comparative scientific methodology provided him with breadth of outlook and a firm foundation for his later experimental and systematic work. As a psychologist he became dissatisfied with the relatively static quality of associationism. He wanted to see if it could be made to account for the now more respectable concept of motivation. To avoid teleology he used the terms "needs" and "goal-directed behavior." Convinced of the value of theorizing, he consistently combined the gathering of empirical data with his step-by-step building of theoretical concepts.

He was wont to start with simple, common-sense terms and convert them gradually into operational definitions. These he tested empirically once more. On the basis of his accumulated data he slowly developed ever more exact conceptual definitions and formal constructs. To meet the new standards of science he insisted from the start that the hypotheses be put in testable form and that the terminology be as exact as possible. Furthermore, every new hypothesis had to fit into his general theory so that contradictions were quickly discovered and became the subjects for new investigations.

The experimental work which proved to be the foundation of a new systematic psychology grew out of his reaction to a series of experiments done in 1910 by Ach, whose scientific abilities he greatly admired, and who, like other colleagues, was then trying to include goal-directed behavior in the psychology of associationism without changing the basic character of the latter. Ach was making experimental use of nonsense syllables to test his concept of *determinierende Tendenz,* a scientific term for "will." Lewin wanted to explore this idea further, because he thought it a way of providing a sound concept of a motivating force which he felt was requisite to any psychological system. Using a similar method he got negative results and proved conclusively that associations do not in themselves provide a motivating force.

Lewin says about his experiments *(Field Theory in Social Science,* p. 5): "They [his experiments] were based on the assumption of the classical law of association as stated by G. E. Müller. The experiments, however, seemed to prove conclusively, contrary to my expectation, that this assumption had to be abandoned or decidedly modified." In order to account for goal-directed behavior it was necessary to distinguish two rather different types of habits (associations): "need habits" (like alcoholism), and "execution habits" (like pulling a lever up rather than down). The first type results from a psychological or physiological need (such as hunger) which demands satisfaction either directly or through substitution and therefore creates a tension which is a source of energy. The execution habit, on the other hand, is itself no source of action; it is equivalent to a "pattern of restraining forces determining a certain path." Without a need or quasi-need the execution habit does not lead to action. He therefore had to produce a modern replacement for the old theory of energy and of instinct. Drawing on physics for a model he concluded that a tension system is always necessary for every mental activity as well as for the reproduction (memory) experiments he was working on. Associationism was thus replaced by a more dynamic concept.

To establish a base line for the new approach he set to work on a series of experiments on the resumption of interrupted tasks. About his plan he wrote: "The first step was an attempt to achieve a more precise conceptual analysis. Dynamically, an 'association' is something like a link in a chain. . . . On the other hand the tendency to bring about action is basic to a need. This property of a need or quasi-need can be represented by coordinating it to a 'system in tension.' By taking this construct seriously and using certain operational definitions, particularly by correlating the 'release of tension' to a 'satisfaction of the need' (or the reaching of the goal), and the setting up of tension to an 'intention' or to a need in 'a state of hunger,' a great number of testable conclusions were made possible" (pp. 5, 6).

For example, if the effect of an intention is the creation of a quasi-need (equivalent to a tension system), then one should assume a fair number of resumptions after interruption. Ovsiankina (1928),[4] who worked with Lewin on this study, found about eighty percent of resumptions. The experiments of another colleague, Zeigarnik (1927),[5] proved that an interrupted task produced greater tendency for recall than an uninterrupted one. She also proved that both tasks were motivated by a force which set up a tendency for recall, and that the result of the conflict between completed and uncompleted tasks might be stated in the form of a quotient.

These two collaborators then went on with him to test experimentally a large variety of derivations from this theory. Eventually they demonstrated that a need or intention may be conceived of as a "system in tension"; that it has the basic property of a tendency to bring about action; that the intensity of a need may be correlated with its force toward action; that it is released only by the satisfaction of that need; and that objects in the environment attain positive or negative valence in proportion to their ability to satisfy that need. This theory could be applied to a wide variety of psychological problems, such as the concepts of frustration, conflict, levels

[4] From Lewin (1951).
[5] *Ibid.*

of reality and irreality, and so on. Lewin found he would eventually be able to explain dynamically the relationship of the interdependent parts of any total psychological field (whether person or group). After a large body of fact and theory had been established he proceeded to apply certain concepts from topological geometry, which enabled him to investigate qualitative relationships of connection and position in cases where these relationships remain unchanged under continuous transformation or stretching. In addition, he formulated a hodological geometry in order to arrive at a rigidly accurate conception of psychological direction.

One of Lewin's basic constructs, borrowed from the new physics, is that of the "field," which he transposed into subjective psychological terms as "the interaction between the person and the environment as it exists (has demonstrable effects) for him." To this construct he gave the name of "the life space." This psychological field is considered as a totality of interdependent parts, a concept which Lewin incorporated from gestalt psychology. By restricting the term "environment" to that part of the objective world which the individual perceives, he created a psychological phenomenology which drew much criticism, but it has important implications for increasing the precision of the psychoanalytic theory of transference. For example, it explains distortions in terms of the individual who distorts, instead of merely in terms of the objects which are distorted. Thus, "she is angry because her mother was hostile" becomes "she is angry because she perceived her mother as hostile." All psychological events or behavior are for Lewin a function of the field. This change has found its parallel in psychoanalysis in the ever more active concept of the ego.

Behavior is derived from the totality of the coexisting facts (dynamic field). A change of behavior in any part of the field changes the entire field. In order to account for changes of behavior with an adequate dynamic theory, Lewin used the biological concept of need and need systems, as explained above. Needs, according to him, had the basic property of a tendency to create tensions. The need, in other words, is a source of action for the purpose of releasing tensions. He also borrowed the concept of force from physics. Force has a vectorial character implying directed energy. The energy is directed toward a goal which has positive valence because it has the capacity to bring about closure and thus release the tensions. These concepts are subsumed in the dynamic theory called "systems in tension." Individuals are considered holistically as a totality of interdependent systems which maintain a dynamic equilibrium (similar to homeostasis). A tendency for change in the direction of equalization of tensions among the systems in one environment is assumed. As Lewin put it, "Every field is influenced by its own tension levels and also by the tensions of every other part of the field. The tension tends to spread out evenly."

One further statement basic to Lewin's field theory concerns contemporaneity. According to this principle the only determinants of behavior at a given time are the properties of the field at that time. Since this theory has sometimes been misconstrued by group therapists to imply that only the here and now is of significance, we must examine it more carefully. It was constructed in the interests of scientific rigor and precision and in order to circumvent the ancient problem of teleology. It was not meant to deny that genetic events are important or that an event from the past may influence the present. It simply considers that a change in any field may leave its trace on that field and thus become a part of the new one. The effect, therefore, is indirect. Lewin's studies of regression are an excellent illustration of his meaning.

In summarizing, we quote from Lewin (1951, p. 92): "The problem of regression, like that of development, includes an historical aspect which refers to the sequence of styles of behavior in the life history, and a systematic aspect which refers to the conditions of the change occurring at a given time. Both questions are entirely legitimate and are necessarily dealt with in a psychological approach to regression." Lewin believed that the aspect studied had to be strictly a function of the goal to be achieved. He himself freely used the historical method in the area of child development, and there is no reason whatever to suppose that he would have been averse to it for therapeutic purposes. In describing his concept of "the time perspective," Lewin gives us further insight into what he means by contemporaneity, i.e., past experience may have an effect on the mood of an individual which will affect his attitude and therefore his achievement in the present. If circumstances, real or imagined, have made him doubtful, then his level of aspiration will be lower, and so on. In like manner the intensity of an individual's wishes (irreality) may determine the activity he exerts to gain an end. In other words, the time perspective includes the psychological past and the psychological future. In this way past and future are seen to be simultaneous parts of the field at a given time.

Lewin's systematic psychology has been called field theory or topological psychology. (For a full description see M. Deutsch in Lindzey's [1954] *Handbook of Social Psychology*.) He preferred to consider it a method which could be systematically used with whatever new data might be presented, rather than a system as such. In so far as it is a system of psychology it is, of course, an open system in accordance with modern scientific requirements.

This construction of a field theoretical method for handling psychological data constituted a large part of Lewin's life work. He did much of the experimental groundwork in Europe and continued it in America, where he came about 1935, by testing it out with groups. His early work was summed up in *A Dynamic Theory of Personality* (1935) and *The Principles of Topological Psychology* (1936). A third book, *Field Theory in Social Science* (1951), explains his theory as he later applied it to groups. It was published posthumously and edited by Cartwright, and forms the major basis of the present summary. Lewin's field theory set three major trends in motion: (1) He founded topological psychology; (2) He influenced certain British psychoanalysts who incorporated his thinking with their group analytic therapy method; (3) He inspired the American social psychologists and, working with them, laid the research foundation for group dynamics.

In 1945 Lewin was made Director of the new "Research Center for Group Dynamics" at the Massachusetts Institute of Technology. Here he and his colleagues engaged in a program of action research in which he continued to apply his knowledge of group processes to social problems in order to solve current practical needs. One of his colleagues was Alex Bavelas, who contributed the now popular concept of "group decision." He conducted an elaborate series of experiments on communication patterns in task-oriented groups (1950). Lewin himself made a study of food habits and the methods of changing them which demonstrated the superiority of group discussion over individual methods of persuasion. This was followed up by Radke and Klisurich who in 1947 conducted experiments which reinforced Lewin's results.

After Lewin's death his Center was moved to the University of

Michigan and became part of the Institute for Social Research. Many other large projects were set in motion and a number of new research centers were formed at various universitiees. Among them were the Research Center for Human Relations at New York University, the Laboratory of Social Relations at Harvard, and the Institute for Research in Social Science at the University of North Carolina. The advantage of such centers has been that they were able to carry out broadly envisioned, systematic work which unified many related smaller studies, and that they were able to develop comprehensive theories from this broad base. This movement itself registered a sweeping change in our higher education, for rigid boundaries between disciplines were broken down in our universities, and for the first time professional studies were admitted into academic curricular psychology.

Another new and heartening development has been the provision of substantial grants for researches by large organizations, such as the National Institute of Mental Health, the Rockefeller Foundation, the Carnegie Corporation, the United States Navy, and others. Equally encouraging is the interest of large business firms like Westinghouse and the Bell Laboratories, which have turned to psychological research for answers to their problems. At long last the confidence of the public in research psychologists has been won and the burden of work shared with those who can afford to finance projects which require an inordinate amount of time and money if they are to be rigorously executed.

World War II gave great impetus both to group dynamics research and to group psychotherapy. The importance of group leadership and group relationships came to be recognized by the military, which encouraged their scientific investigation. Concurrently the need for returning psychoneurotics to the lines as often and as fast as possible made recourse to the rather new method of group therapy imperative. Psychologists were called upon by the armed forces and they were, fortunately, ready to meet the contingency. They established their status in both therapy and research.

DEFINITION AND BOUNDARIES OF GROUP DYNAMICS

After the war, group therapy and group dynamics continued to grow. While group therapy was adapted for use in hospitals, clinics, and private practice, big industry and university psychology

departments collaborated in continuing the study of group properties and processes. With the consequent enormous expansion in
the latter area, the term group dynamics was widely applied and
eventually became so diffuse as to blur its meaning. It was apt to
refer either to a vague, unbounded field covering all these endeavors or to one or another specific segment of it. It has, e.g., been
used to refer to the group processes themselves, to the theoretical
formulations of one or another of its leading psychologists, or to
the methods of changing group behavior. It has even been used to
refer to the techniques of one particular program, such as buzz
sessions, role playing, or group decision as developed by institutes
held by the National Training Laboratories, which were another
outgrowth of action research. (See Chapter III.)

Enthusiasm ran so high in some quarters that a hint of religious
fervor intruded itself here and there in the otherwise sober scientific literature. But group dynamics continues to be legitimately understood as that field of specialization which is interested in increasing our knowledge of group life, of its processes, its special
phenomena, and its particular laws, and in the practical application of this knowledge to specific situations in politics, industry,
delinquency, training, education, and other fields. Group dynamicists continued to define the group as a structure that emerges from
individuals in constant dynamic interaction with one another. The
individuals are considered to be interdependent parts of a larger
whole which is different from the sum of its parts (Lewin, 1951).

Of fundamental significance is the recognition that the group
restructures itself in a "continuous process of adaptation of individuals to one another and to their mutual problems. The consequence of this mutual adaptation in groups is a set or complex of
differentiations, integrations, and ever more complex patterns of
organization" (Bonner, 1959). Although we have couched the theory in Lewinian terms this connotation of dynamic interaction constitutes the basic principle of the large majority of approaches to
the study of groups regardless of the discipline or the profession
which engages in it. Another such basic finding common to all the
researches is the circularity of causal interactions, which remains
consistent. It has become even more clear that the old way of studying variables two at a time is not practicable for the complex group
phenomenon. Instead, a configuration of related variables must be

sought. The goal then becomes that of discovering a constancy of relationships among crucial variables rather than merely the similarity between elements in a situation. These three principles provide a fundamental unity for the entire field of group dynamics, and this unity in turn provides the basis for compatibility with psychoanalytic group therapy. For the above principles which are explicitly stated by group dynamics are implicit in Freudian group psychology, even though they have not been expressly articulated.

III Group Dynamics Phenomena
Significant for Therapy

Surveying the research findings in the field of group dynamics proved, in itself, an arduous task. At first I had hoped to extract from their vast numbers those which might provide a representative sampling of the total field. But since a majority of the studies dealt with overt, group determined behavior in well structured groups which had a definite external goal, most of the specific researches had little bearing on the problems confronting group therapy, which is our major theme. It seemed wiser to limit the discussion to those group phenomena which have relevance for group therapy and which will throw light on the issues involved in applying group dynamics concepts to therapy groups. There is no doubt that group determined phenomena, i.e., group goals, group structure, group standards and pressure, leadership, cohesive and destructive forces, atmosphere, and role distribution do occur and in all kinds of groups. In analytic therapy groups, the therapeutic process sometimes makes use of them and sometimes cuts through them. The most pertinent problem to which we may address ourselves is, what precautions must be taken in applying group dynamic findings to therapy groups? Cartwright (1960, p. 43) articulates a general rule which the group therapist might well consider: "The understandable tendency of an investigator to generalize his findings from a particular setting to groups in general is another source of confusion. It is a legitimate objective of group dynamicists to construct a theory applicable to all types of groups, but this does not mean that any particular finding will be applicable to all groups in all conceivable settings. The task of deriving general principles from diverse findings is a most difficult one. It is the essential nature of a general law that it specifies what effects may be anticipated under specified conditions. The achievement of such a law demands, therefore, that great care be exercised in specifying the conditions which generate any particular findings. Only confusion will result unless one is careful to determine what limits should be imposed upon findings from a particular type of investigation or a particular type of group. Such different findings, when properly conceived, can be made to supplement one another in a comprehensive theory." (See also Durkin, 1957.)

Following this wise precaution, one must keep in mind the following basic premises: (1) a therapy group is relatively unstructured; (2) it does not have concrete external goals; (3) the members are patients who have come to an expert authority for personal help of the kind which requires the examination of unconscious motivation; (4) therapeutic process will tend to cut across the group processes.

For example, the group goal is a key factor in determining the pattern which will develop among the interdependent group variables in all kinds of groups. It plays an important role in prescribing the nature of the leadership, the standards to be adopted, the degree of pressure to be encouraged, the path-to-the-goal, decision making, and the nature of the interaction. As soon as the definition of the term "group goal" is examined, we shall have an idea of the complexities involved in transposing group dynamic concepts to therapy groups.

Cartwright's (1960) definition of the group goal demonstrates the point. He rules out the shared goals of a number of people, such as the goal of three men who court one young lady, and that of five committee members who all want to go home early. Neither, he says, can be said to be a real goal. Cartwright believes that a group goal must be defined at the group level of description, as individual goals are formally defined at the individual level. In order to arrive at such a definition he affirms that one must "start with the group at least at a first level of approximation as an undifferentiated entity which at any given time has a location in an environment. The goal may then be defined as a preferred location for the group toward which it may move or locomote. In order for a group to change its location to a preferred one it is usually necessary for it to perform a sequence of group activities. Such a sequence may be thought of as a path through the group's environment, toward its goal. The process by which one path-goal structure acquires concomitant potency for the group may be called a group decision" (p. 347).

Does the therapy group have such a goal? In the first place only the therapist can be said to have a clear-cut goal, for he knows best what mental health is and how the group may bring it about. For a rather long period individual group members care very little about the aims of the other members. The individual patient ostensibly joins a group at the behest of the therapist "to get well," but we know that the patient's unconscious goal is merely to be relieved of his anxiety and to reestablish the neurotic equilibrium which has been disturbed. If the therapist wishes to bring about any real sharing of his goal he must repeatedly analyze the patient's unconscious neurotic goal, i.e., his resistance. Therefore, maintaining that all members are concerned with improving their emotional health would be a superficial and inaccurate statement, totally lacking in the precise analysis which the group dynamicists themselves would consider essential.

Even if the therapist's goal alone is considered, complications arise, for he must have specific aims in mind for each individual patient. For example, his goal for one member may be to help him become more spontaneous in expressing emotions; another must be helped to control his immediate desires. One patient must dig deep, just to find out what his desires really are. Yet there are those who must learn to think less and act more, and others who must learn to think carefully before taking action. These are aspects of the goals which the therapist has for each individual. They may not be lumped together.While some of the members may come to articulate them in specific terms, others may actually achieve them without becoming aware of them.

The differences now become very clear. The therapy group cannot be thought of as having a goal of its own until a good deal of therapeutic work has been done. Although the dilemma of the three men and a girl and the tired committee members is not that of the group therapist, the fundamental conditions are so unique that they preclude any easy application of the findings of one to the other.

It follows that group decision, which is the preferred path-to-the-goal in most ordinary groups, is inappropriate under the conditions of therapy groups, for in them group decision can at best signify group assent by the members who have confidence in their chosen leader. Minor decisions, such as time of meeting, may be left to the group, but those that involve the basic tenets of the therapeutic process must be the responsibility of the leader. The members select him because of his skill and willingly surrender to him the right to make decisions having to do with the treatment process. That is not to say that they cannot make other decisions for themselves. They must, for instance, reserve the right to withdraw from treatment if they are convinced they have the wrong therapist. This, however, is usually an individual matter. It would be difficult to imagine a group coming to the decision to drop their therapist and choose another. Individuals do so from time to time, sometimes for good reasons and sometimes to their own detriment.

All kinds of groups tend to put pressure on members to accept the standards of the leader, and the therapist as well as other group leaders therefore have this in common, that they all set up the best possible conditions for reaching their goals during the first sessions. There are certain similarities between the optimal group atmosphere in an ordinary group, and the optimal group analytic situation. But there are also some differences, as we shall see.

Deutsch (1949), a prominent social psychologist interested in understanding and controlling social processes, has made an experimental study to test the hypothesis that a cooperative social situation is more conducive to getting a group to reach an external goal (solving a series of puzzles) than a competitive one. Not only was Deutsch's experimental design worked out with the greatest care, but it was preceded by the most detailed conceptual analysis of the situation, the terms to be used, and their logical and psychological implications. His research is well worth reading in the original, if only to learn how meticulously the research scientists approach matters that the group therapists only too easily and mistakenly take for granted. Deutsch's results are convincing. He gives ample evidence to show that an atmosphere of cooperativeness in the work group is more conducive to productivity and communication than one in which the interaction is on a competitive basis.

Only a minor amount of conceptual analysis is sufficient to indicate that to minimize competition would be contraindicated in a therapy group because it would reinforce the tendency for conflict avoidance, and it is essential that the members feel free to express all their socially unacceptable feelings. Permissiveness must take precedence over cooperativeness whenever the goal is therapy. After conflicts have been repeatedly experienced and their components analyzed, the therapy group tends to become spontaneously more cooperative.

Similarly Fourezios, Hutt, and Guetzkow (1950) demonstrate that self-oriented needs work against group movement, yet in the therapy group these are the very needs that must be explored, for unless they come fully into the open they cannot be effectively analyzed, and so resolved. Furthermore, experience has proved that if the therapist is skillful in making his interpretations the group will thrive on the full expression of these needs, and will move dynamically on its path, not in spite of them but because of their frank expression. I recall a situation in one of my first heterosexual groups in which each member openly admitted, much to my consternation, that he couldn't care less what happened to the other members. I soon discovered that this expression and acceptance of narcissistic attitudes was the important first step in working together therapeutically. It was as if the repeated assertion of their infantile narcissism without admonishment or retribution helped them give up their desperate defense of it.

Because leadership has been studied in so many different types of groups, no truly comprehensive theory of it has as yet been achieved by the group dynamicists. Yet the change from a substantive to a dynamic view is apparent. The former notion of innate leadership qualities has been almost completely replaced by the idea that leadership is a function of the group which derives from the relationship between the personality of the leader, the members, and the conditions under which they work together.

As illustrations of the way the social psychologists attack the problem of defining leadership, two outstanding group dynamics theorists may be cited. Bales (1950) concludes that leadership depends upon an individual's access to the resources necessary to achieve the group goal, his identification with the group, and his influence on the members. Cattell (1948) proposes that any member of a group exerts leadership to the extent that properties of the group (to which he gives the term syntality) are modified by his presence in it. Group therapists who give serious consideration to such definitions cannot in all due conscience simply take a finding as to the effect of a certain type of leadership on productivity in a problem solving group, apply it to their therapy groups, and expect it to work effectively. They must ask what differences in the concept of leadership are made by the single fact that the therapist has far more complete access to resources than do the members. Leadership may still be seen as a group function, but designated and member leadership must be distinguished from each other.

Some studies seem to describe ideal leadership and omit the power element, while others stress just that factor. This is due to the variations in the situations that are studied. Investigators of problem solving groups are not likely to be affected by power struggles as those who make field studies of community organizations.

When we examine the concept of the leader's power in relation to therapy groups we find that confusion arises whenever the distinction between authoritativeness and authoritarianism is ignored. There are therapists who seem to be so jealous of their interpretive power that their groups miss out on membership participation in this function. Worse, the members' spontaneous emotional interaction is curtailed if they are encouraged to be submissive. Other therapists deny their realistic authority and consequently play so passive a role that they do not deal appropriately with resistance. If one keeps in mind that there is a role differentiation between realistic authority and the unrealistic intrusion of omnipotent fantasies, these problems are minimized.

Lewin's introduction of an ideological principle, that of democracy, into scientific investigations has also added to the confusion of this issue. The Lewin, Lippitt, and White study, which showed the superiority of democratic over laissez-faire and autocratic leadership, started a trend. It was followed by the field studies of Kahn and Katz (1953) which demonstrate that "the full motivation of workers in a complex organizational system can be tapped only when some system of functional representation assures them of an element of control in the larger organization as well as in the smaller groups." Preston and Heintz (1949) found that "changes of opinion in discussion groups were more easily brought about by means of participatory than by supervisory leadership." One very common finding seems to be that although autocratic leadership may at times increase productivity, it decreases group morale, and may in the long run also interfere with that productivity.

This general trend is brought into question by other investigations, such as those by Berkowitz (1953), who made a very careful and thorough study of governmental and industrial conferences which showed that the more the chairman took over the leadership the more satisfied the members were with the conference. But Bonner reconciles this in his conclusion (1959) that "people do not object to strong leadership provided they know they can participate and take the initiative if they wish."

Since most group therapists strive for active membership participation it would seem that these findings might indeed be taken at face value and automatically applied in therapy groups. Yet closer inspection definitely indicates the necessity of a more discriminating use of concepts. For instance, if the therapist is so democratic that he allows hilarious chatter, endless reminiscences, too many dreams, and even too much mutual analysis to continue at length, he is likely to miss its resistive character and fail to use his realistic power to set the group in motion again.

Acting in a democratic way may actually obscure the members' problems concerning authority, and his own as well. An exaggerated democratic reaction could indicate a reaction formation to unconscious power needs on the part of the therapist. A true democratic feeling will reveal itself rather in the therapist's nonverbal communications and requires no particular emphasis, especially in a democratic culture. The therapeutically valent factor here has to do with the therapist's freedom from unconscious omnipotent needs.

The warning often repeated by group dynamicists that leadership varies according to the situation in which it occurs, unfortunately is sometimes ignored by well meaning but undiscriminating group therapists. Impressed by the findings concerning democratic leadership they tend to roll up their shirt sleeves and assume a cozy "call me Joe" expression, mistaking this for a therapeutic measure.

Cohesiveness has been another of the most widely studied group dimensions, and its relationship to a number of other variables, such as group atmosphere and uniformity of standards, has been established. Festinger, Schacter and Back (1950), who are prominent contributors to this subject, made an investigation of a number of dwellers in housing projects and discovered that distance and other physical environmental factors affected the formation of cohesive social groups within the units. They showed that uniformity of standards of behavior is closely related to cohesiveness, and gave substantial evidence that the more cohesive the group, the more the norms of its members are affected. On the other hand, the more uniform the behavior of the members, the more cohesive the group atmosphere is shown to be.

These studies are characteristic of a larger majority of the group dynamics investigations, especially of the early years, and they are therefore of relatively little interest to group therapy. It is more important that group therapists take into account the limitations of the cohesiveness principle. As the transferences develop in the therapy group, a family-like atmosphere and a strong cohesiveness may indeed develop which will for a time prove therapeutically useful. But if the neurotic transferences are not fully analyzed the family atmosphere can become so comfortable and easy for the members (in so far as they derive infantile gratification from the other members) that they cling to their therapy group instead of venturing forth into the outside world to make more realistic and satisfying relationships.

There have been several different approaches to the empirical study of structure and several theories have emerged. Group structure can be viewed in so many ways that the multitudinous findings lack coherence. Cartwright and Zander (1960) bring some order into the picture by pointing out the rather general acceptance of the thinking of Linton,[1] who emphasized the distinction between the static organizational aspects of structure (status as a collection of rights and duties) and its dynamic role

---

[1] In Cartwright and Zander (1960).

aspects (putting the rights and duties into effect in one's own way). Linton also showed that structure may be studied in terms of (1) interpersonal relationships, (2) communication, and (3) power. The relationships among these three types of structure remain an important area for investigation.

The interpersonal type of structure has been studied largely by sociometric methods. Glanzer and Glaser (1959) pointed out that such studies could be treated mathematically in the form of matrices. Festinger (1949) and Ross and Harary (1955) put this theory into practice and proved its validity. These methods represent major methodological progress. For instance, Guetzkow (1960) shows the effect of the various structural dimensions on the development of the roles which individual members assume in the group. The studies of Lippitt et al. (1952) have even attempted to illuminate the psychoanalytic concept of identification. They show the enhancing effect of prestige on contagion. As personality factors and unconscious motivation are brought in, the group dynamics studies and the interest of the group dynamicists draw closer, as we shall show in the next chapter.

Bales' (1950) interaction theory brings group dynamics closer to interpersonal psychoanalytic theory. He discusses the reason for the development of structure in groups from the point of view of the members' motivations, and perceives the process as a means of reducing tensions which arise in a group when the members interfere with one another's activity. His belief is that "it is to the advantage of every individual in a group to stabilize the potential activity of others toward him, favorably if possible, but in any case in such a way that he can predict it. Structure thus partially solves the problems of interaction which might result from interpersonal conflict. The resolution of such conflicts becomes stabilized in the structural hierarchy. Each individual finds his place in that hierarchy according to the way in which the norms of behavior he has learned from other group situations fit in with the goal of the new group."

Both therapy and training groups which focus on the latent emotional meaning of behavior corroborate Bales' conclusions as to the causes for structuring and the mechanisms used in the struggle for position. Phenomenologically each member may be observed to bring with him not only his potential capacities for the work to be done by the group, but a repertoire of values and role behavior which he has learned in other groups. Members are under apparent tensions and seem to jockey for position. Gradually each member's patterns of behavior, his attitudes, and his capacities are revealed. These are either accepted or rejected by the others according to whether they will help or hinder the achievement of the particular goal. At the same time their personal prestige is tested in relation to one another until the position of each is implicitly determined.

Bales' theoretical position is quite compatible with Freudian group psychology. Indeed, Freud also made the statement that organization (structure) provides groups with the very characteristics of control which the ego provides for the individual. Both men seem to have drawn similar conclusions from their observations.

The criteria of the applicability of group dynamics findings to therapy group must be based on an analysis of the particular situation. We have begun to see that group dynamics which was at first interested only in group process and group-determined phenomena gradually became interested in the individual factors which are involved in group interaction. In Chapter IV we shall investigate their growing interest in depth factors as well. Movement in this direction augurs well for the eventual harmony beween group dynamic and psychoanalytic group psychology.

IV Recent Developments in
Group Dynamics

A comparison of the 1960 edition of Cartwright and Zander with that of 1953 gives a fair idea of research trends in recent years. Many of the older experiments, such as those of Lewin, Lippitt, and White, and of Festinger, Schacter, and Bach, are still included and seem to be on the way to attaining the status of classics. But there are several new names among the authors. The work of Deutsch and Gerard on the effect of group influence on individual judgments, for example, and of Fiedler on the effect of the leader's psychological distance on the group, as well as that of Guetzkow on role differentiation, are new. The section on cohesiveness is longer than it was and concerns itself with the factors that bring about cohesiveness rather than its effects. The section headings are also indicative of some new trends. The one originally entitled "Leadership" has been changed to "Leadership and Group Performance"; "Goals and Locomotion" is now "Individual Motives and Group Goals." The latter indicates what is for us the most pertinent change—an increase of interest in individual and personality factors. Bonner's book, *Group Dynamics* (1959), also reflects this trend by its inclusion of chapters on role dynamics, group and personality dynamics, and even group therapy. Group dynamics and group therapy have definitely moved much closer together.

A vast amount of additional information has been given, but

more significant is the increase in coherence in this previously rather chaotic field. Although the variety of theoretical approaches still attests to its youthful vigor, there is a beginning of convergence among them. March and Simon published a book called *Organizations* (1958)[1] in which they have developed "maps" showing the relationships among the significant variables reported by different investigators and how these may be combined. Cartwright says these firmly establish the assumption that "a fully adequate understanding of the determinants of group life will always involve a network of causal relationships." This assumption of circularity rather than a linear principle of cause and effect relationship between two single factors is consistent with Lewinian theory and provides a unifying pattern for the whole field. It augurs well for the possibility of its future internal theoretical integration.

Of even greater significance to us is the tendency toward a rapprochement of the two basic, complementary ideologies. Just as Foulkes and Anthony have brought group dynamic theory to the attention of the American analytic group therapists, Bion and Ezriel have introduced psychoanalytic concepts into the American group dynamics research movement. Those group dynamicists who had already become interested in the personality factors of group behavior had found the interpersonal school of Sullivan, with its phenomenological approach, more congenial than Freudian depth psychology. The impact of Bion's social psychology with its Kleinian roots greatly extended the dimension of depth and necessitated the introduction of a higher level of inference than had been customary among social psychologists.

The well-known social psychologist Herbert Thelen, with his co-workers[2] was the first to put Bion's group psychoanalytic concepts to experimental test. I believe their work marks a momentous occasion in the history of social science. It proved once and for all

---

[1] According to Cartwright and Zander (1960).

[2] Stock and Thelen (1958) have published their findings in a book called *Emotional Dynamics and Group Culture*. See also Thelen et al. (1954). Other accounts may be found in Volume III of S. Koch's (1959) *Psychology: A Study of Science* and in Leonard D. White's (1956) *The State of the Social Sciences*.

that very high level abstractions could successfully be put to experimental test. Neither psychoanalysts nor analytic group therapists need any longer rely on clinical evidence and observation alone. Conversely, group dynamicists need not limit themselves to directly observable overt data. If it was possible to convert the highly complex and vaguely worded abstractions of Bion into operational terms, it would certainly not be difficult to apply the same technique to the more clearly stated perceptions of Freud. The phenomenological base (the empirical data) need in no way be sacrificed in order to gain deeper insight into the intangibles of human behavior. Because Thelen's research provides a sound methodology for coping experimentally with high level psychoanalytic abstractions it is of vital importance to group psychology and merits detailed description here.

Hill[3] reports on the collaborative efforts of the Human Dynamics Laboratory Team to interpret Bion's concepts and put them on an operational basis. Since I was fortunate in having a copy of Hill's excellent account I drew freely on it, as well as on Thelen's own reports in preparing the present summary.

Thelen had noticed the regular occurrence of two levels of functioning in his problem-solving experiments and had characterized the one as "work" and the other as "emotionality." He became interested in their similarity to what Bion called the "work" versus the "basic assumptions" groups, and was determined to test these concepts.

Bion's concepts (1948, 1949, 1951) had provided information on three levels of group operation which he considered essential to his point of view. These are: (1) total group operation; (2) relation of individuals to the group process; and (3) relation of subgroups to group process (with which we are not here engaged).

(1) Bion starts with the group as an undifferentiated whole and then gradually analyzes out its interdependent parts. While there is nothing contradictory in this design to Freudian group psychology, Freud approached it from the side of the individual; and for this reason Bion's method was much more appropriate to Thelen's group dynamic research. Thelen's group understood

---

[3] See W. F. Hill (ed.) (1961), *Collected Papers on Group Psychotherapy*.

Bion's central postulate to be that "at any given time the pattern of group behavior is concerned chiefly with one emotional problem," (i.e., either dependency, or fight-flight, or pairing). This underlying psychological state could be identified through its behavioral expression. Although many other trends may be observed, the possibility of focusing on one such central trend was a simplifying device which gave a certain necessary degree of unity and coherence to interpreting the behavior of the group as a whole.

(2) In order to relate individual factors to group behavior Bion used the ideas of valency and cooperation. Valency was defined as an unlearned, instinctive potentiality for expressing emotional character and through this for interacting with others in a specific situation. Cooperation was defined as the analogous force for the participation of individuals in the work group. It is conceived as an acquired drive which compels individuals to be socially responsive and responsible mature group members.[4]

In order to proceed experimentally, Thelen's group made the fundamental assumption that detectable affect may be expressed by the individual in his verbalizations to the group and that the emotionality in the group as a whole must ultimately have its source in such personal feelings. They found that in the common matrix of the group emotion, all the members may be seen to share the same concern and to express it behaviorally. By assessing the valency and cooperation patterns they could detect the way in which each member participates in any given pattern of group interaction. Relating the individual and group factors brought them potentially much closer to the Freudian and interpersonal schools in which individuals' personality factors are of primary importance, for both Bion and the social psychologists had focused almost exclusively on those of the group. Emphasis on the individual factors also made the methodology practicable for therapists for whom dealing with individuals is a sine qua non.

The two levels of functioning were handled in the following

---

[4] This latter hypothesis is far from being generally accepted but was plausible and certainly useful for methodological purposes. We ourselves are not concerned at the moment with the validity of these concepts but in what can be done with them experimentally. Refinement of conceptualization may be left to the future.

way. Bion used the construct of "group culture" to describe the behavioral events which are the result of the "psychological state of the group," and the construct "basic assumption" (the members act as if they wanted certain emotional gratifications) to describe the motivation which gives rise to that state. He postulated a work culture which was defined by Thelen as "that aspect of group activity which is associated with the performance of a task, which is related to reality, and whose methods are rational."[5] This definition makes it possible to include, among the legitimate group tasks, process problems, such as working out interpersonal relations, as well as more cognitive questions. Thus both training and therapy groups can be studied.

Bion postulates three emotional cultures:[6] (1) that in which the group acts as if it were looking for a leader who would gratify its dependency needs; (2) that which demonstrates its need for fight-flight, and (3) that which demonstrates its need to pair off.

These two categories of culture—work and basic assumptions—may occur together in a number of different relations. Work always appears in some combination with one form of emotionality. Either of them may be dominant at any given time. In a mature group the relationship will have developed considerable stability, with work and emotional character well integrated. In such groups emotions are not expressed but are channelled into some means of expression so that they may be integrated with the work task.

Thelen et al. worked out specific behavioral classifications[7] to correspond to the basic assumptions, forming their decisions from detailed empirical data derived from concrete group situations. As a result of this preliminary work they decided to separate Bion's fight from flight, so that they came out with four classes of emotionality. Definitions were established both generally (dynamically) and in terms of specific behaviors (operationally) which typically fall within each category. They then worked out four

[5] This would appear to be the equivalent of the Freudian concept of the ego, the reality principle, and its expression in secondary process.

[6] The emotional cultures are unlearned, instinctive processes, corresponding to the Freudian id, as expressed in primary process.

[7] It will be interesting to see how these categories, by no means to be regarded as final, continue to undergo changes in the theories of group development. As constructs they are expendable and the way is left open to modifications by later investigators.

parallel qualities of work behavior, which Bion had not done, so that the two dimensions might be recorded and summarized on a graph.

So much for the conceptualizations which provide the material for Thelen's investigation. On the basis of careful scientific procedure, valid systems of observing and rating were then developed.[8] All observers and raters were trained until the categories were internalized and two separate observations were regularly made. The results of the two dimensions were then measured on an additional graph. Both time and verbal units could be used. This system makes it possible to measure process in large or small amounts of time, so that one session or a series of sessions may be included. To serve as an instrument for prediction a "Q" Sort and a Sentence Completion test based on Bion's concepts were constructed, which made it possible to identify valency patterns. For a complete description of this work, Thelen's book and Hill's collected papers are recommended. I have tried to excerpt from them only the most salient features.

Although we are concerned here with group psychology rather than with group psychotherapy, it is interesting to see how this methodology may become the modus operandi for research in group psychotherapy. Hill himself moved from group dynamics to group psychotherapy, which he studied with Elmore Martin. He continued his research, using therapy groups, and together with Martin developed a theory of group development (1957). He and I. S. Hill also worked out the Hill and Hill Interaction Matrix, according to which therapy group process may be assessed and measured. He based his model on the work of the Thelen group which he modified in order to adapt it to group therapy. It, too, is available on application to the Provo State Hospital, Utah.

Another valuable research on group therapy which came from the field of group dynamics is reported in a number of papers by Whitman, Lieberman and Stock (1958, 1960, 1962). Their investigation was carried out at the University of Chicago and was supported by an N.I.M.H. grant. In order to adapt group dynamic principles, especially the concept of the group-as-a-whole, to meet

[8] Participating in the development of the behavioral rating system were: S. Ben-Zeev, A. J. McPherson, R. Rodgers, D. Stock, and H. Thelen.

group therapeutic needs, they utilized T. French's psychoanalytic theory of "focal conflict." They defined the group focal conflict as consisting of a "shared disturbing motive or wish which exists in opposition to a shared reactive motive or fear." They perceived the group as using its energies (much as an individual does) to strive unconsciously toward the resolution of its focal conflict and to arrive at some generally acceptable solution which will simultaneously alleviate fears and allow for some gratification of the disturbing motive. They assume that the successive material of a group session is comprised of elements in a process akin to free association. The manifest content is understood to have a symbolic reference to the here-and-now situation. Comments made by individual patients are seen as having a personal meaning but at the same time to have relevance for the emerging group conflict. In other words, each comment is shaped or influenced in some manner by the immediate interactive situation in the group. The verbal content, as well as the nonverbal behavior, pace, rhythm, and mood are regarded as elements in the associative process. By looking for the relevance of these associations for the focal group conflict they are able to identify the underlying coherence in all the diverse elements.

During the period in which a group focal conflict is emerging it is likely to exist outside the awareness of the patients; but as the group moves, the character of the shared wishes and fears may come into awareness. The therapists interpret each session in terms of this conflict. Their goal is to arrive at its solution. Both sides must be clarified before its resolution can occur.

Their data bear out these assumptions. They have devised a procedure for analyzing the sessions which they believe can be duplicated by independent observers and which permits some degree of prediction of what will occur in the sessions. They have demonstrated that their method can explain group behavior, the individual's relationship to it, and the reasons for deviant behavior. They have, for example, made a study of the cues, both verbal and nonverbal which enables them to sort out the purely personal meaning of each bit of participation in the interaction and also its implications for the group conflict. More recently they have also discovered a way of studying the therapist's interventions by testing the relationship beween its applicability to the focal conflict and its effect on the group's reaction.

Their work has been placed in the section for research rather than described as a typical group therapy method for the reason that it is still in its experimental stage and is continuously being developed. Not enough time has elapsed to find out whether its therapeutic results are comparable to other forms of group therapy. It is my impression, which the authors seem to share, that their results are proving therapeutically satisfactory, and I am confident that a sound method is in the making. Only clinical appraisal over a long period will determine the ultimate outcome.

Through more recent correspondence with Stock, I have had access to material on the further development and elaboration of their ideas which she and Lieberman are in the process of preparing for publication. As a result of their increasing experience with therapy groups they seem to be putting greater emphasis on the role of the members as patients. Consequently individual and group factors are now considered by them to be of equal importance. They have also studied the role of the therapist in further detail.

Of this work Stock, in a personal communication to me, wrote: "In the book (forthcoming) we deal with the group processes as the context in which therapy occurs, with the individual patient in the group (especially from the point of view of his impact on the group forces and the impact of the group upon him) and with the therapist's role and function. The over-all philosophy is that it is important to attend both to the group forces and to the individual in order to utilize the unique opportunities which a group offers for therapeutic change.

"As we have examined more closely the character of the therapist's role, we have come to the recognition that interpretations of the group focal conflict are only one of a number of possible devices which the therapist may utilize to manage and exploit the group forces for therapeutic purposes. In the book we develop the idea that certain kinds of group solutions are therapeutically beneficial to the patients while others may be therapeutically undesirable or damaging. For example, a group solution which allows for the free and open expression of feelings is regarded as therapeutically beneficial. On the contrary, solutions which involve denial, displacement, scapegoating, turn-taking, and so on, are regarded as therapeutically undesirable. We define the group culture as the body of solutions on which the group is operating. Thus, a group which is operating on a body of therapeutically desirable solutions is maintaining appropriate cultural conditions, i.e., cultural conditions which contribute to a positive therapeutic experience. One of the major tasks of the therapist is to establish and maintain these appropriate culture conditions. Another is to establish and maintain conditions of safety in the group such that individual members feel free to take risks and expose themselves. Finally a third major task is to manage and exploit group processes for the benefit of the individual patients. By this we mean keeping an eye on the position of the various patients vis-à-vis the group forces and being alert to individuals who may be harmed by them, as well as being alert to the opportunities which the group forces provide for interpretation. One form of interpretation (and in this our position is similar to that of Ezriel) is the one which refers to the prevailing wishes and fears and perhaps the prevailing so-lution, but also points out to each individual the unique stand which he is taking with reference to the group focal conflict and solution . . . . it is reasonable to say that we feel that a therapist who is in touch with the character of the over-all group forces and with the position of each patient vis-à-vis them is in the best position to utilize the unique qualities of the group situation for the benefit of individual patients."

It is my impression that social psychologists who start from a purely research point of view to do group therapy inevitably re-spond increasingly to the needs of the patients who have come for help and soon add therapeutic aims to their primarily research goals. For instance, in their early investigations, Stock et al. are content to report that the group arrives at a solution which is ac-ceptable to the group as such. But to be satisfied with such a global change is a far cry from the goal of the leader who is first and fore-most a therapist and who wishes to reach an optimal rather than a compromise solution for each member. In order to achieve this end he must deal with each member's unique motivation and with his consequent mode of participation in the interaction. And this is exactly what Stock and Lieberman have done in their later work. In the course of therapeutic experience and later research their method has moved toward that of analytic group therapy.

On the other hand, no matter how well satisfied the analytic group therapist may be with the effectiveness of analyzing the intragroup transference and resistance he will find that an awakened perception of the total group through a concept such as "group focal conflict" will add a dimension to his vision, highlight that content which is of central import at any given point, and give character to the details of each individual's participation in it. It will sharpen his perception of the connection between any given event and his therapeutic goal for each member. Moreover, by acting as a guide to the direction of therapeutic movement such a group concept will minimize the time lost in going off on tangents.

What Stock and Lieberman have to say (above) about the therapist's role in creating a therapeutic group atmosphere articulates an essential (but heretofore often neglected) attitude for those who wish to utilize group dynamic principles for therapeutic purposes. They are in effect stating in group dynamic terms what analytic group therapists mean by setting up a group analytic situation. Similarly their development of the therapists' functions is probably roughly equivalent to the analytic group therapists' use of transference and resistance in the group. On the whole, both schools of thought utilize the human relations processes which occur in a group. Their conceptualizations differ because one approaches these from the point of view of the group, the other, from that of the individual, and each uses the language that their parent disciplines have developed. This is merely my conclusion and must, of course, be subjected to more serious scrutiny.

Stock's statement that the nuclear conflict has no bearing on groups is related to her exclusive emphasis on the here and now, and constitutes one of the major differences between her work and analytic group psychotherapy. The nuclear conflict lies at the base of personality and derives from the earliest phases of life. To plan on its eventual analysis and resolution would inevitably bring a great deal of history into the therapeutic process.

RESEARCH AND THEORIES BASED ON LEADERSHIP TRAINING GROUPS

According to Leland Bradford's account, the organization called The National Training Laboratories developed as result of "the conscious use of primary group processes which increasingly characterized social practice in America in the past generation."

Its work bears on our subject. The first training group was held at a workshop in New Britain, Connecticut, in 1946. It was sponsored by the Connecticut Interracial Commission, the Connecticut Department of Education, and the Research Center for Group Dynamics then located at the Massachusetts Institute of Technology at Cambridge, Mass. There was a training team (Kenneth Benne, Ronald Lippitt, and Leland Bradford) and a research team (Kurt Lewin, and Ronald Lippitt). This work was in the tradition of Lewin's Action Research and was the precursor of the National Training Laboratories Institutes held annually thereafter at Bethel, Maine, and later at other centers. K. Lewin, as the leader of the group, arranged meetings for the discussion of the reports' recordings, and observed processes the effects of which on the participant are described by Benne (Bradford, 1964) as electric. Bradford says that "a potentially powerful medium and process of reeducation had been thus inadvertently hit upon. It seemed to be capable of permitting members to achieve highly meaningful learnings about themselves and about group behavior and development."[9]

It was as though these group psychologists had discovered out of their own experience the dynamic effect of bringing to light the meaning of group process and of the members' latent interpersonal feelings in group situations. From then on, they accumulated a wealth of empirical data and engaged in numerous research projects. Of special interest to us are the theories of group development which grew out of this experience, especially those of Bennis and Benne (1958), who, by their conclusion that the group goes through the same epigenetic phases as does the individual, have brought analytic group psychotherapy and group dynamic group psychology into close relationship. These theoreticians, like the Thelen group, have worked not merely with the phenomenological data but have incorporated certain of Bion's psychoanalytic conceptualizations in modified form, as well as certain constructs of interpersonal theory. As we shall see from a review of their work, they have provided a potential basis for harmonizing group dynamic, Bionic, and Freudian psychoanalytic group psychology.

Using Bion's formulations about group psychology, Bennis and Shepard (1956)[10] approached their behavioral data with the

[9] This paragraph is based on a chapter in Bradford et al. (1964).
[10] This is an extension of the Bennis and Shepard paper (1956).

question in mind as to what anxiety areas seemed to cause trouble in the group relationships by interfering with the valid communication necessary to solve the problems of the training group. These areas of anxiety seem to fall into (1) relations with authority (this included Bion's dependency upon and its obverse rebellion against authority figures), and (2) peer relationships among the members pertaining to emotional closeness or intimacy, which Bion called pairing. They, like Thelen, dropped the fight-flight category, which they felt characterized tendencies of the members to maintain stereotyped orientation (resistance). It does not require a great conceptual jump from these "areas of anxiety in interpersonal relations" to conflicts deriving from Freudian stages of psychosexual development which affect and interfere with the development of object relations. The problems with authority can be thought of as arising out of conflicts in the preoedipal stages, while those of intimacy among peers derive from oedipal problems which must be resolved before successful "pairing" can take place. (The concept of pairing and intimacy is broader than sexual relationships but must include them.)

Once again it seems important not to become too concerned with the specific conceptualizations and the terminology employed nor the question as to how exact a parallel may actually be drawn between these and the Freudian constructs. Nor are any conclusions to be drawn about group therapy at this point. It is the basic structure of this kind of thinking which presents exciting possibilities to the group psychological theorist. The vision of a bridge connecting group dynamics with Freudian psychoanalysis may be extravagant. To fulfill it will require a tremendous amount of conceptual analysis and experimental testing, but it is beyond all question plausible enough to warrant serious consideration.

Because of their significance for an over-all group psychology both the Bennis and the Benne articles are worth summarizing. On the basis of the most careful observation and analysis Bennis has found that the group as a whole moved regularly from preoccupation with authority to preoccupation with personal relations. Each of these phases falls into three subphases determined by the ambivalence of orientation both of the individuals and of the group as a whole in each area. In the first phase the group moves from (a) submissiveness, to (b) rebellion, and comes to a

resolution in (c) independence. In the second phase, the movement is from identification in subphase (a) to self-identity in (b),
and finally to resolution in the acceptance of interdependence (c).

In order to bring the individual personality factors into relation
with the total group preoccupation, two similar areas of concern
have been identified in the individual members. These are called
dependence and personal intimacy. Each individual has characteristic patterns of relating to authority and these are reflected
in his participation in the group problem. Some of the members
have submissive dependent patterns which they express through
urgent compulsive need for a strong leader or clear-cut rules.
These members dominate the first subphase. Others have aggressive, defiant or counterdependent patterns and they tend to become leaders in the second subphase. Their resentment and rebelliousness remains latent. Each individual may, of course, have any
number of further variations of pattern derived from his particular
life experience, but these are not of concern here. Thirdly, there
are the unconflicted members who may exhibit either or both of
these characteristics but to a smaller degree and without compul-
sivity. They become the chief agents for group locomotion and take
the lead in the third subphase, in which a breakthrough is made
and the dependency-authority conflict is resolved. In the second
phase (intimacy) a similar movement occurs. There are individuals
whose pattern of relating to others is overpersonal and those who
exhibit an underpersonal pattern, and there are the unconflicted.
These indicate the degree and intensity of closeness each person
desires.[11]

Bennis' description of the actual process of group movement
illustrates how these aspects of relationship operate interde-
pendently in the course of group development. He says the first
sessions are filled with attempts to ward off anxiety. The security-
seeking behavior is group shared. Sometimes it is shifted from the
need for help from the protecting leader to the need for some form
of structure, or to a search for a common goal. The behavioral signs,
however, show that the real (latent) anxiety concerns the feelings
toward the leader, who is seen as omnipotent. On the surface the

[11] Besides their meaning for group development these findings make a distinct
contribution to a deeper understanding of the nature of leadership and also
have connotations for the selection of members for group composition.

dependence is apparent in behavior which asks his help or strives to please him (according to the member's notion of what the leader would approve). Even during this first phase there is secretly also some resentment toward the leader because of fear of his power and the fantasy that he wishes to manipulate them for his own purposes, but it is generally kept in abeyance until subphase two. An interpretation by the leader as to the nature of the immediate unconscious preoccupation is likely to be firmly denied by the membership, although their behavior usually reveals that the comment has been registered.

In the second subphase the counterdependent members begin to rebel against the leader. They may criticize him obliquely or openly; they may ignore him or lead him to give opinions only to prove him wrong. Or they may oust him. The secret wish for his omnipotent protection remains but now *this* aspect is in abeyance. The atmosphere of the group is one of disappointment, hostility, suspicion of his motives, and rebellion.

In the third phase a resolution of the conflict takes place. Mutual relations among the members of similar patterns have strengthened them. The permissiveness of the leader has given them assurance and the meaning of his interpretations has had its subliminal effect. It is at this point that the non-conflicted members take over. Whereas they have been vainly striving for conciliation and compromise, they now assume leadership in breaking through the contradictory alternatives by getting the group to be responsible for itself. The leader who has been directly challenged is now seen in more realistic proportions as an expert resource person. The group can proceed with its work. On the emotional level it will now move on toward the problems of member-member intimacy. It seems that the problem of affectional ties among members cannot be adequately worked on until those of dependence toward authority are resolved.

The subphases and resolution of the intimacy problems run a similar course.[12] Bennis suggests that these phases overlap much more than his description indicates and that it is probably more accurate to think of them as cycles, with the major problems

[12] For further information about these, the reader is referred to the Bennis and Shepard article (1956).

emerging recurrently with deepening understanding rather than as representations of a thesis-antithesis-resolution dialectic. He also warns that although a variety of investigators seem to be converging toward the basic direction of this theory, the possibility is that it is based on a self-fulfilling prophecy in which the leader's concentration on these particular areas may bias what he finds.

In a companion essay Benne also discusses aspects of group development. Without presenting a theory he operates on somewhat similar assumptions as Bennis. He describes the group as a social system and the aspects of conflict as a series of polarizations which the members encounter and convert into a paradox which can then be handled by the group. Noting the complexity of the training group's goal [which includes (1) conscious work production, (2) group formation and reformation, and (3) learning], he views its movement as a "progressive differentiation and integration of these goals." The membership divides into factions of those who want form and work production, and those who resist agenda and structure and want to discuss feelings and relationships in free floating interchange. A third faction, to be supported by the leader, tries for compromise and for recognition of the reality of both goals. Such recognition constitutes the valid learning that can be achieved in training group experience. Benne structures his training groups by describing briefly the goals, his role, and the members' prospective participation. He keeps the learning objective well in mind. The complex goal can best be furthered, he says, "through realistic recognition, clarification, and interpretation by the leader of the plight of the group and of its members. Only through such a process can the unworkable polarizations about goal and goallessness be converted into manageable paradoxes ... "

He then presents several polarities and shows how they can be resolved. The first is between group and individual rights and responsibilities and is resolved in the paradox that groups are best served when members maintain their rights, and individuals flourish best when the group rights are served by them. A second polarity is that between comfort and growth; a third, between authority and freedom. He believes that the group comes to a provisional solution but that any particular polarization may appear at a later time if the conditions reactivate it. Certain learning is possible. The group as a whole may come through the training group experience to accept the difficulties and paradoxes inherent in all social living. Individuals may learn about their personal quirks and blind spots that interfere with self growth. They may learn to accept their limitations if they are unchangeable, change them if it is possible, or move into therapy if that is indicated.

In spite of their quite individual ways of approaching and conceptualizing the problems of group development, Benne and Bennis can be seen to touch on the same basic points. Both deal with dependence, as shown by the members' anxiety about lack of structure and by their relationship to authority; both deal with intermember affectual relationships; and both recognize that they have not exhausted the possibilities of interpretation and problems which are resolved during the two-week period are likely to return.

Schutz, on whose thinking Bennis based some of his ideas, has proceeded to weave these Bionic-interpersonal views into the fabric of the modern theory of psychological epigenesis outlined by the psychoanalytic ego psychologists. He has added a third phase of group development, representing the need for "inclusion" which accomplishes this purpose. It is equivalent to the Freudian oral stage and is prefixed to the other two. Because Schutz explains group and individual psychology on the same principles, and because he utilizes the phases of psychosexual development and their ego correlates in a way which is capable of combining the various conceptual systems, it seems to offer the best foundation so far available for our attempt to integrate our theories into one overall system of group psychology. I therefore consider it essential to review his thinking at it is described in his book called *FIRO* (1958a).

His work reflects his rigorous training under the scientific philosophers, Hans Reichenbach and Abraham Kaplan; his thoroughgoing knowledge of Freudian psychoanalysis and its extension in the tenets of ego psychology; and his training in group therapy under Elvin Semrad, the eminent Boston psychoanalyst. In his introduction to *FIRO* he writes, "After leaving the University of California, I underwent another thrill. I discovered that Freud's psychoanalytic theory was a great deal richer and more sophisticated than its critics led me to believe. Strangely enough, it seemed to me that the writings of Freud had a great deal in common with the writings of logicians and scientific philosophers. Both were remarkable for their penetration, for seeing through a maze of complication and confusion and selecting out those elements and their configurations that made the whole problem simple—even obvious in the more successful cases. It was certainly true that Freud's theory could be criticized on the basis of its lack of experimental support, but this always impressed me as an uneasy criticism, one in which the critic knew somehow that Freud would probably turn out to be largely correct."

Schutz regards as his theoretical goal the creation of a model toward which systematizing efforts may be aimed. He therefore leaves his system open for further changes as new empirical observations are made. He states that the basic postulates of any theory express the most fundamental ideas embodied in that theory and outlines the ones that he intends to use. His first is called the Postulate of Interpersonal Needs, and states that every individual has three such needs: inclusion, control, and affection. It is apparent that these three parallel the needs of the oral, anal, and oedipal phases of psychoanalysis. He finds that these three needs compose a sufficient set of areas of interpersonal behavior for the prediction and explanation of interpersonal phenomena. This statement clearly indicates his intention to deal primarily with ego correlates of the psychosexual phases and with the way in which these are translated into object relations.

In the second postulate, called the "Postulate of Relational Continuity," he accounts for transference. It states that "an individual's expressed interpersonal behavior will be similar to the behavior he experienced in his earliest interpersonal relations, usually with his parents. It functions according to two principles: (1) the Principle of Constancy: when he perceives his adult position to be similar to his own position in his original parent-child relationship, his adult behavior co-varies positively (i.e., varies concomitantly in a statistically significant sense) with his childhood behavior toward his parents (or significant others). (2) The Principle of Identification: when he perceives his adult position in an interpersonal situation to be similar to his parents' position in his parent-child relation, his adult behavior co-varies with the behavior of his parents (or significant others) toward him when he was a child." We shall see in Part II of the present volume how frequently in our groups these two aspects of transference occur.

Schutz also presents two postulates of importance for group psychology. The first is the Postulate of Group Development, which states, "The formation and development of two or more people into an interpersonal relation (i.e., a group) always follows the same sequence. Under this postulate fall two principles: (1) For the time period starting with the group's beginning... the predominant area of interaction begins with inclusion, is followed by control, and finally by affection. (2) This cycle may recur."

The second is the Postulate of Compatibility and states: "If the compatibility of group H is greater than that of another group, M, then the goal achievement of H will exceed that of group M." Group interaction during any time interval may be described as taking place predominantly in the area of inclusion, of control, or of affection. In this section Schutz makes a distinction between "wanted behavior" and "expressed behavior" for each stage and these categories signify the degree of passivity or activity of an individual's behavior in relation to getting interpersonal satisfaction in the group in any given area. Compatibility, then, is measured both as to the dimension of the need and in the way the need is handled. The first is called area compatibility; the second, reciprocal (i.e., complementary) compatibility. For the total group the term interchange compatibility is used and it, too, may be measured.

Schutz has also developed a measuring instrument called FIRO-B, designed to evaluate behavior in these three crucial areas of interpersonal behavior. In Chapter IV of his book he describes this instrument and shows the specific ways in which the tests are related to the theoretical framework and to the subsequent empirical results derived from its application. He thus provides a means for the further experimental investigation of group behavior.

It is not our purpose here to evaluate this system, nor to suggest that it be adopted by group psychologists in general. Our interest lies primarily in the fact that it demonstrates the feasibility of devising a scientifically sound, systematic theoretical orientation which combines the Freudian, the interpersonal and the group dynamics (Bionic) approach to group psychology, which is productive of a progression of hypotheses, and provides the means for putting these to experimental test. Here is a worthy model for an eventual group psychological theory.

Taken together, all these recent developments in group dynamics have prepared the way for infinitely better communication between psychologists of the several disciplines and schools of thought. They have shown that the abstractions used by psychoanalytic group therapists and those group dynamicists, while originating on different levels, can be put on the same plane for experimental purposes. The vexing question remains as to how this rapprochement between two group psychologies will bring about better understanding among group psychotherapists of different schools, but reciprocal influence between two great complementary psychological ideologies has been established and the prospects for future collaboration are exciting.

V Illustration of Group Development Theories: Experience in a Leadership Training Group

During the summer of 1961 it was my privilege to become a participant observer in a training group at Bethel, Maine. It turned out to be a very rewarding experience. I had anticipated that among research psychologists there would be an interesting but somewhat cool and detached atmosphere, where scientific attitudes took precedence over human considerations. I learned almost immediately that the leader to whose group I had been assigned had a stereotype in mind for me, too. He expected a rather irritating and disruptive female therapist who would specialize in informing the members what they were "really thinking." He was distinctly worried about having me in his group, and not a little apprehensive about the prospects for his peace of mind. The chief administrator took the precaution of suggesting that I remain a silent observer who would politely evade the direct questions which would no doubt be asked me, whereupon I became worried myself. I didn't think I could manage the role of silent member and at the same time feared that if I could accomplish this feat my purpose in coming would be defeated. However, at our first meeting, preliminary to the group sessions, the leader and I both recognized that our fantasies had quite misled us.

I was introduced to the group and they gave their consent to my becoming a full-fledged member. Some school administrators from grade to college level, a few "Y" executives, a neurologist, two ministers, several industrial executives, and one other woman, a teacher, constituted the membership. There were about fourteen of us. The leader[1] was easygoing and emotionally responsive, and interacted with the group so naturally that although he did not answer questions or introduce topics we were hardly aware of his role. His co-trainer[2] was of a very different temperament and had a correspondingly different conception of his role, more in keeping with my original idea of the leader's attitude. He was very quiet, expressed no feelings or reactions, and intervened only to make an interpretation of what he thought was the emotional preoccupation of the group as a whole. Since his comments were usually on a fairly deep level the group tended to deny what he said. For example, when we were struggling with hostile dependency feelings he tried to put the problem in terms of family relationships, which the members completely rejected. And once, when we were nearing the end of our two-week period and he noted an atmosphere of depression, he related it to our losing people close to us. They refused to admit it. It is true that such an explanation is usually denied, but it is also true that later events give evidence that it was registered.

The group responded very warmly to the chief trainer's method of free and candid interaction with them, much preferring it to the co-trainer's detachment. The reason for this choice is not exactly clear, for the difference between their status and personalities cut across that between their methods. This confusion, together with the friendliness of the leader, probably contributed to the members' displacement of their resentment onto the second in command. There seemed to me to be no question that a more anonymous role on the part of the leader would have had greater research value, but the goal of learning, in so short a period, was probably better served by a leader who interacted and de-emphasized his authority role.

Although I had come in the middle of the first week I was able to observe some of the mutual testing out that occurs in a new group. I assume that my late entry reawakened such reactions, especially as the members knew I was a therapist. They seemed to

[1] Chris Argyris, Ph.D., Yale University.
[2] Arthur Cohen, Ph.D., Harvard University.

find it very hard to give up their usual status designations and status-protection modes of behavior. They could not readily modify their habitual bearing, manner, or mode of speach. Nevertheless, as a group they were beginning to respond to the standards of behavior expected by the leader. The fact that some of the members had heard about the Bethel idea from former members added to the pressure they put on their less "sophisticated" peers to adopt new norms.

It seemed apparent to me that the members were dealing with the anxiety usually aroused in the early stages of any group meeting. At first they strengthened their usual character defenses; then as they began to realize that their old techniques were not acceptable in the new group they became much more anxious. There was a general feeling of unrest and querulousness and a frequent expression of doubt about achieving their objective in coming to a "leadership training institute." Their attempts to gain security by establishing agenda or rules of procedure were not encouraged by the leaders. This increased anxiety probably served to accelerate both learning and the acceptance of different standards. The necessity for them to determine what the leader wanted and to try to produce it increased appreciably.

There were many variations in the way the members dealt with their anxiety and these clearly reflected the individual character development. One whom we shall call Bill (he was an executive in a war industry) brought up the question of how to diminish the anxiety of his men, who were constantly reminded of the possibility of diaster but not allowed to mention to anyone the nature and implications of their work. He asked if they should not be encouraged to air their feelings among themselves, under leadership. It seemed a perfectly rational question and it was completely baffling to him that the leader refused to answer it. The group, which sympathized with him, took up his problem, asked many questions, gave advice, and gradually came to realize that it was his own anxiety that was at the core of his difficulty. This fact was readily inferred from his behavior in the group, for he was restless, dejected, and irritable. Yet he denied being anxious, and said he was thoroughly frustrated and angry that we should try to get to his feelings instead of telling him what to do. The group pressed on until the leader felt it better to divert its interest to another member. This man had become the spontaneous leader in this discussion, and he was at the moment ready to express his own severe anxiety, which he did in terms of concern about the welfare of his family, from whom he was for this period separated. Bill became even more sullen and restless. His hostility was openly expressed toward another man, who was certainly trying to help him and who had until then played the role of the nonconforming scapegoat in the group.

Another participant, Bob, an oil executive, had marked outward poise but was relatively quiet during the early days of the group. While the more overtly dependent members kept asking for answers and evinced many forms of behavior calculated to please the leader, Bob either chimed in occasionally to back one of them up, suggested his own answer, or made a veiled criticism of the leader's apparent lack of "know-how." He managed to keep everyone friendly both toward him and one another, as if he were already preparing for the later period when he was to become the leader of the outspoken rebellion against the Institute's methods (the second subphase). Once this took place, and his open hostility had been tolerated, he laughingly spoke of the "let's kill the leader" movement. The defiance and control of the anal character became quite evident in him, as did Bill's orally-determined, infantile fury, clearly associated with denial and helplessness.

Little by little the questioning of the leader and hope for answers diminished and increasing criticism took their place. The more aggressive (counterdependent) members took the lead. Resentment was at first expressed toward the Institute, then toward the assistant leader, and finally, albeit reluctantly, toward the leader himself. The group then seemed to reach a new stage and the members began to discuss freely among themselves their relationships, their problems, and various events which took place at the Institute and in our group.

During this third subphase, in which we seemed to transcend the dichotomy between dependence and counterdependence to interdependence, personal relations developed among us. The topics of discussion also markedly changed, and clearly had to do with problems of distance or closeness among peers, although those of authority figures continued, too. A Swiss minister, for example, had found it difficult to become a part of our group. He smiled frequently in a friendly way but said little; and we experienced him as being distant and aloof. One day, however, he brought before us a problem he had encountered in his work with the children of his parish. He felt he had failed to combine handling the disciplinary problems of the children with that of diplomatic relationships with their parents. What became apparent (as it always did in the group) was that his problem at home was closely related to his problem in our group. The common denominator for the two situations was the man's character and the consequent attitudes he unconsciously displayed in his relationships. To me it seemed clear that he suffered inwardly from too great a distance between his ego ideal and his inability to realize its demands, and that problems which derived from this bind were revealed in his inability to assert himself and were obviously interfering with his ability to relate warmly with his peers as well. His unconscious fantasies of omnipotence were subtly conveyed by his bearing and manner. On the other hand was an inability to assert himself firmly when the occasion demanded it. The combination played havoc with him. All this was, of course, not analyzed as it would have been in a therapy group, but merely bringing up the problem brought him into interaction with it and with us. The ensuing crosscurrents of the conversation and feelings visibly engaged him emotionally. (Incidentally, we also supplied him with various bits of advice from which he might, if he saw fit, choose his course.) His relationship with the group improved and it was obvious that many of the attitudes, now for the first time expressed openly toward him, gave him some insight into the aloofness of which he had not been aware.

This incident brought to focus my own criticism of the training method. It seemed to me that to discourage this man from talking about the "there and then" was to miss the core of his problem as badly as if we had not talked about the "here and now." I made the point that it seemed to be the clear-cut and crucial linkage between the "here and now" and the "there and then" that counted in situations like these, and that it might very well be the insight into that connection which was the decisive factor for change. Both the leader and the group received my comments warmly, and I felt more than ever accepted in spite of the lively intellectual argument which followed.

It was in the next experience that I became vividly impressed with my special reaction to the group as a whole quite apart from my relationship with its individual members. We were assigned to second groups, called "N" groups, in order to supply the data for some additional research by the leaders, the purpose of which we were not aware. Almost all the members experienced a sharp heightening of group loyalties and affection for the members of their original group, and I was no exception. I suddenly felt I was a member of the very best group, actually missed it and was extremely happy to get back to it.

I examined my feelings to the individual members and realized that with one or two exceptions they were not strong enough to account for this attachment. Even my liking for the leader, though it might have been displaced to the group as such, seemed insufficient to explain the situation. I could no longer personally question the concept of the group as a total entity which extended beyond the sum of its parts.

Differences between therapy and training methods also showed up distinctly. At Bethel there was no exploration of the member's anxiety or its origin and no discussion of other aspects of their lives. Only interpersonal feelings evidenced in the immediate sessions were subject to comment. Moreover, if there was any sign of pathological reaction the leader reassured the member in question and deftly steered toward another subject.

It was also very clear that the training group method is appropriate to the purpose for which it was originated, i.e., to change systems rather than individuals. To accomplish this, individuals must of course also change in some respects; but their problems need not be and in all likelihood cannot be thus resolved. Therapeutic changes take place, but not therapy. The group movement proceeds and the group as such changes.

The training leaders are very well aware of this difference and in no wise claim to do therapy. The total experience confirmed my theories about the basic similarity of all groups regardless of their goal. It demonstrated the plausibility of the theories of group development which the National Training Laboratories had been developing, and it particularly affirmed the hypothesis that groups follow the same psychological principles that individuals do. It reinforced my conclusion that the framework of the phases of development, if expanded to include the growth of the ego and object relations, is suitable to a comprehensive group psychological theory.

VI Psychoanalytic Contributions
Toward Convergence

For a long time social psychologists and group therapists pursued their studies of group behavior in relative disregard of one another. Because each worked on a different level of abstraction, they had little interest in each other's results. Among group therapists the general impression seemed to be that the theoretical foundations of field theory and those of psychoanalysis were antagonistic.

Yet Lewin himself had called attention to their compatibility (1937). And J. F. Brown, a systematic psychologist of the topological school, with a comprehensive knowledge of psychoanalytic theory, had elaborated the thesis in some detail (1937). He reasoned as follows: (1) both theories are dynamic, holistic and functional. He noted that (2) they see the human individual as an organism in an environment. Although they differ in the weight given to society, biology, and the intrapsychic, they both agree that the individual is a sociopsycho-biological organism. (3) They both see the organism as a supersummative whole. (4) They agree that growth and personality genesis become matters of restructuralization or differentiation out of a global whole. This view is opposed to mechanism. (5) They invent theoretical constructs in order to arrive at a systematized science. (6) They posit some dynamic force to account for activity, i.e., they stress the problem of motivation. (7) They agree that motivation is blocked by social or physical barriers; (8) that all symptoms have a cause, a significance and an economy; (9) that some sources of motivation are unknown. (10) They both use the hypothetico-deductive method which allows for the theoretical constructs such as libido, ego, vector, life space. (11) Both observe behavior and coordinate it into theory in order to integrate the facts.

The differences, he says, are such that they can be decided by clinical or experimental evidence. Psychology had made notable advances since Freud pioneered in the second scientific revolution. More precise constructs such as the concept of the field theory, and better theories of energy, could be formulated. Yet Brown feels it should be "obvious that psychoanalysis adheres to the concept of the individual as a self-regulating system, the constant restructuralization of which is economical in nature," and that "we must distinguish between the organismic theories of Freud and Lewin and the atomistic, mechanistic approach of Wundt and Kraepelin."

Some of the statements Freud made in his *Group Psychology and the Analysis of the Ego* (1921) immediately corroborate Brown's views and indicate that they apply to group as well as to individual psychoanalytic psychology.

Freud writes, "The contrast between individual psychology and social or group psychology, which at first glance may seem to be full of significance, loses a great deal of its sharpness when it is examined more closely. It is true that individual psychology is concerned with the individual man and explores the path by which he seeks to find satisfaction for his instincts; but only rarely and under certain exceptional conditions is individual psychology in a position to disregard the relations of this individual to others ..." (Freud, 1921, p. 2).

This view makes possible the mobility between individual and group psychological concepts which is requisite to the very existence of psychoanalytic group psychotherapy.

In elaborating on McDougall's theories, Freud (1921, p. 27) made it clear that "reciprocal influence between the members" was for him a basic qualification for defining a group. Thus he implied the reflexive nature of the group relationships which the group dynamicists make explicit. His subscription to the organismic view is again indicated by a comment (p. 32) in which he underlines Trotter's remark that "the tendency toward the formation of groups is biologically a continuation of the multicellular character of all higher organisms." Freud suggests (p. 32) "that he [Trotter] implicitly advocates the notion of continuity between the individual and the group as two orders of organism."[1]

The significant fact that our major premises are compatible seems incontrovertible. We share adherence to the basic tenets of an organismic view. This does not, of course, mean that we all adhere to a particular organismic theory. As Hall and Lindzey (1954) point out, "What Goldstein finds in the organism is not precisely what Allport or Freud finds there." It means, rather, that we share the common attitude that groups, like individuals, are such organisms, and like them have the capacity for restructuring themselves by means of self-correction through the assembling of information from the surround; that their inner relations are of a reflexive rather than a lineal nature; and that multiple causation is a fact with which we must learn to deal effectively both in therapy and in research.

The first steps toward concretizing the possibilities for convergence were taken by the group dynamicists. The recent work of those social scientists who have been doing research in a group therapy context and with the data of training groups actually does provide the beginnings of a group psychology which is congenial to the thinking of the analytic group psychotherapists. It has the capacity of being developed into a sound theoretical framework within which to apply the several varieties of group therapy. Many group dynamicists combined the techniques and terminology of interpersonal psychoanalysis rather than the Freudian techniques with Bionic theory (See Chapter IV). H. Thelen, W. Bennis, C. Argyris are examples. A few brought in Freudian concepts. G. Bach made his bow to Freud in terms of family transference, but relied much more on interpreting the group dynamics and the here and now interpersonal relations. D. Stock and her colleagues employed Thomas French's psychoanalytic theory of focal conflict.

---

[1] Freud had already expressed the hope of finding a way to influence the masses through psychoanalysis. He wrote (1910): "We expect to gain the authority of the community in general and thus to achieve the more far-reaching prophylaxis against neurotic disorders." Present-day training and therapy groups fulfill this prediction.

Meanwhile, analytic group therapists with a predominantly Freudian orientation had been largely pre-occupied with applying psychoanalytic techniques to groups of patients. Their interest in group psychology as such, even Freud's presentation of it (which was by his own account only a partial one) was at best secondary in their actual work. And until very recently most of them paid little attention to the developments in the field of group dynamics. But there were those who kept abreast of the broader field of group behavior. S. R. Slavson (1953, 1956) was one of them. He presented both viewpoints but, because he was primarily concerned with therapeutic techniques and who should apply them to groups, he drew a hard and fast line between the two disciplines and reinforced the cleavage between them. It was S. Scheidlinger who first called attention to Brown's propositions and who emphasized the generally ignored fact that, in spite of their different goals, the two fields had a mutual interest in the group psychological phenomena. He had (1952b) listed and described what he considered group relevant psychoanalytic propositions in contradistinction to the primarily group therapeutic factors. By including the individual personality and the group factors among these, he went beyond the group-individual dichotomy that was in the making. Later (1960) he reviewed the relationship between the two fields,[2] and pointed out the complementary relationship between group dynamics and Freudian group psychology. The one interests itself in the group, he said, the other in the individual; the one in the present, the other in the past; the one in the overt, the other in the latent phenomena. Unfortunately his suggestions were not followed immediately, but today these differences have been reduced to a mere matter of emphasis. Both groups are interested in all these phenomena.

Durkin (1957) further investigated the relationship between the two fields. Following through on Carthwright's opinion that it was a mistake to assume that findings based on one type of group can be directly applied to another, I compared the specific conditions which hold in therapy groups to those of work groups in order to show how a different constellation of variables necessitates different rules for dealing with the same group phenomena. For

[2] He also provided us with one of the few adequate critiques of Bion's theories.

example, because of the nature of the goal and the established path to that goal, democratic leadership, which is most effective in groups, must take second place to therapeutic considerations in decision making in therapy groups. This examination of comparative conditions is continued in the present volume (Chapter III).

Edward Glover, an outstanding practicing psychoanalyst and theoretician, showed how adherence to certain psychoanalytic principles would greatly enrich a comprehensive group psychology. In a chapter concerning the frontiers of psychoanalysis, he writes (Glover, 1956, p. 433): "There seems no reason to suppose that the metapsychological principles found so useful in the case of the individual mind should not be applied to group phenomena. This implies that three distinct approaches should be made to each problem—dynamic, economic, and structural, leading up to an examination of the technique whereby the group succeeds in maintaining its organization in spite of the turbulent forces with which it has to deal. In this connection it is essential to find a set of energy-measures comparable with those that are available in the case of the individual. . . . We may also assume that the same forces and the same types of controlling mechanisms operate in the group and following this assumption it would appear essential to decode the end-products of group activity in terms of their unconscious components, a task which again would require the cooperation of the psychoanalyst." And later (p. 434), "For it is not only the mental history of the individual adult that lies buried in the mind of the child, but also the mental history of the race. It was one of the virtues of Freud's formulations regarding mental disorders that they could be plausibly correlated with reconstructions of racial development; the best examples being of course his correlation of the obsessional neuroses with the animistic and magical phase of mental development of primitive man, and his suggestion that hysterical states are atavistic. . . . This correlation between the mental disorders of adult life, the predisposition to them developed during early childhood, the early unconscious phases of mental evolution of the race leads to the further assumption that major unconscious mental conflicts of the individual adult correspond to difficult phases of adaptation in racial history." The interprofessional project we envision would be the loser if these dimensions were to be excluded.

The most comprehensive effort to construct a system of group (and individual) psychology based on an organismic view and including the Freudian principles is that of Schutz (1958b, 1961), which is described in Chapter IV. His blend of Freudian, interpersonal, and group dynamic (Bionic) social psychology is both ingenious and sound.

Schutz not only coordinated the Bennis and Shepard theory of group development with Freud's psychosexual phases, but defined such major concepts as transference and identification in operational terms, and in language that would be acceptable to both group dynamicists and the interpersonal schools. In other words, he took definite steps to concretize an integrated group psychology in depth. Furthermore, his FIRO-B tests provide an instrument for testing all the hypotheses which may be derived from his theory, and the means for repeating any of his experimental proofs. Moreover, his work has been systematic enough to demonstrate how Glover's requirements—that the dynamic, economic, and structural approaches be utilized—might be met. For instance, in following through on his hypothesis that the group follows the same psychological principles as the individual, Schutz (1961) demonstrates that the leadership function of a group may be coordinated with the ego function of the individual. In doing so he, in a sense, provides evidence for Freud's idea (1921) that the group, in developing its structure, gradually takes over the functions of the ego, which the individuals who compose it yielded when they became its members.

Schutz (1961) shows how leadership as a function is exercised by anyone, whether it be the designated leader or a member, and how it develops through the interplay of outer reality with personal needs and with the conflict-free areas of the personality. He makes a special point of demonstrating how the leader exercises the adaptive functions of the group through the available intelligence, perceptual ability, motility, and action, in order to adapt it to the external world. The leader, he says, helps the group deal with its internal interpersonal needs by gratifying or channeling them in order to accomplish its task roles. He has arrived at these conclusions by research in which he applied his FIRO theory and the FIRO-B tests. In other words, he provides both a logical and a technical means for testing out his theory that the group and the individual are organisms which operate on the same principles, and the consequent propositions of that theory as well.

In the division of social and community psychiatry at the Albert Einstein College of Medicine, Harris Peck and his colleagues have come to an almost identical conclusion. They have been carrying out another broadly envisioned research program, in connection with their training and service facilities, which points in the same general direction. It is operating under a long-term NIMH grant and consists of (1) a group process section and (2) a clinical center for family and small groups. In this way the goals of theory, training, and service are implemented in constant interaction. One of the primary purposes of the program is to fill the conceptual gap that exists between the intrapsychic and the societal levels and has long impeded progress in the field of mental health. In pursuing these goals, Peck and his colleagues conduct a series of seminars among various levels of trainees (residents, nurses, social workers, etc.) to study group process in relation to both individual and group phenomena. They hope to discover improved modes of operating the ward personnel, and to raise the level of competence in group and individual task roles. In their search for suitable definitions of mental health requisite to a more scientific and practicable mental hygiene program, they have found Marie Jahoda's criteria relevant to their purpose. For instance, one of these is "accessibility of self to consciousness." They are able to show that changes in the functioning of groups and of individuals result from the members' ability to acknowledge unconscious information regarding events, feelings, ideas, or impulses. They also find that such changes are the function not only of the individual's history, but of the group's readiness to accept the material. Furthermore, they discovered that the individuals' readiness in a new group was also partly a function of the attitudes prevailing in former groups of which they had been a part (Peck, 1963).

Peck and his colleagues see the dynamics of the small group as a possible means of bridging the gap between the psychoanalytic and epidemiological points of view and of providing techniques which may be adapted to the solution of intergroup problems. One of Peck's basic hypotheses is significantly identical with that which Schutz has proposed. The Albert Einstein group calls it "individual group psychological isomorphism." It is defined simply as:

"the psychological organization of groups is fundamentally similar to that of individuals." Peck warns that he does not mean that
their organization is identical.

Harris B. Peck, Melvin Roman, Seymour Kaplan, and Gerald
Bauman have been engaged in psychological research with therapy
groups in which certain propositions arising out of the Individual
Group Psychological Isomorphism (I.G.P.I.) hypothesis have been
tested experimentally. Roman and Bauman (1961) worked out a design for testing the hypothesis that the same considerations which
determine the competence of an individual are applicable to the
group. Using a technique of interaction testing, they provide inter-
related sets of data giving information about the intellectual and
personality characteristics of the group as an entity. Each member
of the group is tested and scored in the standard manner. Following
this, the group members are tested together with the instruction
that they are to produce responses acceptable to all. The test protocol obtained from the group is scored and interpreted as though it
had been obtained from an individual, and test results are based on
intensive quantitative and qualitative analysis of the data, and on
comparisons based on both individual and interaction test material. Peck feels that the hypothesis of I.G.P.I. (i.e., that the group
protocol may be treated as if it had been obtained from an individual) is promising but needs further validation.

In summary, his view is that the small group is a psychological
entity capable of delineating its own purposes, boundaries, identity, and relation with the outer environment and its own com-
ponent units. He sees the I.G.P.I. hypothesis as a useful base for
approaching problems concerning the relationship between groups
and individuals. It provides a way of shifting back and forth between the group and the individual and of describing the ongoing
processes in comparable terms and within a common reality.

In general, Peck's work is geared somewhat more in the direction
of practice, while that of Schutz is aimed primarily at creating a
theoretically sound, open system of psychology which will encom-
pass both the individual and the group. Both are using the same
basic premise and both are finding it productive. Both feel that a
great deal of continued research is in order before definitive statements may be made, but they are optimistic about the final out-

come. This kind of convergence is a significant indication of to-day's *avant-garde* trends.

We are at the moment much concerned with individual-group similarity. There are those who object (Slavson, Schwartz, Wolf). However, no one has denied that there are also significant differences. An individual is not a group; nor is a group an individual. The propositions we have been reviewing were developed especial-ly for the purpose of enabling us to move from one integrative level to another. The problem at hand is simply whether or not a group belongs to the same order of psychological systems as does the in-dividual.

Wolf and Schwartz (1960) take a strong stand against the empha-sis on their similarity, to wit: "To misapply individual psycholo-gical concepts as explanatory for the group is to destroy the op-erational and phenomenological characteristics of group entity. It's just as inappropriate to misapply social psychological constructs as explanatory for the individual ... any attempt to make these [group] laws fit the individual is to propagate a mystique." To be sure these critics do not give evidence for their statements, but the burden of proof is always on the initiators of a new hypothesis, so we shall have to provide both logical and empirical evidence to combat their criticism. Nevertheless, a broad theoretical frame-work for a scientific group psychology which is capable of encom-passing all points of view is in the making, and a number of ana-lytic group therapists have contributed to it.

Because of the growing rapprochement between group dynamics and analytic group psychotherapy, I felt it was worth reviewing Freud's (1921) *Group Psychology and the Analysis of the Ego* with this in mind, in order to discover whether it might provide further contributions to the comprehensive group psychology we have en-visioned. The results were startling. They suggested a reformula-tion, based on Freud's own ideas, which would bridge the gap be-tween his older theories and those of Bion which the group dynamicists had adapted. They are reported in the next chapter.

VII Review and Reformulation of Freudian Group Psychology

Freud was one of the first to present a dynamic group psychology. Beginning with an assessment of the then current theories of the sociologists and social psychologists, such as Le Bon, Trotter, and McDougall, he applied his psychoanalytic theory to group behavior. A decade was to pass before a more empirical sociology and an experimental social psychology came to a degree of maturity, and two decades before group dynamics, as we know it, was well established. Freud's formulations, partially anchored though they were in nineteenth century biology, give evidence also of the newer trends.

It has always seemed strange to me that the contributions of so eminent a psychologist should have been received with such relatively little enthusiasm in his day and have stimulated neither breadth nor depth of interest among group psychotherapists twenty years later. However, we know that in his day there was almost no interest in group psychotherapy. Recently analytic group therapists have been more interested in applying his therapeutic techniques than in studying group psychology. They wanted to *use* groups, not to learn about them. They took what he had to say for granted and seemed unaware of, or disinterested in, elaborating on the more subtle implications of his comments.

And there were other reasons: Freud frankly limited himself to choosing, out of the entire literature on groups, only a few points which were of particular interest to depth psychology. He concentrated on the *libidinal aspects;* and although *Beyond the Pleasure Principle* had been published the previous year, he merely implied that in group psychology aggressive motives might play a role comparable to the libidinal ones. His style contributed, too, to the indifferent reception of his beliefs. He frequently used the trick of following along the reasoning of the authors he was presenting, appearing to agree with them, only to disprove their premises in the end in favor of his own. Nor was he averse to questioning his first conclusion, and overthrowing it to present a second and even a third. This procedure, excellent for permitting the student to follow his reasoning and determine its validity for himself, becomes confusing for those readers who, years later, wish to grasp the main point of his argument. Such readers, though their attitude be indefensible, are likely to select the wrong conclusions and distort the meanings. And so it appears to have happened.

His writing, usually clear and concise, became harder to follow when he began to probe a new theme. His examples oscillated from clinical descriptions to statements based on assumptions concerning their original derivation. Because he himself was still groping for answers and never achieved true closure for the brilliant new configuration that was in the making, the most valuable part of the book was less than convincing. Partly for these reasons, and partly because most analytic group therapists tried to follow the principles of individual psychoanalysis, little use was made of the new ideas that were embryonic in the volume.

Freud accepted the contemporary opinion that emotional intensity is heightened and intellectual activity decreased in members of ephemeral groups, and that even the members of better organized groups endow their leader with extraordinary prestige and evince a high degree of suggestibility. He probed this puzzling phenomenon of emotional contagion. His unique contribution consisted in investigating its causes in depth, according to psychoanalytic principles. The first thesis of his group psychology was a clear, unequivocal, and almost too simple application of libido theory to group behavior. Suggestibility was shown to grow (1) out of the members' libidinal but aim-inhibited drives to the leader and (2) from their mutual identifications through this common tie. Object relations among the members were said to "prop them-selves up" upon these identifications. Potentially ambivalent, these could then turn either into love or hate. Usually in groups hate seems to be repressed because of love for the leader. In his day these two points made a valuable contribution to group psychology be-cause love relations had not previously been mentioned as a factor and the whole question of motivation was still a new subject for social science (Freud, 1921).

Freud himself felt that his first two hypotheses were inadequate and began a search for a more substantial explanation of the com-pliance of individuals to groups. That they do it, "Ihnen zu Liebe," did not, to him, seem sufficient. He hoped to find an answer by in-vestigating the subject of identification which he felt was in any case insufficiently understood. A third hypothesis did indeed emerge from this effort. It stated that members tend to substitute the leader for their own ego ideal. This new idea opened up fertile territory. It led to further investigation of the role of preoedipal factors, and to the not yet fully understood realm of the archaic ego and superego. Today it provides us with material for a refor-mulation of his group theory in modern terms. But Freud's con-centration on the oedipal situation prevented him and others from bringing these newer aspects of his contribution into clear focus.

His preliminary investigation produced a clear-cut operational definition of identification. He stated it as the wish "to be like another" as distinguished from object love or "the wish to *have* another." Moving toward a conceptual definition, he differentiated between the two processes on the basis of whether the tie was the subject or the object of the ego. Next he articulated three forms of identification. There is the original form of emotional tie with an object, achieved by the mechanism of introjection. Second, when an object is lost or given up, the subject may regress to introjecting it. A third, much later derivative is identification with "every new perception of a common quality shared with some other person who is not an object of the sexual instinct." "The more important this common quality is," he wrote, "the more successful may this partial identification become. It may represent the beginning of a new tie," and the mutual tie between members of a group is such an identification, based upon an important common emotional quality.

He turned next to the important distinction between that form of identification in which the object is introjected, and a second process in which the subject substitutes the object for the ego ideal.[1] On the latter he based his third hypothesis for group psychology. "Suggestibility," he said, "is increased by the fact that each member gives up his own ego ideal and adopts that of the leader. A group from this standpoint may be regarded as a number of individuals who have taken the same object for their ego ideal and who have consequently identified themselves with one another in their ego."

But he was not yet satisfied. There was a missing link. He wrote: "There is still a great deal in it which we must recognize as unexplained and mystical. It contains an element of *paralysis*[2] derived from the relation between someone with superior power and someone who is without power and helpless—which may afford a transition to the hypnosis of terror which occurs in animals. The manner in which it is produced and its relationship to sleep are not clear; and the puzzling way in which some people are subject to it while others resist it completely points to some factor which perhaps alone makes possible the purity of the attitudes of the libido which it exhibits" (Freud, 1921, p. 79).

Because he had not fully realized the preoedipal implications of his observations, Freud then fell back on an analogy with the primal horde to account for the group's mysterious power over its members. In the horde, the father is all powerful and the others must obey. So magic and dangerous is his power that the others cannot even look upon him directly. But in the end he is killed and eaten, and the primal horde is thereby transformed into a fraternity of brothers. Freud conceived of the group as a revival of the primal horde.

One cannot deny that this theory brings a modicum of coherence to our understanding of group phenomena. The members' expectations that the leader is omnipotent, the inevitable hostility they sooner or later express toward him, no matter what his leadership tactics may be, and particularly the extraordinary compliance of

---

[1] These might be the equivalents of Klein's introjective and projective identification.
[2] Italics mine.

the members to him and to the group as a whole, can all be comprehended in its light. But from a scientific point of view, the horde theory is far from convincing. When it becomes necessary to use one unprovable, even untestable hypothesis to prove another, we stand on shaky ground, especially when it is also impossible to explain the mechanics of the connection between them. The horde theory is, at best, expendable. Freudian analytic group therapists have accordingly shied away from it. He himself admitted from the start that it was only an hypothesis and laughed with a critic who referred to it as a "Just-So-Story" (Freud, 1921, p. 90).

Dissatisfied with the evidence as it stood, Freud undertook to strengthen his theory by drawing a parallel between the power of the horde father, the hypnotist, and the father of the family in order to explain the mysteriousness of the group's power. The characteristic of uncanniness, he said, "suggests something old and familiar that has undergone repression." Expatiating on Ferenczi's discovery that the hypnotist, in putting the subject to sleep, uses the soothing tactics of the mother or the threatening ones of the father in order to gain the power which the parent once had over the child, Freud wrote, "The hypnotist awakens in the subject a portion of his archaic inheritance which had also made him compliant towards his parents and which he had experienced in an individual reanimation in his relation to his father; what is thus awakened is the idea of a paramount and dangerous personality, towards whom only a passive-masochistic attitude is possible, to whom one's will has to be surrendered..." (Freud, 1921, p. 99).

One wonders at this point why he had to resort to the primal horde and to the hypnotist at all, since the alternative ontogenetic hypothesis suggested by his material, also based on the family analogy, would have been scientifically more acceptable. Why, in other words, did Freud assume it was the relation to the father that was "reanimated," while he overlooked the obvious fact that the first compelling power in human experience is the mother? Surely the neonate's mother must evoke just such an image,[3] for it is she who unwittingly destroys his narcissistic bliss and who must bring to his awareness the deprivations and limitations of reality, as well

[3] To be distinguished from the good image which the sustaining function evokes.

as her love and sustenance. This seemingly cruel, powerful aspect of the mother image is subsequently largely repressed, but its deep-seated effect can later be demonstrated in those cases which come up for analysis. Such a theory not only puts us in the useful position of having access to observable facts to test the hypothesis but of having at our disposal a bona fide mechanism to explain how it works in the concept of transference, the function of which in determining the adult's behavior has been firmly established.

Freud's overarching concern with the oedipal situation here again determined his selection. His choice of the horde father as "proof" was in line with the startling oedipal discoveries he had made in working with hysterics and was favored by the particular condition of his time and place, nineteenth-century Vienna. The behavior of little boys in America today would cast doubt upon it. Since that time, developmental psychology and psychoanalytic research have given us sufficient information concerning the first months of life to allow us to realize their tremendous and perhaps primary influence on adult behavior. I do not mean to underrate the unconscious libidinal aspects of the oedipal situation, but rather to bring into proper focus the preoedipal factors, especially that of the power element in the mother-child relationship, and their connection with early ego and superego development and with group psychology.

Any attempt to articulate a theory which depends upon reconstructing preverbal material is precarious. However, without such hypotheses one cannot make progress in understanding this significant phase of life. The hypothesis through which I hope to connect the adult's reaction to groups with the neonate's earliest interaction with his mother grows out of a conception of that period of his life which is based on a mixture of observed fact, established inference, and assumption. In order to test the reasonableness and plausibility of this hypothesis it will therefore be necessary to describe in detail this conception of that interaction. I shall try, without hope of complete success, to avoid the error of adult morphism, for empathic observation of infants must be translated into adult words if we are to bridge their wordless experience. At this stage of our theory building, then, we must expect to fall short of the scientific precision we ultimately hope to achieve. Much more needs to be learned about that period and the task is not made easier by the fact that we have to deal with a transition stage in the infant's life in which psychological reactions are beginning to emerge alongside the purely physiological.[4] Nevertheless we must make the attempt, for to be overly cautious at this point, where our objective is to penetrate the mysteries of preverbal behavior, would severely block our progress.

Let us imagine, with the help of recent research, clinical experience, and common sense, what the early situation was like. At first the "other" could only be perceived rather globally as "something out there which comes and goes." Two very primitive qualities of the other must have been differentiated rather early with a perception of a crucial relationship. They would have concerned size and power. We can easily believe that one of the first wordlessly discovered relationships must have been experienced as the equivalent of "me little, other big." Then the big other must gradually have come to be sensed as the one who determined whether gratification or frustration was to be experienced, for as soon as his magic gestures proved to have only limited effectiveness, he found himself not in control of his situation. Whether her presence was related to food, warmth, and comfort or to frustration and discomfort she, rather than he, controlled it. A much more complex but still wordless notion must then have come into being, something like "me little, can't," "other big, can." Thus bit by bit the image, now rapidly emerging as mother, was built, and she became the prototype for all later "different" ones.

We cannot avoid the conclusion that this aspect of his experience with the mother must have been a terrifying and infuriating experience. How could the infant have experienced differently her intrusion into his state of narcissistic bliss? He was forced to become aware of his separateness, his littleness, his helplessness, and his almost absolute dependence upon someone who was different, had different wishes, and often obstructed the fulfillment of his own. And how could he have responded as it became evident in the ensuing months and years that she continued to make demands on him which were alien to his baby wishes? He must have supposed that he had to yield or have his supplies cut off, yet that he must

---

[4] Although I believe the very earliest psychological reactions are of tremendous significance for later life, I do not go so far as M. Klein in assuming that ego, superego, and full-fledged psychological reactions begin at birth.

fight her demands in order to maintain his identity. A crucial conflict was born which had a lasting influence on the nature of his
object relationships.

Although we are concentrating on the frustrating aspect of the
mother-infant relationship, we must not forget that the gratifying
aspects of it went hand in hand with it. In fact, as one or the other
of these aspects were dominant in the child's experience a generalized emotional stance toward life must have been developed in
some such terms as "someone out there loves me" or "someone out
there hates me," or, perhaps more often, a confusing mixture of
the two.

In the first or "oral" stage the struggle was begun in order to preserve the existence of the newly discovered self and was presumably
carried on in terms of the crucial experiences of that age. It was a
devour or be devoured world. The fact that there was also a loving
image of the other only played into the infant's desire to yield to
her wishes; but to preserve his identity he had somehow to hold off
or control the powerful one. Ambivalence resulted. In the second
stage the "other," who had by now definitely become "mother,"
was still a loving refuge, but she was in control and still made demands. Control of behavior became the central issue. The conflict
ensued in anal terms, but many other problems with parental authority arose as well, for there were demands that the child be
polite, wash, brush his teeth, and learn an overwhelming assort-
ment of other things. The third stage was, of course, complicated
by the triangular libidinal situation, in which the mixture of libidinal and power needs might easily create a hopelessly entangled
confusion. According to Bergler (1952), the father not only played
his part in the libinal aspects of the oedipal drama, but often in-
herited the role of the controlling dangerous preoedipal mother,
while she was cast into the helpless submissive role. If the conflict
remained unresolved, it was presently carried into school and interfered with other authority relations. Often it was even injected
into peer relationships in a repetitive process of status assessment.
Both the libidinal and the self-preservative needs continued to be
pursued and they were often used in a defensive way, one against
the other.

The very earliest solution was not, of course, carried over in its
entirety. At each stage of ego development the child was able to

perceive reality a little more accurately than before and to adapt his behavior accordingly. Modifications of pattern consequently took place. But on each occasion his behavior carried over traces of the earlier adaptation and reflected something of the particular stance he had adopted toward it. Similar modifications might continue to be made in later life, though the underlying attitude remains. The present-day response, except in cases of extreme regression, is repeated, but in modern dress. The adult's response, including his attitude and behavior in the group, will be distorted to the degree to which the old anxiety is stirred up, and his mode of behavior will reflect the nature of his old solution.

Starting from this plausible analysis I submit as a prerequisite to my hypothesis that it was the frustrating preoedipal mother whom the infant perceived as a "paramount and dangerous personality toward whom only a passive masochistic attitude was possible and to whom one's will had to be surrendered" (Freud, 1921, p. 99) and that it was identification with the two aspects of the mother which accounts for the contrasting aspects of the ego ideal and superego. The hypothesis by which I propose to connect the infantile interaction with group formation has grown out of many years of clinical experience with individual children, adults, and groups; and while this work has been carried on within the framework of a Freudian orientation, it has been continually stimulated by the examination of the concepts and techniques of other schools of thought. It may be stated as follows: The idea of a group activates in the adult individual traces of the preoedipal mother image and the fears connected with it, causing him to become relatively submissive to the group and unusually suggestible.

For example, Frank said about his group, "They seemed like a pack of wolves, ready to devour me." Another young man of phallic orientation, who seemed to have transformed the earlier narcissistic fear into one which was suitable to the period which had been crucial for him, explained his marked anxiety one day by saying, "I'm awfully nervous today . . . expecting the sharp tongues of the women to slice me up piece by piece, I guess"; and he smiled feebly. A voyeuristic patient in another group expected repeatedly that it would "undress her with its many eyes"; another, that it would "expose his shame."

The process of transference in cases such as these seems to occur in two separate steps: (1) The idea of a group, i.e., a large totality of unknown power, conjures up the harsh, preoedipal mother image,[5] reactivating the individual's narcissistic fear of her, and (2) the individual perceives the group accordingly in distorted fashion, and behaves toward it in a way that resembles his mode of reacting to his mother, but in "modern dress." Characteristically, the opposing compulsive traits of submission and opposition are included, one gaining ascendance at a time.

It was not until I reread Freud's *Group Psychology* that I realized how well the material in this volume alone would have provided an adequate foundation for this hypothesis. Because I believe that my expansion and reformulation of Freud's group psychology is not only consonant with our clinical data but makes it possible to bridge over one of the major gaps between it and the theories of the Washington School[6] and that it will also bring us to a clear understanding of the most recent theories of the social psychologists (predominantly Kleinian and Sullivanian) concerning group development (Chapter IV), I shall present this evidence as I see it.

In the discussion of identification on which Freud based his conclusion that the individual substitutes the leader for his own ego ideal, he refers chiefly to earlier papers which deal with (1) preverbal (preoedipal) factors, and (2) with the formation and nature of the ego ideal. In this way what happened during the oral period is closely tied in with what happens to the adult individual when he joins a group.

Concerning the first he says that identification "behaves like a derivative of the first oral phase of organization of the libido, in which the object that we long for and prize is assimilated by eating and is in that way annihilated as such" (Freud, 1921, p. 61). The implication is self-explanatory. The prototype for identification is the taking in of the outer world during the oral phase, by eating. It could of course also be taken in (i.e., introjected) through the other sense organs as is indicated, for example, in the analysis of scopophilic cases.

Freud (1921, p. 68) re-examines certain orally regressed cases

[5] Narcissistic anxiety was presumably at first a response to the forces over which he had no control and only later attached to the image of mother.

[6] Here are emphasized the importance of early mother/child relationships and the significance of the power element in human relationships.

which illustrate the reversion in adulthood from object love to identification with the object via introjection. He related these to the original division of the ego. "But these melancholias also show us something else, which may be of importance to our later discussions. They show us the ego divided, fallen into two pieces, one of which rages against the second. This second piece is the one which has been altered by introjection and which contains the lost object. But the piece which behaves so cruelly is not unknown to us either. It comprises conscience—a critical faculty within the ego, which even in normal times takes up a critical attitude towards the ego, though never so relentlessly and so unjustifiably. On previous occasions we have been driven to the hypothesis ('On Narcissism' and 'Mourning and Melancholia') that some such faculty develops in our ego which may cut itself off from the rest of the ego and come into conflict with it."

There are two important points here which illuminate the relationship between what happened in the oral phase and what happens when an individual joins a group. The cases show that identification with an object brings about a division in the ego. Since the regression in these cases of melancholia is clearly back to the oral-dependent period the assumption would not be out of order that the original division of the ego must have occurred during that period. That is exactly what his reference to "On Narcissism" shows.

I submit that something similar again occurs when the individual yields to the group. Since an object relationship with the leader is sure to meet with opposition by the members it is replaced at least to some extent by identification. This is in the area of his values, i.e., his ego ideal (superego). This same point of view is expressed by Anna Freud (1936, p. 124) when she discusses the defense mechanism, "identification with the aggressor." She writes that this is a "by no means uncommon stage in the normal development of a superego," and again (p. 128) when she explains how projection of guilt goes hand in hand with identification with the aggressor. "An ego which with the aid of the defense mechanism of projection develops along this particular line (i.e., identification with the aggressor) introjects the authorities to whose criticism it is exposed and incorporates them in the superego. It is then able to project its prohibited impulses outwards" (p. 155).

Experience with the first stages of therapy groups seems to bear

out her statement. The parallel is reinforced when she shows
(p. 156) how the child's fantasy of what the grownups will do en-
hances the "objective anxiety" which is the "precursor" of the
superego, so that "its connection with reality becomes ever looser."
We, too, find that the prospective group patient's fantasy of what
the group's attitude to him will be is far more frightening than the
reality. Real experience ameliorates this fear. Only consistent
analysis brings about basic change in a structure which was developed in very early childhood and is now only being repeated.

Freud (1921) goes on to describe the nature of the ego ideal, and
we continue the quotation given above (from p. 69). "We have
called it 'the ego ideal' and by way of functions we have ascribed
to it self-observation, the moral conscience, the censorship of
dreams, and the chief influence in repression. We have said that it
is the heir to the original narcissism in which the childish ego
found its self-sufficiency; it gradually gathers up from the influences of the enviroment the demands which that environment
makes upon the ego and which the ego cannot always rise to, so
that a man when he cannot be satisfied with his ego itself, may
nevertheless be able to find satisfaction in the ego ideal which has
been differentiated out of the ego. In delusions of observation, as
we have further shown, the disintegration of this faculty has become patent and has thus revealed its origin in the influence of
superior powers, and above all of parents."

We are not here so much concerned with the benign part of the
ego ideal (later superego) except to recall that it too may have
been brought about largely by a process of identification with the
good all-giving part of the mother which the child took over in
his attempt to keep a fantasy of omnipotence, and which in
therapy groups he seems at first to project on the leader rather than
the group. Our immediate concern is with the frustrating aspect of
the mother who is perceived as harsh and cruel, a veritable
"aggressor" with whom the child identifies and which accounts
for the cruel aspect of that ego ideal, and which as an adult it will
be prone to project onto the group as a whole.

According to Freud, the identification in melancholia is with
the lost object and reinforces the gradient within the ego. It is
essentially a superego identification. It is with the aggressor,
i.e., with the bad, rejecting mother, and once it is internalized it is

hostile to the rest of the ego. This view would account for the harshness of the archaic superego, and in cases of melancholia would mean that ego is hated, sometimes to the point of extinction, by the internalized aggressor (harsh aspect of early superego) rather than the other way around. Freud speaks of the object as being rejected in these cases but is it not more consistent with clinical data to say that the ego feels rejected by the object? It is in that sense that the object is lost.

If we reconstruct how the gradient in the ego came about during that early period of transition from primary narcissism to the acceptance of reality it would in essence resemble what follows. When the infant could no longer experience itself as omnipotent and perfect it must have imputed that quality to the world outside which soon came to be represented by the mother. Since painful feelings were first projected while the good ones were introjected, two images of the "one out there" must have formed, both of which were reintrojected to form a gradient in the ego, i.e., the beginnings of the ego ideal. These may be thought of as precursors of the superego, and this early development may then be connected with the individual's attitude toward the group, as we have shown.

Freud seems indeed to have provided us with a good deal of material concerning preoedipal events which give backing for this hypothesis. But he himself did not make the same inferences from it. It was only in the light of more recent psychoanalytic theories and my own clinical data from group psychotherapy that I drew my own conclusions.

Clinical experience with analytic psychotherapy groups very definitely suggests that the processes with which we are concerned are much more complex than he implied in this volume. For instance:

(1) The individual does not just take over the leader in place of his own ego ideal: a complicated transference is set up through which this occurs.

(2) Neither the infant nor the adult neurotic seems to be as inactive as Freud implies. Both toward his mother and toward the group the individual acts not merely submissively but ambivalently. He is passive but he is active too. He is compliant and de-

fiant, dependent and counterdependent. Whereas submission is in
the service of his libidinal satisfaction, a need to fight for his individuality is pressing him too. As an infant he spit, screamed,
kicked, and learned to use his passivity to control. Later as a small
child he used withholding or incontinence to fight with "the one
he saw as an aggressor." In the therapeutic group he uses whatever
defenses have evolved out of his original crude protective measures
as strong resistance to the leader's therapeutic efforts.

(3) In the therapy group too we see plainly that there is always
interaction between the leader and the members and that the
group standards result not entirely from accepting those of the
leader but also from a struggle among the members concerning
their values. It is in this way, after the first pseudo-acceptance, that
the group's standards are taken over by the individual to modify
his own ego ideal. It must be admitted that the leader's ideas prove
to be the most weighty single element in this interaction.

(4) Group therapy experience gives evidence of still another
complexity. The individual member's reaction to the leader and to
the group is by no means always similar because of identification
with the same love object. At the beginning the members, with the
exception, perhaps, of the most paranoid, tend to perceive the
therapist in the image of the good all-giving omnipotent mother.
They expect final answers and formulae for cure from him and seem
willing to accept whatever he says. During that period they are
likely to be very much afraid of the group as a whole. As they gradually become disappointed in the therapist's magical power they
become angry that he will not "wave his wand" in their behalf, and
begin to cast him in the role of the bad mother. Individuals differ
greatly, of course, as to how long they persist in idealizing the
therapist. Eventually, with the help of experience in the group and
analysis of their conflicts, they begin to see the therapist much
more realistically and become more able to treat him as a peer.
Concurrently, as they come into deeper contact with the individual
group members, reality mingles with their original distorted image
and modifies their reactions to the group as a whole. But this does
not happen until the transferences have been analyzed and the entire process is well in process of being worked through.

The following examples illustrate the fact that the leader and
the group come to represent these figures (as they do many others)

interchangeably. John suffered from a harsh but corruptible maternal superego. He had some anal defenses against his oral conflicts in the defiant aspects of his character. He perceived me only very briefly and superficially as the ideal giving mother. During the first visit or two he was very ingratiating, but as soon as he discovered that this policy did not elicit the usual response he got from women he began to display signs of passive resistance. The material he discussed during this period was his inability as a youngster to attend to his school work. In the early days of the group which he joined about a year later, many signs of passive resistance reappeared. Both its members and I represented childhood authorities, which were eventually traced to the infantile fear of the mother, and her intrusion on his narcissism. He often showed his placating side to the group. Once he went to the extent of bringing a bag of apples to the session after they had become angry with him. The defiance was revealed in his chronic lateness, unexplained absences, forgetting their names, or even upsetting stories he told them which elicited their genuine sympathy. In all they sensed him as extremely arrogant and took him to task for it, thus opening the way to analyzing these traits. After that he began to work through his conflict with authority, with the result that he handled his business affairs much more successfully. He came to recognize that self-defeat was the real effect of his apparent "omnipotence." After a while he could tell us that he was beginning to appreciate the group because they, like the therapist, were his best hold on good common sense. The following year after vacation he came back in an anxious state of mind, admitting that he had hardly been able to wait for the group sessions to start because he had been getting lazy and negligent about his work and was frequently tempted to drink too much and to "fool around." He said he felt relieved now that we were together again because he knew they would help him to act more realistically. It was clear that both the group and I represented his ego during this period.

(5) A final complexity, as important as any of these, is the fact that Freud implied, but never incorporated into his theory, the importance of a power element in the infant's relationship with his mother. He refers to it (1921, p. 79) when he speaks of an "element of paralysis derived from the relation between someone with superior power and someone who is without power and helpless."

And he does so again when he tries to connect the power of the horde father, the hypnotist, and the father of the family in order to explain the mystery of the group's power. Clinical experience seems to show that this element must be considered *pari passu* with the libidinal factor in understanding his infantile experience with the mother and in explaining his adult object relationships. It is only after his struggle over power is normalized that mature love is possible. Freud did not connect it with the mother, nor did he incorporate it into his theory. The Washington School made these facts a foundation stone of their divergence from Freudian theory, second in importance only to their quarrel with his libido theory. It is a gap which need not continue to exist.

If we wish to build a comprehensive, modern, psychoanalytically oriented theory of group psychology we must also study the role of the aggressive forces. Freud had already published *Beyond the Pleasure Principle,* but he refrained from a full discussion of aggression in groups. One may look in vain for the word "aggression" or "aggressive forces" in the index, which merely includes "hatred." He is intent chiefly on showing how the libidinal ties function to neutralize aggression in the group.

We are quite ready to grant the neutralizing role of the libidinal ties but contend that their effect is more limited than he indicates. He himself explicitly stated that with neurotics there is a defusion of instincts,[7] that it is therefore difficult for them to participate in groups, and that neurosis has a disintegrating effect on groups. In therapy groups, then, we can expect defusion and must be prepared to deal with it. He was, of course, speaking of autocratic groups in an autocratic society. In a democratic environment the libidinal ties do not play so successful a role even in ordinary well-organized groups. The aggressive forces have to be kept at bay by other leadership skills than mere force of authority lest their disruptive effect will work toward disintegration. For instance, we know that in the army, although the libidinal ties do function to neutralize aggression, our democratic society allows for a certain amount of griping which acts as a safety valve. But as the last war showed, even this, together with the libidinal ties, was not always sufficient for purposes of morale. The psychologists were called in

---

[7] He referred to sexual instincts, but the same would hold true for aggression.

to help solve this problem. In our therapy groups we have also found that although the libidinal ties to the leader do play an important role, defusion takes place nevertheless, because we are dealing with neurotics.

The data from our analytic therapy groups also readily confirm Freud's description of the manner in which repression of the aggressive factors is brought about in groups. Although he uses the model of the family his description applies perfectly to therapy groups. He says, for example, "competition for parents' (leaders') love is usually repressed when such feelings threaten the child's (member's) relationship to the parent. In its place a demand for equality and justice appears which is a kind of reaction formation to the hostility. The aim of killing the sibling has been repressed with the help of reaction formations" (1920, p. 86). But recent experience with both training and therapy groups demonstrates that such repressions are frequently superficial. Signs of the underlying hostility are easily detectable even though they may be well camouflaged. Hostility rises quickly and disproportionately to the surface whenever a member detects or imagines preferences on the part of the therapist, with the result that equality and justice come into question frequently.

For this reason we cannot go along with his conclusion that hostility "vanishes" in groups. In analytic therapy with neurotics we are impelled to probe more deeply into the meaning and function of aggression, for the unfortunate conviction is soon forced upon us that "Love is Not Enough." Our patients have come to us for the very reason that they have lost their ability to win or even to accept love when it is offered them. The process of neutralization has been seriously interfered with in our members and if we wish to help them to love again it is incumbent on us to discover how and why this has happened and by what means we can make it possible.

We can underwrite the following quotation only if the idea of the permanence of the repression is deleted:

"But the whole of this intolerance vanishes, temporarily or permanently, as a result of the formation of a group, and in a group. So long as a group formation persists or so far as it extends, individuals behave as though they were uniform, tolerate other people's peculiarities, put themselves on an equal level with them, and have no feeling of aversion towards them. Such a limitation of

narcissism can, according to our theoretical views, only be produced by one factor, a libidinal tie with other people. Love for oneself knows only one barrier—love for others, love for objects . . ."
(1920, p. 55).

In order to prove his point that "libidinal ties are what characterize a group" (1920, p. 54) Freud examines the "feelings of
aversion and hostility" which develop in all close human relations,
and which "have first to be eliminated by repression." He admits
that "the same thing happens when men come together in larger
units."

It is of extreme interest to our theory that Freud in speculating
on the "undisguised antipathies and aversion which people feel
towards strangers with whom they have to do," says that "in these
feelings we may recognize the expression of self-love—of narcissism." And we are increasingly impressed by the applicability of
this insight for therapy groups. He continues, "This self-love works
for the self-assertion of the individual and behaves as though the
occurrence of any divergence from his own particular lines of development involved a criticism of them and a demand for their al-
teration. We do not know why such sensitiveness should have been
directed to just these details of differentiation; but it is unmistaka-
ble that in this whole connection men give evidence of a readiness
for hatred, an aggressiveness, the source of which is unknown and
to which one is tempted to ascribe an elementary character" (1920,
pp. 55-56, fn. to his polarity theory).

We believe that our investigations have provided an answer to
this question. The first strange but significant other in his life, the
one whom he first discovered, through frustrations, to be different
from himself, against whom he was so powerless, and whom he
was bound in childhood to experience as critical and demanding,
was, of course, the preoedipal mother, whom Freud seems to have
ignored (repressed?) in favor of the oedipal father.

It is the reawakening of this old narcissistic fear that is reactivated as soon as the possibility of joining a therapy group is
mentioned to a patient, and that continues to threaten him
throughout his early sessions and recur at intervals later. For the
group is a totality of strange others, the full extent of whose power
and intentions in relation to himself he cannot assess. He imagines
they will be critical and demanding and render him helpless. It is

no wonder that the adult ego which finds itself invaded by anxiety and helpless anger stemming from the past projects its destructive anger to the group and tends to yield with apparent meekness to the group will, in order to avoid imagined injury.

If we keep in mind our hypothesis that the group recalls the image of the preoedipal mother while we turn the searchlight away from the, in itself, significant enough role of the libidinal factors where Freud had rather tenaciously focussed it, we are rewarded by an illuminating transformation. Our change of perspective has the startling effect of a figure-ground puzzle. Freud's ventured inference about the relationship between an individual's hatred of the stranger and his narcissism instead of remaining incidental, suddenly takes on major significance for group psychology. It suggests a plausible explanation for the thinly veiled hostility which is a defense against anxiety and which most observers of groups admit hovers over the membership during its early stages, ready to flame out if conditions allow it.[8]

It is at this point that we must pick up the theme of the power factor which we mentioned earlier. Freud had indicated its existence but connected it with the role of the father toward the helpless child. Our hypothesis connects it primarily to just this relation of the helpless baby to the mother on which it is totally dependent. In our group members there comes to light, not only the need to submit but also the opposite need to fight for identity of existence and for control against the mother's power. It seems to have been this second need that interfered with their capacity to allow the libidinal ties to develop fully or to utilize them effectively. Even as adults these same needs, frequently converted into need for status, drive them unduly and interfere in their attempt to make object relationships. Their behavior in therapy groups substantiates these statements.

If we believe that in transference many individuals are later seen in distorted fashion in the image of the powerful mother then we

[8] In this connection it is interesting to compare the observations of the leaders of training and human relations groups which presumably have a normal membership. They have come to the conclusion that the group in its development goes through stages similar to that of the individual; and their empirical data have shown that these groups cannot solve problems of love and intimacy before they learn how to handle problems of aggression over power and status. (See Chapter IV.)

can well understand their anxious submissiveness to the group and the hatred that attends this necessary precaution. We can also understand their early attempts to be agreeable and try to structure the interaction in the conventional ways they have been accustomed to use. And we are not surprised to find that these maneuvers merely disguise deeper rumblings of fear and hatred (which bring about "fight and flight"). They camouflage the deep-rooted narcissistic fear embedded in man's basic distrust of anyone different from himself.

It may be that we have found a clue to the distressing pervasiveness of power and status problems in our society. Hostility to the foreigner, cocktail party conversations, and our incessant one-up-manship are representative. It would seem that no one entirely solves this conflict, including "well-analyzed" individuals. It may be that these elements have simply not been analyzed out with sufficient thoroughness, or even that it would be impossible to do so because of the irremediable condition of man who is for so long a period helplessly dependent upon his parents. We do know that when this factor is dealt with in depth and with full recognition of its origin the defensiveness and power struggle may be ameliorated. I am not under the delusion that such a course can bring about a miracle, but group therapy may prove to be an effective "specific" remedy for it.

It seems to me likely that it is this same problem with which Burrow (1928) was struggling, to which he assigned societal causes, and for which he demonstrated measurable physiological effects (strain around the eyes and forehead). His phyloanalysis was a project in learning how to become aware of the problem and to deal with its restrictive emotional effects by combining analytic and physiological means. He saw the phenomenon as a reflexive one between the therapist and the patient that must be worked on cooperatively. His followers continued to use his theories, working on the problem with both organized and natural groups. Some experiments were carried on in a living situation where no real distinction was made between therapist and patient, and continuous verbal interchange took place (Burrow, 1928; Syz, 1961).

Although Freud did not bring to closure his many penetrating insights into the preoedipal aspects of development and their importance for group formation, and could not therefore perceive their full significance, he did sense that their implications were greater than he himself had grasped, for he wrote:

"We are aware that what we have been able to contribute toward the explanation of the libidinal structure of groups leads back to the distinction between the ego and the ego ideal and to the double kind of tie which this makes possible—identification and substitution of the object for the ego ideal. The assumption of this kind of a differentiation grade (*Stufe*) in the ego as a first step in an analysis of the ego must gradually establish its justification in the most various regions of psychology. In my paper, 'Introduction to Narcissism,' I have put together all the pathological material that could at the moment be used in support of this separation. But it may be expected that when we penetrate deeper into the psychology of the psychoses its significance will be discovered to be far greater." He was aware, then, that what he has had to say here was likely to bring about many changes in his theory as a whole (1921, pp. 102 ff.).

This prediction has come true. Ego psychology has contributed enormously to the understanding of the very early development of the child by the rigorous observation of small infants, children, and psychotics. More psychoanalysts are gradually joining the ranks of those who are attempting experimental elaboration of some of the basic hypotheses concerning preoedipality and early ego and superego development which Freud has given us. We need only mention some of the most prominent of them, such as Kris, Hartmann, Bychowski, Rapaport, Bellak, and Colby to realize the possibilities of the future. Others, like Klein, Bergler, and Lampl-de Groot have worked out clinical elaborations.

In this much more modest study I, too, have "established justification" for his study of the gradient in the ego by demonstrating its applicability in the area of group psychology. More than that, by suggesting certain changes of emphasis in Freud's contribution, I have attempted to synthesize his views of the group with other current theories, with the hope of formulating a single, modern group psychology.

In the light of this new perspective, the parallel between Freud's psychosexual phases (and their ego equivalents) and Bion's "basic assumptions" and his "psychotic group" becomes apparent. Bion's dependency assumption, Schutz's "inclusion" and Freud's oral phenomena can be sheltered, as it were, under the same umbrella. Freud's anal drives and the defenses against them fit in with Bennis' phase of authority relations, and with Bion's "fight-flight" category.[9] Freud's oedipal behavior seems to be equivalent to Bion's "pairing."

A group psychology, which worked out the details of such a compromise using the ego correlates of the psychosexual phases as a foundation and adopting a mutually acceptable scientific terminology, would provide a sound, flexible and enormously productive base for collaborative operations.

[9] The group dynamicists have sometimes put "fight-flight" into a separate category which is equivalent to "resistance." Another possibility would be to break them up into "fight" when referring to rebellion against authority, and leave "flight" as comparable to resistance. However, the details must be left to future investigators.

VIII Are Our Differences Reconcilable?
An Evaluation

Before we give endorsement to any integrated group psychology, it will be necessary to re-examine certain important theoretical
differences. Unfortunately, conceptual convictions about neurosis
and its cure have been allowed to intrude on theories about the
nature of group behavior per se. Failure to distinguish between
them has created an unnecessary obstacle. Actually, there is much
less divergence among us than appears at first glance, but in order
to assess the plausibility of a synthesis we must turn our attention
to the debatable concepts. Three such differences of opinion seem
to have assumed the proportions of a dichotomy. They concern:
(1) the definition of the group as a dynamic whole, (2) the nature of
the group processes, (3) the principle of contemporaneity.

THE GROUP *qua* GROUP

The supersummative character of the group has persistently en-
gendered controversy among group therapists. Group dynamic
therapists make a *sine qua non* of both their group therapy and
group psychology. Although the same definition of a group has
been consistently implied in Freud's writings, analytic group therapists tend either to ignore it or take it for granted in their therapeutic endeavors. Existential group therapists, because they put a

great deal of emphasis on holism, unquestionably conceive of the group in this way; but because they perceive the therapist as the central figure and chief source of therapy, they may be assumed to take an intermediate position.

The field theoretic view of the group could actually serve as a unifying concept for a mutual theory of group psychology, but for some reason when we are challenged as therapists we not only argue about the therapeutic value of this definition but tend to lose our perspective as group psychologists.

Each school's strong convictions seem to have grown out of the circumstances that have brought it to its present position. The entire purpose of the social scientists had been to study the nature of the group. They were not interested in its therapeutic potential. Even when they did put it to practical use as in action research, they were thinking more about changing systems-in-action than individual personality. They wanted to alter such social systems in education, in industry, in community life. Never having been closely involved with the dynamics of therapy, they were the more impressed by their discovery that the group was a power field which might be used to create social change. Although they recognized that individuals were influenced by the group, their interest in the particular individual was minimal. They regarded the group both as a source of change and as its object. Even in recent years their aim in leadership training institutes has been to train the leaders to return to their communities and effect changes in the way in which their respective groups functioned. Public opinion was the ultimate goal. For them the fact that this change works through certain alterations in individuals is of secondary consequence.

The situation out of which American analytic group psychotherapy emerged was quite different. These therapists were well entrenched in psychoanalytic thinking and in the habit of employing the highly dynamic analytic process as their method. When they found they could apply that method in small groups, they did not require and therefore did not search out new sources of dynamic leverage. For this reason they all experienced the added stimulus of the group situation, but did not feel the need to conceptualize it as a new "group force." Nor did they pay much attention when the social scientists began to write about group dynamics and to provide a whole new set of group-oriented concepts. They remained geared primarily to the interpersonal aspects of individual psychodynamics and felt justified in this choice because it was, after all, the individual whose health was at stake. As they attained experience and facility in doing therapy in the group situation, they increasingly made use of the facets it provided, but they did not distinguish its unitary nature as a therapeutic force. Those who, like Hulse, conceived of the interaction as a network of transferences came very close to the "group-as-a-whole" idea. Yet in therapy this network continued to be merely a background from which the significant intragroup transferences were selected for analysis. These analytic group therapists remained confident of their method and believed that their therapeutic results registered its effectiveness. When they searched for greater efficacy they did so within their own conceptual framework. For better or worse the group as such remained for them a highly desirable medium rather than a therapeutic agent in its own right.

Slavson (1953) raised a valid therapeutically oriented question which deserves the most serious investigation. Speaking as a therapist he maintains that the difference between analytic and group dynamic methods of therapy are definitely irreconcilable. He sums it up as follows: "The question whether we deal in group therapy with the group as a unitary entity, or with the individuals, that is, the patients in them, as individuals, may well determine the course of its development as a science and as a therapeutic tool." He asks whether patients improve "merely by virtue of their adjustment to a group, because of its 'influence' on them, or because of the relationships they establish with fellow members. Or whether the improvement is a result of personality changes that accrue from the release of anxiety previously bound up in neurotic nucleus originating in childhood, the insight they acquire, and the new self-image that emerges?"

We might also ask whether the individual can respond as fully and change as completely, characterwise, when the interpretations are made to the group as a whole? Or is there danger that he will go along with the group as it resolves its group conflict in order to be accepted by merely allowing the other side of his ambivalence to function, or by changing his defenses? If so, is it not possible that he will yield to group standards under its pressure while he is a

member, but remain motivated by his conflicts and revert to form
under different circumstances? Does this argument hold if the
group and individual aspects are combined as in Stock's (Chapter
IV) method? Can the therapist, for example, really bring about
the structural change in the individual patient if he deals with his
basic conflicts as these become a group preoccupation?

It seems to me that the individual member will unquestionably
be reached in such a group. Certainly he will cease to be a deterrent
to the group movement and he may be substantially helped. But it
may very well be necessary to work through his problems in specific
tailor-made fashion in terms of his own unique life experience together with their emotional nuances, and that this must occur repeatedly and in great detail before he can give up his major defensive system and achieve real character change. However, Slavson
would be the first to admit that once these therapeutic considerations are laid aside, there remains no real disagreement about the
nature and definition of the group as a dynamic entity with interdependent parts. It is the therapeutic factors that obscure our perception of the group psychologic elements.

THE GROUP PROCESSES

The problem concerning the definition of the group processes is
somewhat different but it too grows out of misunderstandings.
Several sources contribute to the confusion which surrounds this
term. Within the field of social science the term group process has
been used interchangeably with group phenomena, with group
forces, and with the more general term group dynamics. No true
conceptual problem is involved, only some imprecision in its usage.
Increased clarity would immediately follow if the term group phenomena were applied to the substantive aspects, group forces when
their vectorial quality is to be indicated, and group dynamics when
reference is made to the total field of scientific investigation. Group
process could then be reserved specifically for the functional aspect
of such group determined phenomena, such as the formation of
standards, the exercise of pressure toward uniformity, role-assign-
ment, subgrouping, and the like.

But the matter is not that simple, for a second source of confusion derives from the difference in the way group dynamicists

and analytic group therapists conceive of the way in which these processes originate. Group dynamicists arrive at the construct by making an abstraction from their empirical observations of group behavior on the group level. They refer to processes which are caused by the group interaction. Analytic group therapists, observing the same behavior, make their observations on the individual level and think of group processes merely as an extension of the way individuals relate in the group situation (i.e., the way in which they translate their intrapsychic processes in their interpersonal relationships). In other words, for them the dynamic processes which are observable in groups are interpersonal and can also occur between two individuals. They give rise to some new feature when several individuals are involved in them, but are not basically different.

The lack of precision in this matter has been compounded because of the too rapid success of both group therapy and, almost concurrently, of group dynamics. These circumstances permitted many self-styled therapists to proceed without clear concepts. As a consequence they impute almost magical powers to the group processes. They appear to regard group interaction as a kind of magic wand, as if all one has to do is bring together a number of people and let them interact, and *ipso facto*, they will get well. The reason? Why, the group processes, of course! A true mystique has been in the making. The unsoundness of this remarkable misapprehension is camouflaged by the fact that the observable behavior of people in groups is misleading to the relatively naïve practitioner. Truly, something is always happening in groups and that something is dynamic. It has the quality of a vector. Some fail to notice that it is not always therapeutic.

The group processes do bring about changes in the behavior of the members, but the effect may be antitherapeutic, as when a single individual finds himself strongly pressured to think and behave in a way that arouses great conflict and anxiety in him and/or results in brain washing. It may be nontherapeutic, as in the kind of impartial discussion groups set up by the League of Women Voters. On the other hand, it may indeed have therapeutic effect if it makes members feel comforted, if it gives them a sense of belonging or an opportunity for self-expression or self-actualization. It may even help improve the individual's perception of reality by

offering him new experiences and more accurate "consensual validation." Analytic group therapists contend that though this
may be therapeutic, it is not therapy. For them only reconstructive
psychotherapy which *resolves pathogenic conflicts* and brings
about basic character changes qualifies as psychotherapy.

Phenomenologically, therapeutic group process seems to consist
of releasing latent emotions in the context of human interaction.
From the beginning this process has been an integral part of psychoanalytic therapy, though not its equivalent. It has recently been
found by the social scientists to be capable of achieving group
change. For instance, training leaders use it in order to relieve
interpersonal emotional tensions which interfere with an assigned
group task, or for the purpose of making the members aware of the
way in which groups function.

THE HERE AND NOW IN GROUP PSYCHOTHERAPY

There has been a tendency to carry the implications of Lewin's
principle of contemporaneity beyond his intention. Group therapists on both sides seem to assume that he minimized the importance of the past. This assumption puts the debate between us on a
false basis. Lewin did not intend to discount the continuity between past and present, but rather to take account of it in a scientifically rigorous fashion. He wanted to increase the precision of
those concepts which had to do with motivation because they still
bore the traces of the teleological thinking which had made them
taboo. This was his systematic position. For research Lewin believed that whether or not the historical as well as the systematic
aspects of theory should be utilized depends upon the investigator's
specific goal. And he himself investigated genetic aspects in his
study of child development.

In the early stages of group dynamic research such inquiry into
the past was clearly not pertinent. The significant issues would
have been obscured by an attempt to include a temporal variable.
The indirect representation of the past in the present field was
sufficient for the problem at hand. Later, after Thelen had shown
that the quality of the group emotion at any given point must ultimately have its source in individual members' expressions of it, this
view became subject to question. It thereafter became a reasonable

hypothesis that each member's valency for the group emotion and his mode of reacting to it are products of his character and therefore of his genetic history. The *members* do have a childhood which can be shown to effect their group communications.

On the other hand, no one knows better than the analytic group therapist that his interpretations must be anchored in the immediacy of the group events. What is transference if not that relationship which exists between patient and therapist, or patient and patient, at that very point where past and present meet? It is in that moment alone that the patient is able to recognize the dysfunctional elements of the past that have remained to disfigure his present relationships. However, the analytic therapist is convinced that this work is not complete unless he takes a second step in which he helps his patient understand the conditions under which his anachronistic patterns came into being and why they were necessary to him at that time, and only then does he begin to lose his desperate need for them. Experience seems to show that it helps the patient overcome his fear of losing his defenses if he realizes that long ago he made the only compromise of which he was capable in order to deal with what must have seemed an intolerable situation. Knowing that he is unnecessarily clinging to solutions which he had to make when he was small, helpless, and unable to comprehend his situation is one link in a chain of events which helps him gain the courage to turn his insight into behavior change. It is for this reason that the analytic group therapists insist on exploring the "there and then." But this fact in no way is an argument against the "here and now." In defending his investigation of the past against criticism, the analytic group therapist was caught in an untenable argument.

Yet we must acknowledge that the group dynamicist who accuses him of delving into the past at the expense of the immediate experience has based his argument on a grain of truth, for some analysts still seem to let their patients futilely wallow at length in the past. It is a heritage from the time when Freud first assumed that a childhood trauma was the chief etiological factor in neurosis. Moreover, after transference analysis became the major focus, detailed investigation of the infantile past proved such a fertile soil for research into psychosexual development that some analysts neglected therapy for the collecting of information. But the fault is rare among group analysts because the present reality makes itself continuously felt. It is difficult in the group to become swamped in the infantile past. Crucial glimpses into the past as it is illuminated in the present must suffice.

The misinterpretation of Lewin's principle of contemporaneity has obscured a substantial area of agreement between group dynamic and analytic group psychologists. Both sides stand to benefit by the correct construction of his idea of the "here and now" issue rather than by indulging in an extremist view. Genetic investigation into the individual member's past would presumably enrich the understanding of his valency in the group and yield increasing predictability concerning the distribution of social roles among the membership. Similarly, if the analytic group psychologist were to redefine transference in concordance with the principle of contemporaneity, he would give precision to a valuable concept which loses much because it is vaguely worded. He would also render it less open to criticism and misunderstanding.

Once again the area of real disagreement is confined to the field of therapy. Future collaborative research in group psychology must be based on an accurate understanding of Lewin's contemporaneity principle, on both sides.

To compare the attitude of the existentialist with that of the other two approaches is almost pointless because they operate on different wave lengths. The very expression "here and now" implies an awareness of time; and the existentialist holds that once man becomes aware of the temporal quality of an experience, the experience itself has already become a memory. To experience temporality implies self-observation and destroys the "wholeness of the experience." As Buber (1948) put it, *"The pure present has no specific consciousness of time."* Yet, in practice, existential group therapists make this semantic compromise. They understand the "here and now" to signify experiencing. They make nonteleological comments on the spot and leave analytic comments until after the experience. The comments of the therapist express his experience and reaction to what is going on in the encounter prior to his understanding of it, whereas interpretation in the usual sense occurs only after the encounter becomes a memory. Actually if the analytic group therapist has a good sense of timing he also will "seize the moment" quite spontaneously, yet know when to withhold his interpretations until the patient is experiencing his transference feelings.

CONCLUSION

The dichotomies with which we seem to be confronted then are not genuine. Once the cobwebs are cleared away, we find ourselves with a common fund of knowledge based on observed phenomena from which inferences have been made on several different levels. Our immediate goal must determine which level of abstraction we choose to use in any given project.

Intensive collaborative research is the only scientifically satisfactory answer to the numerous problems which such a challenge conjures up. There are at least three major areas open for this kind of research at present. The first amounts to a continuation of the study of group dynamics in a therapy group context. It should not be confused with group therapy research. In such a project the social scientist may be expected to benefit from consultation with group therapists on the psychoanalytic concepts and techniques to be used. Research design, no matter how carefully conceived, will not produce valid results if the therapy is not clear-cut and well executed. The therapeutic process is the variable which must be kept as constant as possible. This can be achieved only if experts do the therapy or at least undertake its supervision.

The second case would consist of research in group therapy by group therapists. In this project the presumably skilled group therapist should turn to the group dynamicist as a consultant on research design and methodology because no matter how good the therapy, nothing can be proved if the design is not rigorous. In both these situations accuracy and constancy will be very difficult to attain, so that we urgently need the experience of the research scientist.

The third area of research is an investigation of the relationship between group dynamic and psychoanalytic concepts. Such an investigation has not yet been seriously undertaken. It would require the most wholehearted and methodical collaboration of the two disciplines on an equal basis. Remaining prejudices and ill-feeling between them would have to be dealt with frankly and openly at every step of the undertaking in order to avoid blocks to progress.

Mutual observation of a variety of types of groups by trained observers within the framework of a tight research design might yield the data for devising productive hypotheses. For example, I submit that given the same empirical data—let us say the behavioral events in a psychotherapy group—it can be demonstrated that (1) the group dynamic concepts are abstractions at the group level while the psychoanalytic concepts are abstractions from the same behavior on an individual level and may therefore be considered equivalent; and (2) the group dynamic abstractions deal with the result of any given behavioral interaction while the psychoanalytic abstractions deal with its cause.

A series of specific concepts could be put to the test. There is, for example, the possible equivalence between resonance and acting in transference. And one might attempt to question whether cohesiveness is the effect of the same behavioral phenomena of which identification and libidinal ties are the cause; or whether a similar relation exists between the disruptive and the aggressive factors. Freud suggested that group structure might legitimately parallel ego function on a group level. Is it not possible that we might interpret the members' well-known submissiveness to group standards and group pressure as the effect of their transference to the group-as-a-whole either as the oedipal father or the preoedipal mother, as I suspect? Another idea has been brought forward that subgrouping is often the outward result of an unconscious liaison between two people whose neurotic needs dovetail. In other words, interlocking transferences are taking place. Scapegoating could, among other things, mean that transference exists between a masochistic member and the group-as-a-whole from whom he elicits sadistic reactions. The group may or may not be displacing angry feelings meant for the leader. I have suggested just one series of problems. Innumerable other hypotheses will come to the reader's mind which are equally in need of investigation.

A word of caution—I have noticed that in our enthusiasm for the rapprochement, there is a tendency to lean over backwards to cooperate. It should not, however, be necessary to behave like new members in a group which is composed of those who are prone to give up too much of their individual thinking. Our mutual venture will not be injured by differences of opinion. In fact, conflict avoidance is contraindicated, as new insights will be born of conflict. A productive partnership cannot thrive on identification. Separateness, being over against the other, is prerequisite to true encounter.

I believe that in taking this stance we shall be better able to provide that most flexible and sensitive collaboration which will be necessary in all three areas of research. It seems reasonable to suppose that the methodological sophistication of the social scientists will, in combination with the analytic group therapists' intimate clinical knowledge of depth psychological concepts, produce a superb research combination. The prospects for the next decade are as challenging as they are stimulating.

IX Horizons in Group Psychology

Because of the tremendous expansion of scientific knowledge in the last three centuries, and its extraordinary acceleration in recent decades, scientists of all disciplines have come to be increasingly sequestered in their separate little corners of the broader domain. Not only the modern physician but the physicist, the engineer, the chemist, and the psychologist are in danger of becoming myopic. We have only to think of the modern psychologist who engages in research on the electronic brain to be able to sense the ease with which one can isolate oneself from the main stream of human events. The clinician may become so engrossed in perfecting his techniques and in helping his patients that he fails to take measure of the larger scientific world to whose past, present, and future he belongs, yet he will be enriched if he keeps it in mind and his patients will not fail to benefit from his more balanced picture of the march of progress.

Over the ages there always have been those whose primary interest lay in searching for unity among the diversity of mankind's interests. The old philosophical problem of the one and the many has lost none of it fascination. As the modern world grows more complex and unity of thought seems increasingly to elude us, new methods of transportation and communication provide the possibility for bringing us together again. In the scientific realm today serious attempts are being made to break down the barriers between the sciences. One of these is the Josiah Macy, Jr. Foundation, which sponsors multiprofessional conferences to "stimulate research and to promote effective communication across the departmental walls which tend to isolate professions and specialties from one another" (Transactions of the Fourth Conference [1957] on Group Processes). Setting aside the question of whether or not basic unity among the sciences is attainable, we could profit by maintaining communication with the wider world. For this we need a common language and a common conceptual framework.

Thus far, mathematics has provided a major avenue of approach to the problem. It gives us a common language in which to communicate. In mathematics man has come closest to realizing his potential for pure abstraction. He has created a concise shorthand which can be used not only to handle calculations concerning enormous quantities of data, and to provide means of checking and correcting for error at every stage of the process, but reaches its maximal degree of precision in communicating its findings to other scientists.

What the average layman often fails to realize is that this succinct means of translation does not actually provide explanations of the phenomena; that it is flexible rather than static and complete; that the rules may be changed by those who employ its processes even though they must be adhered to once they are adopted for a given endeavor. Nor does he always realize that there are any number of numerical systems, that there are other geometries besides the Euclidian. Though the layman meets them in their final state, mathematical systems start with intuitive hypotheses and become abstract fact only after long testing. The mathematician, like the scientist, puts his faith in his intuition. He must have the perseverance to keep testing his hypotheses and the fortitude to eliminate them if they are proved false. It is at this point that he and the scientist must part company with the trail blazer and the mystic.

I am far from insisting that the psychotherapist or any other skilled technician needs to utilize mathematics, but only wish to suggest that an enlightened acquaintance with what the theory builder in science can do when he adopts the tools of mathematics will broaden his outlook and give him the opportunity to play the role of sophisticated observer in any interdisciplinary research project.

One may well ask how so abstract a discipline as mathematics can be of use in a largely qualitative social science like psychology. The question of quantification has in fact long presented a problem in that field. Once it was actually frowned upon because of the nature of the material. But, since Weber and Fechner proved its usefulness in the nineteenth century, it has had a somewhat obstructive premium put upon it. Until recently quantitative analysis continued to be generally perceived as an opposite to qualitative analysis in psychology. Only in our present age of relativity did quantitative and qualitative processes come to be regarded as complementary. The behavioral sciences have recently been going through the same struggle which had been fought out centuries before by the physical sciences (Lewin, 1951). In psychology, the statistical approach has moved in leaps and bounds since the coming of the electronic computors.

Lewin's topological psychology illustrates the way in which mathematical procedures may be capable of dealing with qualitative data. He insisted that constructs should not be left at an operational stage (i.e., true to the observable facts according to the experiencing person), but should be made true to the basic mathematical interrelationships of his total theory. He decided to use the theories of a non-Euclidian geometry, called topology, which is capable of transposing the concepts of physical to those of subjective space. Psychology has to deal with related, coexisting facts which have a subjective position in relation to one another (Lewin, 1951, pp. 151-152). Where the logic of topology failed, as it did in dealing with dynamic problems of direction, distance, or force, he applied a "more specific geometry . . . called hodological space." This, he says, "permits us to speak in a mathematically precise manner of equality and differences of direction and of changes in distance without presupposing the measurement of physical direction and distance which is usually not possible in a psychological field."

More recently the application of mathematical theorizing has given rise to a new and very stimulating approach to psychotherapy. We know it as "communications theory"; and among its outstanding achievements have been its new insights into the etiology and treatment of schizophrenia, and the family therapy described in Chapter XX. Its effect on the psychiatric thinking of our day may be noted in the accounts given by Ruesch and Bateson (1951) and by Ruesch (1961).

What is less generally known is that the communications approach to therapy is derived from the hard core mathematical communication theory which was originally worked out by telecommunications engineers for the purpose of dealing with the mass of data which were piling up in the fields of telegraphy, telephone, radio, television, radar, etc. As such, it was a strictly mathematical theory, based on the study of these technical "systems." It had to do with the signals that were transmitted, with the quantity of relationships among such signals, and with their informational content abstracted from all specific human uses. It was concerned with the question of *how much* information rather than *what* information. It has, in this form, nothing whatever to do with the human beings who might be involved at either end of the transmission, nor with the meaning of the signals that were transmitted. In Britain the name "information theory" is reserved for this hardcore communication theory, while in America the terms are used interchangeably, which gives rise to some confusion.

Early in the nineteen forties, Norbert Wiener gathered about him at Harvard University a number of philosophers, scientists, and mathematicians who were interested in extending the principles involved in "engineering communications theories" to the biological sciences, which dealt with communication in self-regulating systems (they were in that respect similar to the telecommunication systems). Wiener et al. pointed to the common phenomena of feedback mechanisms and self-regulating systems in various branches of science, similar to that of the steam engine and the thermostat. In biology, for example, there were such physiological mechanisms as bodily homeostasis and the central nervous system. The common element always resides in the communication of information for purposes of self-stabilizing control systems. The analogy refers to function rather than, as is frequently thought, to structure. Wiener and his group gave this field of study the name of cybernetics because it derived from the Greek word for steersman.

The mathematical theory as such had nothing to do with human communication but it did have the potential of being transposed into the language of meaning, i.e., into the essence of human communication. Within this area of its usuage there are three distinct levels: (1) the syntactic, which deals with signs and the relations between signs; (2) the semantic, which deals with the relations between signs and their designata; (3) and the pragmatic, which deals with the aspects which involve the sign users. It is only in the last connection that communications theory becomes a part of psychology and psychotherapy (Cherry, 1961).

The special instance of group psychotherapy is an exceptionally intriguing one. For if we accept the Lewinian theory of the group as a dynamic unity of interdependent parts it is not difficult to take the further step of viewing each part (member) as having feedback capacity. The total feedback may then be seen as a stabilizing mechanism for the whole group. In this sense all groups may be considered homeostatic systems. The kind and direction of change that occurs in each would depend upon the purpose for which it was formed and the skill of its leader. The therapeutic group, for example, may be considered to have the function of self-correction of the members' distortions by means of group feedback. The concept of consensual validation is obviously closely akin to this view. Both interpersonal and communications theorists view the human being and the group as primarily self-correcting, self-regulating systems.

Since all schools of group psychotherapy are primarily concerned with the way the members' personality problems are reflected in the intragroup communication, it would not be unreasonable to suggest the possibility that communications theory might well provide us with a common language which could be used as the medium of intellectual exchange in joint investigations. Developing such a project would require the utmost caution. Group therapists would have the twofold task of acquiring meticulously thorough understanding of the new terminology and assessing most carefully the dangers of losing the finer nuances of meaning as they translate their old concepts into new terms. One warning against undue enthusiasm comes from a communications expert. Bar-Hillel writes: "The concepts and terminology of statistical communication, i.e., information theory, have been applied by impatient scientists in various fields in which the information was used presystematically, in a semantic or even in a pragmatic sense. Because of its popularity the study of communications must continually be evaluated.[1] Its meaning for other disciplines such as linguistics, sociology, and semantics is by no means evidence that there is any basis for more than the recognition of some common ground which promises fertility. Very little has yet been proved" (quotation taken from Cherry [1961]).

Because of its reliance on a much higher level of inference Freudian psychoanalytic group psychology may at first glance seem unsuitable for participation in such an attempt to find a common terminology. Actually this characteristic need not stand in the way. Cherry (1961) reminds us that there is no difference in kind from the other schools because " ... even the simplest observations include some form of inference and purely behavioristic description of human communication puts severe restrictions on the aspects to be examined." And we have already shown that psychoanalysis fits into any organismic approach and that its concepts can be successfully translated into operational terms. However, Freudian analytic group psychologists must, on their part, be prepared to reformulate their propositions in precisely worded and testable hypotheses. As an analytic group therapist with convictions about the effectiveness of the basic Freudian theory and its technique of analyzing transference and resistance in the group, but also with almost daily clinical evidence of the need for more precise terminology, I feel inclined to make a strong case for the inclusion of the Freudian contributions to our ultimate group psychological theory.

[1] A timely and rather interesting example of the pitfalls may be seen in the way some scientists speak about the "electronic brain." Much information is being gathered about the human brain through the study of electric computers. It is a logical continuation of activities which were subjects of interest in the seventeenth century's attempt to see man as a kind of machine. Ross Ashby's *Design for a Brain* gives an indication of the technological advances that have intervened. Popular descriptions make us acutely aware of the lingering tendency to put animistic interpretations on such analogies, but no communications engineer calls the new computers brains. They know that the human brain is far more complex and flexible than any computer, which merely performs such mechanical work more rapidly than the human brain is capable of doing. The computor cannot perform without programming. It does not reason. Nevertheless, there is usefulness in the analogy between mechanical and physiological self-regulating systems, relying on feedback (Cherry, 1961).

The work of Schutz and of Peck provides concrete evidence that this can be accomplished. Neither utilizes the concepts and language of communications theory. They offer us an alternative. Schutz's terminology is firmly grounded in basic Freudian theory but is expressed in a well chosen combination of interpersonal and ego psychological language. Peck's work, described in Chapter VI, likewise offers the basis for a comprehensive group and individual psychology couched in psychoanalytic ego psychological terms. He and his colleagues have used Rapaport's psychoanalytic model of individual behavior as the basis for their formulations about the group. One of their basic principles is that the "behavior of groups as well as individuals develops as an epigenetic prcess, through a sequence of developmental crises whose solution depends as much on the solutions of previous crises as on the environmental provisions which meet it." They go along with Erikson (1959) in perceiving "the developmental task as an expression, not only of the individual's biogenesis but also of the group's potential adaptiveness. The societal norms are perceived not as being grafted on the genetically asocial individual by "discipline" and "socialization"; but it is believed "that the society into which the individual is born makes him its member by influencing the manner in which he and his small group interact in the collective solution of tasks posed by each phase of his and their epigenetic development" (quoted from the mimeographed description of the family and small group research program).

The striking similarity between Peck's thinking and that of Schutz, and the group development theories of Bennis and Shepard, Benne, and my own conclusions[2] regarding the central importance of an epigenetic schema in group as well as individual psychology, seems to hold promise of an eventual agreement on group theory. The existence of two separate terminologies (the communications and the ego psychological), each of which could be used as a common language, signifies that the tools for the interdisciplinary investigation requisite to formulating such a comprehensive theory of group psychology are at hand. The groundwork for it has already begun. The goal we really have in common is to pool our knowledge about group psychology and to find a way of collaborating in our future research in order to extend that body

[2] See Chapter XII.

of information on which we all draw and which we utilize in different ways according to our specific purposes. The task before us is not an easy one, for there are old dichotomies to transcend and new learnings to be digested, while due care is taken to preserve those well established theories and techniques which still serve one or another discipline effectively. However, we have sound cause for optimism in our attempt to coordinate our various approaches to meet the needs of a civilization so based on group process, as is our world in the twentieth century.

PART II

Group Psychotherapy

Introduction

Finding a principle for classifying what seemed, at first glance, to be a large variety of group therapy methods posed somewhat of a problem. The movement had mushroomed so rapidly that conceptualization had not kept pace with practice. I decided to leave to historians the earliest forerunners, the inspirational-repressive therapies like that of Pratt, and Trigant Burrow's very interesting phyloanalysis which was investigatory in purpose and included therapists, family, and friends as well as patients. It seemed better to include only methods which are currently used. *Progress in Neuropsychiatry* listed eighty-nine group therapy articles in the thirties, sixty-nine of which were published between 1936 and 1940. Few of us in the early years realized how much work was in progress for, like other discoveries group therapy seemed to be responding to the *Zeitgeist*. It was started quite independently in a number of different places. Most of the pioneers used psychoanalytic knowledge, but in a number of different ways. Louis Wender, for example, became the father-leader of the small hospital groups with whom he was working as chief psychiatrist; Paul Schilder used analytic techniques with groups of patients in Bellevue Hospital; S. R. Slavson, coming from the field of progressive education, developed activity therapy which was consonant with psychoanalytic principles but did not use interpretive techniques. Alexander

Wolf was doing group analysis. Durkin, Glatzer, and Hirsch began to apply John Levy's relationship therapy using analytic interpretations with groups of mothers and children who were in treatment at the Brooklyn Juvenile Protective Association. Thus each of these pioneers gradually developed his own modifications of psychoanalytic method based partly on his training and partly on his perception of the situation with which he was dealing.

Jacob Moreno had already begun to use psychodrama, an action method based on the principles of group interaction rather than on psychoanalysis.

During that first flush of success, articles on group therapy were characterized by their emphasis on the excellence of the results and the experimenter's own findings. Each author reported descriptively on what he was doing without reference to the concepts and methods of others in the field. The literature read as if there were a common definition of group therapy. Actually there was none. There were as many kinds of group therapy as there were therapists. There was therapy by the group, in the group, and to the group. The common denominator was the utilization of the group, but precisely how it was used was by no means clearly defined. On the whole, the pathfinders were cautiously scientific in their attitude toward their work, but before long less well-trained therapists came into the field who seemed to use the group as a panacea for all emotional ills.

Gradually, increased interaction among group therapists began to take place with the result that the differences between them were stressed more and more. Often minor disparities in technique which did not really change basic concepts were overemphasized and schisms were created where none were necessary. An example was the disagreement between Wolf and those analytic group therapists who did not use alternate meetings. Meanwhile, the ranks were rapidly increasing. Seven hundred thirty articles were listed in the forties, the majority after 1945 (Corsini, 1957). The large majority of these were still based on psychoanalytic thinking. But there was also Moreno, who was including audience discussion in his psychodramatic method, and Carl Rogers who applied his client-centered therapy to groups.

I searched for a principle of classification that would delineate the major differences in a dynamically meaningful way and yet absorb the minor disagreements. Because the therapist's own personality is deeply involved in selecting his method of training, and therefore of treatment, it seemed wise to approach the project from this angle. Since so large a contingent came from among individual psychoanalytically oriented therapists, the possibility arose immediately of listing the various forms of analytic group therapy. But by the turn of the fifth decade, the group-dynamic and the existential methods of group therapy had made their appearance and suggested a different method of organization.

Psychoanalytic group psychotherapy has many subdivisions, including all the differences in orientation to which we have become accustomed in individual psychoanalysis. It goes without saying that the old differences among analytic group therapists persisted in the groups. Some analytic schools continued to ignore libido theory, to emphasize interpersonal factors and to replace biological with cultural emphasis (see Munroe, 1955).

In 1956 the Thirteenth Annual Conference of the American Group Psychotherapy Association featured papers on group psychotherapy as viewed by Freudian, Adlerian, Jungian, Horney, and Sullivanian schools of psychoanalysis. The papers were published in the *International Journal of Group Psychotherapy* in 1957. Each of these schools welcomed certain attributes of the group setting and used that medium in its own characteristic way.

Sullivanians saw the group "as an effective laboratory to explore and vividly verify one's patterns of interpersonal reaction as a prelude to learning their historical perspective and eventually changing one's behavior" (Goldman, 1957). Those who follow Horney's thinking found that "the group can help appreciably to modify the member's exaggerated self-idealization and distorted concepts of the world which come from childhood. In its striving toward a cooperative mutuality it can, under the therapist's guidance, develop a healthy feeling of belongingness in the members based on the essential humanness of each" (Rose, 1957).

For the older Freudian point of view, the group represents a family *par excellence*. The old neurotic conflicts may be relived and solved in the more permissive new family, the group. Where catharsis and regression are relied upon as the significant therapeutic agents, the group offers increased emotional stimulation. For the more modern psychoanalytic ego psychologist, it offers an extraordinarily sensitive milieu for the mutual exploration both of defensive character structure and of healthy adaptive functions. It lends the members both support and opportunity for growth.

Those of us who bring more emphasis to the resolution of pre-oedipal conflicts find that the group not only facilitates character analysis, but provides a useful ally in detecting the role of the archaic precursors of the superego in its strange self-defeating alliance with the members' narcissistic fantasies of omnipotence. Group members seem to be quick to grasp this aspect in fellow members, and in pointing it out in the group gradually learn to apply this knowledge to themselves.

It might seem appropriate, therefore, in a book on methods of group psychotherapy, to describe in detail the way in which the different schools of psychoanalysis apply their theories to therapy groups. However, a significant new trend had been in the making which changed the constellation completely. Social scientists whose researches had brought into being the new field of group dynamics, and British psychoanalysts who had adopted Lewinian field theory began to utilize group dynamic principles with groups of patients. Analytic group therapists, including at first myself, raised the question as to whether group dynamics qualify as therapeutic process. This became a highly controversial subject, the issues of which were badly confused by lack of understanding (see Part I). What became increasingly clear, in my investigation, was the fact that—whether we liked it or not—an increasing number of accredited individuals were practicing a method of group therapy which was based as solidly on the foundation of group dynamics as analytic group psychotherapy was based on psychoanalysis. I have therefore included it as one of the major contemporary methods, and subsumed the psychoanalytic schools under the unitary caption, "Analytic Group Psychotherapy."

My choice proved consonant with current developments. In 1957, for the first time, the *International Journal* devoted an issue to a series of papers on group dynamics and group psychotherapy. Although the majority of analytic group therapists at that time opposed the application of group dynamics as a therapeutic process, I was convinced that a new chapter in the history of group therapy had begun. I went along with this shift of direction.

During the fifties, the effect of the humanistic rebellion against the psychoanalytic "system" and its techniques had also begun to make itself felt in group psychotherapy circles. A number of former psychoanalytic therapists (from various schools) who were discontented with analytic techniques, and some who were not analytic and still more discontented, were searching for a more effective and intuitive method. They fashioned an experiential type of group psychotherapy for themselves and gradually moved in the direction of existentialism. They put group therapy on an ontological rather than a purely psychogenetic foundation, but differed among themselves as to their way of applying the philosophy and in how much they continued to use psychoanalytic concepts. Although the adherents of this school are not many in number, and although we do not yet know how widespread or permanent it will become, its impact has been marked enough to make it mandatory to include existential therapy as one of the major approaches.

Of still more recent origin was the introduction of communications theory and its particular progeny, family therapy, into the world of group psychotherapy. We do not know whether this form of therapy will remain as a school of thought or will merge with other schools. But in 1964 its voice is too strong to omit it from any current survey of group psychotherapy.

It will be apparent to the reader that it is impossible to make a clear-cut and absolute classification of group methods. The theoretical orientations differ fundamentally; but to some degree they also overlap, and many therapists combine several techniques. The compatibility of both the Sullivanian and the Adlerian analytic group therapies with group dynamics makes for a certain amount of merging, and that between the analytic thinking of Horney and Fromm with existential thinking has a similar effect. However, if we do not take the classifications too literally, and make use of them instead of "believing" in them, they will serve to achieve clarity about our clinical differences and pave the way for a more precise description of group therapy theory. I have tried to present each of these methods as objectively as possible.

In addition to a serious attempt to comprehend each method intellectually, I have also striven to gain an empathic experiential understanding of them. For example, I participated in an existential group as a patient, and in a group dynamics training group as a participant observer. I tried to record each kind of group therapy from the point of view of the school it represented. Unfortunately, I am sure my bias will nevertheless become apparent, and I must rely on the reader to believe in my good will, and discount for human frailty.

Unfortunately, too, there are so many variations in conceptual emphasis and in style of working that an exhaustive account of each school could not be achieved. Instead, I reported on the work of typical and outstanding representatives of each point of view. Naturally, my particular version of analytic group psychotherapy received the most emphasis; and, although I know that my psychoanalytically minded colleagues will differ with me in a number of respects, I believe that we have in common the simple basic fact that we adhere strictly to analyzing transference and resistance in the group in order to bring about basic personality change in the individual members.

My goal in Part II, however, was not simply to describe methods of group therapy, but to clarify our conceptual differences in order to reduce our too prevalent misunderstandings of one another's theoretical positions. Chapter X is therefore devoted to a preliminary survey of the chief sources of confusion among us.

X Some Misunderstood Concepts

"Truth can be begotten from error but seldom if ever from confusion."
S. R. Slavson (1953)

We have seen that it is impractical and perhaps inadvisable to attempt to integrate disparate theories of psychopathology and its cure. Nevertheless understanding the different philosophies of therapy and accepting the real differences are essential if group therapists are to contribute meaningfully, in the way they are uniquely qualified to, to an interdisciplinary program of research in group behavior. Ironically, this is difficult in our field, which relies so heavily on good communication. Even members of the same school seem to have trouble in coming to agreement on such fundamental concepts as transference and countertransference. Ostensibly clear-cut exposition intended by an author of one school to convey a particular meaning is likely to be misinterpreted and criticized by readers of another. It seems we fall prey to a common human tendency to take our basic assumptions for granted, to remain unaware that we are doing so, and then to judge others' theories by our own premises, instead of examining theirs. Confusion ensues.

In the creative arts, lack of logical rigor does not particularly matter, but science cannot flourish in such comfortable apathy and illusion. Actually therapy is a border area. As therapists we are required to function both ways. In practice, intuition and artistic skill are very important, but when we are constructing a concep-

121

tual framework within which to practice our skills, scientific rigor becomes a necessity. It has been suggested that perhaps our patients gain more from the therapist's conviction than from the insight based on conceptual understanding of their conflicts. But in spite of the indubitable importance of the relationship within which therapy takes place, I believe this notion is only a consequence of the present imperfect state of our knowledge.

Meanwhile, the need to be right is very strong. When we look deeper for the source of this striking but quite irrational disposition to defend our theoretical positions with something akin to religious fervor, we sometimes speculate that we share a deeply rooted narcissistic investment in our conceptual frameworks. Nevertheless an effort to overcome it is indicated at this time of increasing interest in interdisciplinary research. At the very least, our differences must be concisely delineated in terms of the assumptions on which they are based, and all possible sources of misunderstanding reduced to a minimum. It may clear the road to make a preliminary survey of some common misunderstandings that have unnecessarily contributed to confusion.

MISCONCEPTIONS CONCERNING ANALYTIC GROUP THERAPY

Since the related branches of social science from which group therapy draws have all been influenced to some degree by the discoveries of Freud, as well as by some strong reactions against them, analytic group therapists have been especially prone both to deep convictions and to being misunderstood. Reliance upon a high level of inference promotes these tendencies. Moreover, the illogic of the unconscious with which it deals is such that clinical experience and/or personal analysis is almost prerequisite to its accurate comprehension.

We inherit some intrinsic sources of confusion from psychoanalysis. The traces of nineteenth-century animistic thinking and the terminological imprecision which is often a product of the very novelty of its discoveries raise doubts in the minds of modern experimental psychologists and other social scientists. For example, colorful clinical descriptions such as "the work of the unconscious," or the "cruelty of the superego," produce the atmosphere of anthropomorphism. The reader who follows the descriptions of how the tripartite structure of the personality functions is more likely than not to visualize a struggle between a weak little man (the ego), a beast (the id), and an unpleasant kind of ghost (the superego)!

The substantive employment of the term "the unconscious" emphasizes the structural rather than the functional aspects of unconscious processes, whereas the latter would be more palatable to the modern scientist. At present both sides of this controversy fail to take full cognizance of the current view of modern physics that structure and function, content and process are simply two aspects of a single phenomenon. Secondly, these critics miss the point that Freud, like Lewin, was referring to psychological rather than to physical space. Perhaps they have been influenced by the knowledge that Freud was interested in finding biological correlates for the psychological phenomena he discovered.

The persistence of traces of nineteenth-century biology despite Freud's effort to break away from it is another case in point. Perhaps the best single example is the libido theory. In spite of his then *avant-garde* ideas Freud was caught in the culture of his time. He may also have been ambivalent in his rebellion against it. For example, he had originally used the German word *Trieb,* meaning drive, yet he did not correct his translators who lapsed into using the less precise term instinct. Moreover, he himself was inconsistent about its use.

The criticisms are of course well taken. The danger they bring to sound theory building comes rather from their implication that the observable data as well as the conceptualizations which too crudely represent them are invalid, and that they must therefore be abandoned. If the criticisms were more carefully screened by the one side, and more seriously examined by the other, as a basis for reformulation, a great deal of confusion could be eliminated. As it is, the persistence in the old terminology puts analytic group therapists in unintended collusion with their critics.

In addition, the rapidity with which theoretical changes followed new empirical findings prevented uniformity in the way concepts were interpreted and applied. It so happens that each crucial change elicited varying responses from psychoanalysts who differed in the emphasis they gave a new hypothesis, the interpretations they made of it, and the way in which they put it into practice. As a result, both analytic and antianalytic group therapy authors have contributed to the confusion by making references to psychoanalytic theory without indicating the year to which they refer. Often they make criticisms which would have been valid about psychoanalysis before 1920.

The development of the ego is representative. The old argument that psychoanalysis (and therefore analytic group therapy) concerns itself too much with the id is still extant, although there has been no reasonable basis for it since the midtwenties, and none whatever since the emergence of ego psychology. Freud, it is true, originally used the term "ego" as an equivalent of what is conscious and viewed it as a weak structure, "a baby riding astride an elephant," and he did, indeed, become almost exclusively absorbed in the study of the id (at that time id referred only to the libido). But he was aware of the significance of the ego and acknowledged Adler's views on this subject even though he did not follow up his study of it for some time. Clinical practice eventually began to force attention to the ego, but only because it was the source of defenses which acted as resistance in treatment. In *The Ego and the Id* Freud (1923) defined it as the active organizer of the mental processes. Perception was considered its basic preoccupation. Thereafter the functional division conscious-unconscious was replaced by that of ego, id, and superego. In *The Problem of Anxiety* Freud (1926) placed the ego on an equal level with the id and granted its autonomous character.

More recently the researches of the ego psychologists Kris, Hartmann and Loewenstein, the studies of Spitz, Bychowski, Erikson, and many others have been filling in the gaps of our understanding of the ego and its range of functions. Their concept of the autonomy of the ego is founded on its origin as a number of inborn adaptive functions. The normally conflict-free functions of perception, thought, judgment, etc., were for the first time given their due place in psychoanalysis. Today such criticism as May's (1958, p. 46), that the ego is essentially passive (which he quotes from Groddeck, a very early writer) is anachronistic and seems an appropriate criticism only of those group therapists who have not kept up with later developments. They miss the indispensable point that the ego is now regularly viewed as "the administrative department of the personality."

Similar sources of error arose after Freud's recognition of the forces of aggression and his formulation, in 1920, of the theory of the life and death instincts. Because psychoanalysts differed sharply among themselves both as to the source of aggression and in their way of dealing with it in treatment, this concept also led to confusion in the literature.

A misunderstanding of Freudian group psychology also occurs. For instance, a paper by a well-known group analyst states that, according to Freud, "behavior is conceived as a function of individual personality. The focus is exclusively on the internal organization of personality. Personality is viewed as an autonomous entity. The characteristic modes of behavior are formulated in the abstract, out of relation to a particular situation. Formulations concerning the intrapsychic organization are not paralleled by corresponding formulation regarding the mode of the interpersonal." And again, "Freud perceived the individual and group as being set against one another. He saw vividly the oppositional aspect but less well the joining aspect of these relations" (Ackerman, 1961, p. 132). Statements like these are misleading and ignore the fact that Freud (1921) took a firm stand on the belief that man is a biopsychosocial being and that individual psychology is at the same time social psychology.

From the existential group therapists comes a different kind of criticism. They frequently accuse analytic group therapists of being too rational. This is indeed puzzling. How is it possible that the method which a mere half-century earlier had opened the doors of psychological science to the irrational is already perceived as being overly rational? In this instance the kernel of truth which lent itself to such a distortion is not hard to find. Freud's own rationality and his compulsiveness (without which he could hardly have achieved so much) probably played their role in determining the sharp emphasis that was later put on perfecting his techniques. He himself once said that he hoped the analytic technique would reach the same degree of precision as the surgeon's knife. Such an attitude might easily have had unacknowledged influence on his followers. The rational means may have become more important to some of them than the goal of bringing the irrational to consciousness. Moreover, the teachers of the next generation sometimes betrayed their own need to be rational in their zeal to perfect the techniques of analysis. Consequently, the novice sometimes learned to cultivate his knowledge of psychodynamics at the expense of the clinical data and tended to rely less on his free-floating attention than was intended. Deterioration of the original spirit of important ideological movements to mere attentiveness to ritual and routine is not new to history. It happened to Christianity and to communism. Heinemann (1953) calls this process "creative alienation." Nevertheless these tendencies on the part of therapists constitute a bewilderment of analytic principles, and critics might more appropriately blame the practitioners than the fundamental principles of the theory.

MISCONCEPTIONS ABOUT GROUP DYNAMICS

The social scientists are open to far less criticism of their methodology and their conceptualizations. Their field-theoretical constructs have first been operationally tested, and then conceptually defined. Their terminology has a higher degree of precision than the Freudian. They are masters of experimental design and their methodology is highly refined. As long as they restricted themselves to research, they offered no challenge and received no criticism from group therapists. It was only when they seemed to be applying group dynamics in place of therapeutic process per se as therapy that their goals were disputed by analytic group therapists. It was then that emotion insidiously crept in alongside valid arguments to distort logic and create confusion.

An article by Wolf and Schwartz (1960) called "The Mystique of Group Dynamics" is an illustration. In it such paragraphs as the following, which we quote verbatim, take their place among other, entirely reasonable discussions of the subject:

"Group Dynamics as psychotherapy is a mystique, because it jumps frames of reference. The social psychologists do not use such terms as group ego, group superego, group id, group mind, group soul, collective unconscious, group resistance, or group transference. The group psychodynamicists who use such terms are trying to reconcile disparate or discrete formulation. They are condensing ideas which are valid in the context of individual psychological theory with perceptions of group processes appropriate to the group. As a consequence, projective distortions, as in dreams, are the result. It is like taking a valid concept, for example, individual physiology, individual respiration or individual perspiration and calling it group physiology, group respiration or group perspiration. Everybody in a group may perspire, but is it group perspiration? Is there a group skin? A group liver? Or a group mind? Can there be an individual mind without an individual nervous system? If we are speaking figuratively let us not act as if it were really so.

"Some group therapists with little or no training in the field of group dynamics have become enamoured of its terminology and non-discriminatively use its technical terms, such as belongingness, togetherness, gregariousness, group loyalty, group contagion, group morale, and group cohesion. This is a problem, too, which fosters the mystique. The group dynamicists mean one thing, the group psychodynamicists, another. . . ."

These authors are scientifically sophisticated. They accept the findings of the American social scientists, namely, that groups do have existence and that group-determined processes do occur within them. They welcome these contributions to our knowledge about the way groups function. They make the distinction which other less informed critics fail to make between group psychology and group psychotherapy. It is only when they discuss therapeutic use of these concepts that the tone of the writing changes and the boundary between fact and interpretation is blurred. They seem to be angry with those who claim therapeutic powers for group dynamics. Their invention of the infelicitous title "group psychodynamicists" succeeds only in adding to the confusion. It does not clearly convey its point that very few group dynamicists engage in therapy. Therefore, the opportunity to correct the erroneous, but very general, impression that group dynamicists regularly engage in group therapy is too easily passed over.

Even those group dynamicists who do engage in therapy insist only that the group forces have therapeutic potential which may be used in combination with an established therapeutic process. At times Wolf and Schwartz seem to be aiming their criticism at the British group dynamics analysts, and it is true that the latter on occasion use animistic terminology. Bion outdoes Freud with his vague, colorful, and esoteric language. Yet if one reads his articles for their clinical value, one finds them so productive that restatement rather than contradiction is indicated. Surely no one doubts that the language must be revised, but the idea behind the words is

not meant to be animistic. Nor would such a criticism be applicable to Foulkes' concept of the "group matrix," nor Ezriel's construct of a "network of intragroup transferences based on a common fantasy." By and large, the British group therapists subscribe
to the Lewinian definition of the group, which is completely objective and supersedes the old animistic concept in a very clear-cut
manner. On this point the exaggeration of a valid argument has
converted it into a distortion.

In caricaturing the analogies between groups and individuals,
Wolf and Schwartz unintentionally reinforce our tendency to
dichotomize. Nobody has actually suggested that the similarity goes
so far as to imply that groups have "a nervous system like that of
the individual." Such emphasis on the distinctions is hardly useful. A less emotional argument, simply underlining the fact that
the group and the individual factors are two aspects of a single set
of phenomena, one of which is more meaningful for group research, the other for group psychotherapy, would be more effective
and less divisive.

MISCONCEPTIONS CONCERNING THE EXPERIENTIAL-EXISTENTIAL SCHOOL OF GROUP PSYCHOTHERAPY

There is as yet so little understanding of this school's group psychotherapy that we can hardly speak of misconceptions. The layman and the average group therapist are far from clear not only
about the meaning of existential philosophy, but also about its
application to therapy. Nevertheless, we might include under this
caption:

1. Many group therapists of other schools still expect to find
that existential therapy, whether applied to individuals or groups,
offers a clear-cut conceptual system and a new technique. The
truth is that its proponents are opposed to the development of too
clearly outlined systems of any kind. What the existentialists present instead is a new point of view. They take a different stance
which goes beyond, and too often ignores, genetic development of
the patient and focuses on the ontological givens of his life. As
May (1958) puts it, they "broaden the base" of psychotherapy by
taking a new philosophic or, more accurately, a metaphysical point
of view.

Sartre, after pointing out the similarities between psychoanalysis and existential analysis, makes the same point in another way. He writes (1948), "They differ most fundamentally in that empirical psychoanalysis has decided upon its own irreducibles instead of allowing this to make itself known in a self-evident situation. The libido and the will to power (aggression) do not appear to us as being beforehand the irreducible limits of the investigation. Nothing prevents us from conceiving a priori of a 'human reality' which would not be reducible to theses.... It [existential analysis] is guided from the start toward a comprehension of being and must not assign itself any other goal than to discover being and the mode of being of the being [of the patient] confronting this being [the analyst]. It will utilize the comprehension of being which characterized the investigator inasmuch as he himself is a human reality. This psychoanalysis has not yet found its Freud." In other words, no specific techniques have been outlined. This ontological view colors their understanding of man, the meaning of neurosis, their way of communicating with their patients, and their goals in psychotherapy.

2.   Another misunderstanding can be said to result from the fact that experiential existential group therapy is the product of a humanism rather than a science. The therapist with this orientation experiences himself more as an artist than a scientist. He is a seeker of freedom, spontaneity and creativity, and so these values are part of his goal for his patients. He prefers a minimum of reasoning and articulation and, in therapy, wishes to identify himself as well as his patient as a living part of the whole of existence. Consequently analysis and articulation of the processes which come into play are secondary for him and tend to follow rather than to produce his therapeutic interventions.

3.   Few group therapists realize that not all existentialists believe in full mutuality between patient and therapist. Those who come from the Jungian School, which has a certain affinity for existentialism, find such mutuality in agreement with their traditional position of the "journey" undertaken together by patient and therapist. Certain experientialists carry this position to its extreme, insisting that the therapist give expression to his own deep-

est feelings, fantasies, and so on, in a full mutual "encounter."
Buber and Sartre hold a somewhat different view. They both recognize the need for a degree of objectivity on the part of the healing professions.

Most other therapists are baffled by this feature of mutuality
and equality between therapist and patient because they are not
aware of the reason for it (i.e., that the assumption upon which it
is based differs from their own). The principle of mutuality is
based on the premise that the therapeutic process depends in large
measure upon fuller experiencing and interchange between therapist and patient. It includes the expectation that the patient learns,
too, by adjusting to the emotions and needs of the therapist. However much one may disagree with this position, one must understand it in order to avoid confusion and to communicate profitably
with experientialist colleagues. In the following chapters an attempt is made to describe each method from the viewpoint of its
practitioners.

XI Relationship Between Individual and Group Psychoanalysis

> *"The strategy is the same but the tactics are different."*
> Max Sherman[1]

Because analytic group psychotherapy applies an old method to a new situation, it draws the fire of criticism from both of its closest neighbors. As we have shown, it falls heir to all the criticisms which experimental psychologists have leveled at psychoanalysis itself. This side is joined by all those who insist that group therapy could stand upon principles which are indigenous to the group situation rather than to known therapeutic principles. They feel that its relationship to traditional psychoanalysis is too anaclitic. On the other side are those somewhat outraged psychoanalysts who cannot believe that the analytic process as they have come to know it in individual treatment can possibly take place in a group. Both of these viewpoints merit detailed exploration.

Certain crucial problems of analytic group psychotherapy have been raised by the constructive appraisal of a highly qualified psychoanalyst, Kubie (1958), whose attitude is friendly but whose mental position is honestly skeptical.

In order to establish a basis for comparison Kubie summarizes what he calls "the essence of usual individual therapeutic process" as follows: "It is an attempt to break down the barriers between unconscious processes on the one hand and preconscious and con-

---

[1] From his opening statement in an address before the Annual Institute of the American Group Psychotherapy Association, January 1960.

scious processes on the other, in an effort to integrate all three systems of psychological functioning. It deals with resistances by interpreting them, as it elicits historical data, and as it works out
transference and countertransference interrelationships so as to
free the patient's production of free associations. It works with
transference, with resistances, with automatic superego processes,
with facts, fantasies, and dreams, always elaborated by means of
the exploring device of free associations. Furthermore this occurs
in a setting which is reduced artificially to two human presences:
the one remaining to the patient as unknown, as poker faced and
poker voiced as is humanly possible, a blank screen, a *tabula rasa,*
on whom the patient can project his conscious, preconscious, and
unconscious fantasies, and to whom the patient will attribute all
manner of appropriate and inappropriate qualities. The analytic
chamber maintains a constancy in the environment and in the relationship which is directly comparable to that which we create in
any experimental procedure, so that any variables which are introduced into the interaction will arrive predominantly from one individual, namely, the patient. To this rule there is only one exception; to wit, the deliberate intrusion by the analyst of that
calculated variable which we call 'interpretation.' Other than his
interpretations the analyst limits the variables which he brings into the situation to that irreducible minimum which his mere presence makes unavoidable. It is in this way that the individual therapeutic situation makes it possible to analyze one unconscious at a
time and not two" (Kubie, 1958, pp. 8-9).

Kubie doubts whether archaic superego figures can be modified
in groups. He doubts whether the group can be used to communicate insights to the individual patients into their individual problems. He further doubts the possibility of unmasking unconscious
linkages in a situation where free association is manifestly impossible. He says: "It is impossible to pretend that we have a true picture of the stream of psychological processes in any individual
unless we have had at least brief random samples of his free associations"; and, "It is impossible to tell what evokes changes in the
transferences in the group where there are so many variables." The
difficulties of communicating insight in a meaningful form to individuals in a group seem to him insuperable. He concludes that
it is "self-evident that group processes depart from our basic ex-

perimental design not in detail alone, but in essence." The difficulty, he says, arises from "the impossibility of controlling sufficient variables in the group therapy situation" (Kubie, 1958).

In order to adapt the analytic process to the group setting, the group therapist has to keep in mind not only his goals but the nature of the concrete situation which will confront him with certain unchangeable facts. It is evident from what Kubie has written that his thinking was proceeding along just these lines. He has offered us a sound goal to follow and one with which we feel at home. The analytic group therapist does indeed aim to pilot the members of his group toward the best possible solutions of their pathogenic conflicts. At the very minimum he hopes to remove some of the distortions with which they came into treatment and to help them develop more satisfactory defenses; at best he hopes for real and pervasive structural and behavior change which comes from the "integration of the three systems of mental functioning." We would agree with Kubie that it is necessary to break down the barriers between unconscious, preconscious, and conscious processes. There is no doubt that our ultimate goal is the same as his. In this and the ensuing chapters we shall try to show that those goals are legitimate and attainable in group therapy, provided we make appropriate adaptations of procedure to meet the changed conditions.

The analytic group therapist's position is based on Freud's definition of the therapeutic process as the analysis of transference and resistance in bringing unconscious material to consciousness (1914a, p. 128). In Kubie's view the techniques of free association and the so-called analytic situation are also integral parts of the process. It is this unnecessary fusing of the essential process with the technical procedures that gives rise to his appropriate doubts as to whether this could take place in groups. We propose to simplify the problem by adhering to Freud's definition and by keeping separate the essential process from those techniques which have been developed to implement it in the individual situation. The problem that remains will then be to determine what changes must be made in the technical procedures so that the process per se will be effective in the group situation and yet not do violence to its basic nature. We are on firm ground here, and indeed are backed by Fenichel (1945, p. 573), who repeats Freud's definition and makes the comment,

"This alone is the criterion. Whether the patient lies down or sits, whether or not certain rituals of procedure are used, does not matter. For psychotics and children as well as for certain character cases, the classical method must be modified. That procedure is the best which provides the best conditions for the analytic task. A 'non-classical procedure', when the classical one is not possible, remains psychoanalysis. It is meaningless to distinguish an 'orthodox' psychoanalysis from an 'unorthodox' one." Neither Freud nor Fenichel, then, insisted upon a fixed mode of implementing the essential process. They left the door open to anyone who would use new techniques so long as he adhered strictly to the analysis of transference and resistance. Freed from the limitations of a particular technique (free association) and of a "scientifically-controlled" analytic situation, the outlook for achieving analysis in a group situation is more encouraging.

One of the immutable facts of the group setting is its inherent incompatibility with the technique of free association. The basic rule will not work. Reality dictates that the therapist must work with ordinary conversation carried on in secondary process. He is denied the fairly direct access to primary process which the individual analyst enjoys via free association. Is there a way around this obstacle? Experience has proved that if we regard the flow of the total conversation, especially its latent elements, as a form of or a substitute for free association, we have a working procedure which is at least as satisfactory as that of the play therapist who observes the child's use of toys in his play room. Psychoanalysis has, of course, long since learned to recognize the signs and symbols of the patient's productions and to translate them into the language of his latent emotions and unconscious motivations. For instance, when patients complain of other doctors, of teachers, nurses, or other ministering or authority figures, they may be assumed, without being aware of it, to be referring to the therapist. Besides such general signals there are also special personal meanings which the therapist soon learns to recognize. Thus, when Phyllis cried, it usually meant that she was giving vent to infantile fury; and whenever Martha spoke of her middle sister she was suffering from superego accusations. From such signals it has proved safe to make inferences regarding the primary process.

Moreover, although inference from the secondary process is his usual source of knowledge of the unconscious, the group therapist also has access to a fair sampling of free associations if he times his requests for them appropriately. Once a patient has become involved in talking about himself in some important area, he may quite naturally lapse into free association. His language even in the group becomes less coherent, logic disappears, and his manner and gestures reveal his underlying feelings. He may make slips in reporting an incident, become confused, contradict himself, or bring in some irrelevant remark. At this usually high-pitched moment of emotion, a gentle nonintrusive request for "what comes to mind about that?" usually bears fruit. Since the whole group is intensely absorbed at such a time, there are not likely to be interruptions, even though the patient in question takes a little time to respond or speaks haltingly or incoherently. Sometimes such bits of free association achieve in a moment what long sequences cannot accomplish on the couch, and they deeply affect the other members as well.

Concerning the analytic situation Kubie says that the group departs from the psychoanalytic experimental design not only in detail but in essence, and that the fault lies with the inability to control sufficient variables. The situation in which the group therapist must work will indeed be in sharp contrast to the sterilized atmosphere of individual analysis. For reality impinges mercilessly on the heretofore sacrosanct relation between the patient and his individual analyst. Characteristically the multiple variables are in constant flux and it is impossible to control the mêlée of human entanglements which exist on all levels. It would be futile to try to match the meticulous design of individual analysis.

But I submit that it is not the rigid control of the variables but the unique quality of the therapeutic relationship itself which is of paramount importance for psychotherapy. Firmly controlled variables are a requisite for experimental research, and it is difficult to prove or disprove a thesis without them, but there is nothing to show that they contribute to therapeutic values. In the early days it was important for the analyst to remain completely anonymous as a personality, so the projective elements of the transference might be clearly demonstrated. But that is assumed nowadays. In the group the transferences are identifiable and analyzable even though they do not occur in "pure culture." Even the patients are soon able to recognize them in others, and later in themselves, with astonishing ease.

Face to face with the powerful emotional responses of the group members, the analyst, it is true, cannot remain totally poker-faced, totally anonymous. Nevertheless he can still control the most crucial variable—his interventions. The nature and form of his interpretations will follow the same principle as that used in individual psychoanalysis. He addresses himself chiefly to the analysis of transference and resistance. Although he must show his face and will be more easily stimulated by the impact of a number of patients in rapid succession (or at once), he need not reduce his anonymity beyond the point of diminishing returns. The fact that he is more stimulated and more vulnerable does not necessitate his becoming personally involved, nor need he ever express his feelings or reveal his experiences and fantasies unless in a special instance he deems it wise. Even Kubie admits that the individual analyst cannot avoid revealing himself minimally. At times he changes his tone of voice, he unwittingly varies the rhythm of his breathing, he even falls asleep. One way or another he betrays his interest, his boredom, his irritation, or his pleasure. The difference in the group is one of degree, not of kind.

The only decisively noxious involvement for the therapist in either situation is that which stems from unrecognized countertransference. And although the group actually does bring countertransference into the open more readily than does individual psychoanalysis, this fact may be counted as an asset, for it prevents the therapist from any tendency to repress his feelings instead of coming to terms with them. The members who are reinforced by their peers in the group are more able to "read" the therapist's state of mind and freer to confront him with their reactions. When they do, he is forced by the weight of numbers to give it more attention. In fact, it is much more difficult to ignore countertransference in the group than it is in the one-to-one situation. Besides, a seasoned group therapist has usually reached the point where he can accept help from the members, and is able to determine what is correct and what is projection in a member's "accusations."

Group therapy fully recognizes its inability to compete with the classical design of individual psychoanalysis. It sets up instead a group analytic situation which is appropriate to its specific conditions. While it must make certain changes, it finds positive contributions inherent in the new conditions.

In order to achieve the maximal freedom of emotional expression in the group, a permissive atmosphere must be established. To accomplish this the therapist takes approximately the same attitudes as the individual analyst. He does not give advice or answer questions, but he is understanding and noncritical, listening much more than talking. At first his comments are planned to help the patients become aware of the acceptability of even their socially undesirable feelings and of the fact that their verbal and nonverbal communications both have latent meaning. Before long the desirable and unique therapeutic climate is achieved.

In the group situation the therapist is aided in this work because the members readily adopt his goal of affective honesty and direct communication as group standards and put pressure on one another to give up their defensiveness in favor of mutual self-examination. As Freud pointed out, the group as a whole has an extraordinary influence on the individuals in it, making them more than usually submissive. The members seem to imbue the group with the function of the superego. Although this attitude must be analyzed out eventually, it helps in the beginning to facilitate good working conditions.

Another unchangeable element in the group setting is the highly subjective and often robust interaction among the members. Since the leader wants to encourage free expression he must allow them to respond to one another in this incalculable way. To make the best therapeutic use of this spontaneity he encourages maximum participation among them. The members barrage one another and the therapist with their feelings and their needs, giving voice to appropriate as well as inappropriate emotions. They make demands, or express irrational thoughts, fantasies, and dreams. Sometimes they gratify one another's needs, sometimes they frustrate one another more sharply than a therapist could possibly do. At one time they may join forces against the therapist; at another, against one of the members. This hardy emotional atmosphere can become a positive contribution to the group analytic situation. It makes a powerful impact on everyone, releasing forces which the therapist may harness for therapeutic purposes. Occasionally the intense emotional transactions themselves create deep-reaching shifts in attitudes which result in real changes in behavior. But such changes are fortuitous and may be temporary or local to the particular group. They may even be antitherapeutic. It is the therapist's responsibility to utilize them therapeutically.

The recurrent periods of emotional intensity provide many occasions in which the heightened tensions create favorable conditions for insight. If the therapist or another member makes an interpretation at that moment when it is clearly alive and disturbing in a new relationship, the chances of its being accepted are increased. It is as if the fire had already been set when the match of interpretation is put to it. The therapist's knowledge, his relative objectivity, and his timing, in unique combination with the subjective emotional power of the group, accelerate the course of therapy.

Another psychoanalyst, Berne (1960), takes the same point of view as those social scientists who would prefer a predominantly group-determined theory and method of group psychotherapy. He feels that group therapy progress is held back by its dependence on "orthodox" psychoanalytic theory, and prevented thereby from developing a "consistent indigenous theory" of its own.

Such theorists apparently take the position that adapting analytic principles to group therapy will automatically exclude the exploration of new and distinct contributions of the group to the theory and practice of group therapy. If this were true, I would agree with them. There is no rationale for an all-or-none "closed" approach. Rigid adherence to psychoanalysis without exploration of new possibilities would indeed stand in the way of progress. On the other hand, discarding established methods without bothering to test their usefulness might very well end disastrously and deprive therapists of valuable procedures. At any rate, the psychoanalyst who is progressive enough to use group therapy is not likely to be that rigid, unless his sole object is to create difficulties for himself! The late Leo Berman, Boston psychoanalyst and group therapist, made a fair and practicable comment pertinent to this question. He wrote, "The regressive potential of the group situation must neither be regarded as its central therapeutic agent nor avoided at all costs." Because the group necessitates attention to reality he felt that "the psychoanalyst who is experienced in the group situation has a better understanding of the reality relationships of those patients whom he also treats individually." He envisioned as the consequence of the extended practice of analytic group therapy "the solution of many ego psychological and sociological problems which would yield new theoretical insights and new techniques for psychoanalysis, and psychotherapy could be attained by research in psychoanalytic group work rather than in individual therapy" (Berman, 1954).

But Berne (1960) was firm in his contention that psychoanalysis cannot be done in groups. It is this thesis to which he devotes most of his article and which we believe we can, on the basis of solid experience, refute. He starts with Rangell's revised definition that "psychoanalysis is a method of therapy whereby conditions are brought about favorable for the development of a transference neurosis, in which the past is restored in the present, in order that, through a systematic interpretative attack on the resistances which oppose it, there occurs a resolution of that neurosis (transference and infantile) to the end of bringing about structural changes in the mental apparatus of the patient to make the latter capable of optimum adaptation to life." (Quoted by Berne [1960] from Rangell [1954].) Berne grants that there are psychoanalytic incidents or incidents which may be interpreted psychoanalytically in the group but insists that "one swallow or a whole flock of swallows do not make a summer." Group therapists, he continues, should therefore "resign" from the terms analysis, psychoanalysis, analytic, and psychoanalytic and substitute some less tendentious word, such as dynamic (Berne, 1960).

Since reality cannot be minimized in the group it is doubtful whether it can legitimately be claimed that complete regressive libidinal and aggressive transference can be achieved, in which the patient's infantile drives are obviously and openly indulged toward the analyst. In this sense there is no transference neurosis.

Is it, then, legitimate to speak of transference and transference analysis in group psychotherapy? We take a firm stand in this matter, for if we examine transference analysis in groups we shall find that it meets Rangell's requirements. We have good reason to insist that in the group the past is restored in the present in all its crucial aspects, that a systematic interpretative attack can be made on the resistances, and that a resolution of the neuroses (transference and libidinal) does occur to the end of bringing about structural changes and better (if not always optimal) adaptation to life.

We may adduce strong theoretical arguments in favor of our position that transference need not be equated with regressive transference. It had been discovered by clinical psychoanalysts that, in spite of all the analytic precautions, the ego even in individual analysis continued its work, and that its defenses regularly became resistances in the course of therapy. They had to be dealt with before the road to the unconscious became passable. As a consequence, the ego psychologists broadened the whole concept of the transference.

Anna Freud (1936) summarized the new position. There are she said, three types of transference—regressive libidinal, defensive, and acting out. The first is the one usually referred to. The second is pertinent to a group psychotherapy. "Not only," she wrote, "do we fill in a gap in the patient's memory of his instinctual life as we may do when interpreting the first type of transference, but we acquire information which completes and fills in the gaps in the history of his ego development, or to put it another way, the history of the transformation through which his instincts have passed. . . . The interpretation of the second type of transference is more fruitful than that of the first type, but it is responsible for most of the technical difficulties which arise between analyst and patient. . . . It is not easy to convince him of the repetitive nature of these phenomena. The form in which they arise is ego syntonic."

The question therefore becomes not whether transference can take place in group therapy but what form does it take? Moreover, the technical difficulties of which Anna Freud wrote were not an obstacle. The patients accept interpretations more willingly from their peers than from the therapist; for the latter, in spite of his efforts to the contrary, may long be regarded as a powerful authority figure who must be held off at all costs. His interpretations, therefore, serve to reactivate the ancient conflicts and the defenses against them, while peers are less threatening when they approach the same anxiety-laden areas.

The ego-alien quality of the defenses was soon demonstrated, a fact which appreciably accelerated therapeutic movement. The group provides five or six targets for each member's neurotic attitudes. When one and the same neurotic pattern is applied inappropriately to several very different individuals, that characteristic lack of discrimination which marks transference attitudes becomes magnified and inescapably clear. Someone has perceptively called the group a "hall of mirrors." It is difficult to avoid seeeing oneself in them. For example, one patient may respond with a certain combination of fear, placation, and rebelliousness to authority figures. He is often shocked to discover how many group members still represent to him the omnipotent parental authority. Even the patient with strong paranoid tendencies is responsive to this situation where he is forced to see himself as others see him. But the therapist must be ready to cope with a possible withdrawal of these patients into vengeful retreat, from which position, instead of absorbing the insight, they may be waiting to strike back.

Group members are keen in detecting in others transference feelings which they hide from themselves, and they are thus provided with an easy, preliminary step toward discovering their own defenses. The members function like so many sensitive antennae in finding the latent meaning of any one member's behavior. When a neurotic pattern is operating, some of them may continue to react with their own neurotic patterns (a kind of member countertransference), but there are usually at least one or two who are not involved in that particular pattern, and it is they who begin to point out its inappropriateness or who support the therapist's policy of exploring it. Usually these transference engagements soon become obvious to the majority and the group acts in unison to help the involved individual understand that past experiences are interfering in his immediate relationships. The group convictions tend to be powerful and hard to resist. (See Chapter XIII for examples.)

The third type of transference, which Anna Freud called acting out, is also more amenable to group analysis. She described it as "an intensification of transference in which the ego behaves wholly as an infantile ego. . . . This is analytically instructive but makes it impossible to bring influence to bear from without and leaves little opportunity for intrapsychic displacement" (A. Freud, 1936).

In the group the patient who is prone to being thus swept into action is repeatedly made to pause by his fellow members. He can accept this from them just because they are his peers and do not, as we have pointed out before, offer the threat that the therapist does.

Moreover, they usually give such a person a great deal of approval and admiration in the early stages when he seems to them to be able to take action spontaneously and freely as neurotics cannot. In a group, therefore, the acting-out patient often learns even better than in individual analysis to bear with his anxiety and restrain himself from plunging into action long enough to observe its irrational quality. Thus, influence from without can help to bring about intrapsychic displacement.

An impulsive young man, who took pride in his sexual acting out and even won status for it in the group during the early sessions, functioned as a natural member leader for a short period. But as soon as he began to make verbal passes at the women in the group, transference aspects of his behavior were investigated under the therapist's leadership. As soon as he recognized that he habitually avoided anxiety by turning to sexual behavior it became much less ego syntonic. Later, when under the stress of anxiety from treatment, he began to report that he was "sleeping around" again, the group took over the therapist's role in a friendly but firm manner by questioning his motivation.

His emotional anchorage in the group was by that time strong enough to enable him to listen to them and even to accept their serious, constructive examination of his motives. His associations made it evident that gratification from his exploits had consisted more in omnipotent fantasies and in warding off imagined destruction by women than in mature sexual satisfaction. It was a revelation to him that sex had been largely in the service of a struggle for self-preservation and power. Beneath his apparently aggressive sexual conduct lay a crushing fear of women. The cognitive shift took place very gradually; nevertheless, it had a dynamic effect in this case. Closer scrutiny of his role as he played it out verbally in the group revealed much more clearly the underlying significance of his exploits than had his edited reports about outside affairs. By combining our sources of information we were able to help him see that he actually allowed himself to be passively exploited by the kind of women who neurotically craved what he offered them. It also became clear that this seemingly self-confident ego-syntonic behavior often brought him a great deal of trouble and frequently meant courting business and family disaster. Only very gradually did he come to realize that the infantile libidinal and omnipotent gratifications his acting out served were minute compared to the pain he caused himself.

A long time was spent in working through; and when eventually he relegated his actions almost entirely to the realm of fantasy, he had to cope with anxiety such as he had never experienced earlier in his career. During these periods the group gave him warm support. I doubt whether he could have accomplished as much as he subsequently did without the group, since he had assiduously kept the therapist in the role of the mother whom he had to try to exploit and charm, but never could approach sexually. It was the younger members who offered an opportunity for investigating his acting out directly.

The following chapters are devoted to the presentation of the conceptual and technical modifications that have been necessary to meet the requirements of the group situation in order to develop an appropriate form of group psychoanalysis. They will also attempt to present a good deal of clinical evidence in support of the position that systematic analysis of transference is possible to provide conclusive proof. As a matter of fact no amount of clinical evidence would suffice this purpose and we do not as yet have adequate means of measuring the therapeutic process, nor the criteria for testing its effects. In this respect, however, analytic group psychotherapy is no worse off than individual psychoanalysis. What we can hope to achieve is a plausible case for our theory.

XII Systematic Analysis of Transference in the Group

My colleagues, Henriette T. Glatzer, Jeanette Hirsch, and I began to do psychotherapy with children and their parents under the direction of Dr. John Levy at the Brooklyn Child Guidance Center.[1] Dr. Levy had developed a modification of psychoanalytic method which would be suitable to treating patients on a once-or twice-a-week basis. He made the assumption, based on psychoanalytic knowledge, that the patients' behavior patterns which had been established in early childhood would appear again in their relationship with the therapist. These behavior patterns, with their attendant attitudes and latent feelings, would be subject to exploration by the therapist for therapeutic purposes. Because it was necessary to deal differently with anxiety when patients were seen so infrequently (Durkin, 1954), he taught a more active technique of intervening. The therapist was to explore the patients' behavior in the relationship including negative and positive transference feelings, and reality relationships. Tracing these feelings back to their origins in the early familial situation was encouraged but primary emphasis was put on the connection between the historical facts and the behavior in the immediate therapeutic relationship.

Dr. Levy's basic rule for the therapist was to "follow the patients' lead." As we did so, the clinical material itself forced us to make more and more psychoanalytic interpretations. Under the supervision of medical psychoanalysts in the following years at the New Rochelle Guidance Clinic (M. Kanzer, G. Pederson-Krag) we grad-

[1] Formerly, Brooklyn Juvenile Protective Association.

ually developed a distinctly psychoanalytic therapy both with individuals and groups. It seemed appropriate to use the terms transference and resistance instead simply of relationship, for transference resistance became the focal point of our investigations and our therapeutic interventions revolved around it. The group situation, however, encouraged us to continue including the reality elements in the relationship, to analyze the "pseudo positive transference phenomena," and to continue to be rather active in dealing with resistance. For these reasons, and because it describes our present analytic group therapeutic method accurately, I have used the term analytic group therapy.

Believing what has since become generally accepted, that transference phenomena occur regularly outside the analytic situation, we made the basic assumption that they would appear in the members' relationships with one another in the group as well as with the therapist, and that whatever behavior patterns the patients had developed in solving their infantile conflicts would sooner or later appear in the therapy group. It remained to be seen in what form the transferred patterns and the unconscious drives which prompted them would make themselves known, and just how they could be analyzed in the group. Because we already had had the experience of applying an analytic method to individual patients who could be seen only once or twice a week, we were convinced that systematic analysis could be carried out successfully in the absence of the traditional procedures of daily on-the-couch analysis. Whether or not our techniques could be further modified to be effective in groups remained to be discovered.

There was no question that resistance would play a part. It would certainly be tied in with all the transferences, and surely new variations of that ubiquitous phenomenon would appear. A more serious problem was whether resistance might not prove to be much more obdurate against interpretation in the new reality-dominated situation. Yet we had to begin with the assumption that it would yield to the usual form of analysis.

We proceeded partly on a trial-and-error basis, expecting to use our training and skill but prepared to meet whatever contingencies might arise. Although we planned to make deviations whenever necessary, we intended to do so only in accordance with the basic psychoanalytic principle of analyzing transference and resistance.

At the beginning, most of us held rather closely to the individual method wherever possible, improvising only when it was necessary. Gradually, we discovered the new dynamic potentials of the group and, cautiously, we began to use them. Later there was criticism that some analytic group therapists adhered to the individual method too rigidly, but it had been apparent from the start that it would be folly to attempt to conduct several individual analyses concurrently, or even to engage in as many separate conversations. Common sense dictated the encouragement of maximum communication among the members.

Our project required that knowledge and training be temporarily relegated to the background. We had to fly by the "seat of our pants" as it were. It was necessary to rely heavily on intuition, empathy, and the ability to experience a multiplicity of relationships while simultaneously grasping their meaning. The task did not seem too formidable. What could be more natural than to be responsive to the relationships among the members as well as those with the therapist? We had only to combine this skill with our usual analytic techniques.

We soon discovered that group therapists do indeed have to be capable of a good deal of spontaneity in relationships while maintaining sufficient distance to make appropriate analytic interventions, for it is only with the single individual that the therapist may, if he is so inclined, calculate scientifically all the elements that will go into his interpretations. He cannot possibly do this for the whole group at once. He will be forced to respond more spontaneously and to trust himself to a greater extent. Nevertheless, the success with which he is able to respond spontaneously, yet analytically, will depend upon how firm a grasp he has on the underlying principles which provide the necessary limitations to it.

Briefly, then, we expected merely to extend a well-practiced skill to a new but very natural human situation. We hoped to learn by experience how to modify our procedures to meet the limitations of group conditions.

CONDITIONS OF TRANSFERENCE IN THE GROUP

Transferences in everyday life tend to be hidden in the tumultuous, subjective interchanges that regularly take place in the outside world. When conditions there become too difficult, problematic behavior is rationalized away, becoming unnoticeable in the chaotic mixture of satisfaction and heartbreak which results from actions intended to achieve, at once, both realistic and irrational goals. Self-deceptions achieve an apparently easy success under these conditions.

In individual psychoanalysis, the chaos of reality is canceled out almost completely. The analyst, under carefully controlled conditions, is enabled to gain direct access to the primary process of his patients by the method of free association. All the old infantile needs will gradually be directed to him. He neither responds like the original family figures, nor tries to give the patients the satisfactions they once missed and for which they still seem to be grieving. To satisfy them would be like trying to fill in the Grand Canyon with grains of sand, for a baby's original libidinal needs and omnipotent fantasies are vast, beyond any human mother's ability to satisfy. Instead, the analyst helps his patients by giving them a chance to relive the old conflicts, to see with adult eyes how their infantile distortions came about, and to realize that they can now find more constructive solutions which will be congruent with reality.

The conditions in which transference phenomena take place in a therapeutic group fall between these two extremes. Since it is not possible to reduce reality to a minimum, the ego plays a role very similar to that which it takes in the world outside, and the balance between the id, ego, and superego functions approximates that norm as well. Communication has to be carried on in secondary process and on the level of the members' defenses. At first glance one might think that the same obstacle that stands in the way of identifying transference in daily life also operates in therapy groups. But if the therapist regards the intercommunications as free associations and searches out their latent intent, he will have no difficulty in identifying transferences in the group. Although their neurotic character may be disguised in apparently rational relationships, he will be able to detect them with ease because of their telltale inappropriateness and disproportionate feeling tone. Furthermore, the permissive atmosphere of the group, the free interaction, and the nature of the therapist's interpretations are calculated to give permeability to the boundaries between conscious, preconscious, and unconscious, so that the latent emotions will rise to the surface.

Transferences will occur among the group members as well as with the therapist. It is natural for the patients to develop transferences to those figures who best represent their infantile subjects. In many cases another member's personality is more conducive to the development of a particular aspect of transference than the therapist's. At the simplest level, if the therapist is a young man and there is an older woman in the group, the latter may become the preferred representative of mother. But it is possible that a young man may be chosen for that role, if he displays certain of mother's characteristics. Secondly, different individuals in the group may represent different family images simultaneously. For example, early in treatment, since the patient's expectations of the therapist are still very high, he might represent an idealized mother, while another member, whom he dislikes, may at the same time represent the bad depriving mother. When the patient is working through an oedipal conflict, one member may represent the rival, another, the loved parent, or either role may be represented by the therapist. The therapist shares his role in this respect with the members, yet on the whole he remains the single most dominant transference figure. The possibilities are almost infinite for the repetition in the relationship with group members of a multitude of very specific meaningful patterns that originated early in the patient's life.

Because, as we anticipated, the members were seldom neutral like the therapist in response to these transferences, and tended to react positively to gratify or negatively to criticize the patient, the latter frequently shifted from one object to another. Thus, the development of the latent affects and drives which were in process tended to be interrupted so often that they could never acquire the unitary quality which individual analysis induces. They appear and must be analyzed in piece-meal fashion.

For example, Anne's positive oedipal feelings to her young male therapist were soon transferred to Arthur, an older man whose voice and manner more closely resembled those of her middle-aged father. The therapist then became the "bad" mother figure for her. Because Arthur saw Anne as a demanding female, he was very critical of her rather than seductive as her father had been. A second displacement to Henry therefore soon occurred. While Anne was treating Henry as if he were the father of her kindergarten years, she was simultaneously exhibiting a good deal of anxiety in relation to Kathy, who was cast in the role of her rival (oedipal mother). At the same time she was beginning to respond to the therapist in the role of the disapproving mother of infancy. In other words, a person may be engaged in several transferential relationships at once.

The repeated interruptions which inevitably occurred as one member or another brought his ideas, his feelings, his problems, or his interpretations to the others, could not be avoided without sacrificing full member participation. The effect was kaleidoscopic. To avoid it, the therapist would have had to conduct a leader-centered group in which he made all the interpretations and did not give the members a chance to come to grips on their own with whatever problem was brought up. The group proved to be very responsive to the therapist's implicit wishes so that if he showed signs of taking over the total responsibility, the members would decrease their participation, and many of the advantages of the group milieu would be lost.

These interruptions were at first disturbing to the patients because the problems discussed were rarely brought to closure during a single session. The members had to become accustomed to an ongoing, open-ended process and to learn with the therapist's help that the real continuity of their discussion was on an emotional rather than factual level. If the threads of their communications were dropped, they were more than likely to be picked up again at another time, either in connection with the same content or with entirely different subject matter. But the same problems and patterns of behavior were repeated until they could eventually be worked through.

Our findings were almost immediately encouraging in that they seemed to testify to the validity of our basic assumptions. Although the patients conversed on a conscious level, they were at the same time giving one another preconscious cues for setting up interacting neurotic patterns of behavior which would ward off, yet secretly express, unconscious infantile drives in disguised form. The therapist had the advantage of observing at first hand a great variety of interpersonal behavior which the individual analyst has to deduce from his patients' secondarily distorted verbal reports about their outside relationships.

These were the intragroup transferences. In them the therapist could discern with the utmost lucidity the way in which each member's intraphysic conflicts were translated into his interpersonal behavior. They added appreciably to his understanding of the patients over and beyond their many transferences to himself.

In one recent group session, for example, Jane and Bob had become very critical of one another. At the slightest provocation, they would carp at each other. It came to a climax one day when another member had brought up a problem about toiletting. Most of them talked freely and on a rather primitive level, but Bob became markedly anxious. After a bit, he shamefacedly complained about his wife's bathroom noises and he couched it in the usual cold mechanical delivery which customarily controlled his anxiety. Jane retired into a sullen slump in her chair. Before he was finished, she threw up her hands and said, "I can't listen—you're so terribly boring." Her manner was disdainful, and she made a pointed but extremely hostile comparison between toiletting and the way he was talking. He called her cheap and disgusting. The rest of the group agreed that he was hard to listen to but they were sympathetic with his attempt to reach us on so painful a topic.

The first move was to get both participants in this incident to turn their criticisms into the feelings which motivated them. After a round of open anger (very unusual for them) with both insisting on the correctness of their position, I commented that they seemed intent on warding off each other's criticisms. One member said, "Who is Bob to you anyway, Jane? You seldom get that angry." This line of inquiry led to the discovery that Jane's "disgusting" comments and her whole purportedly Bohemian way of life touched off in Bob the unacceptable childish body feelings which he had learned to repress. He summoned up a defensive rage to ward off Jane who reactivated his infantile sexuality. Jane's sharp criticism of him was a re-enactment of her struggle against her parents' middle-class attitudes. Her Bohemianism was her attempt to rebel against them. Bob and Jane were counterparts in conflict. Each had externalized one aspect of themselves in the other. At a deeper level, each also represented the other one's mother—but that was not the crucial point at the moment. Through the analysis of their mutual transference relationship they were able to come into closer touch with themselves, and to become more accepting of a formerly rejected infantile part. The psychic balance shifted. It was evidenced by Bob's now much more genuine way of talking with us, and Jane's changing from a critical and maneuvering person into a more compassionate woman. This was not of course a one-shot conversion. We had already done considerable work with defenses, such as Bob's manner of speech, and Jane's apparent need to manipulate. It was rather one of those crucial experiences in which a number of conflicts are resolved simultaneously by a cognitive shift which brings about a new and healthier behavioral configuration.

If such acting out in transference is not explored by either the therapist or the members, it will go on indefinitely until the rest of the group becomes restless, irritated and eventually resistant. We found that such underlying infantile feelings come more quickly to a head with peers in the group than with the therapist. Once they are recognized, there seems to be little need or available time for either the underlying rage or the libidinal drives to be lived out in protracted fashion.[2] They may, however, recur until they are eventually worked through.

Significantly, we discovered that, as a matter of fact, the entire range of each member's transference possibilities was, in the long run, manifested in the group interaction. Careful observation made it possible to extract from the intricate transference network a picture of each member's personality structure and the necessary clues to his personal history.

Still another dimension of therapy was discovered because the members were consistently encouraged to full participation in the interaction. Not only did their subjective emotional reactions reinforce[3] one another to give vitality and immediacy to their transference experiences, but their ability to recognize latent motivation came to the fore and gave them a share in the therapist's interpretive role. This was very helpful to the therapist and it played an integral part in the group's progress, and it was in itself an ego-strengthening experience for the contributors as well.

[2] For those who need more time for this, combined group and individual therapy is recommended (Sager, 1960).

[3] A mild form of group "contagion."

It goes without saying that, in a reality-oriented atmosphere such as the therapy group, many real relationships untarnished by neurotic transference also took place. They too added a dimension, for although they were not necessarily analyzed, they could be underlined and encouraged. For some patients they provided a necessary and conspicuous contribution to ego growth.

We found, of course, that resistance did occur in its usual manifold ways and included, as we had anticipated, some new group-determined forms. For instance, it was relatively easy for two members engaged in a mutual voyeuristic-exhibitionistic transference to act out verbally while appearing to produce important "material." We soon learned that, in detecting resistance in the group, it is even more important than usual to examine not only the content but what the patients are doing with it. During the early sessions the defenses and therefore resistance were often heightened because of the presence of strangers, but they soon yielded to the permissive therapeutic atmosphere. After a while, the very profusion of the defenses served to loosen up the boundaries between the conscious and the preconscious, the preconscious and the unconscious processes, with the result that they became more fully susceptible to analysis.

We also found that the group members frequently helped us to deal with resistance. They differed so much among themselves as to the nature and extent of their resistance that at any given point there was likely to be a nucleus of patients who had sufficient positive motivation to aid in detecting and dealing with the "fight-flight" maneuvers of the others. Generally speaking, too, the members quickly adopted the group standards concerning willingness for self-examination and tended to put pressure on one another to conform to them. They were therefore inclined to become irritated with those who were defensive, and warmly supportive to those who faced their anxiety openly and were willing to reveal themselves. Thus they became our allies in promoting therapeutic movement.

The actual difficulties we experienced in our task of adapting our method to the group situation were, then, not overwhelming. The same kind of response to analytic interventions seemed to occur within groups as those we had encountered in working with individuals. When resistance was analyzed, the heretofore preconscious emotions would come to the surface—sometimes with dramatic effect because the experience was so highly intensified by the group's participation in it. As expected, a recognition of the inappropriateness of the behavior in question for the present situation followed. What was different enough to raise our doubts, was the fact that the periods of emotional reliving could never last very long because of the urgencies of other members' desires to pursue their own problems. But we found that, on the whole, the impossibility of protracted regression did not detract from the meaningfulness of the experience.

The biggest problem was "the fragmentized transference." It required an appropriate modification of our analytic techniques. It was necessary to adapt our timing to the group conditions. If we adhered to the principle of intervening when transference turned into resistance, we found ourselves considerably more active because that situation naturally occurred with greater frequency in the group than it had in the relationship between only two people. The intervention would not hit its mark if it were made before the participants realized that they were sharing a familiar and repetitive emotional experience of some import. Yet it was necessary to comment promptly at that moment when the feelings were openly in operation, at the center of the stage, and before the exchange was superseded by others who wanted the floor.

Gradually the transference manifestations are traced to their origins, but only as the movement of the whole group permits. They can, of course, never be as assiduously pursued as in individual treatment.[4] Consequently, the course which each member's progressive self-understanding takes is more devious. On the other hand, the working-through process is reinforced by the fact that all members are working together. With so many witnesses, for instance, a member is quickly reminded if he tends to repress his insights or to reincorporate them into his neurotic system (for example, by converting them into material for superego accusations and behaving as if his worst and irremediable faults had just been pointed out to him). Patterns of defensive behavior will shift rapidly with the ebb and flow of the interaction during the working-through process, but they will be repeated and analyzed many times in many different contexts. Eventually, there occurs a gradu-

[4] That is why combined treatment is often the best choice.

al progression toward increased insight and decreased neurotic re-enactment of transferences with each member proceeding at his own pace.

Another example may perhaps illustrate how the total membership can become involved through one member's transference relationship. Eve used to produce long-winded, very logical rationalizations whenever she was afraid of expressing irrational anger. The first time she was questioned, she rather easily recalled how afraid she had been of her father. She said that if she dared to express anger or talk back to him, he would explode in what had seemed a ferocious manner. She had learned to give him very logical arguments whenever she wanted something from him. She could usually win any argument with him in this way. One day soon afterwards, Eve responded to Hank, an attractive older man, in the same respectful but devoted manner, which had been her more usual everyday attitude toward her father. Another girl, Ann, had developed a very frankly erotic interest in Hank and tended to pester him with questions about his feelings for her. He always answered that he liked her, but his greater emotional involvement with Eve was obvious. Ann became more and more upset until one day she began to weep. Questioned, she expressed a curiously combined jealousy and admiration of Eve, and with the help of the group was able to get a glimpse of the repressed jealousy she had once experienced toward her sister who was favored by the father, but whom she had ostensibly always admired. Eve, who had formerly implied disdainfully that Ann was not very bright, now became quite solicitous of her.

The others suggested that she felt guilty toward Ann and had, for this reason, become protective and also much more restrained with Hank. Now it was Eve's turn to weep, and she poured out a long story of how she had always succeeded by her clever talk in making her mother look like the stupid materialistic one in the family, while she and her father were the bright idealistic ones. Worse, her father had been in cahoots with her. Now she suddenly felt sorry for her mother who seemed to her quite frail and vulnerable. Like a chain of fire, the other members now recalled forgotten incidents of their childhood relationships with their parents. Through participation in the experience of Hank and Ann, they too came to acknowledge certain feelings which they had long ignored, yet had felt vaguely uncomfortable about. Helen, particularly, evinced deep-seated distrust of her mother and acted it out through her relationship to me. It seemed she experienced every interpretation of mine as a mortal criticism. She had never realized how large a role distrust had played in her life. During one session, when she was complaining bitterly about her mother's behavior toward her, she spent an inordinately long time justifying herself for her anger. Eve said to her, "Helen, you sound as if you were in court. Do you think we wouldn't like you unless you had unassailable reasons for being angry?" Helen was taken aback. After a pause, she agreed that as usual she expected criticism. Eve said, "You know, I guessed that because it is the real reason why I used to give my father those long logical arguments. I really felt that if I didn't, he would criticize me for wanting the new dress— or whatever it was. Besides, I had convinced him mother was the materialistic one, so I felt I was playing dirty tennis anyway." Until now rationality had been ego-syntonic for both girls and served to keep their feelings in abeyance and their infantile conflicts concealed. The others were very interested and reassured Helen that they wouldn't consider her wrong even if she was angry without a cause. Helen felt relieved.

In summary, the transference manifestations proved to be identifiable in the group, and susceptible to analysis. However, they were "fragmentized" and had to be analyzed piece-meal. A change in the timing of interpretations was thereby necessitated. But as the intragroup transferences were gradually unraveled, all aspects of each member's transference possibilities could be worked through. It proved to be the form of transference and the timing of the interventions that were different in the group rather than the basic process of analyzing transference and resistance.

DEVELOPMENT OF A CONCEPTUAL FRAMEWORK

However well our group patients seemed to be responding in practice, the "fragmentized transference" still remained a theoretical problem which required a solution. Did the process of consistently analyzing its manifold aspects contribute to an already chaotic situation? Was group therapy in this form merely another version of "wild analysis"? How systematic could this crazy-quilt type of analysis be? Could it bring about the resolution of psychogenic conflicts and eventuate in synthesis and ego integration? Experience seemed to be giving a favorable answer, but the empirical data did not lend themselves immediately to constructive theoretical conceptualization.

I believe that one of the difficulties was that in conceptualizing the process of analytic group psychotherapy, we still relied too literally upon individual analysis. We are accustomed to thinking in terms of the libidinal regressive transference. We had forgotten that when Freud first came upon the phenomenon, it consisted in the tendency of individuals to repeat the past in the present. It had not yet been cultivated and nurtured by minimizing reality in the analytic chamber. Only after that did complete libidinal regression take place so that it became customary to speak of *"the* transference" as if it were an entity which lay dormant in an individual waiting for an analyst to come along. In therapy groups we found the phenomenon more as Freud first knew it and as it occurred in daily life. We too cultivated it, in a sense, by repeatedly paying attention to it, but it was impossible to go as far in facilitating it as in individual analysis. It was a mistake therefore to perceive it always in terms of a different situation and to speak of its manisfestations in the group by saying "the transference is split up" or "fragmentized."

As the years passed, some therapists responded to the mass of transferential emotional entanglements among the group members by seeing in their very profuseness the possibility of inducing regression, which then became the keynote of the group analysis. Others found unity in perceiving the group as a family and encouraged the reliving of old conflicts in order to find new solutions in the new and better family of the group. Still others relinquished any attempt to make transference analysis the key to therapeutic progress. They adopted a more passive role and relied chiefly on the group interaction to bring about changes.

A number of us preferred to take another course. The enormous number and variety of transference phenomena was impressive, but the encouraging realization had emerged that in the cross-currents of the latent intercommunications every aspect of each individual's entire transference repertoire seemed eventually to be evoked and to yield to analysis. During the course of the therapeutic process his behavior patterns, as displayed in the many transference manifestations, fell into place to form a fair picture of his total personality. The profuse and seemingly haphazard clinical data, viewed in this way, took on some semblance of structure which made the systematic transference analysis seem to be a reasonable goal.

Gradually we also became aware that the many varied defensive maneuvers which each individual manifested in his transference behavior showed a certain cohesiveness. They seemed to form an identifiable configuration, a loose, but nevertheless organized system of interlocking defenses which guard what Kubie (1958) called the patient's central emotional position. Roughly equivalent to the Adlerian concept, "the life style," this defense system includes not only the primary defense mechanisms described by Anna Freud, but a wide range of defensive operations and those built-in character traits that protect the patient from the eruption of unbearable underlying anxiety. It is tantamount to his basic character structure, and reflects the balance of id, ego, and superego forces within him.

This central defensive core seems to be best portrayed in the role which each member plays in the group. The role, of course, has many variations of its main theme. It may even appear in reverse. For instance, a person with a status problem who generally assumes the guise of a leader may treat those he considers of lower status arrogantly and those whom he sees as above him, with subservience. My own recognition of the relationship between role and character came quite accidentally from a discussion of one of my early groups with Dr. Geraldine Pederson-Krag. With penetrating insight, she designated one of the members of my group as "the good little girl," another as "the hatchet woman," and a third, "the misanthrope." Although her designations obviously oversimplified the extremely complex facts, they provided me with valuable clues for formulating a series of related interpretive hypotheses. I continued to work along these lines without at first being aware of their theoretical significance. The empirical results suggested that what she had given me was a rough clue to the basic defense system of each member. This hypothesis was tested out on the specific phenomenological data, which progressively corroborated it. It served to give cohesive direction to the interpretations

and to make orderly progress possible. I was enabled to cut
through the mass of loosely related communications and behavior
in a way which proved to be meaningful for the patients. Systematic analysis of the transferences became a real possibility.

It soon became clear that a structured conceptual framework
was beginning to take shape, which gave meaning and consistency
to the analysis of the multiple group transferences. But although
the analysis of character defenses provides direction, it is not intended to constitute character analysis in the sense in which Wil-
helm Reich (1933) described it. The total character of each member is simply used to give unification to what might otherwise be a
haphazard series of transference interpretations. The clues must,
of course, come from the clinical data itself and be understood in
the light of the psychoanalytic theory of character.

Looking back, this development does not seem surprising, for it
has become a matter of record that a rather large percentage of the
group population we treat consists of character problems.[5] It had
become necessary, quite apart from theoretical considerations, to
engage in the analysis of a great many ego-syntonic character traits
because they formed a predominant portion of the patient's defenses and were displayed freely in the intragroup relationships.

These neurotic character traits of the patients may rightly be
included under the category of transference because, like other defense mechanisms, they bring the past into the present. But they
occur in encapsulated form. They are compromise formations
which represent both sides of the original conflicts they attempted
to solve. Deeply embedded in the personality, these defenses have
become the habitual attitudes of an individual. As attributes of
persons, they have acquired a certain consistency of pattern. In
adult life, they play their transferential part in many relationships
with comparatively little regard for the specific object as such. This
is one reason why the group in which so many objects are available is such a good medium.

This form of transference is identifiable in terms of the behavior
and of the subject rather than of the underlying drive and its new
object. An example was Alice, who behaved naïvely whenever the

[5] Experience shows that the general approach works very well also with
variety of symptomatic neuroses such as impotence, work inhibitions, asthma,
and the like.

subject of sex was discussed. This behavior was quite independent
of who brought up the subject. She was nicknamed Alice in Won-
derland. The hidden drive was, of course, her infantile sexual
curiosity. When she finally recognized the reason for her naïve behavior, she became very flushed and embarrassed and immediately
said, "Oh, now I know why I'm always after my children—I have to
know everything they are doing or saying. I've really always—
wanted—to know what——what the grownups were doing—Oh,
Oh, it comes to me now—that closed door that made me so mad."
She did not live out her sexual curiosity for any period of time,
either outside or in the group, but her behavior changed when she
took a knowledgeable part in the next discussion of sex, and she
reported that she was now able to leave her children alone.

That the definition of "character" coincides with that of the
structure of the ego is to be taken for granted. "Character, as the
habitual mode of bringing into harmony the tasks presented by the
internal demands and by the external world, is necessarily a function of the constant, organized, and integrating part of the personality which is the ego; indeed, ego was defined as that part of
the organism that handles the communications between the instinctual demands and the external world. The question of character would thus be the question of when and how the ego acquires
the qualities by which it habitually adjusts itself to the demands
of the instinctual drives and the external world, and later also of
the superego" (Fenichel, 1945, p. 467).

Fenichel also points out what has become increasingly obvious
in our groups, that the concept of character has a broader scope
than just the "modes of defenses.... It serves an adaptive function.
The ego not only protects but it reacts. It selects, according to
Waelder's law of multiple function, that which gives the most satisfaction for the least expenditure of effort; and it organizes the in-
coming stimuli and the outgoing impulses." Only the *destructive*,
neurotic transference elements must be analyzed out. The others
which are healthy are regularly strengthened by group experience.

We are not restricted to the level of consciousness when we work
with groups, nor to the functions of the ego. It is plain that, as
Fenichel mentions, the ego cannot be understood without a knowledge of what is warded off, of what is selected, organized or repressed. In fact, it is by utilizing this information that analytic

group therapy is able to throw light on the development of the ego, ferret out the underlying conflicts, help first to reactivate and then to resolve them, and finally to reintegrate the infantile drives so that a more effective distribution of energy results.

Unlike symptoms, the character traits have succeeded well in their purpose of binding the anxiety which the patient's continued awareness of the conflicts would have kept disturbingly alive. They are, as it were, "the frozen residues of former conflicts" (Fenichel, 1945; W. Reich, 1933). For this reason, it is necessary to select as group members only those with whom it seems possible to revive the original anxiety. Our criterion has, in general, consisted of judging (in individual interviews or during the early stages of the group) whether the defensive traits loosen up in a reassuring situation and become more restrictive when they are threatened. If this holds true, we can be fairly sure that there is enough mobility to warrant group treatment. The majority of our members therefore has some degree of flexibility. Neurotic characters who are too deeply frozen in to be analyzed impede the group and should be screened out.

As I pursued the analysis of the defensive transference (including the character defenses), the clinical material kept leading directly back to the members' most crucial infantile experiences (conflicts). It became possible to identify those particular phases of development which had most significantly influenced the nature of their personalities. The drives and the defenses common to each period and the character traits based upon them were discovered to be registered indelibly in the personalities of the members, and it was not difficult to determine very early in the group proceedings which phase had been decisive for each person, had in effect tied his particular albatross about his neck. The greedy, complaining patient showed his orality; the "Mrs. Craig" gave evidence of her anal character structure; the girl who flirted and became insulted at the response she elicited revealed her basically hysterical orientation. Each was found to be trapped by his own neurotic defenses. What solution of his infantile conflicts each had achieved was clearly shown in the group explorations to depend not only on the biological impulses that pressed him at the time, but also on the demands of his parents, and very considerably upon the innate capacities which he was able to bring to his problem and the way in which his early achievements were received by his upbringers. The outcome seems to depend on an interaction among all these factors and the situation in which they occur. It is a mistake to reduce them to a single cause.

The members had usually experienced so much in common that the investigations of such historical material brought about very lively discussions and the participants came to feel very close to one another. Since they were acquainted with one another's present predicaments, had lived through the same stages and suffered the same conflicts, they were very much interested in comparing the circumstances under which their difficulties started, how each one had felt, and what they had done about it. These were rarely monologues; rather, they consisted of shared communications in which all participated and the focus shifted rapidly back and forth from past to present and also from one member to another.

It soon became evident that all members could profit from one another's analytic experience and could share in the subsequent growth, with the result that the whole experience became very meaningful to them all. Because each individual had solved his conflicts according to his unique capacity and experience, the members were able also to stimulate one another and to broaden their horizons as they worked together. It goes without saying that it is necessary to analyze with the utmost care the variations as well as the common elements and to keep the connections between past and present constantly in the forefront. Examples to substantiate these claims will be adduced in the next chapter.

Continued clinical testing of this theoretical approach made it progressively apparent that the psychoanalytic theory of character, taken together with that of psychosexual development, would provide an eminently suitable framework within which to achieve a systematic transference analysis of the individual members in the context of their group interaction. And so we added another essential feature to the emerging conceptual framework for analytic group therapy.

Just as we have been indebted to the psychoanalytic theory of character and have been able to contribute toward it, we have a reciprocal relationship to the psychoanalytic theory of psychosexual development. When Freud first formulated his theory of psychosexual development, he thought of it primarily in libidinal terms.

The other early writers, like Abraham and Mack-Brunswick, continued in the same way. We have often drawn on their findings in order to interpret our data, but because of our unique opportunity to observe adults in the process of developing new object relations in an analytically oriented situation, we were able also to contribute to the theory. Because our observations were made in a milieu in which reality could not be discounted, we became acutely aware of the magnitude of the role of ego development in determining the character and therefore the modes of adult interpersonal behavior. We could, through the defenses, gage the strength of the ego, and we hypothesized a correlation between its sturdiness and early developmental factors, and between its weaknesses and the obstructions to its development at each phase. For this reason we are heartily in accord with E. H. Erikson in the firm belief that the theory of psychosexual development must be expanded to include the ego correlates of each phase.

In scrutinizing the clinical material with respect to ego development, we found ourselves generally in accord with the work of the psychoanalytic ego psychologists. We found many of their studies useful in gaining further insight into our data, and were able to confirm others. A few examples might illustrate the point. The work of Bychowski (1952) in which he compares the behavior of psychotics with that of very small children, and is able to shed a good deal of light on early ego and superego functioning, was extremely interesting to us. Its applicability to our data proved that much of what he had to say need not be limited to psychotics and children, but showed up in more disguised form in neurotic character as well. I was reminded of Bion's discovery of the "psychotic group" which lay beneath the "basic assumptions group" (see Chapter XVIII). We could also discern in our members the importance of the patients' constitutional tendencies for determining the way in which they coped with situations, such as their inclination for activity or passivity which Fries (1935) had demonstrated. Such factors appeared to determine how the infant would respond to his caretaker's behavior, and hence helped to determine the kinds of defenses he would develop.

It would be impossible to recount even the most pertinent studies on the development of the ego and the reader who is interested has only to consult *The Psychoanalytic Study of the Child* (Eissler et al., 1945-1963). Excellent articles by Kris, Hartmann, and Loewenstein are recorded in almost every volume. For our present purposes, however, we must return to the material derived from our therapy groups.

With surprising frequency, the modes of behavior employed in dealing with object (interpersonal) relations in the therapy group seemed, upon exploration, to originate at the time when reality first began to intrude on the infant's primary narcissism. The consequent problems around identity, autonomy, and status seemed to be poorly resolved yet extremely important to them. They were still struggling for these goals, albeit in a way that generally achieved very unsatisfactory results, i.e., a lay vistor to any group in its early stages could not but be impressed with the amount of "one-upmanship" that insinuated itself into the communications. Only its ineffectiveness distinguished it from its counterpart in society. Our observer might well have mistaken it for a game of "one-downmanship," for the players were obviously trying to avoid the very self-knowledge they had joined the group to achieve. He might have heard one member setting himself up as the assistant therapist, restricting his contributions to making interpretations for other members, another countering every interpretation with "Well, it's not really as simple as that," or "Of course, I've already solved that problem." The less psychologically sophisticated patients play the game in the more banal social way, referring to their possessions, their achievements, namedropping, and so on.

A good deal of hidden envy and infantile rage is detectable in comments of this kind, pointing to the original power struggle with the parents. Like any other form of resistance, this too must become the target of exploration for therapeutic purposes. Usually it may be traced to deeply embedded infantile images of the impotent "self" and the powerful "significant other." These regularly bear the mark of the time when the perceptual apparatus functioned in global fashion and the capacity for comprehension and judgment was negligible. Accordingly, they helped to distort the individual's present-day self-concept, and his perception of others. Frequently, they also impeded his ability to take mature action.

For example, the members would repeatedly become aware, during conversations with others, outside or within the group, that they felt like small children trying to cope with adults. This held equally true for those who appeared to be well poised and for those who were visibly nervous. Some told of a feeling of not knowing as much as the "other"; some actually experienced it in terms of physical size, as if they were indeed still little. Each indicated his specific variations of the theme and all of them at times suffered a profound sense of helplessness. Their dreams corroborated the phenomenon, and elaborated on it or reversed it, but with the same features greatly exaggerated and distorted (all the usual dream mechanisms came into play). The theme, "little helpless me, and big, powerful you" persisted in all of them. The ego's work consisted of trying to "beat" or "control" their opponents (who were often not, in any real sense, opponents at all) with whatever inadequate measures the ego had at its disposal. Not infrequently, however, they retreated to a position comparable to "If you can't beat 'em, join 'em."

As the impotent infantile rage and the defensive "hostility" it generated were gradually brought to light in these vain attempts to solve old hurts in new situations, the patients became freer to express their feelings more directly. They also learned to distinguish between the old helpless rage and realistic present-day anger. Only then could they assert themselves aggressively at the right time instead of feeling aggrieved and building up resentment. The energy which had been bound in such self-defeating maneuvers slowly became more available for constructive self-actualization.

We have been impressed with the amount of evidence we accumulated that the aggressive drives and the conflicts over identity, autonomy, and status have been every bit as decisive in bringing about neurotic development as have the libidinal drives. (In actuality, they are usually intermixed, or either one may be used as a defense to ward off the other.) In exploring the ego defenses as assiduously as possible, we uncovered innumerable threatening unconscious fantasies, often dealing with witchlike characters whose activities identified them as symbols for the preoedipal mother in her role of frustrator and chastiser. Since they stem from a period in which there was little discrimination between the sexes, they are frequently represented by men as well as women. These too bear the stamp of the phase of life from which they stem and vary in intensity and bizarreness accordingly. Since the fantasies of the more orally regressed patients are at once more available, more graphic, and more primitive, I chose such a patient, Ned, to illustrate how they exert an influence on dreams, on the character, and on family and group relationships.

Ned was a young painter who could not bring himself to earn a living and was therefore completely dependent on his parents. On the surface, he was usually irritable with his mother, but he reported that until recently he had idealized her. "When I was a child," he said, "the lights seemed to go on when she came home." There was also evidence that he identified with her and that his relationship had been close to symbiotic all through his teens. He had never been able to experience himself fully as a separate individual.

During his second year in the group, Ned brought in a dream in which he was running through the woods, chased by a leopard which was intent on devouring him. After a few random associations, he said he had no idea why he suddenly recalled that his mother used to pretend to eat him up when he was a baby. He had a kind of tingling, frightened feeling about it, but it was one of his favorite memories. The other members of his group were interested and soon began to recall similar incidents and to express resentful feelings toward their mothers. Ned became conspicuously quiet. He had not dared to face his infantile, impotent rage. The following week he was absent. When he returned he said he had not been sure he could make it, but he had been particularly nervous all week and supposed he had better come in spite of his fear. One of the women asked him what he meant by that remark. He answered, "I keep thinking the group is like a whole pack of leopards who will tear me apart if I give myself away." One of the things which had upset him was his mother's having told him to take down a picture he had just painted and hung on his wall. He was angry with her. Upon being questioned, he admitted he had not only taken it down, but had immediately discontinued the series of primitive paintings he was doing. Further questioning brought the reluctant admission that he had been painting a fairy tale series. He was unwittingly using his paintings as an adjunct to therapy, getting closer to his infantile rage through a nonverbal medium which actually gave him more scope and less responsibility than verbalizing it. In this instance it also served to frighten his mother into rejecting behavior, for he had painted a pretty little girl chewing on a man's arm. She could not tolerate the anxiety it caused her. The group was upset; but, because they had developed a good working relationship, they began, under considerable tension, to associate to the incident. Eventually, the whole group was drawn into reminiscences of their parents' injustices. The talk was sprinkled with oral connotations such as, "They are always chewing me out," or "She wanted to swallow me up." He seemed much more at ease as he now joined their talk about parents. He told them that as a child he had assumed a submissive role in pleasing his mother by appearing to be always cheerful and polite, while repressing rage. After his paranoid fears and his anger had been ventilated, he could begin to assess the difference between his truly difficult reality and the exaggerated fantasies her anxiety touched off in him. Gradually he was enabled to perceive both himself and others more realistically. His fantasies and his dreams became correspondingly less disturbing.

In our example, we can see the persistence of early identification, of the narcissistic fears, and of the images of self and other which grew out of the infant's first deflating encounter with reality and remained to create later distortions. Such defensive attitudes and behaviors are of course reformulated at each phase of development according to the child's changing reality and his maturing ego functions, but their original intent persists. Deep basic distrust can be disguised but not overcome except through analysis. Although these narcissistic conflicts can only be reconstructed, never recalled except in their later revised anal or phallic forms, I believe that they are basic sources of neurotic character and must be consistently and persistently brought to light. The group situation illuminates them more clearly than does individual analysis because they can be detected in the wide variety of interpersonal attitudes in which they are encapsulated, and because in the group the patient's attitudes toward authority stand out in vivid contrast to those he exhibits with peers.

Whenever one makes working hypotheses concerning the intangible preoedipal phenomena, a high level of inference must be employed. Our own speculations about the clinical data obtained from group therapy have often been stimulated by the relatively few authors who have investigated this area. At times we have corroborated certain of their conclusions—in some cases quite unexpectedly—at other points we have added to them, and occasionally disagreed. As Glatzer (1959a, 1959b, 1962) pointed out, Freud (1931) noted the infant's insatiable greed and hypothesized a causal connection between his anxiety and anger at his inevitable disappointment in his mother and his later paranoid fears of her. We repeatedly came upon traces of those fears, but found that narcissistic blows, as well as real or fantasied libidinal deprivation, were involved in them. Mack-Brunswick (1940) commented on this negative reaction of the infant to his active controlling mother, at a time when he was in a necessarily passive position in relation to her. That theme turned out to be ubiquitous in our groups. In general, little attention had been given to this aspect of Freudian theory, but it has been increasingly capturing the interest of psychoanalytic writers in recent years. Lampl-de Groot (1963) contrasted the oedipal with the preoedipal image of the mother. Theodora Abel (1964) presented clinical evidence of the confusion which the oral-oedipal patterns caused in her patients of varying cultural milieus.

Among the authors who concern themselves with reconstructing their patient's experiences with the preoedipal mother, I have selected two for comment because their particular hypotheses have received, on the whole, less attention than others, yet have proved to be productive in group therapy. One of these is Melanie Klein. She was particularly impressed with the massive hostile-aggressive reactions of the very young children she treated (1932), which she felt were derived from a period of paranoid anxiety. That anxiety seems to be reflected in the group members' transferences to the therapist, who is seen as depriving and/or threatening. The significance which Melanie Klein (1957) attaches to the infant's envy and gratitude as a response to his mother's power to supply milk and love puts flesh and bones on the Freudian doctrine of how hostility is neutralized. It seems to account for some of the healthy as well as the neurotic aspects of the behavior of our therapy group population. Moreover, the distinction she makes between the actual behavior of the mother and the child's inaccurate perception of it, which is carried so often into adulthood, seems to add a significant dimension to therapeutic technique. We have found it effective in demonstrating to patients the way in which they themselves contribute to these distortions.

Another author who, on the basis of wide clinical experience, has made some penetrating observations concerning the infant's pre-verbal dyadic experience is Edmund Bergler. He has built on what Freud and Ferenczi wrote about the problems of narcissism and the infant's fantasy of omnipotence, and demonstrated how difficult it is for the human being to relinquish it. Experience in a therapy group soon gives support to this position. Bergler feels that the adult neurotic has taken the "good mother" for granted and re-sponded chiefly to the "ogress" who intruded into his primary narcissism to threaten his sense of omnipotence; that his exagger-ated fears of this "bad mother" are easily reactivated, and his image of her projected onto any likely candidate. The case of Ned is an example of this. It also occurs almost universally, in modified form, in neurotic group patients.

Contrary to Bergler, I find that the group members also fre-quently reflect the infantile images of the kind and loving pre-oedipal mother and that these contribute largely to their healthy aspects and their serviceable character traits. Like Klein, Bergler emphasizes the neurotic's subjective infantile distortion of the parental image. According to his theory of masochism, the patient saves a shred of his omnipotent fantasy by repeatedly, but unwit-tingly, recreating in transference the original "deprivation" by the bad mother and then libidinizing the consequent suffering. In do-ing so he pereptuates his psychopathology (Bergler, 1949). The group members seem to grasp this concept and frequently use it themselves.

For instance, Maury, whose mother sounded truly like a witch, complained again and again that he was a helpless victim to her endless inordinate demands upon him. The group members in-sisted that he used her tenacity as an alibi; that she would not die, as he feared, if he refused; and that it was he who unwittingly chose to do her bidding instead of establishing his independence of her. He could recognize that he was "wallowing" in his misery. They added that he could find more realistic ways of helping her which did not drain him so completely. They used his dreams to convince him, for in them he continued his grievances, making them far more grotesque than the bitter reality. He saw the point, and it was the beginning of a crucial change in him. Of course, a good deal of working through was required.

Laura, who had a harmless but clinging little old mother of whose yearly visit she was pathologically in fear, caught her first glimpse of her own self-hypnotic attitude when she grasped the meaning of Maury's self-deception. Gradually, she too began to examine her hidden motivation, to relinquish her self-pity, and to move toward independence.

The large proportion of harshly critical and punitive attitudes toward the self and others which occur in the multiple group transferences, the persistent expectation of criticism and punishment from the therapist, and the fact that these attitudes are regularly traceable to early oral and anal experiences with the mother (or caretaker, and in some instances with the father), suggest that the superego passes through developmental stages parallel to those of the ego. So much work needs to be done in this area before any definitive statements can be made about it, that a fuller discussion must be left for another occasion. Nevertheless, I feel that our clinical material gives sufficient evidence of the dynamic influence of these prestages of the superego on present behavior to warrant a recommendation that the attitudes in question be considered as superego correlates of the psychosexual phases of development, and that they be considered seriously for inclusion in any comprehensive epigenetic theory of mental development.

Although these clinical hypotheses concerning preverbal experiences have proved stimulating and productive, caution is especially necessary in drawing theoretical conclusions of this nature from the data. The model offered by the psychoanalytic ego psychologists for increasing precision in studying an area which has seemed to defy accurate observation, and to depend so heavily on reconstruction and inference, is recommended as a guide for this purpose. For example, Kris, Hartmann, and Loewenstein (1946) warn us that *all* crucial variables must be taken into account before drawing conclusions concerning early mental development. Among them: the nature of the deprivation, its timing in relation to the maturation of the ego apparatuses, the mode of its administration, and the child's own tolerance must be included. Following their example will serve to prevent the construction of either an inadequately founded or a reductionist theory.

To summarize, by adopting the psychoanalytic theory of character and expanding the psychosexual theory of development to meet the needs of the group situation we have been able to construct, on the basis of our clinical findings, a conceptual framework for group therapy within which we achieve a systematic analysis of each member's entire transference repertoire in conjunction with those of the other group members.

XIII Role of the Therapist

GETTING THE GROUP OFF THE GROUND

The therapist's initial aims are to set up an atmosphere which will be conducive to free and candid emotional interaction among the members and give them some idea of what his relationship with them is going to be. What he says and the way he says it will distinguish his designated function from that of a teacher, adviser, magic healer, or whatever else he may represent in their fantasy. In a spirit of empathy he will accept the role of therapist which they have asked him to take. Theirs will be a partnership designed to fathom the unconscious processes that have been interfering with their lives. During the course of it they will repeatedly make neurotic demands on him to play other parts. He must recognize what these roles are and analyze rather than accept or reject them.

On the first day he will, in one way or another, structure the situation for the patients. Some therapists, like Bion, do this by default and simply wait for the members to begin. Others like Stephen de Schill have written up detailed booklets of instructions for them to read before entering the group. Wolf (1949-1950), after seeing each member individually a number of times, spends several sessions preparing the group for actual treatment. Mann (1953) makes what he considers a contract with his groups. The members are to say as nearly as possible what comes to mind and the thera-

171

pist intervenes chiefly when the communication among them becomes blocked. This practice is akin to my own approach, although I do not necessarily articulate it. While some therapists feel obligated to give the group members a detailed idea of the goal and procedure of treatment, my experience has shown that most preliminary explanation is futile and the sessions themselves must reveal the nature of the process in which they are involved. I may say, "All of you here have some difficulties you would like to clear up, and together we are going to try to get at the cause of your troubles. I believe I can help you best if you will try to say whatever is on your mind."

The next step depends somewhat on the purpose and plan for the particular group. If it is made up of beginners who are not going to be in individual treatment, the therapist may want to ask if any of them would like to bring up a specific problem. This would be done not so much to solve the problem as to start the ball rolling. It might well lead them to ask questions; and the way these are handled will then begin to set the group therapeutic process in motion. If the group is to be in combined group and individual treatment, or is composed of people in the last stage of therapy, I prefer to accent the immediate feelings and relationships among the members and might ask, "How did you feel about coming today?"

Such questions usually suffice to draw verbal responses, but if there should be none the therapist might speculate, "I have a feeling that all of you are so quiet because coming to a group like this has made you nervous." Another alternative is to take the role of catalyst, saying, "You may be surprised to know that I, too, am a little nervous the first time I meet a new group." Then he must be prepared to deal with both their overt and latent reactions to his remark.

Meanwhile, the therapist will convey by his choice of interventions, and especially by the manner and tone in which he makes them, what the character of the therapeutic relationship with him will be like. Unless the members are experienced in the ways of therapy they will barrage him with requests for answers, for advice, and for immediate solutions. This will be a difficult time for the beginner and for the therapist who feels compelled to give whatever is asked of him. But the opportunity to set the direction of the therapeutic process must not be missed. Although the members press him with great urgency he will refrain from responding to the overt content, for his true value to them lies in helping them to become aware of the latent meanings. He will repeatedly turn back the questions to them for consideration in order to get further light on their problems, so that together they can come to understand the underlying feeling which is significant at the moment. It is the *way* in which he communicates with them in this project that will, in the end, convince them that his true motivation is not to withhold but to help in the special way that only he can, although it is different from that to which they have been accustomed. They may well misinterpret his motive in terms of their transferences and are sure to express some discontent with him. It is important to explore these reactions by getting the members to talk about them more fully. Or perhaps the therapist can follow through with some comment such as, "You may be disappointed in me because I don't answer your questions." Or, "I have a feeling you are protecting me from criticism just now" (Durkin, 1954). This part of the therapist's function is particularly important, for it indicates clearly that he is neither a teacher nor an omnipotent helper. The way it is done will show that he is not an outsider who, with his superior knowledge, is pointing out that he knows what they do not, but that he will use their communications to help them understand themselves, and that he will be candid, as he hopes they will be too.

On the whole, it is best to do the same with personal questions about himself. However, there may be occasions when he may consider it best to answer a factual question briefly, as a matter of courtesy. If a patient asks me whether I have children, I may say, "Yes, two, but they are grown up now," and then try to explore the reason for the question. The therapist might continue, "Could it be that you were wondering if I could understand your problem because I do (or don't) have children; am married or not married; am Jewish or not Jewish; and so on?" Their answers may open up important areas for them as well as penetrate hidden barriers to communication.

In the first weeks, as the members begin to talk about themselves and to react toward one another, he will occasionally make comments which convince them of his understanding. A man who rails against his wife may reveal in the way he talks that he feels, without quite realizing it, unfairly treated. The therapist may say, "You seem to feel she is very unfair to you." Thus the member comes one step closer to himself and has been given something more valuable than the "answers" he thought he wanted. Group members gradually begin to understand that something new and unique is happening which touches them deeply.

One of the simplest and easiest ways to help the patients understand their unconscious motivations is by commenting on their lateness, absence, or silence. Often a novice shirks this task for fear of appearing critical in public. Some students at New York University once explained that they were afraid to hurt their patients' feelings, but it turned out that it was their own hurt pride they feared to expose. The therapist should keep in mind that if he really does not feel annoyed by this natural phenomenon, he will find a way to word his comment so that it will not be embarrassing or painful. If he does he must examine his reasons. He will find it useful to explore his own feelings, since what is worrying him may well be worrying the members too. His own fear that the group is about to break up may be their fear, too, or they may simply be responding to his anxiety. In any event, it will help them to talk about it. Further, it may yield a good deal of insight if he asks them to relate their fantasies about such situations. This holds true for any group problem.

Another revelation to the members comes from the realization that their nonverbal reactions are important and often carry truer messages than what they say. Early in the sessions, therefore, the therapist may call attention to some bodily reaction and use it to stimulate the interaction. Noticing that John, for instance, is smiling a little to himself (or frowning, or stirring restlessly) he might say, "I notice you are smiling, John. Would you be willing to tell us what you were thinking?" The therapist's tone of voice and manner will indicate that his intent is friendly and helpful, rather than intrusive or pressuring. And he will always leave the patient a loophole for graceful escape if it turns out he is not ready to answer the question. It may prove useful to have the other members give their impressions.

These comments may be made to individuals but all the members will be listening and responding in their particular fashion. He will often encourage them to tune in on their own wave lengths if they can. He may address a comment to the group if there is evidence of some common tension, attitude, or feeling. If the therapist senses something which he cannot quite understand in their communications, he should feel free to admit it and request their help in determining what is going on.

Disguised or open expression of doubt is to be expected. It may be directed to the therapist, the institution, or the method. "I can't see why talking does any good" is a common example, or it may be displaced in a patient's criticism of his dentist or doctor. A forward member may bring out such doubts quite directly, and he can then be used as a focus for surfacing the more disguised reactions of the others. Often the patients cover up their doubts by insisting that they merely prefer individual therapy. The therapist must try to sense their real motivation and aid them in getting closer to it. It goes without saying that the group therapist does not defend his method against such doubts but persists in bringing them into the open. Here, as in every other intervention, the therapist who wants maximum member participation involves the whole group in any discussion as far as possible, and if possible elicits from them whatever they are experiencing before he makes his own clarifying comments.

One of the basic feelings common to all (including the therapist) will be the anxiety derived from the primitive narcissistic fear of meeting with a group of strangers. The fears may be hidden, but the protective measures themselves will be easily recognized as such by the trained therapist. If they are not brought to light they may block the road to spontaneity and candor in future communications and inhibit therapeutic movement. The fears are universal and the need to hide them is equally so. The top layer of the defense is very likely to take some socially acceptable form, such as undue modesty or concern for others. Or the members may compete by using the usual status symbols to test their relative positions in the group. Below the surface, however, there is likely to be found a diffuse hostility whose function is to counteract the underlying narcissistic fear and distrust of one another. As Mann (1955) has emphasized, no true group cohesion will develop before this early hostility is brought to light. The problems for which they have come must wait until it has been sounded out and at least temporarily allayed. Eventually the superficial defenses, the hos-

tility, and the underlying narcissistic anxiety **must all be explored.**
Which aspects are to be dealt with first depends upon the therapist's clinical judgment.

This early anxiety can be understood at many levels from the
most superficial fear of exposure to the deepest paranoid terrors.
Although the therapist may be acquainted with its sources, he will
begin by exploring only the external defenses and their meaning
for the immediate situation. If he begins in this way the members
will have no difficulty understanding what is happening. They will
come to recognize and acknowledge their anxiety and the need to
build up devices for hiding it will diminish. As soon as this has
been accomplished the group will be able to move on to an exploration of some of the more immediate problems for which they
came. As therapy progresses new manifestations of this kind of
anxiety will appear from time to time at different levels and can be
investigated one step at a time.

In one of my groups the interplay among five personalities
brought out some typical disturbances in this area.

Ned was a borderline case. His narcissistic fantasy, articulated
only many months later, was calculated to bolster his waning self-
esteem. He felt he could play the casual sophisticate among what
he considered inferiors without revealing his problems. What we
saw in the first few sessions was his effort to play that role to the
hilt. Occasionally, when its smooth surface was threatened, there
burst from him as from a safety valve such a stream of wisecracks
that his long buried hostility was clearly revealed. His accompanying anxiety was evident in a number of other physical signs such as
tightness of the jaw, slight tremors in his voice, and restlessness of
his body, all of which belied the elaborate casual front he presented, but which acted as a barometer for the therapist.

Netta was a plump, jolly, apparently warmhearted girl who appeared to be interested in everyone. She seemed perfectly poised;
and only I knew, because she told me, that she was frightened to
death of joining the group. She had developed a certain façade in
her professional career which she now wore so successfully in the
group that only the extreme degree of her sweetness gave me a clue
to her unconscious hostility. She feared that her utter lack of success as a woman would become public knowledge if she relaxed
in the slightest degree.

Jack was also a success professionally. He could talk freely and understandingly with the others, but there was frequently a stiff intellectual tone in his conversations. Because he was a psychologist and knew something of psychotherapy, he assumed a leading role during the first sessions, trying to get the group to move in what he thought would be the approved direction. But the defensive nature of his self-assigned task was exposed by the fact that he would ask perfunctory questions which prevented spontaneous responses. Without realizing it, he also used his know-how subtly to attack others. For instance, he was the first to upset Ned's shaky equilibrium by saying in a sarcastic tone of voice, "Sounds like you don't belong here because you have no problems."

Cynthia was a beautiful young woman who tended to chatter in a light, sophisticated style which disguised the fact the she was really a very bright girl. She cooperated fully with Ned's defense, and cleverly found a purely intellectual answer to explain her reason for coming so that she might appease Jack and yet bolster Ned's and her own defenses. She performed a skillful juggling act. She had apparently learned quite early in life to outwit her father with logic, and she used it now. Father had responded to this maneuver by giving her whatever she wanted. Thus unconscious incestuous fantasies were stimulated and, of course, accompanied by undue guilt toward her mother. Without being aware of it she kept her voice, her conversation, and her feelings on a very superficial level in order to avoid the depth of her unconscious despair over the conflict. But the oedipal problem was a veneer for oral conflicts and only much later did we discover her basic core of paranoid distrust of everyone. As she succeeded in faking compliance with Jack, the unconscious cues between them were quickly set for a father-daughter transference which could not, of course, be touched for the present.

Ned became more than ever restless under these conditions. But in spite of signalling his anxiety directly he drew enough support from Cynthia to make clever sarcastic comments about Jack's manners, his speech, and his dress. (Example of hostility and humor used as defense.) His barbs did not hit the target at this time because Jack lived blissfully in a different social world. Nevertheless the tensions of unacknowledged anger between the two men were disturbing everyone and Netta quickly took over a role that was to be characteristic of her. She made sympathetic and reassuring remarks to all and changed the subject. Pouring oil on troubled waters was an ego-syntonic pattern of defense which had worked with her parents and she thought to please the therapist by using it here while simultaneously avoiding open anger.

Dick, a member who spoke very little at first, seized on the neutral subject which Netta then brought up, to make comments that would have been approved in his Madison Avenue world, seeking to ingratiate himself with Ned by witticisms and to strike a rational note with Jack and Cynthia. The three partook in unwitting collusion against therapeutic movement.

A group which is allowed to continue in this defensive way because the therapist believes that the interaction will in itself be therapeutic may waste much time. Passivity is contraindicated in the face of resistance. The therapist may be impeded by his own dread of open conflict and anxiety. If the group is so constituted that the members themselves keep it moving in spite of him, it may seem to progress, but in the long run it will become resistively cohesive or break up. If the goal is reconstructive, it is imperative that the therapist begin to explore the defenses and bring out the concealed anxiety during the first weeks or months of treatment. As Mann (1953) points out, it is the resulting awareness among the members of common feelings (in this case, anxiety), rather than common problems or goals, that is the first step toward working seriously together.

I commented on how quickly they were all ready to use Netta's reassurance, and her attempt to change the subject, and wondered why. There was a moment of silence and then a variety of expressive questioning glances could be seen among the group. Netta was the only one to show open anxiety. Her facial expression was worried, almost tearful. (We learned later that she felt unfairly rejected by me for her good offices but dared not admit this so early in our relationship.) She said rather poutingly that she knew she shouldn't have come because she always managed to do the wrong thing.

I had the choice at this point of picking up her annoyance and tying it in with that of the other members, or exploring further the anxiety she had expressed and which was also present in all of them. I decided intuitively that anxiety about starting in a group was the more immediate concern. I must also have been responding to the fact that for most of them outright anger was so deeply prohibited that it probably would have to be denied or rationalized at this time. Furthermore, quite consciously, I reasoned that opening up their angry feelings, if successful, would lead them too abruptly into problems which they were not ready to discuss and bring about a hopeless bickering atmosphere they were not prepared to comprehend. I said to Netta, therefore, that I thought she was not the only one who felt nervous in the group today. Then I turned to the others and added, "How about that? I have a feeling you are all a little tense in this new situation." The group readily launched into exchanges on the subject. Immediately they came closer to the important feeling they were trying to ignore, and at the same time closer to one another in the realization of their common experience. Each had something to say about his reaction to being in the group but for the moment they restricted themselves to a quite superficial understanding of it. They talked in terms of not wanting to be thought too neurotic, of making a poor showing, or of the fear of talking in front of people. But even on this level their relief at these admissions was obvious and permitted a degree of therapeutic movement. At least they now knew their fears were mutual. They had their first knowledge concerning hidden feelings, and experienced the group as a safe place to acknowledge them.

In other groups where there is more homogeneity of defensive patterns they may all join in a tight defensive maneuver (on a preconscious level, of course). When this happens, I know that I have to be more active in breaking through it, whether it be a case of sewing circle chitchat, a discussion of the right way to bring up children, or a verbal fencing match.

As their therapist I knew that I would encounter similar anxiety again on increasingly deeper levels until the major conflicts were resolved. In this particular group the second step came a month or two later during a session in which Jack and Dick, whose rivalry had come more and more into the open, competed in questioning Ned's suave behavior. No amount of playing the game on Cynthia's part, nor Netta's soothing gestures, could prevent Ned from retreating into impenetrable silence. During the middle of the session, after a good bit of shifting around in his seat, Ned got up and started to leave without explanation. When Netta asked him if anything was the matter he began to explode, but his anger quickly fizzled out and he admitted that he was just plain panicky. This brought out expressions of anxiety from the others on a somewhat deeper plane. Jack said, "You have nothing on me—I expect to get my head chopped off all the time." As others chimed in, Ned found himself succumbing to their invitations to stay and join them. At once Netta related a fantasy she had had on the way over in which an accident had occurred to me, and all the members of the group were free to go home. With Netta in the role of the "bell cow" they took the first steps in expressing more openly their feelings to me, and revealing how their narcissistic fears influenced their relationships with authority. It goes without saying that at this point only the therapist understands the connection with narcissism.

As time goes on the members reveal a great variety of feelings and begin to establish relationships with one another and with the therapist. These may be examined, provided preconscious derivatives have already appeared in the group interaction, and provided they are pertinent to the group's immediate preoccupation. During this period, too, the therapist will gradually become acquainted with the group members as human beings. He will be storing up for future use cues as to the nature of the relationships (both transferential and realistic), the areas of anxiety which seem to be crucial for them as individuals, and the mechanisms each member uses to cope with his conflicts as they obtrude into his object relations.

Since the narcissistic fears have their origin in the loss of omnipotence, it is no wonder that the phenomena of omnipotence appear in the group. At the beginning the members will very likely endow the therapist with omnipotence, as they once regarded their parents. It is for this reason they expect him to be in possession of all the answers. As he recognizes this unconscious infantile need in them he will deal with it according to his best clinical judgment. Since their projection of omnipotence on the parental figure grew out of their own feeling of helplessness during a period of absolute dependence, he may judge it necessary not to disrupt this illusion prematurely nor to deny their accompanying dependent needs even though his long-run policy must be to help them overcome both the dependence and their fantasies of omnipotence. But he must also distinguish between this infantile fantasy and the real-

istic expectation of him as an expert authority. It is in responding
to the latter that he will address himself in appropriate interventions. Unless his own omnipotent needs remain unresolved he will
be likely to deal with theirs in a realistic manner.

Once the therapeutic atmosphere and the relationships have
been established, the therapist will become relatively more passive.
He will allow the interaction among the members to take over and
the intragroup transferences to develop. He will intervene chiefly
to deal with resistance, and to help loosen the fixed boundaries between conscious and preconscious and unconscious which are revealed in their communications.

In attempting this complex task the novice may fall back on his
knowledge of psychodynamics instead of relating to his patient as
a human being in trouble. As he becomes less anxious he learns to
be guided by his perception of what the members individually and
as a group are actually experiencing, and his sensitivity to the
amount of anxiety and tension in the group increases with clinical
experience.

Meanwhile, the therapist's personality and sincerity will be apparent to the members and will play an important role in the
group therapy process. Presumably his group will come to feel that
he respects them as human beings and understands their conflicts
but will remain firm in fighting their neurotic trends and refuse
to participate in the roles they assign him. The latter task may be
difficult because those members who feel deprived may become
very angry with him. But yielding to their neurotic needs will be a
false boon for them. For example, I recall a bitterly complaining
patient in one of my groups who became incensed when I refrained
from joining him in his self-pity. He accused me of not being understanding. In earlier days he would have won that round with
me! I said nothing, but the group began to question his attitude.

The friendly way in which the therapist shows them that he understands their unconscious subterfuges and their self-deceptions
will eventually render the more superficial defenses unnecessary,
so that their communication gradually becomes more candid and
direct. What kind of person the therapist is, as well as what he says,
will in this way play a role in the therapeutic process. His interpretations will have maximal value in the context of a good relationship. As the members experience some relief from tension and

learn that they need not be afraid of anxiety they become increasingly able to bear tensions in the group. Tension will tend to rise,
be resolved, fall, and rise again in a cyclical pattern as more and
more aspects of their problems come up for inspection.

There are many ways of insuring full member participation
aside from the basic principle of letting the group interaction proceed except when it reflects resistance. For example, the therapist
takes it for granted that the group itself will deal with any material
that an individual member brings up for discussion. If the members do not pick it up or if someone changes the subject he may ask
why. Or he may ask for their reactions to the material or to the person and his manner of telling it. In the process he brings them all
into closer relationship. He may also welcome their interpretations
if they give them. In the case of dreams these will very often be projections of their own fantasies and reveal what the meaning of the
dream would have been if they had dreamed it. The members' interpretations may be extremely valuable both for this reason and
because they can be helpful to the patient in question; but there is
a limit to their usefulness, and the therapist must be attuned to it.
Analytic comments by members are frequently indicative of resistance and must be dealt with as such.

Similarly the therapist may throw open to the group for general
discussion any problematic group manifestation such as restlessness, boredom, flatness, heaviness, or circularity of content. If he
feels perplexed about what is going on, he may say so and ask for
help in determining its meaning.

If the therapist also consistently makes connections between each
member's reports about outside events and his intragroup relationships, and between present group situations and the past, noting
similarities, differences, and changes, he will facilitate group integration while analyzing the individual members. All such methods of stimulating the interaction and focusing on the group are
important because they create a highly sensitive atmosphere in
which innumerable shadings and fine nuances of meaning become
increasingly perceptible.

If the therapist has set the direction of the group interaction, the
members will be able to carry on by themselves for extended,
though variable, periods of time, blending the dual functions of ex
pressing their reactions freely to one another while at the same

time helping one another to become aware of latent meanings which appear among their transferential relationships.

Before many weeks the character of the group communications will change. The purely social aspects which sometimes predominate in the beginning will be converted into working relationships; the pupil-teacher attitudes to the therapist will change to patient-therapist attitudes. Deeper therapy has probably begun in the sense that the members' pathogenic conflicts have already appeared in the transferences, and the preparatory steps toward analyzing them have been taken. The major line of each member's defensive system will have become apparent. In other words, the first phase has now passed unnoticeably into the second prolonged and difficult phase of transference and resistance analysis.

The Analysis of Transference in the Clinical Practice of Group Psychotherapy

The distinction made by Anna Freud between the regressive and the defensive transference has been useful in conceptualizing the vicissitudes of transference in group therapy. Experience with groups seems to indicate that it would be more accurate to speak of the defensive and the regressive aspects of transference and of the libidinal and aggressive forces which appear in them and may constitute the underlying drive or be employed in the service of its defensive elements. Except for theoretical purposes one cannot completely separate these two forms or aspects of transference. Both appear in individual and in group analysis. It is a question of which predominates. It is only for theoretical purposes therefore that we speak of the systematic analysis of the defensive transference. These concepts are merely abstractions which are useful for describing and explaining clinically observable behavior.

In recent years a number of group therapists who are either not familiar with nor sympathetic to psychoanalysis have relied almost solely on the ventilation of feelings in a permissive atmosphere for therapeutic movement instead of using transference analysis as the chief instrument. They consider these concepts too intellectual and mistakenly think that their clinical application must likewise be cut and dried. But catharsis has long since been found insufficient for producing lasting personality change, and the conceptualizations are intended only as a kind of shorthand to facilitate theoretical understanding, not as a way of communicating with patients.

In the clinical setting the therapist can very easily translate his concepts into the language of common sense and employ a natural and simple way of speaking with the group members. He does not cease to be a human being or put on a mask in order to engage in group analysis, but he does differentiate his role from that of the patients. It is his task to keep the interaction going and, with a degree of consistency consonant with a relaxed atmosphere, direct the members' attention to what they are experiencing, and to the ways in which they interact with others. If he considers a member's interpersonal communication unrealistic or inappropriate, i.e., transferential in character, he encourages its further exploration with the group. He hopes gradually to help the members understand how inextricably the past has been involved in distorting their perception of the present, and to make it possible for them to disconnect this linkage.

The therapist may begin by calling a member's attention to some neurotic bit of interpersonal behavior. He relies on his empathy and intuition for selecting the appropriate starting point. If he cannot sense "where his patient is," his comment is likely to get lost. His entire theoretical knowledge and clinical experience will determine what he will say in the group, but the situation and his personality will influence the way he makes his comments, in the same way that these factors influence the members. Ideally he explores behavior which is both meaningful for the individual and central to the group's emotional interest at the time. Being human, however, he often misses the bull's eye and considers his purpose achieved if he elicits a discussion which will at least lead to further understanding.

He may start very simply. Mrs. F recently came into a new inexperienced group. One of the first stories she told registered her low self-esteem. She had planned what was for her a big undertaking. She had phoned a shopkeeper whom she knew personally for an appointment to try on suits. He knew that her time and money were limited, yet he kept her waiting and then showed her only suits that were well beyond her price range. However, she could not bring herself to tell him of her disappointment because it was based on her belief that his other customers were wealthier and therefore more important to him. She faked friendliness and finally made an excuse to leave, determined never to go to his shop again. She asked the group if we thought she had done the right thing, quoting a friend who said she should have told him off and insisted on her rights. In the lively discussion that followed a variety of responses to this kind of situation was expressed. The answers gave many clues to the defenses which the different members used in coping with status problems, and revealed a rather general preoccupation with this dilemma. Twice during the discussion Mrs. F, who seemed to be the group spokesman at this time, pointed out to another woman, Mrs. C, that she was too self-derogatory. When she referred again to her own lack of importance to the shopkeeper I asked, "Who is underrating herself now?" In the following interchange the members used examples which revealed much more about their various modes of relationships. I had occasion to "wonder why" some of them judged themselves by the standards of others rather than their own.

It was apparent from Mrs. F's lessened tensions and changed expression at the close of the session that she was immensely relieved, but I expected this kind of problem to be repeated many times in transference before she achieved a change of attitude that would endure. Because an unresolved infantile conflict kept remotivating this behavior she was bound to repeat it and only a resolution of the conflict would eradicate it.

Noting her self-effacing attitude, her doubts about her unexpressed anger, her comment to Mrs. C, and her ingratiating manner with the group, I tentatively adopted the hypothesis that Mrs. F suffered from a type of status problem which began in the days when she was little and helpless and dependent on the big people who seemed to have power over her. Such conflicts have to do with a struggle for selfhood, for power or control, and usually involve a considerable deposit of rage and guilt, because suitable forms of aggression were not then available. Among the primary mechanisms which Mrs. F had apparently used to cope with "the big ones" was identification with the aggressor's values. She got along with people whose status she considered higher by being inagratiating, and expressed her rage only in a secret "revenge" ("I won't go back to him again") which unfortunately hurt her more than it did them. (She got no suit at wholesale.) I predicted that she would probably form many transference relations of this kind in the group.

Ordinarily I wait until such transferences develop, but in this case I felt she was ready for a preliminary step which would prepare her for better understanding later. I did not respond at all to her request for opinions nor to the resentment she felt, but directed my comment to her defense. To get out the underlying feeling first would probably only bring to the surface the other side of her ambivalence. I foresaw that these aspects of her conflict would emerge eventually and my intention was to listen and observe her group relationships in order to test the hypothesis. If I was wrong there was no harm done, but if I was right the major direction of the analysis was set, for the time being. Once the defenses were worked through the underlying emotions could be expected to come freely to the fore. The likelihood was that the hostility would turn out to be a second line of defense which blocked her ability to utilize her normal aggression.

Among the factors that made me choose that particular sample of interpersonal behavior for intervention was the fact that the subject had aroused a very lively interaction and there were many signs that the problem was a general one. Our experience in this respect reinforces the group dynamicists' theories of group development which state that problems of authority have to be dealt with before the group moves on to problems of intimacy. (See Chapter IV.)

In spite of what we have said about the fragmentized transferences, there is nevertheless a certain tendency for a number of transference objects to become stabilized. If there are enough of these there may also develop a kind of family transference to the total group. This tendency depends somewhat on the proportion of group members who resemble family figures rather closely for one another. Groups differ a good deal as to how seriously the family image is cultivated. Where cotherapists are used they are likely to be seen as parents and to encourage the viewpoint. Occasionally one or two patients have special needs for bringing about this situation and the others follow along with them to some degree. In other cases it is the therapist who views the group as a family and encourages the persistence of this transference. His rationale may be that the therapy group will be a better family than the original one and will help to change the patient's feelings and outlook by providing the love and acceptance he seems to desire. But this seems to me to contaminate the role of the analytic therapist, which is neither to accept nor to reject the transference roles that are projected on to him but to restrict himself to analyzing them. The long-range aim, of course, is not merely to recognize the transference but to eliminate it.

In one of my groups two members contributed to prolonging the family transference resistance. Barney, who had an unusually trying childhood as an orphan, shunted about among his relatives, was one of them. I had asked him, after a long period of individual treatment, to join one of my groups in order to make available to him an opportunity for reality testing in a protected atmosphere, for he was still quite distrustful of people and was afraid of giving up his defenses long after he understood them. His parents had deserted him and he felt very lonely and rejected in the series of foster homes to which he had been sent. Telling the group his story had been an ordeal but had created strong bonds with them. He often spoke about how much he liked his "new family"—the group. Actually this notion interfered with analysis because he had to try to maintain the illusion that the family members were "ideal" and to suppress his own "bad" feelings. But the good feeling it gave him may have been very helpful in building up trust in others. For a while I respected it as a necessity for him. But in spite of his attitude, there were occasions when the past injected itself into the present too forcefully to be ignored. For example, from the beginning one of the members, Rita, had been very attractive to him. She was gallant and chic (like the mother he had pictured to himself). She dressed in a flamboyant though sometimes sloppy manner. He admired the former and usually forced himself to suppress his disgust with the latter, which might bring to consciousness his fantasy that his mother was a prostitute and the unwelcome fury this thought aroused in him. One day when Rita favored another man with her attention, Barney's anger was out of all proportion to the incident. He had a way of turning anger into criticism and scolded her now very much the way he usually criticized his wife's housekeeping at those times when he felt rejected by her. It was a displacement to a different area for purposes of avoiding deeper pain. As the members inquired about his irrational behavior toward Rita he became more and more illogical, producing a variety of rather bizarre associations. Among them was a fantasy that Rita was a prostitute. From that point he generalized about the irresponsibility of women—they had, according to his distorted view of the moment, no right to be mothers. He supported his argument with an incident which he thought gave a clear indication of how his wife's neglect had caused their child to have an accident. Another group member, a woman who had always been fond of Barney, reminded him that he sounded for all the world like a little boy who felt neglected by his mommy. He had already acquired some insight into his distrust of women but now suddenly the connecting link between past and present hit him more vividly than ever before. He took a deep breath and shook his head. "My God," he said, "I am jealous; don't tell me I've been on that kick again." Somehow the group incident in which mother, wife, and Rita were one and the same person gave his insight an added dimension.

In the next session he apologized to Rita and said that he had always liked her and really respected her. Then he told the group that he had been mean and spiteful to his wife, too, lately, but that since the previous week the atmosphere at home had suddenly cleared. He beamed. This was a very different Barney from the one we had known. The experience seemed to integrate several partial insights for him. It marked the beginning of the end of his treatment, and we began to see significant and consistent changes in his outlook as well as his behavior.

In the same group Grace had so persistently regarded Ben as her brother that I realized she must have libidinized this transference. In order to hide what was going on with him, she talked of the group as a family, although her other transference objects changed often and easily. Grace had started out by hating Ben as she had once hated her brother. Once the defensive nature of this hostility had been examined, Ben became an idealized sexual object and she told us many fantasies she had about him. But there was an air of unreality about the way she talked and she seemed to avoid any real relationship with him. Continuing her fantasies about him helped her avoid facing her repressed incestuous feelings. No matter how often she recognized that he represented her brother she kept the distortion going. The telling of the fantasies itself was eroticized. She had appeared to be so free in talking about them that the group was surprised that after she had sparked off a rather intense discussion of sexual matters among them, she promptly had a dream which revealed deep-seated guilt about sexual feelings. She dreamed she suffered from cancer in her uterus, which had, however, already been removed! Her associations led among other things to her realization that she equated a man's penis with a club with which she would be torn apart. Ben's immediate frank expression of revulsion shocked her but seemed to break the confusion she had built up between fantasy and reality. He became a person rather than a transference object. For a while she related to the group members more realistically and actually acquired a boy friend with whom she indulged in some love-making. But before long she began to complain about coming to the group. She insisted that some things should not be talked about there. The members made her see that she was just running away and talked with her about why she was doing it. They guessed it had to do with sex. It finally turned out that she still did not want to talk about sex realistically in the group because she wanted to get her kicks out of her fantasies, instead of being made to face her incestuous feelings. Several of the members now revealed that they had been puzzled by the fact that she always seemed to relish listening to sexy talk. Someone said that when two of the men got into a rather violent argument one day her face had taken on a dreamy, absorbed expression. She answered that it had been exciting, like witnessing two bulls fighting—maybe over her. Ben then said, "I haven't dared to say it before but maybe it will be useful now. You often sit there moving your body—sort of squeezing and shifting around as if you were masturbating." Not surprisingly Grace was terribly upset and at the point of tears. She later told us she had thought of running out of the room. But the others reached out warmly to her and talked about their own masturbatory experiences which helped her feel less isolated. Eventually I summed up. "I guess it's more fun to experience those exciting forbidden feelings than to talk about them. No wonder you haven't been wanting to come here lately." The back of the resistance was now broken and she began to test out realistic relationships in the group again. It was only after this incident in which the sub-surface connections between her physical experience and her insight were loosened

that the brother transference began to break up. The libidinization
of the transference had been securely lodged in the musculature.

It goes without saying that the group was deeply involved in
Grace's experience. Her fantasies tended to evoke theirs, and her
dream brought their own fears to the surface. The situation was
consistently meaningful and quite intense. Once these two persistent transferences had been resolved there was little further talk
about the group as a family.

So much of what has been written about transference, both in
individual and in group analysis, has been in terms of its object
that these few examples may be sufficient to show how the therapist's role as transference object is shared in the group and what
the advantages of this circumstance are. It has been mentioned
that the mass of apparently disparate transference manifestations
required that we modify the technique of analysis. We found that
we could give coherence to the process if we organized it in terms
of each person's defensive system, which is derived from the way in
which he passed through the phases of development. Since all the
members have gone through these stages our modification was capable of bringing harmony into the analysis of all the members.

The way in which this form of analytic group therapy is applied
in practice is well illustrated, I believe, by the following detailed
example.

Leslie was an intelligent and charming woman in her early forties who started in individual analysis. Her problems included a
rather severe sexual constriction and a hidden but profound dependency upon her husband. At first impression her ego appeared
quite strong, for she had learned to turn her abilities to an active
mastery of external realities in order to ward off fear and anxiety
concerning this inner passivity. This excessive need to get things
done had become a well established part of her character and
might have been regarded purely as an adaptive use of her potentials were it not for its abnormal intensity, the very evident need
for constant approval that accompanied it, and the fact that very
minimal self-regard had been built up in proportion to her considerable achievements. She was ceaselessly driven by this inner
compulsion to increase her performances and win fresh approval.

Leslie had worked hard with me individually and had made appreciable progress, but she could not seem to break through her

idealized mother transference to me. Her deeply entrenched character pattern of overcompliance and submissiveness to authority
hardly varied. It was clothed in such a charming and sophisticated
manner that it had become ego syntonic and difficult to dislodge.
Superficially she accepted every one of my interpretations without
question and even worked hard putting them to use. With her
idealized transference to me as support she was able to examine
her relationship with her mother. Before long she discovered that
under her nagging attitude toward that lady she nursed a bitter
resentment, and for this she felt guilty. She compensated by an
overconcerned and self-sacrificing attentiveness which in turn
brought about self-pity and fed the anger. The vicious circle was
complete. Holding fast to her positive transference to me she
poured out the rational aspects of her anger to the mother who,
she declared, had opposed everything she ever liked—her friends,
her piano, her painting, and so on. She ventilated this facet of her
hostility, the pressure was reduced, and the relationship temporarily improved. But so far she had clung to the rational reasons for
her anger and continued to repress her irrational infantile rage
and fear. It was because these were so drastic and deep seated that
she could not break through her idealization of the therapist,
which served as a defense both against her impotent rage and the
anxiety which attended it. Since a private examination of my own
possible countertransference resistance produced only negative indications, I suggested that she join one of my groups and continue
in combined therapy. She accepted in her characteristically oblig-
ing way.

One would not have known from her gracious behavior during
the first sessions that she had made an immediate transference to
the group as a whole as if it were a single, overpowering person. I
was aware of her inner anxiety because of her body rigidity, which
regularly meant that she was controlling strong anxiety. It was if
she were saying, "If I sit very still, and don't even breathe, nothing
can happen to me." In the group she denied any anxiety, and told
me in her next individual session that she had been too ashamed to
admit this concern. Later she was able to tell them that she thought
they would jump on her if they knew how frightened she was.

Leslie's major defense was vested in the role of the good girl,
overlaid with a veneer of sophistication that served several pur-

poses. On the one hand, it continuously warded off her fear of authority figures by winning their approval; on the other, she acted like a good mother toward her peers—with but few exceptions. The truth was she was protective toward her peers as she had been with her little sister, and thus built up her self-esteem. In cases where the lower-status person was in any way needy or pitiable, Leslie went to great extremes to be kind. She was acting out the way she felt her mother should have acted toward her (as she secretly pictured herself). This role became the unifying axis for her analysis in the group.

The first area of her behavior which was questioned by the members was her unvarying thoughtfulness toward them, individually and as a group. After a trial period of popularity Leslie had found herself criticized for always being the one to get up and move a chair, close a window, give advice, express sympathy, or even offer material help. She became puzzled and distressed at their doubts about her sincerity. George, a rather defiant non-conformist, had been irritated with her from the beginning and described her as a "damned goodygood." Mat, who at first appreciated her attentions, became worried as he began to feel, because of his own guilt, that she would expect him to live up to her expectations. After experiencing a period of feeling terribly hurt by their lack of appreciation, her behavior gradually lost its ego-syntonic quality. The disproportionate anxiety with which she responded made her willing to investigate its meaning.

They reminded her, she said, of her parents, who never really appreciated her earnest efforts either. At that point a screen memory occurred. She began to weep as she told us how her mother had once had her pet cat killed. A woman who did that was capable of doing anything, she asserted, and at this accusation she quite suddenly lost altogether her usually poised manner. It was the group's first clue to her deep-seated fear; and even though the members could not grasp, as the therapist did, Leslie's approach to her irrational helpless fury, they sensed the existence of a long-buried agitation. Her rationalized anger had merely scratched the surface. Her sobbing, childish and uncontrollable, continued.

Later, she said she was amazed that they had accepted her so warmly, for she had expected them to deride her if she cried. It was a constructive learning experience for her. But while it modified her fears somewhat, the defensive patterns of her behavior would keep returning until the underlying conflict was resolved. As time went on, through other transference experiences we gained deeper understanding of her character in terms of her specific life experiences. One day when she was again upset and crying (the crying turned out to be a way of warding off expected cruelty and at the same time symbolized incontinent infantile fury), Ben, to whom she had been attracted, became very restless, sighed repeatedly, and finally spat out, "Oh, for heaven's sake, quit yammering; you make me nervous." I asked very quietly if she could tell us what she was thinking to herself as she cried, and she haltingly told us how, when she was little, she felt she could never go to her parents for comfort because they would get nervous and upset, just as Ben had. Whenever she wanted something, acted childishly, or needed help, she had felt forced to contain herself. Without realizing it, she had made it a practice never to ask for anything for herself and never to appear irrational. Because of her self-containment her husband and other people around her could not know her needs and therefore tended to validate her fears. She therefore usually felt unrewarded for her tremendous efforts to please. This neurotic need interfered considerably with an otherwise good marital relationship.

Through her reactions to Rita we learned about another aspect of her character and its causes. Rita represented the pampered, dependent, lazy little sister who "got away with it."

Leslie's envy had been replaced by an overprotective attitude, but occasionally she burst forth with indignation when the sister did not show appreciation. When Rita evinced the same easygoing side of her character, and yet succeeded in winning the group's admiration, Leslie reversed roles with the bad mother and provoked the group's resentment.

More important, the group also began to explore her attitude toward me. They soon pointed out that she seemed to defend me against all criticism, to echo everything I said, and often to voice my ideas before I got around to do so myself. She was, once more, deeply hurt and offended. Everyone joined in the tempting subject of the therapist as authoritative parent. The contrasting attitudes toward me made for some lively and enlightening interaction. It climaxed one day when George's recurrent paranoid projection to me of the bad mother was under discussion. He reported strong feelings and deep fantasies in which his mother and I were confused as witch women. Leslie was shocked. The incident reactivated some of her own repressed fantasies, but her defenses were immediately redoubled. Only she, and Mat who took this opportunity to show up George, defended me. The others relished the chance to bring out their rebellious feelings about authority figures, but they joined in denying the validity of the paranoid projections. Leslie was puzzled and very anxious. She turned to me for an answer. She said they confused her. Was she to fight me? Whatever she did in the group seemed to be wrong—and now they and I were leaving her out on a limb—not knowing what to do. George, who himself had been helped during the discussion to see that his attitude toward me was really meant for his mother, became calmer and more judicious. He was able now to show her just how much she required parental approval, and how she could, if she made up her mind to, decide for herself what was right. She was angry and turned again to me. I did not answer her question, but said it was a good idea to think over what had been said. She was outraged, and spent several individual and group sessions expressing open frustration, irrational anger, and infantile rage at me. But she did not cry and when the anger was spent she felt a new wholeness in herself which stood her in good stead as we continued to work through this tenacious problem. Bits of otherwise puzzling behavior began shortly to fall into place. She gave examples of her habit of telephoning her husband before making a decision, apparently wanting approval but clearly eliciting the opposite. Once when she had dismissed a maid because the girl's family problems interfered with her work, she felt guilty and called him up, only to be reprimanded. The group was able to point out many incidents she had reported in which by anticipating his disapproval she had actually brought it about, and they showed her similar instances in her group behavior. She was greatly affected when she finally realized that her efforts to win approval served an unconscious need to be rejected.

Gradually, she developed much more self-esteem and became able to ask for what she wanted without "settling for peanuts," as the group called it. She began also to cultivate her hobbies to the point of achieving outstanding success. She was better able to assert herself with her husband without always ending up in a clinging, begging, "don't leave me" position. But the basic defense was hard to eradicate and took endless working through.

As the stultifying effects of her ambivalent preoedipal mother transference to me and to her husband markedly decreased, Leslie gained real self-confidence. She became more spontaneous in general and was now for the first time really drawn into the group's frank discussions of sexual relationships. Just being able to break her private taboo on using the language of sexuality had a liberating effect. This seriously constricted area began slowly to open up and she gained greater freedom in the marital relationship than she had previously dared to enjoy.

Each member of the group is, in somewhat the same way, soon understood in terms of the basic organization of his defenses. Once the underlying drives and their irrational emotions have been recognized the long process of working through and reality testing follows. As the group engages itself with the solution of one member's problems all have an opportunity to examine their own ways of dealing with related areas of anxiety and conflict. So George's paranoid projection, Rita's open defiance of parental discipline, and Barney's basic distrust of women were all investigated in relation to Leslie's problems. Each in turn became the central figure for short periods.

One therapeutically significant discovery emerged from observing group process. The member who talked with the group about a problem he was having at home inadvertently provided a clue to the character defenses which were producing his trouble and carrying his transference resistance. Usually that clue consisted in his manner of telling the problem. His transference to the group as a whole tends to be identical with the one that is operative at home and is detectable in his mood, his manner, his voice, and his gestures and posture.

Harry, for instance, complained that his wife repeatedly refused to listen to him when he wanted to talk to her about his business problems. Greg, another group member, was immediately able to show him by his own reaction how he was eliciting the same indifferent response from the group because he told his story in a dull, droning, overly-detailed fashion. Did he talk in that listless, heavy way with his wife? Jack was so intellectual and superior with the group that he earned the name of professor, and was often laughed out of court. Whenever he intensified this character defense, the members became furious with him. One girl, usually very perceptive, who identified very much with his wife, said to him, "No wonder you complain that Evie has irrational fits of temper. If you were my husband I'd kill you. I just bet you keep implying she's stupid, and then if she gets upset you pull this cool, superior, indifferent attitude. There's nothing worse than a man who won't fight back. It makes you crawl the walls." These remarks hit home.

In another group a former homosexual came in a depressed mood because he could not get an erection with a girl with whom he was having an affair. He slouched in his chair and complained that he was helpless and hopeless and would never make it. Almost every member tried to react to his problem either with feelings, or questions, or suggestions. He brushed them away one by one with a joke, a blank expression, a "yes, but," or switch of subject. Finally one girl burst out, "All right, I've had it, you make me sick. Here we are trying to help you out and you seem to be getting a kick out of turning us down." Another said, "You win! I'll bet you do the same thing with your girl—you let her stew." A third said, "Yeah, you know it's like we're all trying to get you an erection and you're busy frustrating us." Everyone laughed, including the subject, for whom the laugh expressed the assent of the unconscious. The subject's entire manner changed and he said, "I get it—only I'll lose my girl. Oh, damn, I'm a fool defeating myself." This kind of discovery often indicates a new direction, for it releases a deep-seated character defense which binds the anxiety.

Such insights on the part of the group members help the patient understand not only what his past experiences have done to him but what he has done with them by way of perpetuating his difficulties. Very often it coincides exactly with what he does with his insights to vitiate their effectiveness, so that he is unable to translate his knowledge into changed behavior. For instance, in a recent group meeting Sam, who had in the first months of therapy been a highly perceptive assistant therapist, with a good sense of humor, was now sitting rather heavily and glumly in his seat with little to say. The subject of siblings had come up and Mat asked him to tell us more about his older brothers. Sam told us again how they used to beat him up cruelly and he gave us some rather hair-raising instances to prove it. And once again one of the women expressed sympathy. But another more perceptive member commented that Sam was telling the story to us as if he were not so much discovering something about himself but rather savoring a tale in which he was cast in the role of the tragic, persecuted hero. Sam was very angry and turned the tables with brilliant sarcasm. Another member said, "You know, you just had to be doing something to make them that bad. I suppose all brothers hit kids, but this is too much." Sam explained that maybe it was because he had been his mother's favorite and he used to run to her for protection. Someone else said, "Oh, I bet that's why everything was just dandy here in the group while you were making a big impression on us. But when Mama Durkin didn't protect you any more you got morose. You sit there on your hands looking like a black cloud, with your lower lip protruding. If anyone says anything you get into a rage." Someone else added that that was why she never dared to say anything to Sam. And another joined in, "Yeah, he's right, you're getting us to beat you up verbally and you sit there feeling sorry for yourself—and superior." Mat said, "You're doing the same thing in the group you used to do at home—get wise to yourself." For the first time Sam took seriously an interpretation made to him by a group member. He sat quietly instead of wisecracking or making intellectual, psychiatric elaborations as he sometimes did. He nodded his head and presently the black expression left his face and he joined the work of the group once more. The remembered events of his life now fell into a new perspective, which included the way he had interpreted them then and what he was still doing with them in the present. The changed configuration brought about some attitude changes.

DEALING WITH RESISTANCE

It is well known that transferences of all types constitute the major form of resistance. All the other varieties of resistance may take place within its framework. In defining transference resistance Fenichel (1945) writes, "It consists of the repetition of previously acquired attitudes in the transference." Obviously this includes the transference of character defenses which, as we have indicated, become a major resistance in group therapy. Again he writes, "The patient misunderstands the present in terms of the past and then, instead of remembering, strives, without recognizing the nature of the action, to relive the past." Therefore, when the therapist analyzes the multiple aspects of transference as they occur in the group he is by definition dealing with resistance. For the rest, Fenichel defines resistance in its broader sense as ". . . anything that prevents the patients from producing material derived from the unconscious." It is no different in group therapy. Anything and everything may be used in the service of resistance, including dreams and free associations. The group situation adds a few special opportunities for its members to prevent unbearable anxiety-provoking material from coming into consciousness. For example, some members try to avoid exposure by their silence, which may remain unnoticed for a while as others take up the slack; or they may act out their voyeurism or exhibitionism while appearing to take an active interest in the affairs of other members; or they may mask their lack of self-involvement by actively participating as adjunct therapists. The members may join forces acting out together verbally while engaging in apparently lively interaction on "interesting" subjects (such as sex). Or they may be doing it without real involvement in response to an interest they have noticed in the therapist in order to keep him happy and avoid facing their conflicts. There is, as a matter of fact, a certain vogue for emphasizing feelings in group therapy, as if the expression of emotion were equivalent to therapeutic movement. Yet very often the emotions expressed can be a part of the defensive armor as are speech blocks. To be sure, it is important for them to be expressed, but only in order that they may be explored. A good deal of what is welcomed by the novice as freedom to express hostility, for example, is really only synthetic anger summoned to ward off some other emotions—perhaps tenderness. The group situation, being a highly stimulating one, is especially prone to this kind of resistance. The more the patients are encouraged to express it the longer they will keep the status quo. As the late Samuel Flowerman once remarked, "You can't judge how much therapy is being done in a group by the amount of excitement that is going on."

Of course, the reverse is not true either. Emotion, thought, and action must all play a part. The inexperienced therapist can easily

miss the repetitive or circular nature of resistance in the group interaction. Only clinical experience will develop a sixth sense in
him which can perceive in this lively veneer the static quality of
resistance. The therapist must be able to recognize that though
lights may be flashing and horns honking nothing is moving. He
must learn to be ceaselessly vigilant in detecting this obstacle to
therapeutic progress, prompt in drawing attention to it, and tactful
in helping the patients understand its meaning in the specific
instance.

A word of warning. Resistance as a term has been much abused,
and in some quarters has come falsely into disrepute. Therapists
who unthinkingly avoid their own frustration sometimes blame
their lack of success on the patient's "resistance" as if this condition
were a willful act of defiance on his part. Glover (1955) reminds us
that resistance is not "an artifact peculiar to analysis even though
the analytic method aggravates its symptoms. It is a common phenomenon of life designed to protect man against being constantly
exposed to acute anxiety over his infantile conflicts." When it occurs within the group situation the therapist need not be aston-
ished, nor must he allow himself to become irritated by the phenomenon. He may, for instance, be forced to conclude that his own
pride is hurt because progress is slow. Once he understands himself
he will be able to work more effectively again. Step by step he helps
the patient break through the resistance and sets the therapeutic
process in movement once more.

Since the analysis of character resistance forms so important a
part of the group analytic process, it will be well to recall Anna
Freud's comments: " In my opinion we do our patients a great in-
justice if we describe these transferred defense reactions as camouflage, or say that he is pulling our leg. . . . The patient is in fact
candid when he gives expression to the impulse or affect in the only
way still open to him, namely in the distorted defensive measure"
(1936). If we wish to help him we must "be where he is" and start
from there. We cannot pit ourselves against him. If resistance is
thus understood, the patient's cooperation in overcoming it will
be easier to achieve.

We have shown how, in the first sessions, the attitudes of doubt
must be analyzed as resistance. If the hidden feelings were brought
into consciousness and temporarily dissolved, the patients were

able to move toward other troublesome hidden feelings and motivations. If their disappointments or resentments are not dealt with,
the members become more and more angry, less capable of revealing themselves, and more strongly resistant. When this happens the
members may show it by long-winded intellectual discussion, or
become restless, or fall into continuous fencing, or talk about apparently appropriate subjects such as their children or families
merely as a way of winning the therapist's approval, but in a
repetitive circular fashion. The therapist will then have another
chance to uncover their resistance. However, this time it will be
necessary to bring what is happening to the attention of the group
as a whole and to solicit their help in getting to the source of the
difficulty. The less resistant members are likely to come to his as-
sistance. Or, if nothing is forthcoming, the therapist may venture
a guess at what the trouble is and then deal with their reactions to
it. Once the resistance is penetrated the ice is broken and the interaction will become more fluent and direct. Of course, renewed
freedom from resistance will not be a fixed asset of the group. Individual members will develop it periodically in accordance with
their own needs and anxieties. Two members might reinforce each
other's resistance in this way. At other times one strongly resistant
member may reinforce the resistance of every other member in
whom it appears and so another group block may occur.

The "unwilling" member will be ready to join forces with anyone who defends himself against therapeutic measures. One such
woman regularly used "reality" in this way. She was quick to give
opinions and good advice, agreeing with one member that it was
no use coming to the therapy group if one's husband refused;
with another, who insisted that it didn't make sense to come with
a cold; and with a third, who stressed that money matters had to
take precedence over emotional difficulties. Two or more members
may "dovetail" in acting out their neurotic drives. Thus a voyeuristic and exhibitionistic team may develop and appear to be active
in expressing feeling when they are really only acting out in transference. This is intermember transference resistance par excellence.
I remember that one young woman regularly baited a particular
man in the group who always rose readily in righteous indignation
to tell her off. If this were accepted as a healthy expression of aggression it would go on repeatedly with no real change occurring.

If it is picked up as transference resistance it will lead to an understanding of the under-the-table motives of both parties to it. The chances are that for each it was a re-enactment of a significant childhood relationship. If it is not examined, it may lead to a stalemate.

The therapist may deal with resistance as soon as he recognizes it in the individual , the pair, or the subgroup, or he may wait until it is fully developed and becomes a substantial group resistance. In the first case the therapeutic process moves more smoothly, less time is lost, and there is less sense of frustration. In the second, far more tension is built up, the group forces are given a chance to become full blown (they *are* the resistance then), and it is taken up as a group phenomenon. The results are indeed dramatic but the *specific* individual significance which differs for each participating member may be lost. In my view, making specific, tailor-made interpretations for each person is the surest way to bring about understanding and change in the group members who have come to the therapist for help as individuals.

A recent group session comes to mind as an example of group resistance in which there were a number of therapists among the patients. The likelihood of using analytic interpretations to avoid anxiety, which is always present, was therefore heightened. Too large a proportion of the members in this particular group found it difficult to express their feelings in a direct and candid fashion. We found ourselves frequently in the situation of stagnation due to defensive intellectualizing. It was one of the members, David, who complained about the group's constricting atmosphere. Celia, one of the worst offenders, was quick to answer the critic. "If that's the way you feel why don't you start us off?" David tried, but found it hard to get the others to go along with him. He suggested that they fine anyone who attempted to tell anyone else what he was thinking or feeling or to make an interpretation. The members went along with him. Since they recognized their resistance I went along, too, saying nothing, but I doubted that a rule could stimulate spontaneity.

A few timid attempts were made to express feelings and were immediately jumped on with expressions of annoyance, which served to bring about the old sense of deadlock. I noticed that here again there was a kind of collusion for the purpose of stopping real investigation of problems. When I brought it up for discussion simply by asking what they thought was happening to us, Celia said angrily that the others acted as if she were required to have only healthy feelings. She complained that they scolded her whenever she dared to say what she was experiencing. John countered that she needn't collapse just because someone didn't approve of her brand of emotions. David began to understand that talking about feelings for feeling's sake would not help. He asked Celia if she didn't agree that they had come to find out how their feelings affected others and what they meant. Celia had to agree, and as a group they came to the conclusion that both candid expression of feelings and willingness to examine them were necessary for progress. The analyst's function is to know when the patients' emotions and their interpretations to one another are genuine, and when they serve the purpose of resistance.

The resistance which is built into the character is of an extremely persistent nature, especially when it is of preverbal origin. It is as if the patient feared he would lose his individuality or his very existence, as if he would fall apart, if he gave up his crucial character defenses. The patient cannot know that the opposite is true and that only when he gives up his armor can he become truly and spontaneously himself. His panic itself can be seen to stem from his original narcissistic fears, and it brings about a tenacious negative therapeutic reaction. The therapist and the rest of the group are frequently perceived as the omnipotent parent who wants to destroy him with hostility or consume him with love.

This attitude became particularly apparent in one group which had just experienced a trying session in which the members clearly faced their need to give up the very foundations of their neurotic character. A number of pertinent dreams were brought up for discussion. One young lady dreamed she was in her old childhood home and found that someone was putting in a new fireplace. She was desperately upset about this although she knew perfectly well that the chimney had long needed to be replaced. Her associations clearly revealed that the symbolism of the fireplace referred to a basic change which involved her sexuality.

Another member dreamed that he and his wife (he had been having sexual difficulties with her which he had only recently and reluctantly discussed in the group) were moving into a new apartment. At the entrance there were a number of people who were somehow dangerous to him and he fought them off. It turned out that this dream had a double meaning. The new house stood for privacy with his wife which he felt the therapy group was trying to invade. But he also felt the group was about to help him change his relationship with her and he was afraid. In the dream he had to prevent them from accomplishing this. A third member had been in the grip of a severe conflict with authority which she repeatedly acted out in her choice of boy friends. She was torn between satisfying her parents' conventional and materialistic standards and defying them by choosing a Bohemian beau. No matter which she chose, she was plagued by the opposite need. In therapy, the group and the therapist alternately represented the parents who wanted her to marry well, and the seducer who urged her not to independence but to open rebellion. When this dilemma was analyzed and the possibility of breaking through the dichotomy opened up she became very anxious and promptly reported the following dream. She was walking along a precipice through a mountain forest with a psychologist friend. The friend wanted her to climb the mountain and she panicked. It was as if it were a matter of life and death to remain on the edge of the precipice.

Since the therapist remains an omnipotent image, such resistance to giving up the neurosis is much better dealt with in a group of peers. In this case each dreamer could see the fallacy of the other's position and so was helped to re-examine his own fear. They are more willing, therefore, to explore the narcissistic sources of that fear. But the resistances which stem from narcissism are extremely persistent and need much working through. Since the tendency toward maintaining the status quo is strong, the therapist must not relinquish his role or rely solely on the group interaction for continued progress. He must be ready to deal with their reluctance to move. In this case I had to intervene several times until each in turn came to see the regressive significance of his rationalizations for standing pat. It was a crucial session and the group began to work with renewed vigor.

Each phase of development seems to have its own characteristic tenacious defenses. The insistence of the narcissistic character on pseudo self-sufficiency may be expressed in an interpersonal atti-

tude: "I don't need you." It is a consequence of his having experienced any intrusion of reality into his primary narcissism as a
threat. He is likely to view even the therapist's most helpful interpretations with apprehension and to exercise every possible device
to avoid "swallowing or digesting it." The passive helplessness of
some orally regressed characters who need to control the weak-
ness is equally hard to overcome. The patient who complains pite-
ously and continuously that he is excluded or rejected, and insists
that he badly needs love although his actions clearly provoke rejection, cannot be reached until he becomes aware of the fact that
his actions speak louder than his words. Similarly the ego-syntonic
defense, hidden in an apparently consuming compassion for the
unfortunate, persists because it offers the secondary gratification
of feeling omnipotent, conveys a hidden reproach to his bad mother (Bergler, 1952), and appears realistically praiseworthy.

Glatzer has written several illuminating articles to show how
these defenses against the early narcissistic wounds appear repeatedly in the adult neurotic population of therapy groups. She believes that the more active group techniques, including those of
the therapist and the reactions and interpretations of the group
members, make more effective inroads on these tenacious resistances than individual psychotherapy. Her clinical examples of
masochism, magic gestures, helplessness, and the way in which they
are handled in the group are convincing (Glatzer, 1959a, 1959b,
1962). My own findings are very much in line with them.

Since the character resistance involved in these transferences is
of preverbal origin and only the vague but pervasive sense of danger remains one must get at them through fantasies and reconstruction. Once their seemingly invalid logic is understood, there
is hope for basic change, but it must be followed through with reality testing and constructive experience. For this purpose the
group situation lends an added impact toward change.

As the second phase of therapy merges into the final one the
transference aspects of the group recede and the reality of the peer
group takes the foreground. Concurrently, blanket reactions of
hostility used for defensive purpose will have become differentiated and give way to many finer nuances of feelings among the members. Self-assertion at the appropriate moment will tend to replace
the tendency to store up resentment, to express it obliquely

when it is unconscious, and explosively when it is conscious. Infantile impotent rage, so prominent in the active transference stage, will be a much rarer occurrence, and will be more quickly recognized and dissipated through insight. With these old neurotic impediments out of the way, new patterns of behavior may be tried out in an empathic but realistic atmosphere. Reality testing is at its height. This does not mean that all transference analysis is over. Those members who once felt their very being threatened by contact with others may now become aware of their difficulty in recognizing peers as peers and relax their tensions with power figures. Old patterns may easily kick up again. In fact, as a member is being prepared for leaving the group, he may be expected to experience a return of old problems, the resistance meaning of which will have to be analyzed carefully before he will be ready to go. So while it is true that the group therapist has to deal with tremendous complications, he will not lack the necessary resources, derived both from individual analytic method and from the group situation itself, for carrying out a systematic analysis of transference and resistance in the group.

XIV An Illustrative Group Session, with Explanatory Comments

From the very first meeting of any group, the interaction will begin to shed light on the basic character patterns of each member. It does not require much probing on the part of the therapist to elicit this information nor does it matter what the subject matter of the conversation is. The basic areas of anxiety for each individual will be revealed as he interacts with others. This is the take-off point for group analysis. The therapist's job is to recognize at what points to intervene and how gradually to renew the connections between the present modes of behavior and the infantile needs so that old conflicts may be resolved in a more mature way.

Therefore, it might be interesting to introduce the members of the recorded group by summing up briefly their ways of presenting themselves in the first few sessions. Then we shall be better equipped to understand the events of the sessions and also get some idea of what transpired in the interim.

From the beginning Jo, a nicely groomed, well-mannered, soft-spoken girl in her late twenties, presented herself as a remarkably well adjusted young woman. Her first reactions to the other members revealed both her intelligence and the adroit way she used her smattering of psychoanalytic knowledge to try to help others while keeping herself emotionally disengaged. She told us she was

206

eager for help and would have preferred individual sessions, but felt she had to refuse to accept financial help from her mother. The other members gave her the approval she was striving for with this statement, but I made note to watch for incidents which would make it possible to explore the true meaning of this "counterde-pendent" attitude.

Jo's ideal behavior was especially geared to keep the approval of female authority figures—in this case the therapist. I felt it was just as well that Jo had started in group therapy, for this defense against her anxiety would be reinforced by individual therapy. Later, when her position in the group had been established, she admitted to them that she was "frightened stiff" of older women and was almost overcome with anxiety when she had to have lunch or a conference with her boss. Her fantasy was that she might "fall into a thousand pieces." Still later, she told us that the only recol-lection she had of her childhood was pulling up the covers over her ears or hiding while her mother and brother fought like wild ani-mals, shrieking and wailing. She played out the role of the ideal mother with Vi, for whom she became the dignified helpful au-thority. She was denying her identification with her mother, re-proaching her, and winning approval of her superego all at once. When the group finally got her to show anger, she made a very mild assertive comment to Vi, and later referred to it as "that time I shrieked at Vi." This exaggeration was only one of many clues that her image of an eternally angry mother, though based on some fact, was severely exaggerated. Actually the woman she saw as stin-gy and unloving had, whatever her shortcomings, worked very hard to give her fatherless children musical and college educations.

When Jo did talk about herself it concerned her problems with men, but she did it with too little emotional involvement to have much meaning. However, before these revelations had taken place her less frozen attitude toward the men in the group gave us op-portunities to begin to unravel some of her problems. Here, too, her verbal behavior was exemplary, but her unacknowledged non-verbal seductiveness gave a clue to what were the unacceptable parts of herself. It helped us fathom the tremendous distance be-tween her behavior and the ideal image she felt she had to uphold. She repeated endlessly her infantile misconception that her father and her brother deserted her, although it was illness and death that had caused their defection. She used sex for the conscious purpose of winning love but was unconsciously driven to make men reject her. Ed once said, "As soon as they get into pussy—it's the beginning of the end."

The other girl in the group, Vi, had presented herself as a pretty, sweet, rather sad *jeune fille* with an air of injured innocence, in spite of the fact that she seemed always to blame herself when things went wrong. She dovetailed immediately with Jo, setting her up as a strong woman to whom she was inferior. Though both flirted with the most aggressive male in the group, Vi was so obviously vulnerable that she stirred only the faintest interest in him. She abdicated almost immediately to Jo. Much later we uncovered a "tragic heroine" fantasy which Vi nourished, in which both the man and her mother knelt at her dying bedside.

Vi turned her attention very soon to Al, the weakest of the three men in the group, with whom she played the giving mother role, but in her unconscious image she identified with his helpless, hopeless "baby" self. At times they reinforced each other's infantile selves, as others tried to jog each one out of their bind. Vi was rather shy with all the members, but became warmly sympathetic when anyone was experiencing pain. We were not surprised, therefore, when she revealed that most of her friends were lame ducks of one kind or another, and that she had a cat whom she overprotected beyond all reason. The group saw the relationship between her treatment of Al, the cat and the suffering members and began to question its meaning. It was a major line of defense. She preserved a false but ego-syntonic self-image of the good Samaritan. Through this behavior she gratified a secret measure of infantile omnipotence and at the same time concealed a reproach to her own mother whom she appeared to worship. Outside she was engaged in a relationship with a sadistic-dependent young man whom her mother disliked. She hoped to gain strength in treatment to win her mother over.

In the group she was very submissive and ingratiating in her relations with the two men she considered strong, and was shocked to learn that this behavior irritated them. They accused her of acting like a low man on the totem pole and of being a sucker. They encouraged her to assert herself more with Jo and me and at home with her mother, and with the boy friend they had learned to hate. Vi responded quickly with changed behavior before her insight actually warranted it. By the end of a year in the group she had declared her independence from her mother and found an apartment of her own; she had given up her nostalgic tie to the deserting boy friend; and when we meet her later we learn that she has found a man who is much kinder to her. She subsequently married him.

In the recorded session we shall see how strange she felt in the role of an independent person who is able to have good things for herself. But she retained a kind of secret smile and a good deal of her "magic gesture" defense. It seemed to me that her fast progress might represent a secret deal with her superego, the therapist, and the group. It was as if she were giving up some of her troubles in order to keep the shreds of her omnipotent fantasies. It would have been interesting to try to keep her in treatment after the two years she spent in combined group and individual therapy, but practical conditions demanded that I support her need to call herself "cured," so she went with my blessing and an invitation to return without feeling embarrassed should she ever need more help. The patient has, of course, the right to decide how well she wants to get. She had little money, a long trip to my office, she was happily married, she became pregnant, and was in general getting along rather well. There was no reason to hold her.

Ed, the most aggressive of the three men, good-looking and in his late thirties, made it obvious from the start that in order to attain his goals he would use his charm to get his way passively. In spite of a good working relationship with him, I most often represented the depriving hated childhood image of his mother, whereas the women in the group were the objects of his oedipal acting out. Their youth, slim figures, and attractiveness disguised the fact that they stood for the damaged oedipal mother. His behavior in the group revealed certain facts that his accounts of outside affairs never touched upon. Vi's willingness to yield bored him, whereas Jo's verbal rebuff made him eager to know her. But whenever either girl became angry with him he quickly began to court her. When someone pointed this out he had his first insight into the deeper and less ego-syntonic motive in his affairs.

His defenses were on the whole counterphobic. He was, for instance, very daring in the water under the most dangerous conditions, his underlying fantasy being that he was swimming near some sharks and succeeded in fighting them off, but continued to fear they might swallow him. Behavior prompted by this fantasy brought him often into serious difficulties. It was easier in the individual sessions to work with his need to bring destruction upon himself and to deal with his omnipotent gratifications in the group. The group challenged him on the many small signs of his arrogance as revealed in his flamboyant manner of entering the room late and drawing attention to himself, his frequent absences, his tendency to forget the members' names, and to forget an event in which he had engaged their sympathy only the week before. He usually tried to laugh off any angry encounter and earned the title "laughing boy" until he got over the habit.

Al, a man of about thirty-three, impressed one first as a very young boy who was unsure of himself, and who in the manner of a friendly puppy wanted to please, and yet was quick to experience criticism and rebuff. He responded to Vi's attention quite happily, but alienated her by his romantic interest in the less responsive and to him unavailable Jo, who gave him a hard time with her ambivalent behavior. His most noticeable characteristic was the striking difference between the way he was able to make acute intelligent observations about others but became practically inarticulate when trying to say something about himself. At such times he would talk in such a floundering and garbled fashion that he quickly lost the attention of the group. Nor could he think through a problem of his own in trying to reach a decision or make a judgment. It was as if a fog had descended and prevented any clear assessment of reality. His bodily movements, described by the group as "flapping around," spoke loudly of his helplessness, his uncertainty, and his passivity. He sat on his spine a good deal of the time, his muscles lax, his shifts of position indeterminate. The invasion of his thinking by his emotional conflicts prevented real insight—for this he substituted "lip service." His ability to follow through with decisions and reality testing was negligible. It seemed best, therefore, to try to work with the ego so that he could cooperate in the analysis.

I was able to utilize the group's impatience with him to make him aware of how this characteristic operated against him. He was furious at first, for he had tended to ignore this defect and think of himself as very articulate and intelligent. When he realized that we were quite ready to grant his intelligence and only wanted him to use it in his own behalf, he began to cooperate in investigating the inconsistency. During the process his secret image of himself as very small (he was actually six feet tall) and helpless came to light. In childhood, helplessness had been Al's only means of winning victories over his mother's demands that he be a "big boy." It had successfully defeated his school teachers and bosses, and was about to conquer the therapist and the group as well. That he was destroying himself in thus securing his own illusion of omnipotence had only begun to register with him since he talked about it with the group. There his lip service (pseudo-compliance) with my interpretations was sharply questioned, and led to his realizing that he had always made it a point to give his mother what she disdainfully called "lip service." This method, he admitted, with a smug little grin, had "fixed her" and given him a chance to indulge secretly in his infantile gratifications and feel justified about it. "No wonder," said Jo, "you're fixing up Dr. Durkin in exactly the same way." Ed pointed out that he was cheating himself. Al laughed, and said, "Oh great, but where do I come in." We noticed that thereafter he used fewer of his mother's truisms, but occasionally slipped back into his helpless feelings and still often "quoted Durkin" in the group discussions instead of thinking for himself.

Hy had been sent by a psychiatrist to join my group because he could not afford individual treatment. After seeing him a few times individually I felt he could not in any case have continued to work this way because of his extreme ambivalence. He presented himself to the group as a paragon of proper behavior. His reaction formations were his major defense against his fear of falling apart. They could not be touched on for some time because there was the possibility of a psychotic break. The group seemed to follow my unspoken lead in this respect. They commented instead on his fear of ever being wrong and his unwillingness to say how he really felt about anyone in the group. We learned that he scorned Al who acted out some of the impulses against which Hy had erected his reaction formations, and was scorned in return as a "square" and a conformer by Al in order to defy his own superego. Hy's apparent aggressiveness was belied by his voice and his posture which indicated that he was really on the brink of giving in to his urge toward passive submission. His bursts of anger at Al were merely the last line of defense.

Hy's inconsistency was questioned by the group. He seemed to be making an implicit appeal for help, but when Jo offered him realistic help she was abruptly brushed off. Vi had tried sympathy and was criticised for her effort. Their complaints made it necessary for Hy to face one of the ways he brought about his own disappointment and discontent.

As I surveyed the group during the early sessions, I felt that in spite of the rather large proportion of narcissism in these five people, there was enough variety of character defenses to stimulate interaction and keep it fairly self-propelling. Al's helplessness would not be tolerated by the others, who had developed their own ways of fighting authority. In their very objections to his passive behavior, they would come to recognize their own dependent needs. Jo's insistent coolness and detachment would be disliked by all and their insistence on her becoming involved would help her break through. After that, it would not be long before we could question her need for presenting such an idealized self-image and hiding those parts of herself she rejected but secretly indulged in— seductiveness, self-pity, infantile rage. Her strong motivation for therapy would prevent the others from indulging in the more obvious resistances such as chatting. She would find a partner to act out her neurotic relationships with men in which she revealed double contradictory communications. Vi's secretiveness would be severely tested by Ed's voyeurism and down-to-earth stress on the concrete immediacy of experience. His own acting out might be admired by the more constricted members but its ego syntonicity would certainly be questioned in the long run. Would Jo fall prey to the temptation to act out outside of the group with him? I must watch for the first signs to help them verbalize their fantasies instead. As it happened, Jo had had her fill of rejections from men; and Vi was too available and clinging to interest him in more than mild flirtation. I have spoken of the clash between Hy and Al. It was bound to help each understand his rejected self in the other. It was a matter therefore of waiting to see these defensive traits reveal themselves in the interaction and to stand ready to explore them at the right moment. If the group did not take the lead at that point, I would have to be ready to do so. There would of course be times when my own knowledge of preconscious derivatives and unconscious motivation would serve to add psychological depth to the common-sense appraisal of each other.

Jo's well adjusted coolness, Vi's sweet submissiveness, Al's helpless confusion, Ed's sexual acting out, and Hy's anxious need to be right and his pseudo-independence would all need to be explored and the underlying conflicts investigated in terms of their specific life experiences. The starting point for each would be when some interchange with another member gave us the clues to these defense patterns and why they were not really working. We knew that they had railroaded Jo into heartbreak after heartbreak; Vi into longwinded sadomasochistic relations with a man; Hy into a hostile dependent relationship with his wife; Al into homosexuality; and Ed into bankruptcy and broken marriages. Our problem was to discover, through their intragroup relationships and behavior, what self-deceptions brought about these disastrous results. If we could find out why they had once seemed necessary and were now mere excess baggage, perhaps they might risk letting down their guards.

The group, which had been discussing sex rather frankly, was in this session preoccupied with the voyeuristic-exhibitionistic aspects of it, probably because of the presence of the recording device. They all seemed to have a good deal of anxiety about gratifying these infantile drives. Since Ed, the impulsive character, was the least controlled and most articulate in expressing them, he acted as the spokesman for the group. He and Jo took the active roles, playing out the exhibitionistic elements while expressing their curiosity verbally in the content of their conversation. The others became the observers. It was as if they saw and heard mother and father together. They were puzzled, anxious, interested, and critical by turns. Vi was relatively quiet. Following a recent very active period, she had made definite progress and was now consolidating her gains, as it were. Al competed briefly with Ed for the active role toward Jo but could not as yet be assertive enough to carry it out. He was disappointed, and expressed his anger destructively by insisting on his interpretation of Ed's behavior although it was not at all in line with the group's interest. Thus he became the deviant, isolating himself somewhat from the group. His way of defeating himself was clear; but since it was neither central to the

group's discussion nor interfering too much with it I did not take
it up at this time. Hy's slowly diminishing struggle to use reality
and rationality to ward off his unacceptable feelings brought him
into the central role at the end of the hour. He began to understand how his hostile dependent attitudes prevented his achievement of mature gratification. The relationship between the way he
behaved with the group members and with his wife and mother
would gradually become clear to him. This was a crucial first step.
The session on the whole showed up the close connection between
the oral and the genital drives and how readily hostility is mobi-
lized as a defense.

It is the author's conclusion, based on a variety of experiences,
that no single recording can actually demonstrate group therapy
process. Tape recordings have the advantage of revealing the messages communicated by the tone of voice, pace, and decibels; but
all the physical postures, movements, and expressions are still missing. And this lack obscures the role of the therapist as much as it
leaves incomplete the interaction among the patients. Nor can a
verbatim recording convey the context of the session in the therapeutic process. Therapy is an ongoing process whose meaning is
obscured when broken up into units. Once an effective analytic
group situation has been established, minor errors and missed opportunities on the part of the therapist are not as destructive as
they may seem to someone who listens to one session out of context.

Our recording of this mixed open group of three men and two
women was made toward the end of the first year. It was the first
of five consecutive tapes and was selected because it seemed fairly
representative of analytic group psychotherapy in process. It
shows, for example, that as meaningful group situations come up,
whether in terms of problems brought up for discussion or in terms
of the immediate group interaction, they are explored by the members, under the leadership of the therapist. The aim is to examine
the present behavior, to show that its distortions and inappropriateness reflect past conflicts which are demonstrably both unnecessary and detrimental in the present. The patients contribute their
reactions, including their emotions, reasoning, and value judgments as frankly as possible; while the therapist deals with resistance and transference when these seem to block the channels of
communication or the therapeutic movement.

For about two weeks the group had known about the plan to record some sessions and of course their reactions to the project had been rather thoroughly explored. I did not ask them to decide for or against this undertaking, but told them of the plan and invited discussion. Their responses ranged from reasonable interest and hope that the experience might help, even though it made them nervous, through a variety of voyeuristic-exhibitionistic reactions and to some evidence of deeper narcissistic pleasure and fears. I had been most concerned with Hy's initial denial that he was not bothered at all. The group got him to admit some concern on the level of a wish to sound good. I did not sound out the probable underlying paranoid anxiety because I felt that his defenses against it were strong enough to hold. I planned to proceed step by step, dealing with further reactions to the recorder as they took place.

As the members arrived on this first day, there was some joking about "being on the air." I joined with them a little and then commented on the tension among us all. On the whole, there was only moderate reaction. However, when there was a moment of uncertainty, it is interesting to note that they began again to talk about the recording. Its covert effect was marked, however, in the pronounced voyeuristic-exhibitionistic material which was produced.

THE SESSION

(The preliminary comments reflected some anxiety about the machine. Then Jo complained that the business of recording was really consuming too much of her precious treatment time which she felt was insufficient anyway, since she was only "in the group." Vi asked her what she meant.)

Jo: Well I told you, you know, that I didn't get enough time. I wish I could be in individual treatment, and now this is more time wasted. (This comment of Jo's ushers in a new direction for her in relation to the group. Up to this time she had presented herself as a well-adjusted person who was able to use her psychiatric knowledge to help other members. She *had* told of her problems with boy friends—about the relationships which always started well and ended in her being rejected and angry. The group had been able to show her some of the ways in which she helped to bring this about, and as a result she was maintaining somewhat more stable relationships. But until we could break through the barrier against feeling, no basic change could be expected. It had been implicit, but not yet acknowledged, that with these men she began as she had in the group, by appearing quite admirable and well adjusted. Slowly she began to feel deprived and then became demanding. That she was actually refusing her mother's help to pay for therapy has been mentioned. Her underlying concept of herself as injured and deprived had been evident to the therapist, but no concrete evidence had made any such interpretation appropriate. In the present session she began for the first time to approach her unconscious envy of others who have more.)

Hy: Well, why don't you talk then ... you came five minutes late, you know?

(Jo looked uncomfortable and a little taken aback.)

Th[1]: What about that, Jo?

Jo: My feeling about the matter is that time itself isn't a particularly real problem. I have a compulsive feeling about it. As Hy said, I could have come here earlier and could have talked more. I mean I have funny ideas about wasting time. (The stirrings of insight begin to break through the intellectual recognition.)

Th: Do you feel that you're not getting enough from us?

Jo: Well, if I had to say it over again I wouldn't say it that way. I would say I'm not getting the time, not that I'm not getting-uh-enough when I do come to therapy. I don't say that is the group—that the group isn't functioning well enough to give me what I want. (Evidently she wanted more from me rather than the group, but she was not yet ready to acknowledge it and there was no need to press her.)

Th: How would you say it now?

Jo: Well, I said it that way last time. My beef is that I'm not in therapy enought. (She was still hiding the "I want more.")

(Vi chuckled—no one else commented.)

Th: What's the matter, Vi?

Vi: I don't know (giggled). Maybe I'm embarrassed at having the opportunity for a private session (giggled). I was saying—I said last week in group that I felt pretty happy about things in general.

[1] Therapist.

And everyone else was unhappy. Now I feel like I shouldn't have private sessions when others don't. (Turned anger against herself.)

Jo: (Giggled too.) It's nice that you're happy and that you have enough money. (Her tone of voice indicated the fundamental but unconscious insincerity of her remarks.)

Vi: Well I don't know. I don't know how to express it. I just get. . . .

Jo: I know what you mean—as I said to you when I was trying to explain my feelings about specific boys—I don't know what the other side of me is. It's so hard for me to say anything. (Laughed slightly.) You know like that time when Dr. Durkin said to describe what your feelings are and she said, "Boy it sounds like an intellectual dissertation!" (She seemed to have some vague awareness of the warded-off feelings.)

Vi: You do sound intellectual. . . .

Hy: I don't think Vi expressed herself clearly in what she was trying to get across.

Vi: It's like what I do when anything good happens—I can't quite believe it can be me. I don't know how to tell you. It's not that I don't want to . . . It's that I can't . . . I feel funny when other people are feeling worse than me. Hearing other people and being with four other people who have been so unhappy the last few weeks even more so than usual. I don't know how to. . . .

Jo: Is that sort of like reaching out to . . . I don't know—to people who are less fortunate than you when you do that. It's kind of a way maybe—it's kind of a way of making yourself unhappy (sensed Vi's masochistic needs).

Vi: Oh, I don't want to become unhappy just because you might be (denial).

Jo: Why did you feel unhappy then?

Vi: No I didn't. I just felt. . . .

Jo: Did you feel guilty?

Vi: I don't think it was guilt either. It was just strange. I don't know what the word is for the way that I felt . . . I'm not. . . . Actually, I don't think I'd offer to say to Jo, "Here you take one of my sessions." I don't feel that bad. I don't know what the word is to describe it. Or maybe it's a different feeling for me. Because usually if I think of myself as being unhappier than other people who are worse off than me, and maybe if I find myself in the strange position of being a little better off, I don't exactly know what to do. (Vi used to make a cult of unhappiness. She is in the process now of learning to accept good things for herself. It's still new and confusing to her.)

Jo: You said that you used to envy me ... and now you make me feel like a poor pathetic thing. (Jo was having to face two opposite images of herself.)

Vi: Well, I—that is, I felt that last week almost was the first time that you really expressed your feelings about yourself.[2] And you weren't just talking about things; and even before that—I mean you gave me different pictures of yourself from what you've seemed like since the beginning of the group.

(Jo looked disconcerted and puzzled. I tested to see if she could move ahead on this.)

Th: (To Jo) You don't like that "pathetic" side of yourself? (Since she wasn't ready, she changed the subject and I felt she must have the right to do this.)

Jo: You know I was thinking after the session last week. I drove Al over to Second Avenue. I was looking for a parking space and he said, as if he would like to extend himself to me a lot, "I'll go on down to the next block with you." And I said, "No, I'll go around," and by the way there was a parking space on the next block you wanted to go down (laughs). Anyway it seemed to me that he had been much friendlier than he had ever been. I was crying last week and was showing a lot of feeling because I was very upset, because I wasn't getting all the attention that I want as my baby self. (Here Jo shifted attention to her rebuff to Al. She'd rather believe herself to be bad than pathetic.)

Ed: Here? (Ed perked up at any kind of emotional expression.)

Jo: Yes, so I burst out crying—at two minutes to seven (ending time). (Her voice was self-derogatory.)

Ed: Hah, you cry and then leave?

Jo: (To Al) But it seemed that you were much warmer to me or you showed much more warmth to me than you ever had before (very quiet) even though I know that you like me, you know.

Al: Well—well I'm sure that this is. . . .

Jo: It's like you were fathering me.

---

[2] Jo had cried.

Al: No, I came closer to talking warmly to you today. (Jo had had a single individual session.) You know when I met you right at the top of the stairs—I mean—It's a feeling I hadn't had for you in a long time ... (Al had for some time given up homosexual experiences. He has been suffering from a problem of impotence with women. In the group he has experienced only tender feelings and fantasies about Jo, but now for the first time he is approaching sexual feelings toward her.)

Th: What feeling, Al? (Wanted to get Al to articulate his feelings.)

Al: I wanted to kiss her—I—she looked sexy.

Ed: You wanted to kiss her in the elevator? (His curiosity and competitiveness were immediately aroused.)

Al: No, downstairs—the elevator was broken and she came up and she was huffing and puffing and her face was suntanned and you know she had a glow—and she walked upstairs. And, you know we exchanged more confidences than I do with the person that usually follows me. And it seemed to me that last week I was no different than I had been any other time. I could be wrong but I don't think so. (Veers away from immediate feeling.)

Jo: I felt it different. And I felt bad that I had refused Al in his effort, you know (laughed) to look around for a parking space, I mean. (She ignored the immediate incident and focused on how refusing she was last week—warding off feeling.)

Al: Well, personally I was well aware of the situation, I asked "Do you want me to or should I?" You know, the same old thing: Don't make a decision until I've asked the question of Mama: Should I? In other words, I didn't say "You leave off here and I'll look for a space" or whatever I wanted to say. I phrased it as a question. (Al gave up the positive move and responded to her unconscious rebuff by falling into an old habit of futile self-criticism. Jo unaware of this looked baffled.)

Th: Do you know what he has been getting at? (Hoped to bring the focus back to Al's positive feelings.)

Jo: Yeah. He can't be decisive. Well I can't be decisive either. When I was decisive and I let him out on his corner I felt bad. I thought that I had pushed away your warmth. (The triple bind. Refuses his immediate feelings, but her manner is seductive and she talks about *last week's* feeling instead of today's.)

Al: Well, I don't know . . . maybe I was so dumb that I didn't dig this . . . well, now . . . I . . . (Al is confused but he still looks interested and flirtatious.)

Jo: I didn't mean an evening (laughs). I meant a parking space (rebuff again). (As soon as the nonverbal message gets to him, she quickly retracts. Here we get a glimpse of her rejection-provoking behavior with men. The group recalls this incident a month or two later in relation to her problems outside.)

Vi: (To Al, who looks hurt). I notice you're sitting back here after your change of seats last week (giggles). (Vi who always feels sorry for "lame ducks" tries to rescue him from Jo's rejection.)

Al: I don't know. Maybe somebody . . . or Durkin should explain to me what all this means. Last Friday I refused to lie down on the couch, and in group I took a different chair. Maybe it's an outward symbol of some sort . . . that I want to change inwardly by external things . . . I can change I suppose. (Here we see Al failing in a struggle to keep his recent increase in self-assertiveness.)

Th: (To Al) How about that? (In response to my encouragement, Al brightened up and asserted himself again.)

Al: I think this one looks radiant today . . . (meaning Jo).

Ed: (Breaks in quickly, and Al allows him to take the lead). Yes . . . very animal . . . straight neck . . . good healthy color . . . then softly, "I'd like to drive you home some night . . . that would be nice". . . . (He touches her arm, then hesitates and looks at the therapist.)

Th: Say whatever comes to your mind, Ed. (Whenever there are signs of an impulse to act out the therapist tries to get at the fantasies which underlie it. In this case I knew it must concern a particular fantasy in which Jo represents his mother's old doll. He used to retreat to the attic with it to masturbate whenever he became anxious. It was usually when he couldn't get what he wanted from his mother. The doll, therefore, was both a symbol and a denial of mother. The group had already learned about this.)

Ed: (Continues to Jo) I'd like to exchange . . . very relaxed and intimate conversation with you. Because I've never had a chance to . . . Couldn't do it . . . Couldn't do this in front of a lot of other people. . . .

Th: What would you say to her if you had the chance?

Ed: (Thinking) I don't know. . . .

Jo: I'm very ill at ease with you, Ed. You know, when we walked out, not last week but the week before, and you were kind of kidding around. (Again Jo prefers last week's episode to the threatening present.)

Ed: What was I kidding around about?

Jo: Oh, well, we were going down in the elevator and you said, "Why don't you go out and get fucked" and uh—

Ed: Why don't I go out and get fucked?

Jo: "Why don't you," meaning me. Why don't I go out and get fucked. You were kind of bantering around. Social gaieties. . . .

Ed: I was probably making out I'd like to do it to you.

Jo: I think, kind of like, I dig your insincerity in a way and I don't know what to do with it, you know, I mean you're the kind of person that I used to react to, you know, I don't want to react in that silly social way. (Jo's manner of speaking indicates her anxiety at facing his urgency.)

Ed: Well, you would like it to be real and I would like it to be real, yet the reality—the thing we're thinking of as a reality—is somehow just not reality, or the thing that I'm thinking of as reality somehow isn't reality . . . It would be—I don't know, somehow it isn't. I can't put my finger on it. (Usually glib enough, Ed flounders and grasps at stereotyped words when he has to face his anxiety instead of acting out.)

Jo: Well, I know—like for me—I don't. I would like someone to come along and say these things and mean them for a change. You know, and—like every guy means it only for the moment. And this is the kind of thing I get messed up with and I don't want it.

Ed: True. (Jo "brings influence to bear" and he is forced to observe himself through her eyes. In individual sessions he keeps me in a different category, and outside he leaves if the girl won't "play.")

Vi: It sounds like myself. I don't know whether I go for that type of person any more or not. I'm lucky if I don't. I guess I'm not really sure whether I do or not. I sort of had a feeling like . . . I was for a while. (Partly identified with Jo, Vi experienced the change which is beginning in herself.)

Al: I take it your romance has got complications all of a sudden?

(Defeated by Ed, Al joins in to interrupt the tête-à-tête and regains self-esteem by attempting the therapist role. Hy sits listening intently but looking anxious.)

Vi: Huh?

Al: You got complications in your romance?

Vi: No, it's going very nice. Everything's going along very well, I feel as if I got away from—well—people like . . . an honest, an honest person who means things when he says them. And I feel lucky.

Th: How do you feel toward Ed right now? (She once flirted with Ed. I wanted to tie her into the immediate group situation and work through a little more.)

Vi: I guess I still have a feeling toward Ed—a little like this feeling I had toward this other fellow I told you about that came to see me one Sunday. I had the satisfaction that he called me again recently and now I have the satisfaction of not wanting to see either him or you (Ed).

Ed: What did he do to make you not want to see him?

Vi: Well, he said he'd call and he didn't call. He's a—uh. . . .

Jo: Is he the guy you had that dream about?

Vi: No. I liked this man very much, I was very attracted to him. And he knew it and he didn't really like me. It was just one of those things where he said I'll call you next week and he finally called three months later on a Sunday. And I don't want him any more and I'm glad that I don't and I'm not interested any more.

Al: Why don't you want him any more?

Ed: Supposing he called you and like—well, he hadn't waited three months? Of course he didn't, but supposing he had. (Ed refers to himself really. He needs to see himself as the star of all stories).

Vi: I probably would have still been interested in him. I mean, if he had called me the week he said he was going to. I would have gone and it would have been different. But I feel that uh, well, in the meantime I found this other guy—which, of course, is the difference. I don't know what I would do if I weren't going with someone else. But actually by not calling me for three months he did insult me. And at least it gives me the satisfaction of turning around and not wanting him. Now, he didn't really want me and I feel a little of that revenge toward Ed, too. . . . (Ed, probably threatened by Vi's repudiation, gets tangled up with the "mike" and regains center of stage. The group laughed).

Jo: (Who has been thinking hard) You know, like what I was thinking—what I would do is—I would want to have somebody like you like me, and I would try to have you like me and I'm just beginning to feel, you know, maybe that it's the wrong type of person. That I'm coming up against something completely no good (dawning insight). Of course, my bit is that I have to have everybody like me. I play up to everybody. (This playing-up behavior, however, is merely a façade to disguise her unconscious compulsion to be rejected. Jo chooses men of whom she is very uncertain either because they are withdrawn or aloof and rejecting. She charms them and then goes to bed with them almost immediately. Thereupon she becomes demanding and begins to present herself as needy and deprived. Once Ed said to her, "As soon as they get into "pussy," it's the beginning of the end. I think you plan it that way.")

Vi: Without regard to liking him, you still want him though? On a permanent, not permanent, but you know.... (Vi is trying to understand her own needs.)

Jo: Well I think with Ed that if he got to liking me, he would stop liking me after a while because his reasons for liking me wouldn't really be sincere. It would be based on his own problems (growing insight).

Vi: Yeah, but what would you want? Would you want him to keep on liking you, more or less permanently or at least for a long time?

Jo: Well that's what I've been thinking—I've been wanting to have people ... but.... (Here we begin to see the struggle between id and superego, which has been unconscious. The ego at the behest of the superego takes over her verbal behavior. She *says* no. Nonverbal and unrecognized seductiveness is, however, observable. In this encounter she begins to examine the two sides of the conflict.)

Jo: (Turns to Ed) Yeah, and at this point I feel flattered and glad, you know, that Ed makes approaches to me and likes me. You know, Ed, or anyone in this situation ... I still can't say always resist, you know, and I still have to ... uh ... to have the ... uh, you (to the therapist) in back of me telling me I should say "no." This makes me see these things very clearly ... I should want....

Th: I think something *in you* feels that "should."

Ed: (Impatient with all this talk) Go on, say yes! Do you want me sexually or would you like to—would you just give yourself sexually because—to please me if I was interested or if I showed an interest in you of a sexual nature.

Jo: I think it's the last and I'm not at a point where I really know what I want.

Hy: That must be very flattering to Ed (hides his envy).

Jo: You know—I don't know what I'd say. I keep thinking of this fella, Lou (the latest boy friend) and I think—suppose he should really want me. I recognize this guy isn't healthy and why can't I say—well this guy isn't healthy—yet I can't say no.

Ed: What do you mean, isn't healthy?

Jo: Well this is the guy who is looking for a perfect image.

Al: You weren't here when she said that he could never really be interested in Jo because she didn't measure up to his ideal . . . of a woman. (A chance to explain to Ed—Al asserts himself where ordinarily he would have withdrawn by now.)

Jo: Well, here's a guy who is constantly looking for an ideal, an image. I've gotten this before. And I can't get away from something I feel is unhealthy, but I still have to want to make him interested in me too. (Realistically Jo is right but such critical dissection of the boy and herself are typical signs of resistance for her.)

Ed: Well, He says he doesn't want you—but he wants you. (Speaking for himself.)

Jo: He doesn't want me but he wants to continue seeing me. He doesn't want to marry me.

Ed: Oh. Does he want to fuck you? (In verbally acting out his curiosity he nevertheless helps the others face the fact that they are evading the sexual thoughts and feelings.)

Jo: (Sighs) No.

Ed: Does that interest you in him sexually?

Jo: Not particularly. I'm not very—not passionately drawn to him. I haven't had much to do with him physically. I wasn't initially attracted to him sexually. You know—but it's just the idea that someone is paying attention to me. You know, even if it isn't a good attention, if it isn't a whole thing . . . I suppose I feel something is better than nothing.

Ed: Let's you and me do something instead. (Again his impulsivity brings the focus to the immediate concrete experience.)

Jo: From the frying pan into the same (laughs). I'm trying to find out why I do these foolish things!

Th: What are you doing with this, Ed? (Trying to make Ed aware of his resistance here. He wants to play rather than work.)

Ed: Oh, I don't know (sighs). I don't know.

Al: It's not like you not to make a comment on it.

Ed: Well, I'm not outside—I'm involved in it.

Al: No—uh, now in here—

Ed: —In a sense I am—so I can't. I'm not thinking—I mean, I'm sort of watching myself or ... (He becomes anxious when he can't go into action.)

Jo: Well, you said you were very interested in why you do this kind of thing to girls, but—I mean, here you came in and started with the social business and with the physical play. Maybe something else is really on your mind. (She refers to his having said he turns to sex when he's anxious.)

Ed: (Avoids facing his anxiety by acting out verbally) Well physically often ... and the idea of your ... like every time when we leave here and you're going off to your place ... like your place would be my attic or something. Your place would be my escape. And somehow you're alone ... and I would love to be—like I say, I would love to talk intimately with you. It's like goofing off in ... somewhere in my past or something ... so I could just feel comfortable for uh ... for a while ... like I know it wouldn't have any lasting significance or anything like that. I mean realistically it's impossible. (He squirms in his seat and gets red.)

Th: What would you do? For example? (Trying to get Ed to continue his fantasy. Once a fantasy is fully conscious it tends to lose dynamic force.)

Ed: What would I do? Well I would ... (sighs) I would go along, you know, to your house, we'd probably stop and have a drink and talk ... and it would be like the feeling of uh—like rapport, something sympathetic or hungry, going back and forth would be established. And we would—um ... it would be compulsive on my part that—I sleep with you. I mean that it would be a strong feeling. I mean like we would go and cook dinner and talk all during the cooking about—I don't know—you know, personal things . . . and . . . we'll make love . . . (sighs) probably—probably—you know—right after dinner. (Laughs.)

(Group laughs, out of anxiety.)

Ed: One story struck me so much like this today. Somebody said: "Did you hear about the sexy mouse?" "What happened?" "Got caught by a pussy!" (Ed laughs.) So the poor little mouse he was caught in a trap, like . . . (Group laughed. The close relationship between the genital and oral drives are illustrated by this joke. His joke reveals this underlying fear of being trapped by the woman, and the fact that the fear is on the level of power rather than adult sexuality.)

Al: I don't know—there's something Ed said there that I don't quite agree with. I don't think we're so much different outside than we are here.(Al feels left out but persists in making his interpretation which is outside of their interest. Thus he further isolates himself.)

Hy: Speak for yourself.

Al: I don't think so (mumbling).

Ed: (To Al) Well, I agree with that—I don't mean in that sense, but except there are so many . . . except here we're talking instead of acting.

Th: And you find it so hard to think about things before doing them?

Ed: Yeah, it's very difficult sometimes. I mean, you ask me to talk about what I would do. It's hard for me to say what we would do because . . . because—I just do things—I don't talk or think too much about it. I do things compulsively. I mean, I would have to sleep with you (to Jo) . . . uh . . . but here I can't. If I did, I don't think I'd be too aware of you as a person thongh I would be aware of you—terribly aware of you at a purely physical level. (Here we see a deepening of insight in Ed to which Jo responds. Shortly after this session Ed began to see Jo as a real person. He said he had never had a woman he really talked to before—except me).

Jo: Yeah (to herself). It makes me very sad when Ed talks because this is the kind of thing I have been accepting from men as real feeling. You know, I've been hoping that it's real . . . and of course it isn't . . . (Getting to the meaning of this behavior helps her recognize the unconscious impulses that she has thought of as realistic before.)

Ed: It's a certain—it's a feeling, but it's not a feeling which could give you any—well, it's a kind of feeling. Sure it's a feeling, but it's not a kind of feeling you can live with.

Jo: Yeah. Well, it's not the kind of feeling that I want. I want to think that men would be in love with me, you know, and would want me permanently and yet I take this kind of thing, you know, hoping that, you know, this was it. But—maybe—it's a good way of not getting it. (All looked very serious. Their voices are low but intense.)

Vi: How can you really tell the difference? In the beginning of a relationship? You don't know whether—I mean, how can you? (She was trying to interpret her own experience through theirs.)

Hy: If she can't she hopes (sarcastically).

Vi: I mean, anyone—I don't mean exactly her— I mean me— how could I tell the difference? I mean I couldn't either.

Hy: Can't you hope also? That's what any of the rest of us do (bitterly).

Jo: Well, I think with somebody like Ed or anybody who acts out a lot, very fast you can . . . you know, begin to suspect that there is something fishy about it because they don't know you. You know, this is the "throwing yourself into it" thing. The girl doesn't mean anything. It could be any girl.

Ed: Yeah, then you can realize you are a symbol for something which isn't quite there or is not quite you.

Jo: Well, I start to carry on before it occurs to me, you know—.

Ed: Yeah?

Jo: That it isn't the man.

Ed: Well, then you are just as unaware of me as I am of you. Under that circumstance . . . you are using me! (He has thought of himself as being aggressive with women. He is just beginning to learn that he is often passively exploited by his counterpart.)

Jo: (Laughed) Yeah.

Th: This is something neither of you usually think of. (Underlining their growing insight.)

Ed: About her being unaware of the "me"? In men?

Th: Yes. The fact that she is doing it just as much as the men are doing it.

Jo: Well, it's hard for me to make myself realize that—because it means that I'm not so nice. (Jo used a good deal of "denial" to preserve her self-image and here began to understand why.)

Ed: Nice-schmice!

Hy: So where then does the reality begin? (Hy's ambivalence showed. Made anxious by this sexual stimulation he tried to put us on an intellectual level. He also wants to get into this discussion and does so in the only way he knows.)

Th: I have a feeling you are all very curious, yet upset, at hearing Ed and Jo talk like this.

Hy: I gather that everyone must be doing something . . . well, playing some sort of role when he does—uh—put his best foot forward toward a young lady—or when a girl does the same sort of thing. So then it's difficult to say just what is reality. Actually I should imagine that this is reality—the fact that people are uncertain of each other and that they don't know what the other person is thinking. Well, that seems to be the reality to me. I don't know what the other thing is.

Vi: I can see where I have a tendency to pretend. I just like the idea of love so much that I force it on that person—even when it isn't there.

Hy: How?

Vi: Well, I mean if I would feel sexually attracted to a man, even if I honestly think—realize—that he hasn't got the real thing—to make me like him . . . I just don't let myself see it . . . or I say it isn't important or it will come, or something.

Th: You're idealizing it? Because plain sex seems wrong to you?

Vi: Yes—So I feel if the sexual part of it is there I feel that the rest of it has to be there as an excuse maybe for feeling that way or. . . .

Hy: That sounds a little unrealistic. (Hy was very tense. He seemed to be warding off sexual stimulation by the group, yet wanting to know and also to reveal his own problems.)

(Jo laughs.)

Ed: Oh, but this is the way she is.

Vi: Just because I want—like I want to be in love so much and I want someone to love me, I do that. And I was thinking that even with J (the former sadistic boy friend) that happened where all these horrible things—I've—I mean I knew that they were happening, but I didn't let myself know that they were so horrible, but they were. Because then I wouldn't be able to—to love him any more, if I recognized them. Or if I could have seen that he really didn't love me . . . (Growing insight for Vi. There was a silence, full of tension. Hy looked at the therapist.)

(After a few minutes:)

Th: Well—Hy—what is it—what are you feeling? (He looks upset, angry.)

Hy: Uh—that's a very nice dress you're wearing (reaction formation).

Th: Thank you—but you seem upset.

Hy: Well—I was sort of curious as to when you were going to make some sort of comment. (He was the spokesman for the "observers" who were puzzled and wanted an answer to their infantile curiosity from me.)

Th: For instance?

Hy: Well—in general. The fact that our conversation of the last—well—fifteen minutes—(Hy's tension has been mounting during the talk about sex. Besides being curious, he has also been wanting to talk himself, yet trying to ward off his unacceptable feelings.)

Th: You feel I should have helped out somehow?

Hy: I was just looking at you, expecting you to say something. (Hy was probably right. I may have been too much involved with the content of the discussion to sense that the "observers" were not only curious but angry with me for letting it go on. At any rate, I was put off by Hy's use of "what is reality," so that I didn't recognize his resistance. Ordinarily I would have said, "You must be disappointed in me." There are a few minutes of silence. Since I still do not deal with Hy's angry resistance, the whole group becomes rather anxious. They quickly attach it to the presence of the recorder and as they talk about it their feelings about me come through again.)

Al: There's going to be a whole blank spot on that record there.

Jo: I was thinking of that too.

(The whole group laughs nervously.)

Ed: What are you going to do with the record? Erase it or keep it and play it back to us?

Th: What do you imagine I might do?

Ed: I was wondering if you would play them for other people? I have worked professionally with people who analyze conversations.

Th: You feel I might betray your confidence?

Hy: (Cynically) At parties only. (All laugh. Hy's rage is evident.)

Al: In that case we better make better records than this ... (All laugh.)

Ed: No, I don't suspect you ... you'd only do it for professional purposes.

Al: Well I don't think that would be breaking confidence particularly. . . .

Th: I guess it would be natural to be worried about why I would do this. . . .

(Their doubts about me in the open, the tension decreased markedly. They now expressed the voyeuristic-exhibitionistic reactions stimulated by the recorder, directly in relation to it.)

Al: I'm more interested in how I would stack up—how I would show up on this thing. Unless I would be really good, you know, I would hate to hear myself.

Ed: Well, why don't you sing?

Al: La, lalala (group laughed).

Ed: He can really sing!

Al: Well, what do you know! I took lessons once—Oh, not for too long. . . .

Hy: Gee, we never heard about that (looked and sounded envious).

Ed: What did you sing—I once learned "Pussy Willow had a Sweetheart" ... that's appropriate, come to think of it. (All laughed).

(They went on for a bit longer, then as I was about to intervene)

Vi: This isn't a show, for heaven's sake! (Tried to bring them back to the reality of the therapeutic work.)

Th: I wonder what it is you are all doing that bothers Vi?

(But the group was carrying on under its own steam and it seemed best to let them go on until the matter came into clearer focus for them naturally, so I didn't press the point.)

Ed: I wish we could take movies. (He was ready to act out again and in doing so verbally he continued to help the others get to feelings they cannot face easily by themselves.)

Hy: You're very photogenic. (He is stonily ambivalent toward Ed.)

Ed: I meant a dirty movie.

Al: Ohhh—(his face changed—he grinned—was ready to join in.)

Jo: You could play the lead (To Ed).

Ed: You and me. (Smiled at Jo.)

Jo: (Giggled) Not I. (The nonverbal and the verbal communication went in opposite directions here. She giggled but tried to deny her sexuality and her exhibitionism.)

Ed: Why not you?

Jo: I don't think of myself as a lead in dirty movies. (The self-image and resistance.)

Ed: No? (responded to the nonverbal).

Jo: In spite of my lurid past I like to think of myself as a very sweet young thing. (Giggled. Recognized her conflict and so prepared the way for resolution.)

Ed: Can you conceive of yourself pictorially making—fucking—you know—fucking and making love?

Jo: I hadn't thought of that. And—I don't like to.

Ed: Did'ja ever make love in front of a mirror?

Hy: How does one make love in front of a mirror? (He is stimulated again.)

Al: I don't know what you're getting at. I mean—there's something that you're getting at that you're not saying. (Feeling excluded, he recognizes hostility in Ed through his own anger.)

Ed: Just asking her. (His interpretation was probably true but it was too far away from consciousness to be understood by him.)

Th: Well, he means what are you doing with this now?

Ed: I don't know, I'm just asking questions. (Preferred not to think about it.)

Hy: He's playing in the attic. (Referring to childhood masturbation and the doll fantasies Ed had told about. Wanted to get back to sex yet frustrated himself by giving lead to Ed.)

Al: No, more than that. (More persistent than usual.)

Ed: I'm experimenting. I want to see their reactions—to look. . . . (Al cleared throat and started to repeat his point.)

Ed: I seriously want to know what other people feel, what they want to do. What women want to do.

Hy: That's an odd sort of question to ask a woman. I've ... (He was envious of Ed's freedom—yet needed to be rational. I made a mental note to be sure to get to Hy later.)

Ed: I've made love in front of a mirror with women and yet I don't know exactly why. Or why they did or why I did myself ... except it was stimulating—to me it was stimulating. And to some people it is and to some it isn't. (He resented having to understand it and yet refused to go on.)

Hy: I was thinking about the question before that, about—making movies.

Al: I was thinking—was the mirror on the ceiling or was it on the wall. (Too stimulated to persist he joined Ed in the "play" and encouraged him.)

Ed: What?

Al: Was the mirror on the ceiling or was it on the wall? (Giggles.)

Ed: On the wall. I couldn't arrange to have it on the ceiling. (Enjoying himself.)

Th: Well, you're very curious, but I got the feeling that you were doing something else with it too. (Hoping he would be able to recognize his desire to shock us.)

Ed: Well, I'm defensive in front of a group of people. Asking some of them do they care for this kind of thing because I can't really make love to her (Jo) in front of a group of people. I can only make sort of a conversational remote. ...

Th: So this is what you were still doing—Hm?

Ed: Yeah, still making love with her.

Th: I think you are all very interested both in seeing and in showing—like when you were little.

Al: I don't know. I had an idea that there was something hostile directed toward Jo, specifically, you know. (Al provided the counterpoint.)

Ed: Hostile?

Al: Yeah. (But the voyeuristic motive was the one he was experiencing. The hostility was unconscious, though implied.)

Hy: May I make a comment at this point? This seems to be a slight playback from last week, when I was sort of looking into what Al was doing. And Al seems to be turning around and using ... those same ... huh ... well, types of media ... playing with it sort of—with other people. (Anxious about sex he turned the tables on Al, thus trying to change the subject.)

(Ed looked upset.)

Th: What do you mean?

Al: Do you think in this particular instance that there is any justification for my saying so? Seems to me that there must have been, because there was a lot of questioning that Ed went through.

Ed: No—I'm growing up sexually because I've been a baby sexually. I've been playing games that I've played all my life.

Ed: No, I don't mean that—(but he went on in a stumbling way —very fidgety again.) It's just—I find—like for all this sexual experience, quote-unquote, that I've had, I know very little about how people have felt about what they were doing because I wasn't terribly aware of what I was feeling myself, because it was a compulsive thing and I just kept doing it. So I seem to—this is something that I should have gone through a hell of a long time ago— about knowing about how people feel about—sex. And yet it was something that I couldn't talk about. And it's only in the last— (coughed)—excuse me—since I've been going through analysis that I've been somehow able to talk even to the extent—which isn't very deep—that I talk about it now. It's sort of like . . . I'm experimenting, which is a little ridiculous and uh . . . (He was becoming aware of the difference between masturbatory sex play and sex in a real relationship.)

Hy: You seem to be going to the other extreme.

Ed: What extreme?

Hy: To shock us! (This is correct. The group and I represent mother.)

Al: No. he seems to me to—(was succeeding in getting the whole group irritated. They ignored him.)

Hy: Well, you say that in the past it was very difficult to talk about sex. Well, here you seem to be going to the—well, what appears to me to be the opposite extreme. And I really don't know you that well—you seem to be talking about these—well almost lurid sort of things—about taking motion pictures and sexual acts and things like that which I'm sure you don't really mean that— just—what it is that—well, as Al says, what it is that you're doing. (Hy took over from Al and the therapist.)

Ed: I'm trying to get closer to it than I have been, that's all. I think. (He acknowledged only the curiosity.)

Th: Do you just want to know more? Are you like a little boy who says to Mommy, "What about it? Who does what to whom?" (This was the level at which I believe Ed was experiencing himself, and so although the others were also correct, I selected this level. He was saying, "My mother didn't let me look enough." The infantile fury at an unconscious level perhaps being acted out here in shocking us.)

Ed: Yeah, momma (to Th) look at my cock and what is it? And what has it got and ... uh ... what do I do with it and how—what goes on in the world with it? And I never had a chance to do this with my mother. I could never tell her whether I masturbated or that I—I used to have dirty books around the house and they would take them and hide them and so I never had like—that emotional relationship with my mother where I could relate or even admit that I—there was such a thing as sex because you know it was dirty and taboo—Jesus Christ! It was taboo! To the extent that when I got a little older and my father would occasionally indulge in a dirty joke and I would be terribly embarrassed ... I wouldn't know how to accept it, in the context of my experience with my mother and father. How could he suddenly tell a dirty joke? (His anger was mounting. He seems to have expected the impossible from his mother.)

(Al was obviously trying to get back in.)

Th: What do you have in mind, Al?

Al: No, somehow I think this whole thing is a little strange because I think Ed is on the defensive when I ask him this question, you know. "What is he doing?" I mean—

Ed: I'm not on the defensive.

Al: You—you took it as uh. . . .

Ed: I took it personally, maybe that's what you mean.

Al: Well, no, uh ... you did take it personally. And you got on the defensive as if I was questioning—you know what your actions are. I mean—you know that there is something wrong with the action of looking at yourself in the mirror. I'm not saying this at all. The only thing I know is that there was a certain play between you two and I thought it was a hostile play because I thought that before, when you and Jo went to tell you that you were the sort of person that she no longer wants ... that you were sort of getting back at her. (This was said more clearly and firmly than Al usually talked, but he was asserting himself at the wrong time and the wrong way.)

Jo: I didn't really say that, I said that Ed was the kind of person I really shouldn't want. But I haven't quite made the break with—

Al: Well, —

Jo: But, uh. . . .

Al: I thought that there was this personal interplay in here where you were using this against her—what she had told you—your anger was behind all your sexual questions toward her. And in other words you didn't really—I mean you weren't really interested in whether she looked at herself in front of the mirror or whether she ever did. But this is just some sort of a way of digging at her. That's only the thing that I felt in it. (Al perceived this deeper motivation because he was angry with Ed. Weeks later we got to it directly, and also at the way Al managed to isolate himself. These were not of central interest today.)

Ed: I really don't see that. (This was said without much expression. He looked puzzled.)

Jo: On the other hand, Ed has been interested, you know in—in. . . .

Ed: Yeah, I was visualizing. I made a movie, I was projecting a movie.

Th: I got a feeling, too, that there was something else in it—as if you were the little boy saying, "See what, I can shock mommy." As if you were taking a little relish in saying these things that nobody else would say.

Ed: Yes, but I don't recall having a feeling of hostility—yes, in the sense that I'm full of hostility to all of them (women). I sort of hit them with my cock, you know—strike at them somehow physically—because—

Th: So making her see herself as the subject of a dirty movie may have been hostile?

Ed: Yeah, I don't know—somehow it's not humiliating. (He denies it.)

Th: No? How do the rest of you experience it?

Ed: Does she seem to think it's humiliating? Because she said "I don't see myself as the heroine of a dirty movie."

Jo: Well, one of the reasons also that I didn't answer was that—because I feel—

Ed: This is not a movie for the world to consume it? It's just a movie for you and I. Two people ... and it's a way of seeing and showing on the ultimate level, I mean, like we act on the stage and we're all displaying ourselves and we want to, and this is a way of displaying ourselves in our more basic natures, like let's get down to the—something more fundamental and show—and see—sex—which is what we're trying to do anyway. So I'm trying to skip too much. Because people ... I want to get sex right down into the—into the—vagina and penis area ... instead of—like the nerve-wracking interlude between, which to me must be nerve-wracking ... the love making—the relationship.... The knowing—the seeing other people and feeling them and getting close to them, in order to make love to them, because I've always avoided this (i.e., real relationships) and wanted to get very close to—the penis—right to the vagina—right to—the things. Because this is what I wanted and not at all the uh ... (tried to justify his rage).

Th: All the subterfuges you felt you got when you were a little boy? (A word Ed has used before to express his frustration.)

Ed: The *nothing* I got when I was a little boy! The *absolute nothing!* (Infantile rage.) So this whole area of getting close to somebody and moving into somebody is very strange to me and very foreign. And so when I was very apprehensive as a little boy when —then I grabbed my cock immediately and played with it. And I can do the same thing ... as an adult with a woman. And I let her do it instead because I don't ... somehow it's not quite as satisfactory as uh ... to sit around and play with yourself—so you have to do it with somebody else. Though it's strictly gratification of myself ... so that (clears throat)....

Th: You are reliving this with Jo but you have never been too aware of what you were doing. (Therapist was trying to pin down something Ed and Jo had glimpsed many times before.)

Ed: I never thought about it at all. (Thoughtfully).

Th: It's almost as if you were a child at home and you were trying to get back at mama. (Enough is enough. I was pushing him too much.)

Ed: Yeah! And here we are, we're part of a group, like this is society. (To Jo) So I could take you and—you and I could go out from society and we could go somewhere else—to a less anxious area. And this would apply to you, too, (to Jo) because you would feel the same way. (Tried to get away from insight and back to "playing.")

Jo: Well that's the thing, I mean, that's one of the reasons I didn't answer because I do the same thing too. (But Jo continues to work.)

Ed: Yes, I'm sure—

Jo: And I didn't know what I—was doing.

Ed: Sure, but you at least can say it here, you know.

Jo: I keep going with men . . . and my mother likes that . . . of course she wants me to get married, but if she really knew about my life she'd die.

Th: So in a way you are pretending to give her what she wants, yet secretly you manage to frustrate her and get revenge on her.

Jo: (Chuckled) (Assent of the unconscious.)

Th: But I have a feeling that you are hurting yourself more than you are her. (Pressed again.)

Jo: Couldn't you open a window in here . . . (Group laughs knowingly. Both are upset by having to face the real meaning of their play and they stop me this way.)

(Ed opened the window and accidentally pulled the curtain down!)

Hy: I was sort of thinking—uh—thinking a few minutes ago of —about what Ed said when he sleeps with a woman all he wants to do is fuck her. He doesn't go through the preliminaries. (Finally mustered up the strength to talk about himself.)

Ed: No, that isn't what I meant. I like to play before—it's romantic—getting down to the physical thing—I don't know—I feel at home there—uh—it's making friends that I guess I'm afraid of. But excuse me, Hy, go ahead.

Hy: I—I didn't get that—(flustered.)

Al: It's the opposite with me—I like the preliminaries more than the act. I mean like when I get with this Jean I was telling you about—it's such a rush—she is in a hurry and I, uh, I get sort of overwhelmed—I don't know why I have to get stuck—sort of take refuge in the preliminaries—like prolonging or stalling. . . .

Hy: (Recovered) I think it's a very essential part of the whole process of whatever is going to happen at the end. And I think that,

well, I don't know—whether—I really don't know if it's so important—but I find it desirable. (Jo laughed, embarrassed.) It's sort of
going through a very exciting novel—and you want to go through
all of these motions, yet you want to finish—and uh—it would be
sort of brutish to push it all aside and, so to speak, get to the meat
of it—like do it in a milk bottle or something. (Struggled against
his primitive sexuality mixed with hostility.)

Al: I don't think it's brutish—I think it's wonderful—I wish I
could.

Hy: I don't know (to Al)—well, go do it in a milk bottle—(made
a grunting noise.)

(Al and Hy were antagonistic. Each hating himself in the other.
Hy's reaction formations were approximately what Al's superego
demands of him. Al on the other hand gave expression to Hy's repressed infantile drives and felt guilty about it.)

Th: Well, that was said with a lot of feeling, Hy.

Hy: Because I think that—uh—

Ed: Did you ever do it in a milk bottle? (Interfered with Hy.)

Hy: I've never done it in a milk bottle.

Al: You haven't? (Laughed)

Hy: No, I'm afraid not.

Ed: D'you ever try?

Hy: Pork barrels or anything like that, no?

Th: What are you trying to express, Hy? (Gave Hy the lead because he was so full of tension and had tried several times to get
in.)

Al: I tried once—I can tell you that.

Hy: No, I think—I think it's very important—all the love and
affection that goes with it. And uh—well, when I think of someone, only thinking of the biological end of it, I—uh—feel that he
only wants to relieve himself, just as I've relieved myself at times—
because of anxiety, but when I'm with a woman I want—I want to
experience all of these different things and let it end up in having
intercourse. But I want all these things that go with it. With the
kissing and the love making. (Responded to therapist's belated recognition of his tension.)

Jo: You still may be talking about establishing a relationship
with the person before that, we don't know.

Ed: Oh, I like sexual foreplay all right, but you are right. I want to get right to the sexual level rather than to be on any other level —like friendship.

Hy: Well, then I misunderstood you, because I thought—

Ed: I'm not going to jump on somebody and stick my cock into them if that's what you're thinking, like a milk bottle. No. (Hy has made him feel misunderstood and Ed was angry.)

Hy: (Cleared throat) Because immediately I thought back to times when—well, in Europe, where I've met prostitutes and I've slept with them. Well, they got undressed and they sat around and —"Well, let's have it, son." That sort of thing repels me. Well, here was the woman and she was there for whatever use I wanted to make of her. And it was awful.

Ed: Well what did you want? Romance? (Still angry.)

Hy: Well, I—to say the least—I was very inexperienced at the time. (Group laughs.) There are a few interesting stories that could go along with that, but we haven't got time enough. (Typically self-deprecating and self-defeating.)

Ed: Not enough tape? (He was still aware of being on the air.)

Th: Sure we have time—and tape. Tell us about it, Hy.

Hy: Yeah. I've always sort of envisioned I was very inexperienced. I had no experience at all before I went to sleep with—uh— a prostitute. And I could have gone to sleep with other women but I was always afraid to. I think I explained the reasons for that last week and in the previous weeks. So here was an opportunity to do whatever I wanted to do and I wanted to be passionate and all the rest of that. And on the very first occasion it took a very interesting turn. I met a girl who was the very same way. She insisted on seeing me again and so on and, uh, when I saw her on the street again at one time she looked very lovely and when I came back to the same place several months later, I didn't want to have a thing to do with her. (Cleared throat.) But she immediately got undressed when I was with her and she expected that, well I was just going to jump on top of her in bed and—bang, bang, and that's the end of it. And that wasn't what I wanted. I wanted to go through all these emotions that I always envisioned. To experience, holding a woman, fondling her, petting her and so on. And uh—

Al: Oohh! My goodness (vicariously).

Ed: (Whistled) Well—

Th: And you gave her all the foreplay, Hy?

Hy: Yeah, and then she said a strange thing to a friend of mine afterwards. I had told her that I had never slept with anyone before and she told my friend that she didn't believe me (cleared throat). Well—I—it's just that—that everything that was—that I had envisioned—everything that I had wanted to do—that was all (laughed slightly). (It would seem that Hy can let himself go only with a woman he feels is of inferior status and who doesn't endanger his self-esteem.)

Ed: You must have brought a bit of romance into the girl's life.

Hy: (Laughed weakly) Yeah, I guess so.

Ed: And she wasn't expecting it. It must have been quite a shock.

Hy: I think he's trying to be funny.

Ed: No! Nooo! What do you think you did?

Hy: Well it's sort of a sore point with me because it's sort of a— I sort of felt that . . . as long as I was paying for it I was entitled to do whatever I wanted to do whether it was adequate or inadequate. Because I didn't want—

Ed: How do you make love to your wife? (A pertinent point but not timely. Still getting back at Hy.)

Hy: Oh, I caress her, I kiss her, I pet her, and I have intercourse with her (allowed himself to be harassed by Ed).

Ed: Same way as with the whore?

Hy: I can't remember—it was . . . A long time ago. About nine years ago or something like that—eight, nine years ago.

Th: What do you have in mind, Ed?

Ed: I was wondering what he really—because he said he didn't remember, and he remembered it—described it, and yet when I associated it with his wife he didn't remember.

Hy: Well, I don't remember all of each and every action that I went through, but when I . . . (was becoming angry).

Ed: I mean the feeling.

Hy: If I had the same sort of feeling toward my wife, when I first slept with my wife?

Ed: How is it now?

Hy: Changed slightly. I still go through all of the emotions. . . . But I think with a strange woman I might be more excited. It would have to depend on the woman, but I . . . (Hy brought his power struggle into the relationship with his wife and it was causing him trouble. He put her on a pedestal and himself in a dependent position. At present she has to support him while he is taking a degree, but the ambivalent attitude exists anyway. He wants to be cared for but he is resentful of any demands from her. Blocked by guilt he cannot assert himself when he should, refuses to "carry his load" and expresses his fury by sulking. Putting her in the role of the preoedipal mother has made inroads in his sexual life with her. He does not want to face his resentment toward her. Here he is acting in the same way with Ed—helpless!)

Jo: Well, it—it sounds kind of funny, you know, that you should have the same kind of emotion that you have with a prostitute that you have with your wife. It sounds as if it's all in you again.

Al: Especially—in view, you know, of what he told us last week. (Had spoken of his anger when his wife asked him to help with the dishes—and his guilty feelings about it.)

Ed: Well it's hardly realistic to have a romantic attitude toward a prostitute.

Th: But is this what you wanted, Hy?

Hy: Wanted what?

Th: Romance? What was it that you wanted so much, Hy, from this girl?

Hy: When I first went to sleep with a woman? Well, I had a sexual desire (cleared throat) Well—a carnal desire. And I'd never experienced this and I felt that I wanted to experience it—and when the opportunities presented themselves I was always embarrassed, flustered, and ashamed, and didn't want to do it. And yet I did want to do it, but didn't. And I was very apprehensive—this time to—with this girl—when uh—this was going to happen. (His fear of trying with women who are his peers was confirmed here.)

Al: It seems to me that you're a little boy looking for love and affection from mother. (Al was using Hy as a kind of proxy to work through his own feelings. Unwittingly he tried to take Hy over a hurdle he could not jump. This is one of the dangers of group therapy by peers; but unless there is too much group pressure, no harm is done. The therapist can help out if necessary.)

Hy: (Sighed) Whoo, what a hot night this is. (Hy was made anxious by Al's attempt to connect this with his feelings for his mother, toward whom he is conscious only of hostility and pity. She is an institutionalized paranoiac. Hy had told us some horrible incidents to show how hostile his mother was to him as a child. Only last week he told us that once when some children came to the house, she refused to give them something to eat and poured a kettle of water down on them instead.)

Al: Yes, but how do you think a little boy feels without that affection?

(Hy clears his throat but cannot talk.)

Th: You felt yourself so unloved by her you turned to your father, didn't you? (He had told us about his much more positive relationship with his father who was an alcoholic, but very kind to him when he was sober. His parents had separated when he was about nine.)

Ed: You deny too much. I believe the fact that you want to get away from your mother so much means that you had some feelings of wanting to get close to her and felt very rejected . . . or. . . .

Hy: I only had the feeling that I couldn't stand her . . . (hostility as defense).

Al: It's the most wonderful thing in the world for a little baby boy to suck a mother's breast. (In a world of his own, his fantasies stimulated by his feeling for Jo, Al did not empathize with Hy. It may indeed be that his hostility toward Hy was operating here.)

Hy: I don't remember doing that—anyway, from what my wife has told me about what goes on at nursery school where she is . . . and from what I've also thought the only thing I ever wanted from my mother was to have her around when I needed her. And I think children of five or preschool age want that same sort of thing—they want that security that mother is standing near, so that if I need her she's there—and I—

Ed: But she wasn't there—and that's why you feel this way.

Th: You can't imagine wanting her to be affectionate—nowadays.

Hy: I sure don't want her to be affectionate to me now. Perhaps my father, yes. With my mother so many other things make me so angry when I think of her that I really don't know—I can't imagine, even—what Al is talking about. I think he's full of shit.

Th: Yes, and when you were little you probably felt she was so mean that you were very angry.

Hy: I just feel that I hate her—both of them really. I'm sorry I ever knew them. Although (laughing) I wouldn't be here now if they didn't "know" each other (doing and undoing).

Ed: I never felt the same way about a whore as—uh—Hy. And at least I can understand his feeling of waiting to get—of . . . of disliking very much the fact that—that's why I never went to whores—although I was not—I'm not putting this on any superior level—

Al: You didn't need them.

Ed: Yes, I—yes, I used other devices—other women.

Hy: I was afraid to use the other devices!

Ed: OK, so I was too, so everybody is.

(Hy cleared his throat.)

Ed: No. I didn't want to because then—I'd have to pay her—like I have to pay you, you know. I mean emotionally I resent paying you (therapist). (In equating me with the prostitute, Ed's underlying hostility to me as the betraying mother was revealed.)

Th: You resent having to pay in any way for being cared for?

Ed: I resent paying for love.

Th: You feel as if it's an unfair demand on you?

Hy: You think you are getting love here?

Ed: Yes—in a sense—emotionally—I mean—like figuratively. Realistically, no—I know that's not what I am here for but—I guess it's what I want—and for nothing.

Hy: I disagree with you entirely—I couldn't care less.

Ed: You sound like you're saying—what kind of asshole are you to think of such a thing—love—

Hy: My only rebuttal is everybody has his own problems and solves them his own way. I don't need love—I only believe that what I am able to do here is express myself as I can't express myself elsewhere, and I'm very grateful for that opportunity. (Again hides behind his rationality.) Although at times I am apprehensive.

Ed: But here this sort of a collective solving of our problems—and part of it is certainly being loved—being accepted and cared about anyway.

Hy: I don't consider that love (his voice broke a little). I don't know what love is. I'm all fucked up any way. (His anxiety breaks through.)

Vi: What's so bad about love? I'm just beginning to be able to enjoy it—even from my mother whom I'm pretty—have been mixed up about.

Hy: I don't know. I can only think of love as between parent and

child—I mean the way I would like to relate to my child—or between husband and wife. But I realize I'm mixed up there too. I
don't know if I can consider trust in another person as a sort of off-
shoot of love. Perhaps it is and I just don't know it but whatever
it is it's gone and I'd like to start fresh. Only it—I can't start fresh
—but that is what I would like to do.

Ed: What is that?

Hy: Well, all the love that I should have had or should have expressed in the past and didn't and so on is all behind me. So I sort
of say—well, let's forget about it and start clean—but—but I can't
start clean—because I'm the end product.

Th: It's all entwined with the past—and that's why talking
about it here can help, so you can start again.

Hy: Yes, I've heard that sermon before (laughed). (Hostility to
me is his defense—and his resistance.)

Ed: You're going to hear it many times more.

Jo: Because it happens to be the right one—after all, that's why
we are here to try to straighten out things from the past that got
our feelings all mixed up.

Hy: But I'm very angry at the past. It's gone and I want to get
rid of it. I don't want to be enmeshed in it any more.

Th: You're like a sore kid that puts up his fists all the time.

Hy: Yeah, yeah, I'm fighting all the way.

Th: So you react to us—and especially to me—by saying no, no,
take it away. I don't need you—I'm a tough guy. And yet really un-
derneath you want so badly all that foreplay in sex which is really
your longing for tenderness.

Hy: You know, I—I almost imagine that in some way I'd like to
hurt you. Verbally or otherwise. I don't know why—

Ed: Almost imagine? Why it's happened! (Group laughs, talks.)

Th: As if I were like your mother. I seem to stand for that person
who denied you.

Hy: (Softened) I guess I do at that—I want to do that to Ed. I
suppose I want to do that to—everyone, with the exception of—
well, possibly Vi at times, too.

Ed: When you dig Vi you'll really take a swing at her, too.

Hy: She's . . . sort of a nice kid . . . that's why.

Ed: She's like a little mouse (to Vi) with a big smile on her face!

Th: Yes, you're sort of taking it out here, what you once felt when you were little. Eventually everyone you get close to gets it.

Hy: Yeah, well at least I've been able to—well—(Thinking of what we talked about last week.) Well—I think I've been able to control that with my wife. And it's very difficult for me to do that with my mother (voice raised, would not be interrupted). With my mother I'm just simmering. I'm afraid of any word that's going to come out because it's going to hurt her and there's no point in hurting her. She's about as damaged as they can be—without being dead (cleared throat).

Al: Yeah, but it's one thing to refuse to see that you did at one time. You still do have this feeling—feeling—this uh ... need for mama.

Hy: And as soon as I think of that need I—(laughed, long pause, became very still and pale.)

Th: You what?

Hy: I suddenly get very angry. Just the fact of having to depend on someone else. They didn't give it to me when I needed it and I don't want it now. I don't need them anymore, I don't want to need them anymore. (Cleared throat—growing insight.)

Th: Or their substitutes.

Hy: Or their substitutes. However, I can recognize them.

Jo: But you do need it—because why do you come here?

Th: I think when you get so angry it's some other feelings you're pushing away.

Hy: I don't know. I want to be loved—but I fight it at the same time.

Th: If somebody were to be tender with you, that might make you feel bad and so you quickly get mad.

Hy: I'm like a little boy, a little five-year-old who wants someone around when he needs them but otherwise he doesn't want them. He doesn't want the—well—

Jo: Well, I'm almost like you. I want to get and yet I don't know whether I want to give. Or if I give it's because I want to give and not because the other person really needs it or because the other person—uh—asks that I give.

Al: There is a grown-up way of looking at it and a kid way of looking at it.

Hy: Now that doesn't seem very mature of me. (The immediate archaic superego reaction tends to negate the insight.)

Al: Well, this is the—isn't it possible that you could be acting the way—

Hy: There's something wrong there.

Th: In other words, the little boy just couldn't get what he wanted and that twisted him in some way.

Hy: (With feeling—almost crying—he rescued himself by talking of a related but less emotional subject.) It's twisted me in all sorts of ways. I was just thinking of something that happened this past week. It's a very small petty thing, but I seem to have blown it up in my mind—to something out of all proportion. Several weeks ago in school they put up a notice about submitting applications for students to apply to some honor society. And it depended on scholarship and so on. And I wanted very much to get into it. And, well, a few days ago I received a letter saying that I had been accepted and so on. And now that I have been, I sort of feel that well —something went wrong, that I wasn't really accepted as I should have been accepted, that I don't really think that I'm bright enough to be accepted that—some other—uh—things entered into it which permitted me—possibly to—be accepted. It's as if, whenever I've—anything has been given to me that I've wanted or tried to get I've felt that (cleared throat) I was undeserving of it or it was something that I shouldn't take. Like when working for my father-in-law or something like that—on a week-end he needs someone there. He'd have to pay someone and yet I'm ashamed to take the money from him because I'm related to him. And so I don't know—I'm not able to—differentiate in my mind just what to take or not to take or if I take I feel that—uh—I'm indebted to someone, that I have to repay them in some way or another. I can't accept it for what it is. And yet I'll be—on the other hand I don't want people to be indebted to me for what I do for them because if I do it, I do it because I want to. Otherwise I wouldn't do it.

(The others are very quiet, intent on what is being said.)

Th: So you can't accept anything nice from someone. Neither love nor recognition. (Ties the two together so as not to lose the feeling.)

Hy: No, I—I feel that—well, either something went wrong— they were being sympathetic to me or nice to me. It was something of which I wasn't deserving (clears throat). I don't know (laughed self-consciously). I don't suppose it makes too much sense.

Th: It makes sense only for someone who once felt he couldn't get what he needed and decided to take nothing.

Hy: I don't want to feel indebted to anyone!

Ed: Ever since you were a child. How could you take if they didn't give to you? You know, so you had to settle for not taking. And then you had to convince yourself that this was your choice. (Ed felt this strongly. He felt the same way but had a different solution. He tried to exploit "the other" and get something for nothing.)

Hy: Well, if I don't take, at least I can—I can look upon them in a hostile manner. I can hope to hurt them at some time or another, and perhaps—well, when I was a child I was hurt when I asked for love. So now, when I get it, I don't believe it or I wonder what's coming after—what they'll want.

Ed: So you don't know whether they're giving or not. They might just be paying—

Hy: So I prefer they don't give at all—and I don't want to be obligated.

Ed: For services rendered—but you are the one who put that connotation on it.

Hy: I don't want all of that. I don't want that turmoil going over in my mind as to whether or not I should be grateful or shouldn't be grateful or whether I should take or not take. I don't want it, let them keep it.

(Both were speaking with a great deal of feeling, reliving past wounds—and of course feeling sorry for themselves, but they were not ready to understand that yet.)

Ed: It's like not knowing when to hit somebody.

Hy: Yeah, man—(sighed deeply). (All tension was gone now.)

Ed: You protect yourself by saying "Fuck you, who needs you," you know?

Hy: (Quietly now) Yeah, it's easier that way.

Th: And you are still saying "who needs you," to us—especially to me.

Hy: I suppose I'd break down and cry if it's—uh—if it were any other way. What else can I do but build up in my mind's image that I made the choice? So at least I can—dream up this fantasy—

Ed: You should have been able to cry a long time ago and you should have been comforted in your crying so that you could have gotten past it but you're still there. Like me, you know?

This session turned out to have been a crucial one for the three major participants. For Ed it provided the deepest recognition of the infantile motives in his impulsive pursuit of the woman and for the first time the voyeuristic elements which were involved in it. Jo began to understand that her choices of men and people were neurotic and to realize that in her neurotic need she had ruled out a large number of men as uninteresting only because they were "there," as she put it. For Hy this session marked the beginning of trust in us. He had shown us his raw feelings and thereafter was under much less pressure to hide them. It was a very small step from which he often retreated, but it was a beginning.

XV Work of Some Experiential-Existential Group Therapists

Existentialism had won its place in the philosophical thought of Europe during the last half of the nineteenth century, but it did not become widely popular nor spread its influence extensively into other fields of thought until well after the First World War. In America it had made almost no impression as a philosophy in the academic world of our great universities until after the Second World War, in spite of the fact that the pragmatism of James and Dewey had much in common with it. Both men dealt concretely rather than abstractly with the immediate problems of man; both saw "truth" as relative to a given situation rather than as absolute and apart from man; but their concepts did not embrace existentialism. Perhaps there was no need for the existentialist challenge in this country, since individualism flourished in philosophy just as it did on the broader front of daily life, and its history had been one of concrete practical affairs, of economic and political security.

Between World Wars, American psychology had continued to lean strongly toward experimental method and mechanistic theory. Most academic psychologists had not yet accepted psychoanalysis as a true science, although a growing number of clinicians were beginning work with it. Among psychotherapists, the overwhelming majority of whom were medical rather than psychological, psychoanalysis was firmly established as a therapeutic method.

After the Second World War, however, the situation changed. With economic and political security threatened, the sovereignty of the individual was also threatened. There was growing uneasiness about the status quo, both in the practical and the academic worlds. In psychology, enthusiasm for mechanistic theory had begun to wane. Hope was running out for an over-all psychology which would be scientific in the manner of the physical sciences. The effectiveness of psychoanalysis as a method of treatment was already being questioned in some quarters. Voices which had been heard earlier in criticism were now joined by others who had independently come to certain therapeutic concepts which dovetailed with those of European existential analysts.

Meanwhile the literature of existentialism had at last been translated into English and the influx of displaced European psychologists helped bring existential thinking into American philosophy and psychology. It was not well known except in the more cosmopolitan areas, and there it was more often hotly contested than well understood. In Europe, on the other hand, existential psychotherapy and analysis had become very widespread indeed.

The contrast between Europe and America in this respect became evident at the Fourth International Congress for Psychotherapy, which was held in Barcelona in September 1958. Its key theme was the comparison between psychoanalysis and existential analysis. The chief contributors to this theme were Europeans. There were a few American existentialists among them, May, Hora, and Mullan, but most of the Americans present talked on other subjects. Most of us were not even adequately prepared to be fully receptive to what they were trying to communicate. (May's book *Existence* [1958] was not available until after our return.) Even those of us who, like myself, had made some effort in this direction were, on the whole, left unanswered and unsatisfied. Perhaps it was because, as Hora said, we were "looking for knowledge as a tool of mastery and skill, instead of for knowledge as enlightenment and understanding." We were, paradoxically, too pragmatic. Nor did the existentialists, it seems to me, make much of an effort to help us understand. They talked their language; we listened in ours and were left to translate it for ourselves. We were amazed at the semantic elaboration of the simple verb "to be." Anxiety, guilt, and despair were familiar words but they seemed not to have quite the accustomed meaning. Communication via monologue, they declared, was reprehensible, but "dialogue" implied authentic existence. To be sure, we were inclined to agree on that last point, but somehow their particular "dialogue" did not reach the target. It simply didn't come through to us. They sounded profound, but didn't become meaningful; yet we were often assured that their lectures were truly dialogic. I had done enough reading to have some idea of the meaning of their implications, but I couldn't see how their profundity played a part in making for more effective therapy, and I wanted to know.

I had to face nonbeing. I was full of despair until I recalled a line from a letter I had received from my son (who was better versed than I in existentialism and the Eastern religions). I was amused as I recalled his comment: "If they tell you what existentialism is, don't believe them; if they don't, believe them but be sure to listen carefully for 'the sound of one hand clapping' (famous Zen Koan)." I talked with many who were in a worse predicament than I. In fact the stately halls of the old university were alive with the whispers of the "uninitiate," who asked, "But what has all this to do with psychotherapy?" On the final morning, the chairman of the plenary session brought our questions to the attention of the speakers and asked them if they would enlighten us. But the speakers, who included some of the great men in existential psychotherapy, only continued to talk in inspired language.

It was May's book, *Existence,* published on our return home, that bridged the gap by giving us their major concepts and solving the riddle by the simple statement that they did not have new techniques; that they were not, in fact, so much interested in techniques as in providing a new way of looking at man in his world—a new philosophy which would deeply change psychotherapy. We had been asking the wrong questions.

May's book provided a valuable starting point for a necessary investigation of the existential therapists' point of view. He is scientifically cautious and warns of the pitfalls to be avoided in embracing the existentialist outlook; but he and his co-authors are committed to the existentialists' views and to their meaningfulness for psychotherapy, and their commitment is deep. They do not question the assumptions. Study of their work also leaves a good many questions and confusion. The time is at hand, therefore, when it

becomes imperative for us to weigh these psychotherapeutic concepts and ask ourselves how far we can substitute them for our
thinking, to what degree we can integrate them into our framework
and at what point we must decide to disagree with them. Let us
examine some concrete examples.

Two principal tributaries, in addition to a number of smaller
currents, have flowed into the main stream of existential group
therapy in the United States. There is, first, the original "experiential" therapy of Whitaker and Malone, which has moved consistently toward the ontological way of thinking, and, second, an
adaptation of the European *Daseinsanalyse*. (A number of other
group therapists, such as Bach and Carl Rogers, who have arrived
at a similar orientation, have done so by pursuing quite different
paths.) In summarizing the main flow, it will be necessary to describe these two courses separately. There are sufficient differences
between them to raise doubt as to whether, over the long run, they
will remain in the same camp, but certain metaphysical assumptions will be apparent.

In truth there are not many existential group therapists in
America, and I hesitated a long time before including their work
as a major approach. But individual existential analysis is a growing movement here and has its own society and journals, and there
seems to be a general trend toward the kind of thinking it represents, revealing perhaps a striving toward something more satisfying, something greater than man,[1] which might help to overcome
the postwar disillusionment. There have been, for example, tendencies to reach out for the transcendental, a return to formal religion, a spurt of interest in the oriental philosophies, and, in psychology, a swing toward the Jungian psychotherapy which had
never before been popular here. At any rate the humanistic elements of existential therapy are making a distinct appeal. Some of
its basic ideas had already been foreshadowed in other schools of
therapy (and, for that matter, in areas which had nothing to do
with psychotherapy at all). For instance, there is an affinity between Jungian and existential analysis. and even before its advent
Jung had stressed the need for greater individualism in treatment
methods and more irrationalism in its aims. Sullivan had spoken

[1] Omnipotence?

out for a more inclusive relationship between therapist and patient. Adlerians had emphasized the necessity for a truly holistic view of man. Rankians had written again and again about the "immediate living experience" of the therapeutic relationship. In all of these there is an implied criticism of psychoanalysis on the basis that it smacks too much of nineteenth-century scientism. What these therapists were striving for seems to be satisfied by the ontological base of existential ideology.

Whitaker and Malone's thinking as described in their book, *The Roots of Psychotherapy* (1953), seems to have made its appeal to a number of psychotherapists who were discontented with psychoanalysis and were independently searching for ways of making the psychotherapeutic experience a more vital and more affective experience. The authors have put their ideas into action in a form of therapy which they call experiential and are teaching their point of view in the Atlanta Psychiatric Clinic in Georgia. Their group psychotherapy is, of course, also experiential. A number of group therapists have adopted this point of view, and the best known are carrying on their work in New York.

As experiential group therapy was presented at various professional meetings, a great wave of criticism was generated among psychoanalytically-oriented group therapists. The climax of the polemics occurred when Wolf and Schwartz presented (and later published in 1958) a series of papers called "Irrational Trends in Psychotherapy." Amusingly enough, those "irrational" therapists who attended the meeting answered their emotionally stirred-up critics in a very calm and "rational" manner. In a subsequent paper Malone et al. (1958) drafted an answer which clarified their basic ideas. They preferred, they said, to be called nonrational. The tone and content of the paper were extremely rational and it was difficult to see great differences between their concept and analytic group therapy as I know it. They view the ideological difference between the two schools of thought as follows:

"The therapist who conceives of man as primarily an intelligent being will deal differently with him than the psychotherapist who sees man as primarily a feeling person, with the intellect as a controlling mechanism. In recent years the various schools of psychotherapy appear to gravitate into either one or the other of these opposing ideologies. We identify an emphasis on the patient's intellect as rational psychotherapy, whereas we identify an emphasis on the feeling experience of the patient as experiential psychotherapy. We consider this an ideological rather than a technical difference." They do not explain why a dichotomy is made between thinking and feeling.

In the same paper Malone et al. summarize what I believe to be the major conceptual difference which influences their technical procedures. They assume transferential and existential dimensions in the psychotherapeutic relationship, and point out that "the existential relationship is not rational but personal, and involves the total responsiveness of the person of the therapist to the person of the patient in the current living situation. The totality of both transferential and existential relationships we call the experiential relationship."

In another article entitled "Spontaneous Interaction in Group Psychotherapy" Whitaker and Warkentin give us much more of the flavor of experiential psychotherapeutic transactions, and their deviation from analytic group therapy becomes evident. Here they demonstrate a clear difference in the technical aspect of group therapy:

"Patients symbolically tend to sit in the same chair and to try to push the therapist into an established position. The therapist may then create opportunities for a freer choice by his unwillingness to accept these rigid patterns. He reinforces any spontaneity in the group. Such a simple thing as the therapist's response to the seating arrangement in a group can catalyze spontaneous interactions. Group A was impassed. The patients repeatedly sat in the same chair. On entering the group the therapist forced himself into a chair between two patients who were transferred to each other. He did this by physically pushing their chairs apart. The group made significant constructive movement in that and subsequent sessions.

"In the same group, an ambulatory schizophrenic patient who was exceedingly shy had always managed to sit as far as possible from a very attractive nymphomaniac. In one session he got up from his chair and with obvious anxiety walked around and sat in a chair next to the girl. The therapist reinforced this 'spontaneous' response by moving next to the patient on the other side.

"Conclusion: The therapist responds to his inner self or he shares the affect of the group on him. Thus the therapist is the most experienced patient present. He can be therapeutic, or he can be the one patient who spends most of the period in his aloneness. He can choose to utilize the help available or do without it. He can be spontaneous and creative only because of this freedom to choose. The choice indicates he is not operating on a compulsive or repetitive basis.

"This same choosing can emerge for the other group members. It is more likely to occur in group therapy because each patient is not constantly faced with the need to speak or relate. In this silence and its comfortable aloneness, the patient is both stimulated to make a choice and also has adequate privacy to arrive at it. He may create an interpersonal experience with other members of the group, or he may revel in the right to experience his own person in all its wellness or all its sickness or both."

Closely related to this way of thinking are the views and practices of Dr. Hugh Mullan of the New York group, whose articulate and prolific writing has given me the opportunity to trace the course of their thinking from its emergence out of psychoanalytic ideology to its present existential frame of reference. In order to insure myself against error or misinterpretation I asked Mullan and his colleague, Dr. Iris Sangiuliano, to read what I wrote and then incorporated their suggestions in what follows.

In 1953 Mullan published a paper on "conflict avoidance," in which he expressed his feeling that not only the patient but the therapist often tends to deny his conflicts as a result of the conviction that he should purge himself of countertransference. This need of the therapist would implicitly reinforce the patient's wish to avoid his conflicts. Heterogeneity in group constitution would help to correct this danger by bringing the behavior of one patient into forceful opposition to another. Conflict makes for therapy. For the same reason, it is the responsibility of the therapist to keep the group in a state of imbalance. Being less in need of safety through conflict avoidance, he must lead his group by steadfastly facing his own conflicts and by wording his interpretations so that they highlight conflict and doubt. There is nothing in this paper which a good Freudian analyst might not have said, but it gives evidence of Mullan's dissatisfaction with the psychoanalyst's prescription that the less countertransference there is, the better the therapy.

In the early fifties, experiential therapists continued to discuss

transference and countertransference from a more or less traditional point of view. In one paper Mullan said that "group therapy
rests on the relationships and their continuing analysis according to
Freud's definition (i.e., the analysis of transference and resistance)." Gradually, however, transference and resistance analysis
diminished in importance for them, and they began to change their
technique in dealing with these phenomena. Instead they felt it
was important for the therapist to instigate the patient's fantasy;
to elicit transference from the patient rather than passively allow
it to develop. They had also become so impressed with the tremendous role played by the therapist's own personality in therapy that
they changed their mode of utilizing it. They encouraged personal
involvement and exercised their emotions to the full instead of attempting to minimize them. Combining these two principles they required the therapist to take the lead in expressing his
own transference feelings and fantasies to the patients. Exploring
the transference thereby became a mutual process and the therapist
was prepared to examine with the patients their mutual fantasies.
As Mullan (1955c) says: "Only this bilateral approach produces
sufficient anxiety to force the patient into a totally new way of responding." And again: "We have given up noninvolvement."

Here it becomes obvious that a basic change in the accepted role
of transference and countertransference was under way. The technique of analyzing transference in the patient while trying for full
awareness of one's own countertransference was abandoned for a
mutual exploration of all the emotions and fantasies, the total behavior of both patient and therapist, and, primarily, the gestalt
formed by this new unit, that of patient-therapist. The narrower
concept of countertransference which refers only to neurotic resid-
uals was given up. By implication also the technique of dealing
with resistance was dropped and replaced by undercutting rather
than analyzing the resistance. Here a sharp break with psychoanalytic method is evident. The experiential therapists had moved
into a distinctive course of their own. The experiential method
had been established.

But, the reader asks, how can the therapist implement such a
method? What does he do to facilitate the bilateral approach? Mullan's answer is that he must disregard the usual consideration of
techniques and the traditional attitude that he should be as im-

personal as possible. If he does this he will find a reservoir of feelings toward his patients coming into consciousness, which are, in any case, the real motivators of how he handles the patient. He is better off if he allows himself a full awareness of them. But awareness alone is not enough. He must also give expression to these feelings, for it is through such expression that he eventually achieves the desirable uninhibited responsiveness in himself and in his patients. In this, experiential therapists believe, lies the key to the therapeutic process. In this way the therapist is helped openly to express, rather than hold back, all such feelings as fear, anger, and depression. Avoidance of these is crippling to the fundamental relationship between humans that must be established among patients and with the therapist. Since the therapist and the patients are considered as differing only in degree and not in kind, it follows that the patient-aspect of the therapist as well as the therapist-aspect of the patients will be acknowledged. For therapeutic effectiveness, in fact, it must not only be acknowledged, but fully realized in the experience they share. This means that the therapist must take the lead in presenting himself as a human being with anxiety, depression, and despair of his own. If not, then he is considered to have been denying his own conflicts and preventing full mutuality in the relationship. By the same token he will have encouraged conflict avoidance in the patients. He cannot then be considered to have "been completely with" the patients. Nor must the therapeutic potential of the patients be ignored, for in being able to give expression to it, the group members grow in self-esteem. They express their therapeutic selves in two ways, primarily when they give full expression of themselves to other members, and to the therapist, and secondly when they make interpretations to one another.

In the course of this interactive process the therapist becomes once more the central figure through which therapy occurs. Although the members experience one another fully too and change dynamically as a result, it is the therapist, with his lesser commitment to the rules and statuses of the culture, who must take the lead in transcending them. Therapy transcends time, place, and status. Through his knowledge of the unconscious he can also lead in instigating mutual fantasying, and because of his greater emotional freedom he can recognize his inner anxieties and socially unacceptable feelings and risk exposing them more fully and sooner than his patients. His role as human being in relation to the others supersedes that of analyst.

Following through on this conviction about the therapeutic process as a predominantly "experiencing" one, these therapists have evolved a new concept of interpretation. Having started with insistence upon the inclusion of feelings and intuition as a source of interpretations, they have moved toward a preference for acting, feeling, and fantasying over analyzing and talking. When the therapist controls his feelings and denies his own conflicts, they believe, he is bound to be remote and distant, hence incapable of full mutuality. When he analyzes, he separates himself from his patient as a human being and treats him as an object. Therefore, the term "analyze" is contaminated and the word "interpretation" takes on a completely new meaning. The old concept of unconscious response of the therapist to the unconscious of the patient is now carried to its nth power. The therapist may analyze out of his unconscious, but he must not be aware of himself as analyzing. Hence the wording of his interpretations becomes far more intuitive than that of the classical analyst. In Mullan's (1955c) words: "As the intellectual function diminishes, anxiety comes up and fantasies are expressed. Only then does interpretation become a total biological function in which all the metabolisms play a part." This kind of interpretation involves extensive emotional interchange. It becomes, indeed, "an affective coming together" in which "two or more participants shift their meanings for each other and see life anew." No other form of interchange, they believe, is capable of causing true psychic movement.

In a paper called "The Group Analyst's Creative Function," printed in the *American Journal of Psychotherapy* (1955b), Mullan sums up his personal conception of the creative nature of the role of the therapist as an artist. It gives us a strong, clear picture of Mullan's goal even though other experiential therapists, because of their individual differences, might behave very differently. They would presumably agree with the idea that it is to the patients' benefit for the therapist to express such uniqueness in conducting therapy. Mullan, in this respect, may be a trailblazer more unique than others. But that is beside the point.

Mullan minimizes the value of intellect and technique, which he claims can too easily hamstring psychological methods. According to him the therapist may "use" scientific knowledge and method, but not rely solely upon them. He must rather "individualize and particularize his therapy through the prism of his emotions." He "moves into the group session" with the single purpose of experiencing himself in relation to others, and "by his own freedom he encourages others." The being and the experience are the creative factors, rather than the "highly over-rated intellectual interpretive effort." He feels the therapist must discourage the patients' tendency to perpetuate the old culture and must stimulate them to create new forms. The therapist is creative in two ways: (1) by experiencing himself completely and (2) by revealing himself freely to his patients even when that includes laying open to view his weaknesses and anxieties just at that point at which his patients expect him to be strong. He can help himself to accomplish this by using language which is not strictly conventional but earthy, pithy, and in terms of the language of his group. Such talking, he feels, brings people together, whereas much conventional or intellectual talk separates them. Interpretations are for Mullan creative productions, which he poetically calls "the brushstrokes of the artist." The right interpretations are not based on knowledge but on deep and total involvement. They should come directly and intuitively from his unconscious, and be made immediately as experienced without fear of the patients' ability to accept them. They include direct symbolic interpretation, and are made somewhat in the manner of Rosen or Sechehaye, and often in Freudian terms.

Similar to his view of interpretation is the experiential therapist's approach to dreams. Dreams, he affirms, best express the non-teleological in man. The latent content of the dream is the essential reality of the dreamer's existence. No secondary reductive analysis of it is important. It illustrates what is, not what should be. It offers a new dimension and includes the irrational, the paradox. A member who expresses his dream in the group is helped to accept his inner being and at the same time he is led, by the very telling of it, out of his isolation into relatedness. The therapist in the group therefore tries to evoke from the other members primarily their emotional reactions to the dream, to the dreamer, and to his telling of his dream, rather than their interpretation of its meaning. The important therapeutic ingredient is not insight into

its content but into the response others have to the dreamer's irrationalities. Nor does the therapist himself attempt to analyze the
dream. He utilizes it as a vital existing phenomenon, very often as
if it were taking place at the moment. He points continually to the
importance of the patient's having dreamed the dream, of his telling it, and of his accepting that irrational part of himself which it
reveals and which he has heretofore rejected.

What the dream expresses is also the keynote for what the therapist strives to develop in the group—the nonteleological aspects of
being. The instruments for achieving this are his insistence on
eliciting conflict, transcending status, and focusing on the living
experience of the group. Conceptualization has to occur after experience. To accomplish this takes several years of being together,
throughout a period of heightening of the transferences and their
resolution. It can be accomplished neither by conceptual analysis
nor by removing defenses. Such techniques merely serve to isolate
the individual further. His therapeutic lever consists of the deep,
mutual responsiveness among the patients and with the therapist
as a member of the group.

By 1958 it had become clear that experiential therapy was gravi-
tating toward existentialism. This is confirmed in a paper by Mullan and Sangiuliano, "Interpretation as Existence in Analysis."
There they say: "We have defined interpretation in the following
way: we believe that interpretation involves a range of behavior,
thinking, feeling, and acting through which two or more participants shift their meaning for one another and see life anew.... Interpretation evolves as a new order of involvement. The member
to member and member-therapist communication is less objective.
There is no technical nor causal concern. There is instead uninhibited responsiveness to the process and to the gestalt. It is the
response to the full being of the patient instead of to selected aspects. In its clearest form this kind of interpretation makes for a
deeper emotional interchange with fuller communication enriching the transaction."

To sum up: Mullan started out with the analysis of the patient's
transference, began to instigate it actively, added the mutual exploration of the countertransference, broadened their concepts to
include the exploration of all the mutual feelings and fantasies of
patient and therapist, and finally minimized analysis in favor of

the full experiencing of the relationship. He changed his concept of interpretation accordingly.

From the point of view of the members the primary element is the patient's experiencing himself in a series of deep emotional relationships. The advantage of the group is the multiplicity possible in this process. The patient lives in the present of the group life. The past, though it may come up frequently, has little meaning therapeutically. Their need to belong is also satisfied. The members are reassured by their sameness at the beginning, but they go on to experience themselves as unique individuals. For each individual member finds himself accepted and respected even after his differences from the others have been fully expressed. His individuality is thus confirmed by his peers, so that he can give up his old, frightened image of himself and emerge as a unique human being. He begins to stand out. The process by which this mutual growth takes place is not an easy one. The dominant mood of the group is often one of despair. But as it proceeds the wishing, desiring self of each member emerges. With the resultant increase in ego strength comes the ability to make responsible decisions. The patient is enabled to shift from self-interest to group interest, not in the spirit of self-sacrifice but with a new willingness to give and take. The capacity for personal closeness gradually replaces the original distrust of his fellow man.

On the basis of our material we may then conclude that the experiential group therapist is no longer trying to help the patient understand how much the past is distorting the present through the analysis of the transference. His plan is to promote change through full mutual involvement in the patient-therapist relationship, which includes the total behavior of both. Instead of focusing on the attempt to dissolve the patient's resistance, the experiential therapist tries to gain direct access to the primary process by taking the lead in exposing his own fantasies, dreams, and emotions. The relationship is bilateral in every sense. Interpretations are therefore of an entirely different order from classical and analytic interpretations.

To summarize: It is my impression that if one follows the historical sequence of the papers of the experiential authors one can recognize first discontent and then protest, together with a searching for new ways of helping the patients. Following this there is a rath-

er rapid progression toward a real break from psychoanalysis and
a new orientation which grows essentially out of their own attitudes and experience, but which is influenced by an exchange of
ideas with other writers who are also groping for new ways of therapy. Through such writings it seems to me that their ideas are confirmed rather than formed. They did not take over the philosophy
of Kierkegaard, Nietzsche, Jaspers, Heidegger, etc., but felt
strengthened by it. It is as if in the literature of existentialism and
the existential analysts, the experientialist authors have recognized
their ideological *Heimat*.

In order to balance our picture of American existential group
psychotherapy I would like to present as a typical example the
work of Thomas Hora, whose dissatisfaction with psychoanalysis
also led him through a progression of changes to existentialism.
Today his writings are much closer to those of the European existential analysts. One feels in him a strong commitment to the
philosophy. Even his manner of writing has the atmosphere of
Heidegger and Buber. His style is, like theirs, somewhat lofty and
profound, yet he presents his theory and his method more clearly
and fully than most of the *Daseins* analysts. In a paper called "Existential Group Psychotherapy" Hora (1959b) gives the reader a
fairly concise idea of the method he uses, and of the way he manages his groups.

Hora says of his own approach, "Contributions of psychoanalytic
group therapy and communications research are integrated into
the broader scheme according to the existential viewpoint and are
utilized implicitly." He specifies that, according to this existential
viewpoint, "Man has to adjust not only to his environment and to
his inner self, but to the 'Fundamental Order of Things'. I interpret this to mean that in doing psychotherapy, one must help the
patient become aware not only of his reactions to his environment
and of his inner needs, but of his responses to certain ontological
factors, that is, to the basic conditions of life in the world into
which he was born. Whereas the psychoanalyst's major focus is on
the beginnings of each individual's life in order to discover,
through a genetic study, how his particular patterns came into being, the existential therapist considers this historical process incidental to therapy. His interest is in the patient's present behavior

and the cognitive bias which underlies his mode. According to the psychoanalyst, the patient's insight into the genetic causes of his neurotic patterns gives him the freedom to change them. According to the existential therapist, awareness of his attitudes toward being and nonbeing wakes him up to his freedom and responsibility to choose between authentic and inauthentic existence.

Hora uses Sartre's term *la condition humaine,* to elucidate the meaning of man's ontological situation. More precisely, *la condition humaine* refers to the fact that each individual is cast into the world without his consent and must leave it in the same way. In the limited and unpredictable span between he has to make the most of his potential in order to live meaningfully. The patient's response to *la condition humaine* is of ultimate importance in determining his way of life. The way in which he accepts "man's fate" becomes the steering element of his existence.

Hora does a service to the average American reader by using this logical and lucid French term for what Heidegger calls "throwness." Heidegger's terminology has a more profound tone and it forces the reader to think beyond the commonplace, but it is highly idiosyncratic and few group therapists would take time to think through his obscurantist writings. The accidental nature of man's "throwness" points clearly to the possibility that any particular being might not have been thrown into life at all. Moreover, that being may at any moment be removed from life. The "dread" that results from facing the possibility of nonbeing is so great that the average man tends to take refuge in "inauthentic existence." The neurotic's way of life seems dedicated to avoidance of this bitter knowledge and it is to this fact that the existential therapist primarily addresses himself. According to his way of thinking the psychoanalyst, because he takes existence for granted, cannot resolve the problems which result from its conditions.

Such ontological considerations are thought by Hora to give rise to a more basic concept of anxiety and of neurosis than that which the psychoanalysts have described. Existential anxiety is the "dread" of ever imminent nonbeing. To avoid this dread, man resorts to futile denial of it and to an endless, frenzied attempt to prove his being, his autonomous self-existence. He uses and exploits his fellow man instead of "being with" him. Real communication fails and gives way to speech and intellectual verbalizations which reflect a useless search for confirmation of the self without facing the truth of what really is. The man who thus falls prey to avoidance of "dread" cannot live an authentic existence. In his endeavor to avoid existential anxiety he builds up a way of being in the world that cannot be authentic because it is set up to evade a basic ontological truth. All defenses, symptoms, and neurotic attitudes are a part of this need to run from the inescapable *condition humaine*. Thus he is led to neurotic anxiety, which becomes manifest in the interpersonal sphere. The patient, in other words, is battered between the Scylla of existential anxiety and the Charybdis of neurotic anxiety. The resolution of his neurotic problems lies in penetrating to their existential core rather than to their historico-genetic sources.

Existential guilt haunts such a person because he does not fulfill his inner human potential. Neurotic guilt follows from his inauthentic modes of being in the world, for they arouse conflict with others and within the self.

Out of these philosophical views arise a new definition and goal for psychotherapy, and changes in the role of the therapist follow. The goal is to enable the patient (1) to face the dread of nonbeing; (2) to free his ability to develop his inner potentialities; and (3) to guide him toward full dialogic relations with others. Therapy is an "enabling process" which emerges from full "encounter" between patient and therapist. The therapist therefore is the pivot of therapy. It is what he is rather than what he does that makes the patient able to change. The therapist begins the therapeutic process with an attempt to comprehend the private meaning of the patient's existence, his way of being in the world. He accepts him wholly, by "letting him be" rather than by analyzing him. "Letting him be" (not to be confused with "leaving him alone") is, according to Heidegger plus Hora, that cognitive attitude which makes it possible for "all that is, to reveal itself in the essence of its being." To accomplish this effectively the therapist has to be capable of "participating with his whole being creatively on an existential level." He engages in a real "encounter" with the patient, and responds by communicating his authentically perceived experiences and reflections on the meaning of the actual situation and of the on-going events of the therapeutic session. The patient, however, must be allowed the freedom to accept or reject such communications. Thus he is given the responsibility of choosing of his own free will to accept or reject his existential task. Therapy becomes a clarifying, elucidating process rather than an analysis.

In contrast to inauthenticity of being is the existential concept of mental health. Hora defines it as "a condition of human existence which finds expression and meaning in a capacity of the individual to fulfill his potentialities through genuine, reciprocal and affirmative communication with his fellow man. This definition provides existential group therapists with a rationale. As Hora (1959b) says: "The group is a veritable proving ground for the realization of authentic existence." In spite of the obviously ideal conditions in a group for illustrating and studying existential concepts, there are but few existential therapists who have taken group therapy seriously. At the beginning the group situation reveals the frenzy which accompanies the patient's inauthentic escape from dread. The members are characteristically full of tension. According to Hora, "When a group of people meet, every participant is exposed to the group atmosphere which is charged with affective currents, for the nature of man's tie with his fellow members is basically affective. The undifferentiated state of affective stimulation creates tension and a need to organize the affect into thoughts. This is experienced as group tension . . . it presses for discharge . . . and results in a need to talk. Language here is used as action, serving the need to discharge inner tension. . . . This talk . . . communicates nothing essential. . . . It is a verbal form of acting out (and) makes it possible for the participants to avoid becoming aware of what they are experiencing." Obviously the group offers the therapist a broad opportunity to understand its members' modes of being-in-the-world. "But," says Hora, "it is something more. It is a laboratory for dialogic relationship among human beings." He now advances beyond the teaching of Heidegger, for whom self-development is the primary goal and "care" (concern) for one's fellow man is a step toward it. He introduces Buber's principle that the development of the self is merely preparatory for dialogic existence, which is the goal of man. He remains inauthentic until he comes into genuine dialogic communion with other human beings. While the aim of dialogic relationship can be met in individual psychotherapy, the group broadens its possibilities immeasurably. It is surely in the group that the "we" can be truly understood and experienced. Group therapy may well be the treatment of choice for the existentialists who follow Martin Buber. Increasing as it obviously does the scope of dialogic experience, it enlarges the capacity for it and serves as a transition period as well. The patient benefits from the shared experience with others who are also struggling for authenticity of being.

In the group, according to Hora, the patients go through stages. First they respond to their own and the group tensions by acting out verbally their needs to avoid the ontological realities. They talk without communicating, without being aware of their anxiety and of their need to avoid the truth. Gradually, with the help of the therapist, they do become aware. Then follow frequent painful periods of silence, when the dread of nothingness is experienced and confronted. At the same time they gradually become free to accept the deeper affective ties with one another. And by becoming free to love they become capable of genuine communion with one another and with the truth of what is. Hora has called group therapy "a process of affirmative togetherness."

Influenced as he is by communications research, Hora finds the proprioceptive system a useful medium for becoming aware of nonverbal experiences. He uses both his own proprioceptive cues and those of the patients to bring about a fuller self-awareness and understanding (phenomenological elucidation) of what is. Although this is Hora's particular way of achieving nonverbal awareness, all of the experientialists use this aspect of experience.

These two contrasting approaches serve to illustrate how differently therapists who share a common concept of ontology, of the meaning of neurosis, and of the process of therapy, may present themselves in clinical practice. The existential method promotes such individual differences.

One more example will emphasize this important point. Dr. Milton Berger tends not to use the verbiage of existentialism and much of what he writes is not easily distinguishable from, say, interpersonal psychoanalysis, yet he consistently reflects the existentialist philosophy. For instance, he says (1960), "There is a time for analyzing, a time for experiencing, even a time for acting out, and most importantly a time for functioning as a human being who is interested in and cares for another human being." He is speaking of crises and emergencies and I know of no analyst who would be unwilling to make exceptions at such times. The difference seems to be that what Berger spells out the rest of us take for granted and perhaps too often ignore. He sums up this point of view when in the same paper he writes, "Technique has to become secondary to humanity in the practice of the art as well as the science of group psychotherapy."

On the question of acting out, Berger's point of view differs sharply from that of psychoanalysis. He sees it primarily as a communication which helps the patient experience what is going on in his group. As such he accepts it phenomenologically, believing it makes available for therapeutic working through what has not previously been available in its true state. It is indeed a communication, but one which falls under the category of resistance from the analytic point of view. The experience which it provides would be regarded by an analytic group therapist as having a stereotyped neurotic quality to be analyzed out. Perhaps both points of view would benefit by making a sharper distinction between acting out and taking action.

In common with analytic group therapists and other existentialists Berger believes that the therapist is "the single most influential person in the therapeutic group structure." For him the distinguishing point, however, is that how and what he is *being* is more important than what he says. The therapist's nonverbal communications reveal his true self. They may be transferential, but they may also be an expression of true communion with his patients. The therapist's anonymity is, for Berger, pure myth, but he does not believe in putting the burden of personal problems on the group members. It is important that "sooner or later the patient does get to know and feel the therapist as a human being, as an authority who can be loving, giving, rejecting, and accepting," for under those conditions he can learn to give up his magical expectations of him (1958b).

In Berger's consistent emphasis that what the therapist and patients *are being* is more important than what they are saying, we see the influence of the ontological point of view. Mutual experiencing seems increasingly to replace the technique of analyzing transference and resistance.

The existential group therapists share a philosophy which each translates into clinical practice according to his unique way of being. They may adhere, in varying degrees, to the concepts and the techniques of psychoanalysis or they may divorce themselves completely from them.

IMPLICATIONS FOR GROUP PSYCHOTHERAPY

In perfecting the psychoanalytic method and imparting it to the next generation of students with such meticulous inflexibility, the Freudians sometimes lose the intended spirit of the therapeutic relationship and tend to regard the patient as an object. Similarly the method of free association had as its original purpose the wish to understand as fully as possible what was going on in the patient, just as Heidegger's phenomenological method was an attempt to enter the patient's world. Listening with free floating attention and a receptive "third ear" was intended to liberate the therapist from ego restrictions and give play to his unconscious reverberations. But the educated spontaneity of this subtly balanced attitude has often been destroyed by the analyst's need to read the patient's psychodynamics accurately. It has resulted at times in "throwing the book at the patient" instead of following his lead. The existentialist's insistence on adhering to the concrete living experience of the patient and his reliance on his own spontaneity and creativity revive the original attitude of psychoanalysis. It is carried to extremes by some who allow themselves absolute freedom in this respect. Whatever one's opinion, the existentialist position may well serve as a beacon to therapists who are so submerged in psychodynamics that they have forgotten the humanity which they have in common with their patients.

There is a difference of opinion among existential therapists as to the full mutuality of the therapist-patient relationship. Mullan's position is that full, complete mutuality is the goal, Sartre (1948), on the other hand, makes a point in his comparison of psychoanalytic and existential analysis of the fact that both methods are alike in insisting "on a strictly objective method, using as documentary evidence the data of reflection as well as the testimony of others."

Buber's position seems to be somewhat equivocal on this subject. Maurice Friedman, Professor of Philosophy and Lecturer at the Washington School of Psychiatry, and the first American to bring us a comprehensive study of Buber's thought, has summarized the problem.[2] He quotes Buber in a stand against the psychoanalytic attitude: "If the therapist is satisfied to analyze the patient—i.e., to bring to light unknown factors from his microcosm . . . then he may be successful in some repair work. At best he may help a soul which is diffused and poor in structure to collect and order itself to some extent. But the real matter, the regeneration of an atrophied personal centre, will not be achieved. This can only be done by one who grasps the buried latent unity of the suffering soul with the great glance of the doctor; and this can only be attained in the person to person attitude of a partner, not by the consideration and examination of an object."

Obviously this criticism would apply only to a misuse of analysis, for, as any one who has read Freud, Glover, or Fenichel can testify, it involves a misinterpretation of Freud's intention. At any rate this kind of rigidity is a far cry from the attitude of the analytic group therapist who is completely open to what is going on in the patient but excludes his own personal feelings, experiences, and neurotic needs as far as possible.

On the other hand, Friedman shows how Buber distinguishes between friendship and love *and* the helping relationships such as teaching or therapy. In the former, inclusion or experiencing the other side is mutual. The helping relationships are, however, necessarily one-sided. The patient cannot equally well experience the relationship from the side of the therapist or the pupil from the side of the teacher without destroying or fundamentally altering it. Friedman, elaborating on Buber, then makes the crucial point that this does not mean that the therapeutic relationship becomes an I/It relationship. Not at all. An I/Thou relationship is as vital to psychotherapy as it is to friendship. It must be founded on mutuality, trust, and partnership in the common situation. But there is a significant distinction between the attitude which the therapist brings into the relationship with his patient and the functional aspect of his therapeutic role. He continues, "The difference is not only that of personal stance, but of role and function, a difference determined by the purpose which led each to enter the re-

[2] From a paper entitled "Dialogue and the Essential We," presented at the American Group Psychotherapy Association, Sixteenth Annual Conference, January, 1959.

lationship. If the goal is a common one—the healing of the patient
—the relationship to that goal differs radically as between therapist and patient, and the healing that takes place depends as much
upon the recognition of that difference as upon the mutuality of
meeting and trust."

"The I/Thou relation," continues Friedman, "must always be
understood in terms of the quite concrete situation and life reality
of those participating in it. The full reality of the concrete situation includes the fact that one is a sick man who has come to the
therapist for help, the other a therapist who is ready to enter the
relationship in order to help.... The therapist's feeling of mutuality is not necessarily equivalent to the actual existence of full
mutuality in the situation.... The scientific impersonalism that
characterized the orthodox conception of the psychoanalyst is rightly rejected by many present day therapists. But this should not
lead us to a sentimental blurring of the essential distinction between therapy and other less structured types of I/Thou relations."

At this point he quotes once more from Buber, who, in *I and
Thou* (1923) wrote, "The psychotherapist, like the educator, must
stand again and again not merely at his own pole in the bipolar
relation, but also with the strength of present realization at the
other pole experience the effect of his own action.... The specific
healing would come to an end the moment the patient thought of,
and succeeded in, practising 'inclusion' and experiencing the event
from the doctor's pole as well. Healing, like educating, is only possible to the one who lives over against *(gegenüber)* the other, and
yet is detached."

My own conclusion is that, in principle, there is a basic irreconcilable difference in this matter, but in practice that difference
diminishes considerably. Here dissimilarities which seem to produce a bimodal curve appear more likely to yield instead clusters
of points on a continuum. For instance, even the most orthodox
analytic group therapist cannot retain complete objectivity or
anonymity in a face-to-face group. He is forced to reveal more of
himself than in the one-to-one situation and he is inevitably drawn
into some engagement with the members.

Meanwhile psychoanalysis has modified its position. The recent
emphasis and new understanding of countertransference that has

been evident in the literature of recent years has had a tendency to loosen up the analytic therapist, who has had a need to repress undesirable feelings to the patient. This makes him freer to explore this matter. A scholarly article by Racker in *The Psychoanalytic Quarterly* (1957) made a much needed distinction between countertransference in the broad sense, according to which some analysts include all feelings they experience to the patient, and in its narrower sense of (a) the acting out of remnants of the therapist's own infantile neurotic reactions to the patient and (b) his neurotic reactions to the patient's transference to him. And there have been many other articles which have brought about a healthier willingness for the therapist to recognize his countertransferential feelings. Even more radical opinions have been voiced in these papers suggesting that the therapist may find it effective at times to utilize his countertransference directly but knowingly with the patients. Racker himself stated that often the therapist's best clue to the patient's real motivation may be his own emotional reaction to it. He says that Lucia Tower makes a practice of openly admitting to her patient her oedipal strivings in order to help him come to grips with his. What is true in individual members of the two schools of thought comes much closer in practice than in theory. However, the analytic group therapist would reveal his own feelings only in specific situations when he felt this would help the patient deal with his own emotions. The experientialist, on the other hand, does so continuously in order to foster full experience with the patient. Thus we must come back to a fundamental difference in principle.

The stand that the therapeutic relationship should be fully mutual has, though we may disagree with it, something to offer the group therapist. In his training the analytic group therapist has been strongly impressed with the dangers of emotional involvement with his patient. He sometimes mistakenly tries to avoid it altogether. Of course this cannot be accomplished and so the eager student is likely to resort unconsciously to repression, to deny any feelings toward the patient rather than inspect them carefully and use them in a positive way to understand him. This kind of repression constricts him and deprives him of spontaneity. It desensitizes his antennae. His awareness that one school of therapists actually welcomes as much feeling about the patient as possible comes as a relief to him and allows him once more to admit the truth that he cannot totally avoid countertransference.

The existentialists' insistence on the patient's right to free choice, including the choice of inauthentic existence, reminds us that the patient also has the right to be ill and that he can get well, with our help, only if he so wishes. We become aware, if we keep this in mind, that we cannot force the patient to become well. We will be less impatient with him and refrain from pressing him and from treating his natural resistance as bad behavior. This is completely in line with the philosophy of the psychoanalyst but we are prone to forget it.

Sartre's doctrine of the individual's responsibility is also a point well taken. There has been an unfortunate tendency in analytic therapy to overstress the role of the parents in the etiology of the neurosis. Somehow a disposition to identify with the patient as a passive victim of his parents' neurotic behavior creeps in. This merely tends to encourage him to feel sorry for himself and so plays into his resistance. The concept that the cause of neurotic behavior was the parents grew out of the original view of the ego as weak and helpless, but since the ego has come to be understood as the administrative department of the personality a change has taken place and the patient is made responsible for his present behavior and of his participation in bringing about his neurosis. Nevertheless there remain those who identify with the patient's helplessness and to these the existentialists offer food for thought.

XVI Some Philosophical Roots of Existential Group Psychotherapy

Existential philosophy began as a protest against systems of philosophy, science, and religion, and as a fight for the restoration of individualism. The pervasive feeling of self-alienation out of which it was born and the struggle for self-realization to which it led gave impetus to this new way of thinking. Its message was carried to the thinking public in the works of poets, novelists, painters, and musicians. They gave it the poignant expression which helped to extend its principles far beyond philosophical circles into the life of the average man. In the form of philosophical anthropology it also invaded the field of psychology and made of it a cultural science with an ontological base. Psychotherapists who adopted its principles instituted far-reaching changes in their theory and practice, and it is for this reason that we must comprehend its meaning.

At present existential group psychotherapy is being practiced in the United States and that fact forces us to challenge not only its proponents' ideology but our own. Nor is it enough that we become vaguely or superficially acquainted with what existential therapists are doing. We must come to grips with their basic premises and not fall prey to the easy solution of disparaging a way of thinking with which we disagree nor rush to embrace an appealing one as a panacea. Many of our patients have been influenced through the various art forms by existential thinking and we must be prepared to understand what it means to them, for their ideology is of course closely related to their character structure. Of broader significance is the fact that if we are going to achieve a sound theoretical foundation for group psychotherapy we must consider the formulations of all the major viewpoints. With less than a clear grasp of the origin, the history, and the philosophical and psychological tenets of existentialism we cannot fairly evaluate its contributions to such a theory.

To attempt a brief review of existentialism is not a simple matter for it is a doctrine that defies definition. Its very nature is violated when we attempt to get at its essence. Yet its formlessness does not deny its existence, for its philosophical meaning does have an inner coherence which stems from a consistent approach to the study of man. Its unity, however, lies not in its content but in its basic stance, so that we shall come closer to its real meaning if we search out its intent rather than attempt its definition.

A brief expedition into the history of philosophy and science will therefore prove illuminating to this question. The log of a complete penetration into this territory would fill several volumes, but we must content ourselves with a glance from a jet flight.

Our first landing in the space-time trip is in medieval times. During that period things were not quite what they seemed. We are accustomed to think of Middle Age man as other-worldly. Some of those who have looked closely at his way of life and habits of thought have come to the conclusion that the emphasis on his spirituality was nothing more than an overcompensation for the acutely experienced needs of his body. Compared to a citizen of the nineteenth century, man in those times experienced the world about him as direct and real. The soul was held in high regard but was thought of as living in the body. In spite of the Church, man of the Middle Ages was not particularly alienated from himself nor from the world around him.

Strangely enough it was the Renaissance thinkers who, in spite of their conscious wish that man would get to know his world better, unwittingly began the process of alienating him from it. It was their assiduous effort to observe their world objectively that caused man, the observer, to disengage himself from what he observed. The process thus set off produced an invaluable scientific tool in the empirical method, but it also brought into being a mechanistic philosophy which, carried to its extreme, started the pendulum swinging back to a new form of vitalism. It is another example of the tendency in history for a movement to bear within itself the seeds which bring about its own destruction and give birth to its opposite.

This section of the story begins with Descartes because he has usually if somewhat arbitrarily been selected as the source of the new trends. In spite of the prior contributions of Harvey, Copernicus, Galileo, and Newton, Descartes was the grand philosopher of the new scientific outlook. He was also the first great Renaissance psychologist. In his *Passions of the Human Soul* (1650), he divided human acts into those of a mechanical and those of a rational nature. It was his concept of rational economic man that became the prototype of nineteenth-century man, who avoided pain and sought pleasure. Freud utilized this concept. For although he rebelled against rationalism and actually gave us one of the most effective weapons against it—the irrational unconscious—he was nevertheless steeped in its principles and could not completely cut himself off from it.

Descartes, who began it, had caught a bear by the tail. The cleavage between self and world, between mind and body, that ensued from his work plagued philosophy and psychology for centuries. That Descartes himself was much distressed by it and tried to find his own way out of the paradox is seldom realized. He actually spent much time searching for an answer and he came to the conclusion that the pineal glands were the seat of the soul, and they transmitted physical stimuli to the soul and impulses from it back to the body. But to no avail; the times were not ready for his brand of interactionism. Instead his "Cogito ergo sum" spearheaded the trend toward modern rationalism which thrived in spite of repeated signs that the opposing force still existed. It culminated two centuries later in Hegel's concept of the World Mind.

Meanwhile, Descartes' consistent emphasis on the necessity of refining methods of achieving abstract truth bore fruit in the empirical method. As the result of the careful observation of facts, the collecting of data, and their submission to mathematical analysis and experiment, great strides were made in the natural sciences. Physics, biology, physiology, and psychology all benefitted from acquaintance with the new method. The seventeenth century had given birth to the new direction of empiricism, rationalism, and mechanism; the eighteenth century saw its fructification. In psychology, Great Britain gave us the experimental method and associationism. But although the star of rationalism was in the ascendant, the Scotch School of Thomas Reid reminds us that the opposing force was nevertheless alive. Reid's insistence that the mind worked actively on what it perceived in the real world, and that a force beyond the observation of the senses was at work, gave evidence for that assumption.

In Germany rational philosophy and empirical science also rose to great heights in these centuries, but the opposing forces in that land were less completely submerged. In philosophy Kant did introduce British empiricism but the German scholars were far more interested in explanatory principles which lay outside the field of experience. Kant's adaptation of the then current "faculty psychology" stopped short of empiricism when it came to "willing and feeling," because he considered them a part of moral and religious reality beyond the field of knowledge. Transcendentalism never quite subsided. Post-Kantian psychology also succumbed to the influence of romantic naturalism. This "Philosophy of Nature" stimulated research into biological facts but was, in practice, much more interested in their spiritual meaning than in the factual data. Its explanatory principle was vitalistic rather than mechanistic.

Empiricism in nineteenth-century Germany reached its mark in the biological sciences. The distinguished work of Helmholtz, E. H. Weber, Fechner, Ebbinghaus, and others brought forth a thoroughgoing experimental physiology which in due course gave birth to a separate experimental psychology. But in the long run the great German empirical achievements appear simply as a figure in the ground of German romanticism.

The evolution of the German university system curiously illuminates the story. Until the early eighteenth century only professional faculties had been recognized in the universities. Then a new faculty for the liberal arts was established. It included all the sciences and the humanities under a Chair in Philosophy. The term *Wissenschaften* which covered mathematics, logic, literature, philology, and esthetics as well as the natural sciences implied a broad view of civilization which had a unifying effect outlasting the fluctuation of rationalism and romanticism. In spite of the fact that in the nineteenth century psychology had attained a chair of its own as a natural science, philosophers still regarded the nature of man as a legitimate part of their territory. Both rationalist and existential philosophers continued, in the twentieth century, to present theories of man to the intellectual world which competed for recognition with experimental psychology. The philosophers considered psychology a cultural science and held that it should aim at finding its laws in a different way from that of the natural sciences. Cultural sciences are interested in meaning and value, in description and understanding, rather than in explanation and causation. Dilthey, for example, was one of the rationalist philosopher-psychologists who conceived of psychology as the very foundation of the cultural sciences. Description and understanding are, according to him, not so much scientific as artistic processes in which the *Struktur-Zusammenhang* (configuration) is more important than the elements. Psychology, he insists, must begin with inner connections. But Ebbinghaus, one of the great German experimental psychologists, challenged Dilthey, contending that psychological facts could very effectively be treated like biological data; that the experimental method and mathematical formulae could be fruitfully applied to these facts, after the manner of the physical sciences; and that laws could be similarly formulated and causal explanations provided. Their controversy became a tremendous stimulus to European thinking for a good part of a century. The existentialists were curiously heirs to Dilthey's point of view although they opposed his rationalism with their new naturalism.

For instance, Karl Jaspers, a psychiatrist turned philosopher, followed Dilthey in stressing the importance of "understanding," but he used the word in the sense of *connaître* rather than *savoir* as Dilthey had meant it. He made the distinction, of vital importance to existentialists, between abstract understanding and the understanding of real occurrences. As a psychiatrist searching for better methods of understanding the patients than the old-time classificatory system provided, he adapted Husserl's method of phenomenology to his purpose. Whereas Husserl had used it for the attainment of abstract truth, he used it to gain more direct apprehension by empathically entering the "patient's world" and experiencing with him the concrete phenomena that constituted it. As a philosopher, he, along with Heidegger, reawakened inter-

est in Kierkegaard's teachings and added the ontological dimension to his psychiatry. For some reason, perhaps because of his
hortatory style of writing, and perhaps because he so completely
embraced the existentialist opposition to system that he was called
der schwebende Philosoph, his work was never as well received as
that of Heidegger.

Interestingly enough Jaspers, and for that matter Heidegger, had
much in common with the psychology of Freud. Both had been
motivated by the desire to overcome the growing self-alienation in
man, as well as the fragmentation in science. Both were absorbed in
searching for the truth about the nature of man and better ways of
arriving at that truth. The method of phenomenology (Jaspers) and
that of free association (Freud) had in common the wish to prevent
the observer from reading his own reality into that of his patients.
But there the similarity ends. Freud wanted to understand and to
explain by finding causes; Jaspers, to achieve direct apprehension
by giving "his full human presence." Freud made biology his base;
Jaspers went a step beyond, to ontology. Freud was systematic; Jaspers eschewed system. Freud avoided philosophical entanglements;
Jaspers made philosophy an integral part of his psychology.

Europe in the nineteenth century was ready for a change. The
birth of existentialism was as inevitable as its volcanic upsurge in
the twentieth. The philosophers who began it responded to an urgent need of the times. All through the nineteenth century the disruption of the previous period of comparative political, social, and
economic harmony and stability was increasingly felt. Europe
moved in a crescendo toward its thundering climax in the First
World War. Existentialism was to be the antidote. To be sure, this
was not the first time such a period of breakdown and transition had
come about. The particular *Zeitgeist* had made visitations to earth
before. Socrates had ushered in a similar era, and so had Pascal.
The existentialists, indeed, claim these two as their precursors. Nor
was this existential thinking entirely new to the world, for most
religions prescribe it, at least in their early phases. But Kierkegaard was the first to use the term existential, while Jaspers was the
first to write about *Existenz Philosophie.* In its broader sense existentialism refers also to the work of the poets, writers, and artists
who reflect its philosophy, depicting the kind of tragicomic world
they see and the plight of those who are trapped in it.

The soil from which existentialism first sprang was an exhausted soil. The nineteenth century was reaping the bitter harvest of the industrial revolution and suffering the impoverishment which followed its economic upheaval. As a result the total patterning of European man's social life was in process of change. The kaleidoscopic shakeup was affecting those very institutions from which man had drawn his earlier unquestioning sense of belonging and security. His "props" were all but taken from under him; his "eternal verities" were crumbling. Moreover, the industrial revolution continued in a kind of chain process, eventuating in the more radical technological changes of the twentieth century. Technology and automatization followed industrialization, and the tail of the comet proved more disruptive than the star. The First World War, which was both the result of these events and itself the cause for even greater disruption, created a receptive mood in Europe for the existential movement. Victim to the whirlwind into whose vortex he had been drawn, man became more than ever estranged from himself, from his fellows, from nature, and from his god. The security of the individual was threatened in every direction. In their now urgent quest for certainty some found new ways; some held ever more rigidly to the old ones; some shipwrecked. In most cases, the individual was swamped; autonomy was sacrificed for security. The average man struggled in conflict, blindly searching for some meaning in life. The artist portrayed his plight in painting, in music, and in literature. Scientists, too, among them Freud, joined in the new search for meaning. But each branch of science was so preoccupied with its own truths that fragmentation rather than unity became the order of those days. Furthermore, the mechanistic science of the age which seemed to satisfy the academic scientist gave little scope to the human longing for certainty and omnipotence.

It is no wonder that the age-old philosophical problem of alienation became acute and very real once more. Neither the rationalist philosopher nor the mechanistic scientist could lead the people out of this human bondage. For they were too steeped in abstractions to deal effectively with concrete problems.

The abstract philosophy of rationalism had come to its climax in Hegel's concept of an "all embracing world mind" which seemed to dissolve individual differences and swallowed up altogether the subject who did the thinking. After Hegel, philosophy in the universities degenerated into a mere history of philosophies. Existing philosophical systems were reviewed and criticized but not deeply questioned. Thus the existentialist philosophy was hoist by its own petard.

Hope came from another quarter. The pendulum had begun to swing back in the early nineteenth century. Kierkegaard, the Danish theologian-philosopher, sensing the growing chaos and despair, had cried out in his own anguish against society's utter disregard for the human individual. To counteract it, he focused his entire thinking on the concrete lived existence of the individual. Conventions, rituals, and abstractions were useless in men's search for identity. Of course he thought of existence primarily in religious terms. It was the existence which "every Christian has to face for himself, for which he alone is responsible in the face of God." For as he said, "If he cannot grasp eternity in an *Augenblick* (wink of an eye) and so find his authentic (i.e., self directed, honest, responsible) existence, the suffering, guilty creature falls into despair." For Kierkegaard, obviously, direct apprehension replaced reason as the true source of knowledge. He reversed the Cartesian formula. "I am, therefore I think", he declared. From having been considered as object, man was now to be the subject.

But Kierkegaard proved to be fifty years ahead of his time. On one occasion he challenged the rationalist philosophers of his day to debate at a special meeting, but nothing came of it. His protests were of no avail. The better part of a century was to go by before his thinking was given a serious hearing in the philosophical world.

A little later Nietzsche also raised his voice in a similar challenge to thinkers. He demanded that they first be individuals, and then rigorously pursue the truth without fear or mental laziness and without recourse to the easy solution of religion. Like Kierkegaard, Nietzsche protested against systems of thought in philosophy or in science, and especially against the rationalist academicians of his day. But unlike him he despised religion and insisted on combining with direct apprehension the careful way of reason in the search for truth. For Nietzsche reason and intuition were equally important. Later still Jaspers and Heidegger revived Kierkegaard's work and emphasized the existential elements of Nietzsche's philosophy. They proposed what they considered a new and vital solution to the urgent problem of man's self-alienation. They founded their teachings on Kierkegaard's principles and thus gave birth to existential philosophy as we know it. By turning away from the purely abstract to the living concrete, man was restored to the center of his world and man's existence to the center of the search for truth. A philosophic revolution had taken place which was to have its repercussion in science, in the arts, and in the life of the average man.

The existentialists challenged the scientific attitudes which had reached their peak in the late nineteenth and early twentieth centuries. For example, they pitted themselves against "scientific" psychology, which they felt had embraced a molecular empiricism; against the mechanists who had sneered at vitalism; and against their assiduous tendency to analyze while soft-pedaling synthesis. Such trends, they felt, made for fragmentation and prevented unity of thought. In their stead they offered their holistic, ontological, cultural psychology, from which existential psychology was derived.

In challenging the ethics of the day, they tried also to reach the common man. They urged the individual to demand autonomy for himself and to give up his frightened security-seeking heteronomy. They exhorted man to awaken to his individuality, his uniqueness, his right to "be," and his responsibility. They urged him to resist engulfment, through fear and laziness, in traditional religious dogma, in the social conventions, or, for that matter, in the collectivism of the Marxian solution to their problem. They declared that the man who faces his own being honestly and fearlessly, and who recognizes his sole responsibility for his decisions, has to experience the anguish of his aloneness in order to come to terms with himself, but his reward will be the discovery of the freedom of authentic existence.

The challenge to the individual of the twentieth century was vividly communicated to him through art and literature. Poets, novelists, dramatists, painters, sculptors, and musicians made use of their uniquely appropriate medium to depict the desperation and loneliness of contemporary man. The content of their works is often mistaken for an attempt to describe the existentialist philosophy, which consequently appeared to be defeatist and passive.

But they do not present the philosophy. They present the trag-icomic predicament of man; his struggle to find meaning in a cha-otic world; the absurdity of the depths to which he descends and the grim heights to which he occasionally rises. They leave to the phi-losophers the job of teaching man to meet his own crises and to find his own solutions. In the form of his work the existential artist also reflects his own strong and sometimes desperate need to find his certainty within himself and to withstand the temptation to yield to fixed standards. This urgent need for identity has some-times caused him to fall prey to a new technical form of self-aliena-tion in which self-expression has reached a point of diminishing returns. When the artist became a victim to his techniques he was sharply curtailed in his ability to communicate. Only the few can then understand him. Unfortunately he thus unwittingly deprives his fellow man of the opportunity to articulate his own visions through appreciation. Gertrude Stein, Jackson Pollack, and per-haps Heidegger fall into this category. For as Goethe's words warn:

> Gern wär Ich Überliefrung los
> Und ganz original;
> Doch ist das Unternehmen gross
> Und führt in manche Qual.[1]

To state it simply, the artist and the writer express the predica-ment of modern man and their own struggle with it. The philoso-pher, the scientist, and particularly the psychotherapist must pro-vide guidance to man in quest of his own solutions.

The Philosophical Cornerstones for Existential Psychology and Psychotherapy

It would be as inappropriate as it is impossible to attempt a phil-osophical treatise on the existential thought of Jaspers, Heideg-ger, Buber, Marcel, Sartre, Berdyaev, Ortega y Gasset, and others.[2] We can do little more in these pages than to try to understand

---

[1] "I would be glad to be entirely original, but such a project is enormous and leads to many troubles."

[2] There are several good histories which can be consulted for further refer-ence and a new bibliography of existential source material. See bibliography.

those basic principles which they held in common and to see how and why they became influential in our own field.

It is the nature of existentialism that its points of similarity lie in function rather than in content, so that there is the widest possible variety of content among its leaders. For instance, we have not only the fighting Protestant Kierkegaard, but the agnostic Heidegger, the atheist Sartre, the Catholic Marcel, and the mystical anarchist Berdyaev. As they differ in religious affiliation, they differ in many other important respects. We are much more interested in their common views on the nature of man which are recurrent and consistent throughout the literature. In order to provide an orientation these might be summarized as follows:

Man is a totality to be understood in the lived concrete rather than in the abstract. Human existence is the center of any knowledge of man. The human individual has freedom of choice and is responsible to himself and to others for his decisions and actions. In taking this choice he may yield to inauthentic submergence in others or find his authentic self in developing his own potentialities. He must face being and nonbeing, and suffer anguish (existential guilt) in doing so.

We shall try to become better acquainted with these "articles of faith," although it would take years of study to become conversant with all their elaborations and variations. I shall try to capture the essence of the thinking of three outstanding philosophers whose influence on group psychotherapy seems to me to be most significant. It has been largely their answer to the problem of man's nature which gave rise to existential analysis and existential psychotherapy. The first is Heidegger, upon whose formulations all other existentialists have drawn considerably; the second is Sartre, who transposed Heidegger's philosophy into the key of his personal experience and style and gave it to a very receptive audience in France; the third is Buber who continued the analysis of existence into the sphere of what he called the interhuman and so touches closely on the interests of psychotherapy.

Martin Heidegger

Heidegger became the existentialist par excellence. Perhaps it was because his inimitable description of authentic and inauthentic

existence *(Dasein)* expressed the longing of the people in that turbulent era between world wars, or perhaps because his subtle, almost mystical concept of the relationship between man's earthly being (existence) and Absolute Being gave them hope of transcending
their pedestrian limitations. Whatever the reason, Heidegger did attract a multitude of apostles. Almost overnight, after the
publication of his *Sein und Zeit* in 1927, he was hailed as the
prophet of existentialism. Interestingly enough he disclaimed that
honor,[3] insisting that his book had been misunderstood. He was,
he said, interested in existence itself only in so far as it was the concrete representation of "Being" (the Absolute). He made it clear
that if he had wished to focus on *Dasein* (existence) he would have
called his book *Dasein und Zeit*. As one author has expressed it,
Heidegger is the existentialist *contre coeur*. Nevertheless all other
existentialists drew heavily upon his works and history's verdict
remains to be heard.

What is more important for us is his enormous influence on psychiatry. A number of psychiatrists from the phenomenological
school of which Minkowski is perhaps the outstanding example,
and some not quite contented psychoanalysts like Binswanger
who were searching for new ideas, seized upon Heidegger's views
of the nature of man and adapted them to their theory and practice of psychotherapy. They called themselves *Daseins Analytiker*
(existential analysts). From them, American psychotherapists like
Antonia Wenkart and Rollo May took example; others like Hora
introduced these ideas into group psychotherapy.

We cannot understand their work nor their influence on existential psychotherapy without studying Heidegger's philosophy in
greater detail. It may help to clarify his relationship to psychotherapy if we consider his work in three related aspects. First, he
gave a new secular expression to Kierkegaard's existential principles. Second, he adapted Husserl's phenomenological method[4] to
the empirical study of man. On the basis of the data collected by

[3] He felt that giving his ideas a name would make them into a system among
other systems.
[4] It is interesting to note that Husserl was a rationalist and his method was
designed to extract the abstract truth. Heidegger transformed it into an instrument for gaining concrete knowledge of man's world by direct apprehension.

this method he classified certain modes or categories of man's be-ing-in-the-world. In the third stage Heidegger embraced transcen-dentalism and established a new metaphysics based on what he came to consider the ecstatic character of *Dasein*. Psychotherapists of the existential school differ as to whether they accept one, two, or all three of these aspects of the master's philosophy. The first provides an attitude which all therapists would be wise to embrace; the second, a method which emphasizes the necessity of empathy with the world as the patient perceives it and provides new cate-gories by which to understand him; the third offers a mystical phi-losophy which opens the door to religion.

The Three Phases of Heidegger's Philosophy

Phase I: A New Stance—The Existential Attitude

After almost a century had passed Heidegger reintroduced the work of Kierkegaard and gave his principles, shorn of their religious as-pect, a place in philosophy. He used these ideas as his springboard. Kierkegaard had said that man is not the simple working out of a plan (essence) but is free to make his own choices. Out of his dread of nonbeing he may choose to submerge himself in the thought of others and lapse into an inauthentic existence. Or, by choosing to face his dread, he may in anguish (the sickness unto death) arrive at a moment *(Augenblick)* of direct apprehension of truth. If he is able to accomplish this goal he establishes an authentic (i.e., re-sponsible) existence for himself.

We must note two major differences between them. (1) For Kierkegaard, truth, referred to the Christian God, for Heidegger it referred to Being. (2) Kierkegaard merely reversed the Cartesian formula. He would have said, "I am, therefore I think." The sub-ject-object dichotomy was highlighted but not resolved. Heidegger thought the problem through to its conclusion. He denied the dichotomy and found a way of transcending it. His definition of existence as "man's-being-in-the-world" gave expression to his new perception that all knowledge is in relation to the man who finds it and cannot be separated from him. There is no truth except in relation to the experiencing man. Hence no dichotomy!

Phase II: A New Method. Phenomenology and
New Categories of Existence

Following Dilthey's formulation that human existence differed from other organic and inorganic existence, Heidegger made a distinction between animal existence *(Vorhandensein)* and the unique personal existence of man which he called *Dasein*. He consistently focused on human existence *(Dasein)* as the starting point of the search for truth. If one wants to know what Being (the Absolute) is, he argued, then one has to begin by analyzing the existence of concrete beings in the world.

In order to analyze *Dasein* empirically, Heidegger adapted Husserl's phenomenological method—but with a difference. Husserl was a rationalist philosopher and his method was for the purpose of insuring objective observation of facts so that their pure essence might be abstracted. According to Heidegger the term "phenomena" is understood "as something that presents itself as the being or meaning of the person in question" *(Das an Ihm Zeigen)*. He therefore applied his method as a means of participating empathically in the existence of others. The analyst was to "let him (the subject) be so that all that is may reveal itself in the essence of its Being." Thus phenomenology takes on a new meaning and becomes identical with ontology. Applied in psychotherapy, this way of listening intuitively implied a new, more equal relationship between therapist and patient.

The phenomena of any individual's being-in-the-world become visible in the mode in which he presents himself. Heidegger noted certain significant modes or categories of existence. The most important of these, he felt, was the temporal one. And within this category the future was to be considered more important than the present. Because existence is chiefly temporal and historical, Heidegger thought it had so far chiefly been regarded in the mode of the present. But he stressed the mode of the future. Becoming is more important than being. Becoming was the keynote too, for the analysts who followed him and for whom present existence was of primary importance. But for Heidegger the temporal dimensions became the key to transcendentalism as well and led him to his deepest interest, metaphysics, which formed the third phase of his work.

It was the second aspect of Heidegger's thinking that had so deep an influence on the psychiatrists. Heidegger gave them a new ontological basis; a new understanding of man in holistic terms; and a method for observing him in what they hoped would be a totally unbiased way. It gave them a fresh concept of neurosis as inauthentic existence, loss of meaning and of self-direction; of neurotic anxiety as man's anguish in facing nonbeing; and of guilt as sensing his inauthenticity and his failure to utilize his potential being. These psychiatrists became known as existential analysts. They continued analyzing the *Dasein* of their patients i.e., their particular way of being-in-the-world. They added to the categories out of their own experience. They also continued to stress the need to see man as a totality and to perceive the particular modes of each man's experience rather than to apply the categories they knew about to the man.

But the project of analyzing categories gave rise to certain dangers, for the undertaking involved the precarious task of systematizing the philosophy which had opposed all systems. The establishment of categories, even those of an ontological nature, of necessity opens the way once more to substantive thinking and to abstraction. Existential philosophizing was becoming a philosophy of Existence, thus courting the very dangers against which it had warned.

Phase III: Transcendentalism

As Heidegger came more and more to stress temporality, existence (being) was consistently conceived of as potential Being. He pointed out the close connection between existence, time, and Being. Existence was regarded as having an ecstatic character, having always the possibility of transcendance into different directions and creating time in doing so. These dimensions for Heidegger point in the direction of the horizons of Being. Through them man may reach an understanding of the truth of Being.

Heidegger has given us a very illuminating analogy to explain his meaning. Philosophy, he says, is like a tree. The branches are the various sciences, the trunk is physics, and the roots are metaphysics. No metaphysics so far has inquired into the soil or ground in which these roots nourish. This has been an error, and as a result philosophers have been able to see Being only in its reflections in *Dasein* of the beings, never to see the truth of Being in its unconcealedness, the Source of Being itself. This is what Heidegger wishes to do. He sees the possibility of arriving at such a new metaphysics through the concept of Time. What we need, he says, is a totally new way of looking at things. Neither common sense nor reason will do. There must be a new form of thinking which he calls *Andenken* and implies a recall of what has been thought. Carrying out this idea he goes back to the thinking of the Presocratics to gain knowledge about the soil which nourished the trees. Re-examining the early Greek words for Being, he discovers the following meaning:

"In being present *(das Wesen dieses Anwesens)* there moves, unrecognized and concealed, present being and duration—in one word, Time. Being, as such, is thus unconcealed owing to Time. Thus Time points to unconcealedness, i.e., the Truth of Being. But the Time of which we should think here is not experienced through the changeful career of beings. Time is evidently of an altogether different nature which has not been recalled by way of the Time concept of metaphysics nor can ever be recalled this way. Thus Time becomes the first name, which is yet to be heeded, of the Truth of Being, which is yet to be experienced." This paragraph is typical of Heidegger's writing.

In this third phase of his work he reveals his deep interest in the transcendental. There is a parallel between the goal of his thinking, that of the theologians, and that of the Jungian interest in the Suprarational. All three are striving for the Unknown Absolute, the Source of Life and Truth. Freud's Life Instinct approaches the same category, and he, like Heidegger, conceived of basic existential polarity, which Freud called the Life and the Death Instinct and Heidegger called Being and Non-Being. Heidegger's final goal was to penetrate the heart of this truth; Freud left that to philosophy.

In studying the ecstatic nature of existence Heidegger left most of the psychotherapists behind. He drew close to the goal implicit in all his writing, which was the establishment of a new "Fundamental Ontology" and a new metaphysics which would explore the source of truth (i.e., the ground of Being) in a way which metaphysics had thus far ignored.

Jean Paul Sartre

There are several reasons for choosing Sartre as our second example of existentialism. It was he who brought Heidegger's philosophy to France. But he thought its principles through from his own experience and presented it in his own unique way. Comparing his views with those of Heidegger illuminates both those which they hold in common and the extraordinary divergence that is possible within the existential framework. Sartre has a truly existential attitude. He is original, and he lives, thinks, and writes in the lived concrete. Compared to him Heidegger and Jaspers seem academic indeed. They think and write about existence; he acts and writes out of his own experience. Sartre also regards psychology as an important aspect of his work. He was a psychotherapist and has written a detailed comparison of existential analysis and psychoanalysis.

Yet it can hardly be said that Sartre has won complete acceptance among existential philosophers. Heidegger refused the title "existentialist" partly because of Sartre, who lost favor with him when he explained the statement that existence precedes essence in such a way that it appeared to be an ontological dictum instead of a merely epistemological one. For Heidegger, Being ontologically precedes existence. Jaspers also scorned Sartre, agreeing with Heidegger that the Frenchman's scholarship was second rate. (Jaspers never quite forgave Sartre for having incorrectly referred to him as a Catholic.) He was also contemptuous of Sartre's "spiritual personality." Lastly, Sartre was too much of a littérateur to be accepted by philosophers as a metaphysician. His brilliant, penetrating style and his very lucidity were held against him by those who were impressed with the abstruseness of Heidegger's writing.

But for the uninitiate, Sartre's clarity is a godsend. He explains with beautiful simplicity the rather difficult solution to the subject-object dichotomy when he says: "Every truth and every action implies a human setting and a human subjectivity." With equal acuity he explains his definition of existentialism. "Here is an object," he writes, "which has been made by an artisan whose inspiration comes from a concept. For the paper cutter essence (the plan) precedes existence. Man, on the other hand, first exists, encounters himself, surges up in the world, and defines himself afterwards."

He is more tough-minded than Heidegger. Like Nietzsche, he takes the rigorous position that man is, in the final analysis, responsible for himself. He cannot fall back on God to explain away nor to expiate his shortcomings. Nor may he have recourse to Heidegger's form of Being, nor to explaining away his problems by his parents' attitudes, as the psychoanalysts do. He writes: "We want a doctrine based on truth, not on a lot of theories full of hope but no reality." "God is generally considered a kind of supernatural artisan," scoffs Sartre, "responsible for the shortcomings of man." It is in this sense that he speaks of man as "forlorn." He has nothing to fall back on. He must make his own decisions, and by these decisions he creates the image of himself for which he alone is responsible. He is, moreover, responsible for all mankind, for "whatever decision he makes and whatever action he takes, he sets up his standards and his values for the world." Sartre uses the example of the army captain who must make a decision for the life and death of his men, and alone is responsible for them. Indeed, he goes a step further, holding that whatever man does or does not do implies a decision. If he evades a choice, he, by that token, makes a negative choice. There is no escape for him.

It is in this context that man is considered to have free choice. There are therefore limitations. One is limited by one's situation (la condition humaine); the "givens" of one's existence. One's only choice might be to say "No," like the man in his short story, "The Wall," who must yield to the Nazis or die. He chooses to die and thereby retains his freedom and his human dignity. Furthermore one is limited by earlier choices. For example, a man may want to get married but find it impossible to do so because of early choices he has made. And lastly, a man cannot, in his choices, transcend human subjectivity. It is in making choices of this nature that man has to face being and nonbeing (l'être et le néant) and achieves authentic existence or remains inauthentic.

Like the other existentialists he eschews the concept of the unconscious. Instead consciousness for him includes a prereflective level on which one may at once know oneself and others. One knows oneself through others because one knows them more directly. Oneself, therefore, is constantly in need of being confirmed by others. But running through his psychology we discover Sartre's preoccupation with the negatives (négatives), so that sadism and masochism play an important role in his concept of intersubjectivity. He sees the relationship between people as primarily negative. The problem becomes how to transform individuals in whom negative attitudes prevail into those who will affirm and recognize the dignity of other persons.

This emphasis on the *négatives* is one of Sartre's greatest weaknesses. He has obviously generalized too much from his personal experience. *La condition humaine* for him was the utterly negative one of the Nazi occupation and he judged the world through his despair. From his immediate situation he drew conclusions about all mankind of all times. As one Catholic critic has written of him, "Sartre forgets the smile on the face of the baby." We get from him, therefore, a onesided picture of existence. Heidegger's outlook was broader and less personal.

To sum up: Sartre follows Heidegger in most of his concepts but interprets them through his own experience. He repeatedly translates Heidegger's abstractions into the concrete, accepting transcendence as a constituent element in man but limiting it to human subjectivity. Man transcends himself, he believes, by projecting himself into a human universe rather than into unity with Absolute Being.

Heidegger is deliberately antilogical, but Sartre cannot escape his typically logical French mind. Heidegger, the philologist subtly plays with the roots and stems of his words, producing an obscurantist style and an atmosphere of profundity. Sartre, in contrast, treats us to the verbal agility of the littérateur, and he is easy to read and to comprehend. One cannot avoid the impression that Heidegger gives us the philosopher's thinking about existence while Sartre is a living example of existential thought. They are illuminatingly complementary.

Martin Buber

If Heidegger may be characterized as the thinker among existentialists and Sartre as the man of action, Buber stands out primarily as the human being. The principles of his philosophical anthropology reveal this distinction. For him the most important category of existence is "the sphere of the in between," which concerns the area of genuine relatedness or communion among men. Buber emphasizes true communion between man and man and carries this beyond the dyadic into the nature of group relationships. What he calls the essential "we" is, for him, the final goal of civilization. By virtue of this emphasis he is of special interest to group psychotherapists.

Holding that what most distinguishes human existence is the capacity of man for interhuman communication and relationships, he recognizes several categories in this area. There is what he calls the "primitive I/Thou" type of relation which may be illustrated by the infant and its mother. It occurs in the beginning when there is no ability in man to distinguish between the self and the other. This would appear to be comparable to the Freudian primary identification. Next, after a certain distance has been established between them so that the self may be able to "stand over against" (gegenüber) the other, two new forms of relatedness may be recognized. One is the I/It relationship in which one individual sets himself over against another, but reserving part of himself directs his attention to the other or to some part of the other. He may observe him, use him, have solicitude (Heidegger's word) for him, exploit him, or do business with him. In contrast is the essential I/Thou category which requires fully mutual, spontaneous, and direct relationship. Contrary to the understanding of some psychotherapists, the I/It relationship is by no means an entirely negative concept for Buber. It is only through that achievement, he says, that the individual may gain all the necessary intellectual knowledge about the world of things, animals, and people. Without it, science would be nonexistent. Only in the world of the interhuman does it interfere if it takes primacy over the I/Thou, because it keeps that relationship from being genuine and complete. Another error common to a superficial understanding of Buber consists in the belief that an emotional relationship is always an I/Thou one. Far from it. Any purely emotional relationship such as might exist between physical lovers may be an I/It one when there is not complete mutuality between them. Thus also two individuals who engage only in a common action, even if that action is for a highly and emotionally charged purpose, but do not share other feelings and thoughts, are still in an I/It relationship.

The mode of communication in a genuine I/Thou relationship is called dialogue. Intrapsychic events are for Buber only the accompaniment of the dialogical. In dialogue there is true meeting between man and man, and through it an individual is confirmed in himself and may find his authentic self. Dialogue depends upon full acceptance and mutuality between two people. In contrast to it monologue lacks genuine meeting between the speaker and the one spoken to. For example, the ordinary cocktail party conversation, in which one person talks, perhaps to prove a point (one-up-manship), while the listener is really waiting for his turn, would be described as concurrent monologue. However, the possibility is not ruled out that "across a crowded room" a true meeting might take place, for even the most fleeting glance may be a meeting of souls. Such a genuine meeting is called "encounter."

Buber's conception of the dialogic differs fundamentally from Heidegger's concept of "care" or solicitude for another and goes beyond it. Buber's idea of solicitude of one individual for another implies an unequal relationship. Heidegger is highly individualistic, his first concern being the emergence of the "essential self." For Buber the self is secondary to what goes on between man and man, and derived from it. Heidegger believes that authentic existence is achieved by finding the genuine self in its relations to Being, while for Buber authentic existence is impossible without a deep awareness and mutuality with the other. Expressed in another way, the genuine self is only a preliminary to the dialogic. And in this experience no part of the self is reserved as it is in "solicitude." As Buber writes, "The authentic self is not the reality nor the goal of human existence, only the indispensable way to the goal. The goal is 'meeting' and all real living is meeting (encounter)."

In this connection Buber adds a new dimension to the problem of "What is Man?" He conceives of a special realm in which such genuine meeting occurs and calls it the "sphere of the in between." It is to be distinguished from the concept of interpersonal relationships as well as from the intrapsychic in man. It refers only to the "place" of true meeting or communion of the I/Thou mode and it has a kind of autonomy. He writes of it: "The between is not an auxiliary construction, but the real place and bearer of what happens between men; it has received no specific attention, because in distinction from the individual soul, it does not exhibit a smooth continuity, but is ever and again reconstituted in accordance with men's meetings with one another; hence what is experienced has been annexed naturally to the continuous elements, the soul and its world." Again he writes: "What is essential does not take place in each of the participants or in a neutral world which includes the two and all other things; but it takes place between them in the most precise sense . . . in a dimension which is accessible only to them both . . . in the understanding of such fleeting, and yet consistent happenings. One must guard oneself against introducing motives of feeling; what happens here cannot be reached by psychological concepts, it is something ontic . . . and can be grasped only in an ontic way."

Of especial significance for group psychotherapists is Buber's concept of "we" which refers to multiple rather than dyadic relationships. It holds top place in his hierarchy of relationships in the sphere of the in between. The "we" is the goal toward which man reaches, the goal of real living or "meeting" in genuine mutuality. The "we," too, has a history. The "primitive we" may be illustrated by primitive societies among whose people there is still a very low degree of individuation and to whom all outsiders are enemies, and it is magic that rules. In contrast lies the goal for the "genuine we" among human beings. This is not a goal that civilization has as yet reached to any degree, as is evidenced by mutual distrust, wars, etc. At present, Buber says, we seem to see only two alternatives clearly, individualism or collectivism. We have looked to these to solve the problem of self-alienation and isolation. "Modern man," he says, "tried to save himself from despair either by glorifying his individualism or by allowing himself to be engulfed completely by massive modern group formations." Buber offers us the alternative which he feels is the true solution, "the essential we!" This alternative begins in the "sphere of the in-between."

To summarize: Out of his personal despair and his bitterness about the religious hypocrisy of his day, the Christian "Protestant" Kierkegaard made his plea that man see himself as an individual and take upon himself the responsibility for his salvation. He believed that the rampant self-alienation of his times had arisen from oversystematization of thought—in religion, in politics, in philosophy. He therefore challenged the abstractions of the rational philosophers by reversing the Cartesian formula upon which he felt these evils had fed. Heidegger and Jaspers espoused Kierkegaard's principles and applied them to philosophy. They went beyond him to resolve the subject-object cleavage which they believed had stultified nineteenth-century science and reduced it to a mere "scientism." They bridged the gap by insisting that all thinking begin with the concrete situation, man-in-an-environment. Jaspers extolled the existential approach and preached against all system. Nevertheless he moved toward system when he constructed the first "philosophy of existence." Heidegger, employing a modification of Husserl's phenomenological method to study the modes of man's existence, began to structure existence by outlining its categories. Thus he moved dangerously nearer to systematizing the new philosophy. He came more and more to consider the "temporal mode" as the most significant category. In his study "Being and Time," he came to the conclusion that man could transcend his existence and unite his being with absolute Being. In this way he led the way to a new transcendentalism. Being was more important to him than existence in the end. Sartre introduced Heidegger's philosophy to France and the rest of the world but he eschewed the transcendental aspects. For him existence was prior, in an absolute sense, to essence. Buber's emphasis on "the sphere between man and man" reinforced the humanistic aspects of existential philosophy. The goal for him was not merely the realization of the individual's potential, but "meeting" with his fellow man. He considered Heidegger's "solicitude" and "I-It" mode of relating to others. For these reasons his thinking was highly pertinent for psychotherapy. His interest in the "Essential We" as distinct from "the primitive we" gave his work particular significance for group therapy.

Psychotherapists who were looking for new dimensions found a new base line in the philosophy of existentialism. They put ontological considerations before the investigation of ontogenetic causation in investigating and treating the emotional ills of man. Whether or not philosophy is a legitimate concern for psychotherapists remains a question. Psychoanalysts do not accept it as such. The Daseins Analysts adapted Heidegger's method for psychotherapeutic purposes. They used it to understand the world in which their patients lived. They perceived their relationship with patients as a "being with" and "letting be." Thus they tried to avoid all bias so that the patients could "reveal their way of being in the world" unencumbered by preconceived notions. Actually, this method was not different in its intent from Freud's method of free association, but revived the goal they felt psychoanalysts tended to forget.

It would lie beyond the realm of possibility to summarize even the major variations with which these existential principles have been applied by the existential analysts. Common techniques have not as yet been formulated and are in any case considered to be of secondary importance to the task of understanding the patient in ontological terms. Former phenomenologists like Minkowski, and Jungians like Gerhart, work quite differently. Medard Boss, on the other hand, applies all the Freudian techniques and dynamic explanations but he sees them in the new light of his comprehension of existence and his understanding of each patient's mode of being in the world. When the patient is thus perceived as a concrete being in an ontological context many concepts take on a different meaning. Neurotic guilt must now be distinguished from existential guilt. Transference is no longer the chief focus of the therapy, although it may be used to help the patient move to authentic existence. Its significance diminishes in the context of the more important human relationship between therapist and patient, or of one existence communicating with another.

XVII Group Process as Therapy:
A Case Illustration

Although there is no school of group dynamic psychotherapy in the United States, there are a number of individuals who have experimentally attempted to apply such a method in connection with research. Among these are Martin Lakin and William H. Dobbs (1962) who were primarily interested in determining the therapeutic potential of the group phenomena, and I am grateful for their permission and that of the *International Journal of Group Psychotherapy* to include the article that follows which describes one of their group sessions and gives verbatim illustrations from it. I believe this will clarify their purposes and help us become acquainted with the role of the group processes in their therapy better than any abstract discussion of method could provide.

We can assume that Lakin and Dobbs operate within a framework of Lewinian systems-in-tension theory; and in a personal communication Lakin indicated that he combined this with Bionic theory. However, at this point we are interested principally in the technical rather than the theoretical aspects of their work. It may further be taken for granted that during the early stages of the group the therapists attempted to set up an optimal group atmosphere to promote free expression of thought and feeling. Permissiveness and democracy, then, were no doubt considered therapeutically favorable ingredients for the group climate.

THE THERAPY GROUP PROMOTES AN HYPOTHESIS OF PSYCHOGENESIS: A STUDY IN GROUP PROCESS

MARTIN LAKIN, Ph.D., *Duke University*

and

WILLIAM H. DOBBS, M.D., *St. Elizabeth's Hospital*

In recent publications by group psychotherapists we have noted an effort to firmly distinguish between aim and processes involved in therapy groups and in training and other "small groups." Students of small groups and training groups have, with a few outstanding exceptions, shown surprisingly little interest in therapy groups. On the other hand a recent review of research and practice in psychotherapy summarizes the present situation in the following terms: "It will be interesting to see how much group dynamicists, group therapists, and communications theorists can get together in the next ten years. They all seem to be talking about similar processes".

One focal issue is whether or not understanding of group process phenomena contributes significantly to an understanding of what promotes therapeutic change. We might break the question down as follows: Are distinctive patterns involving pairing, standard setting, deviancy, intimacy, leadership and the like discernible in therapy groups? If such patterns obtain in therapy groups, what functions do they serve for individual members? What is the relationship between the emergence of such patterns and therapist activity and orientation? Most importantly, can the "group dynamics" or process patterns be related to the therapeutic effort and assessed in terms of benefit or harm to the patient?

We have posed a problem or rather a series of issues, which we wish to illustrate by reference to clinical experience. We have selected one group session. It is representative. The meeting which we have selected for analysis occurred during the routine course of treatment of an outpatient group which had been functioning for some five months prior to this session. It is an open, heterogeneous group, with respect to age, sex, and diagnostic classification. Meetings are held once weekly for an hour and fifteen minutes, and members are expected to come directly into the meeting room which is open a few minutes before the meeting. Sessions are routinely tape-recorded for use in teaching and/or research analysis.

The group therapist of the particular group we are going to consider is one of the authors. He takes little verbal part in communication between members so long as communication goes on.

The members of the group, whose identities are disguised, are as follows:

Mrs. Strong is a twenty-six-year-old housewife and mother of three children whose husband attends school and manages a business after school hours. About six months prior to psychiatric consultation she had been seen by a number of physicians because of headaches; symptoms which had been present five years, but which had become more acute following the birth of her third child. Eventually a psychologically oriented internist developed a continuing psychotherapeutic relationship with her, but after six months referred her because of increase in her symptoms and suggestions of impending panic state. After three evaluation interviews she was invited to attend the group. The present session was her ninth.

Dr. Logan is a forty-year-old physician who is married and the father of two children. During the three years prior to this contact he had been admitted on several occasions for fairly prolonged hospitalizations for severe depressive episodes. These episodes were accompanied by heavy alcoholic intake, and by use of addictive drugs. He had been treated prior to referral with intensive individual psychotherapy for about six months by another therapist, and was able to function in his profession, but still had difficulty in controlling his alcohol and drug intake. Also, apparently related to his depressions was a severe marital conflict. His wife seemed to him to be a dominating, controlling person with whom he felt helpless to deal. After two evaluation interviews he was invited to the group. The present session was his thirteenth.

Mrs. Braddock is a thirty-year-old housewife and mother of two children whose husband is a teacher. She had gone through two periods of individual psychotherapy of about one year each with two different therapists. Her major complaints centered around difficulties in establishing a satisfactory relationship with her husband. She was prone to violent temper outbursts, a desire for social isolation, and conflicts over her role as a housewife. After a trial period of individual psychotherapy for nine months with relatively little improvement, and a strong suspicion that she used the personal relationship in psychotherapy as a weapon against her husband, she was invited to the group. This was her nineteenth session.

Mr. Kress is a thirty-five-year-old married engineer and father of seven children. He was seen for evaluation in two joint interviews with his wife who had had brief psychiatric treatment for a severe conversion reaction headache following the birth of her last child. During the course of her treatment Mr. Kress had become more anxious and disturbed about their marital conflict. They were both invited to attend the group. Mrs. Kress came only once, and then discontinued, claiming that she was well and needed no further treatment. He continued, however, and this was his twelfth session.

Mr. Mann is a thirty-seven-year-old married mechanical worker who is the father of five children, two of them by a previous unsuccessful marriage. He was referred following a recent hospital admission, his second in recent years, and still evidenced a great amount of subjective anxiety. He had had difficulty settling down in any one job since adolescence, and had held many jobs. He seemed to have no difficulty in obtaining good jobs, but seemed inevitably to either get into difficulties with authority figures or else simply become dissatisfied and leave a position. He had difficulty accepting responsibility in general. In addition, he had open marital conflicts with his wife. Repeated attempts had been made to engage him in individual psychotherapy for the past seven years. However, he has been unable to stick with a therapist for longer than a few sessions before discontinuing treatment. He has been seen by five different psychotherapists on an outpatient basis, in addition to his hospital experiences.

The opening of the session finds two individuals alone prior to the entry of the other group members and the therapist. They discuss the question of personal responsibility. Mr. Mann admits he has been able to get out of all responsibilities. Mr. Kress admits that he too has avoided personal responsibility. They agree that it is necessary for them to assume responsibility in order to feel at peace with themselves. Mr. Mann says with some urgency that group psychotherapy is really very important for him now [1 and/or 2].[1]

Mrs. Strong and the therapist come into the room. Two things of significance immediately occur. Mrs. Strong tries to disrupt the pairing between Mr. Kress and Mr. Mann. She interjects in an insistent tone with respect to a receptacle in the room. "Is this supposed to be an ash tray?" She demands a reply from the other two members. That her concern with the ash tray is minimal is evidenced by the fact that when she is questioned as to her wish to smoke or to use it, she denies that she has any interest in it. [3]

The second thing of note was Mr. Kress' initial response to the therapist. Mr. Kress turned to him and asked whether the group had been demoted inasmuch as they had been transferred from a larger room to a smaller one. His own embarrassed laugh accompanied this question put to the therapist. Mr. Kress' guilt about his felt lack of progress determines this question. He worries about the therapist's approval or disapproval. [4]

Following the interruption by Mrs. Strong and the entrance of Mrs. Braddock, Mr. Kress attempts to regain the thread of the previous conversation with Mr. Mann. Again personal responsibility is the focus of their discussion. There is a forceful interjection once more by Mrs. Strong. She begins to complain about her headache symptoms. After a brief pause, members of the group show simul-

[1] The numbers 1-10 refer to my comments at the end of this chapter, pp. 308-310.

taneous "sympathetic" and "analytic" attitudes. There occurs a long series of questions of Mrs. Strong with respect to the possible psychological causes of her complaints. Mrs. Strong bursts out after a series of questions in impatience, "I have not felt well for nine whole months!" [5]

Mrs. Strong correctly perceives the group as an arena to which one can bring one's complaints and one's troubles. However, it is also apparent that she wishes to dominate group attention. A group characteristically responds with ambivalence to this kind of approach. On the one hand the group's purpose is defined in terms of its therapeutic goals for individual members. On the other hand, any group resents attempts to gain the attention by an individual member.

A characteristic of therapy groups is their concern about the therapist's attitude. Because of the frustration of the dependent demand for leadership in a therapy group there may be overt hostility against the therapist. Sometimes, however, there is a kind of taking over of "therapist-like" roles and behaviors, that is, behaviors which the patients imagine are those the therapist might reward them for taking. Mr. Mann, who had been paired with Mr. Kress prior to the entrance of the others, pairs once more with Mr. Kress in the attempt to play the role of the therapist. In a verbatim account of one effort to deal with Mrs. Strong's problem we may distinguish between the complementary roles assumed by Mr. Kress and by Mr. Mann.

Kress: Perhaps it is something you push back, something you didn't want to remember.

Strong: My ears feel as though they were strained, my throat feels as though it is being strained all the time.

Mann: Do you have any fears of these being physiological?

Strong: I have not felt well for five years!

Mann: Really?

Strong: My eyes are getting jumpy.

Kress: How do they move when they get like that, up and down or sideways?

Mann: Have you been given reassurance that it wasn't psychological?

Strong: [Tells about visit of repairman to repair furnace and her difficulty in talking with him.]

Kress: But you could talk to him! [with emphasis but sympathetically].

Strong: Sometimes I get so I can hardly hold my head up!

Kress: But you can hold it up! [with emphasis but sympathetically].

Mann: You never felt that this was emotional? How about now?

Strong: I read in a magazine about a girl who had her back nerves severed, I got the hell scared out of me.

Kress: You know that is a pretty scary thing! [with emphasis and support].

The two patients, Mr. Mann and Mr. Kress, maintain their pairing relationship in their assumption of complementary "therapist-like" roles. Mr. Kress tends to provide the support, reassurance, and warmth, while Mr. Mann tends to provide the interrogation and probing of the patient's defenses.

Mrs. Strong becomes increasingly defensive and resistive toward the efforts of the two would-be therapists, particularly toward the probing by Mr. Mann, as illustrated in the following interchange:

Mann: Even though you might not want to say it, have you ever been given any evidence that it might not be an emotional thing—I mean by anybody other than Dr. Dobbs?

Strong: Nobody other than Dr. Dobbs.

Mann: He might be wrong.

Strong: I had my head X-rayed.

Mann: You had what?

Strong: What did you think I said, my head torn off? [embarrassed laughter].

Mann: You saw another doctor. He sent you to Dr. Dobbs, why? I mean, *he was a regular doctor!* [with emphasis]. He had done a lot of physical exams on you. Why did he send you?

Strong: Yes, he checked the blood pressure and all that, but I was asked for [pause] . . . they recommended [pause] . . . I went to another doctor. He said I had migraine. He was shooting some stuff in my head. I don't know what [with irritation]. Anyway, they asked if I wanted to see a psychiatrist and I said okay.

Dr. Logan enters the room. His being a physician offers the group a convenient point of organization from which to investigate Mrs. Strong's symptoms from a physical point of view. There occurs, in fact, an abortive attempt in this direction. Although the group again approaches the somatic aspects under the impact of Dr. Logan's questions, they appear to reject the somatic hypothesis. Even Dr. Logan gives up his professional attitude toward Mrs. Strong's problem and joins what crystallizes as a group psychosomatic orientation toward her symptoms.

We may consider why the group seems to see as its task the "conversion" of Mrs. Strong. The group discussion in this particular session began with a flavor characterized by the theme of personal responsibility. One member demanded attention while at the same time rejecting the "group theme." The group members attempt to explore this in relationship to a therapist who, in their view, refuses to lead. Hence they assume a leadership role and become zealous "psychologizers" themselves. They are zealous in attacking Mrs. Strong's symptoms, using what they see as a psychotherapeutic orientation. That is to say, it appears they avidly desire to prove to the therapist and to themselves that they are fulfilling what they see as the therapist's demands for them in this group therapy situation. It is appropriate to recall that Mr. Kress had wondered if the group were being demoted for failure on its part to live up to the expectations of the therapist. One mode of fulfilling their idea of therapist expectations while at the same time avoiding self-revelation is to explore a convenient target offered by one of the group members. They may also simultaneously "legally" express hostility against an attention-seeking member. Thus, they adopt a militant psychogenic hypothesis with regard to Mrs. Strong. When Mrs. Strong continues to reject this hypothesis, it is reinforced in the interest of group cohesion. To the extent that she departs from the theme preferred by the group she has become a deviate from the group. She desires the support and attention but denies the definition of the group's purpose.

As the session progresses, overt expressions of skeptical disbelief are reflected in the comments of the group members. Even Mr. Kress has become less supportive and more probing. The following segment is illustrative:

Strong:	It feels like I have a steel plate in my head.
Kress:	Did you have a prolonged illness as a child?
Strong:	No.
Mann:	Did anybody in your family have a prolonged illness?
Strong:	My sister just about had Bright's disease.
Mann:	Maybe a brother or sister might have been sick and have gotten a lot of favors.
Strong:	You think I am jealous? [6]
Mann:	Not consciously. It's not a question of your being aware of it or conscious of it. If it was conscious you would deny it. Maybe it's unconscious.
Kress:	[supports this] You'd think of it in a different form or feel it in a different way.
Braddock:	You haven't gained anything by this, have you?
Mann:	You have to know what she wants to gain before you know whether she has gained or not.
Strong:	It never leaves me, this pain.
Dr. Logan:	Never? [incredulous].
Kress:	Yet you said before that this week you had one morning that you didn't have any headaches.
Strong:	Just fifteen minutes!

With defensiveness manifested by Mrs. Strong, the group grows more hostile. At this, Mrs. Strong describes more bizarre symptoms. For instance, she reports the fact that she finds it hard to swallow, that her eyeballs are getting jumpy, that even sitting in the room, she experiences many of the symptoms. In the following segment, her tone of voice has much of a reproachful quality to it.

Strong: Now look, I have had my chin paralyzed.
Braddock: Is that unusual?
Strong: The other day a neighbor came to use my washer and I felt so bad that I thought my head was going to pop off before she left. I felt like I had no head up there.
Dr. Logan: Did you have buzzing in your ears? [caustically].
Strong: I felt as though I couldn't see. People would have thought I was drunk.
Dr. Logan: Do you feel like you have a headache now?
Strong: [with emphasis] Even sitting here it feels like my stomach is tight. I feel paralyzed. My head feels like it is full of something its not supposed to be! It feels heavy! [7]

Mrs. Strong's resentment toward the group pressure is obvious in her responses. In a sense, she seems to be saying to the group members: "I have exposed myself and see how shamefully you treat me; I am getting worse rather than better by exposing myself to you" [8]. Cartwright and Zander point out that two of the functions that uniformities among group members may serve are: (a) to help the group accomplish its purpose, and (b) to help the group maintain itself as a group. Mrs. Strong's refusal to accept a psychogenic hypothesis with reference to her own problems is a threat to this group in terms of its developing standards.

Any group may be committed to a certain way of looking at events. It happens that this group insists upon a psychosomatic view at this particular time. We have already indicated that this view relates to the perceived role of the therapist and the feelings of the patients about their relationships to him. They are in essence trying to make a good "show" of it. An individual who deviates from the basic assumption threatens the whole structure of the relationships to the therapist and to each other. It is for this reason that they enter upon the attempt to convert Mrs. Strong with all the enthusiasm of a "brain washing" team at work.

If this were the totality of Mrs. Strong's relationship to the group the end result might be nontherapeutic or even harmful. Such deviation and the reaction to it in a nontherapy setting might well result in expulsion from the group. However, it should be emphasized that her presentation of her symptoms provides an important and convenient "projecting" point for the therapy group as a whole. That is to say, various group members can relate to Mrs. Strong's position on the basis of their own problems. It will be recalled that Mr. Kress early in the session encourages Mrs. Strong to explore the area of personal responsibility with his reference to: "Perhaps it's something you felt you should have done that you have not done." Mr. Mann, harping on the psychogenic issue, offers Mrs. Strong the unconscious as a loophole by which she can agree to the group standard but at the same time avoid personal responsibility. It is significant in view of his psychopathic background that this individual should, more than any other member of the group, propose the theory of unconscious motivation as explanatory in this case. Mrs. Braddock attempts to explore the possible secondary gain the patient has achieved. This is a major problem for her. Also, and characteristic for Mrs. Braddock, she wonders how the patient felt about her own self-concept.

Although apparently only attacking Mrs. Strong's denial of psychological factors, the individual members actually project their own problems and attitudes into the discussion. This may well provide a convenient and nonthreatening mode of self-revelation. Three of the four other members gain something from Mrs. Strong's continued participation and *perhaps even from her pattern of deviancy*. It may be for this reason that the remaining group member initiates an alternate way of relating to this patient. The following segment illustrates a transition to a different approach.

Kress:	Then how do you feel about the questions we are asking you?
Strong:	I don't mind a bit. [general laughter]. My eyes have just gotten worse. [9]
Dr. Logan:	[caustically] Maybe you just need your specs changed.
Strong:	[exasperatingly] I just got them changed.
Dr. Logan:	Then change them again! [again in exasperation]. [10]
Kress:	Let's get back to the lady who visited with you. Were you afraid that she might pry into your private life?
Strong:	No, we were talking about our in-laws. Our in-laws giving us everything.
Dr. Logan:	That might be part of the trouble.
Strong:	We couldn't live without my in-laws, not that they suffer from it. His mother makes doggone good money.
Dr. Logan:	It's good money from mommy. I still can't get over the bitter feeling. [He describes own problem with father-in-law.] Papa would bill me a periodic statement. It made me feel real mean.
Kress:	How did you find out you felt that way?
Dr. Logan:	[Describes numerous hospitalizations and attempts to

gain alleviation through excessive use of alcohol. His manner is sincere and his mood of despair obvious in his tone of voice.]

With the introduction of the problem of support from in-laws, Dr. Logan, who had become caustically critical of Mrs. Strong's presentation of herself, finally resonates to a problem he has keenly experienced himself. After probing into Dr. Logan's feelings and discovery that they are genuinely and deeply felt, the group alters profoundly its attacking, scapegoating, and diagnosing frame of reference. Now others join in a mutually exploratory interaction concerning the relationship of each to dependency figures. They begin to talk about their feelings toward their wives and husbands with considerable intensity.

This section is noteworthy in that the pairing interactions are not limited to Mr. Kress and Mr. Mann, but also include Mrs. Braddock and Dr. Logan, who discover that they have reciprocal and similar feelings of fear and anger toward their respective spouses. Dr. Logan says: "I am afraid of my wife. Some people can tell their wives to go to hell but I brood about it." Mrs. Braddock then discusses the relationship between herself and her husband. "My husband is scared of my bad temper." Mr. Mann also finally drops his role of self-appointed inquisitor and comes in at this point with the experience with his own wife. He recounts how she gets angry and throws things at him, and how frightened he is of her. Mrs. Strong listens for a change. She asks questions with regard to the others' experiences, and makes a few comments which show that she has been paying close attention to what has been said.

The theme of marital frustrations and active participation by all the members characterize the rest of the meeting until the therapist calls it to a close.

A summary of the events of this meeting emphasizes the primary role of process analysis in comprehending the interaction pattern among the group members. A pairing interaction was disrupted by an attention-seeker. The theme of the pair was supported by other group members and a developing group standard was at least tentatively accepted by the others, with the exception of the attention-seeker. In the absence of overt therapist commitment the group members pre-empted therapist-like roles in application of the group standard. The pattern of deviancy of one "disruptive" member was highlighted. This served simultaneously needs to please a symbolized concept of the therapist, to be aggressive and hostile toward a disruptive deviate, and to have a convenient projective object for covert expression of personal problems. The result was a frontal, "brain-washing" approach which was probably nontherapeutic for the deviate. One member's overt response in terms of actual personal experiences and feelings breaks the pattern and helps to establish a shift in group standards, pairing pattern, and leadership, and thus enables the group to regain a measure of therapeutic direction.

Are the processes we have illustrated in one group session operant in all therapy group sessions? The discovery of the effects upon different individual patients of the different group processes may lead to a more precise articulation of what may be therapeutic and what may be nontherapeutic in group psychotherapy. The relative verbal inactivity of the therapist in this session emphasizes the group-determined properties. In this session the therapist intervened in response to a direct question put to him early in the session, once again to support the deviate when she appeared to need it and to request it and, finally, to close the session. Would a more "active" therapist intervention decisively alter group processes? This would seem to be a very important area of investigation.

The illustrative material we have presented reflects the process patterns involved in therapy groups, and, we believe, emphasizes the need for application of group dynamics research and theoretical tools to the problems of group therapy. Elucidation and study of the effects of the various processes described and the discovery of others may lead to a better conceptualization and discrimination of the effects of group psychotherapy.

SUMMARY

The authors have analyzed the group interactions in a single session of a therapy group. Verbatim material is utilized to illustrate the interactions.

A patient aggressively presents her somatic symptoms to the group and appeals for support yet simultaneously rejects the group hypothesis concerning the psychogenic basis of the symptoms. The initial response of the group to the problem of deviancy from the basic group assumptions is comparable to that described in nontherapy groups. The frustrations of group members in attempting to resolve the problem through pressure and attack and the final successful resolution of the conflict are phenomena which may occur frequently in therapy groups. The authors have made use of theory from small groups dynamics to render more comprehensible the problems of process analysis in therapy groups and to pose the question of differential effects of various group processes.

COMMENTS FROM THE VIEWPOINT OF ANALYTIC GROUP PSYCHOTHERAPY

The authors have given their analysis of the therapeutic process and expressed their interest in knowing how a more active form of therapy might have changed the progress of events. Aware of the

limitations of such an attempt, I shall nevertheless venture to speculate on what I might have done in the same situation and what
might have happened as a result.

It must be kept in mind, of course, that I would have been influenced by my own immediate relationship to the situation and with
the individuals in it, including my possible countertransferential
attitudes. I might, therefore, have responded somewhat differently
to the live situation. It is quite possible, for example, that I might
have been too irritated with the "deviant" to question the pressure
that was put upon her. The following, then, are the points at which
I might have intervened and my reasons for doing so. I have marked
each such spot in the session with a number corresponding to my
comments:

(1) I would probably have explored the ambivalent feelings of
Mr. Mann and Mr. Kress about responsibility when this came up
in the session and sought to find their latent meaning in relationship to recent group events. I would then have used specific comments and nonverbal indications as cues on how to word my questions. If Mr. Mann smiled secretly when he said he had always been
able to get out of responsibilities, I might have asked if it were possible that he derived some satisfaction from this accomplishment.

(2) I would undoubtedly have followed through by scrutinizing
the question of how Mr. Mann hoped to use therapy in this matter,
merely asking, "How do you mean, Mr. Mann?"

(3) I might have "wondered" whether Mrs. Strong had some
definite reaction about the "twosome" which was so busily engaged
in conversation when she came in. If, as one might anticipate, she
denied having any at all, I might then have commented that I had
thought it possible because her interruption had, in fact, stopped
them. A reaction to this from her would be likely. The manner in
which I spoke would, I hope, have been sympathetic and casual,
not accusing. I would have expected the group to take it from there,
and have kept in mind the possibility that she might subsequently
need to be guarded from too much pressure from the members to
express her feelings. I might even have had to cushion her against
it. I often find it necessary to ask the group why it is so eager to press
an individual in this way, and the verbal and nonverbal responses
prove to be valuable in bringing to light the members' areas of
anxiety and transference needs for which analysis is indicated.

(4) If I had thought, as this therapist did, that the two men were competing for my approval, I would have looked for some way of sounding out this idea. I would do so in a manner that would not force them into a defensive position, for I believe that the way comments are made is a crucial factor in whether or not they can be accepted. The patient is not nearly as likely to be defensive if the therapist's motives are seen to be purely therapeutic.

(5) I would probably have intervened in the lengthy attempt to "convert" Mrs. Strong, because I regard her attitude as resistance. However, this might never have been necessary if comment "4" had succeeded in breaking through the resistance, as I believe it would.

In analytic group therapy there is no such thing as "absence of therapist commitment." It is, however, commitment to analyzing rather than either to gratifying or frustrating dependency or other neurotic needs. The patients soon learn to share the therapist's role to some extent, and such interpretive comments are acceptable unless an apparent "interfering" motive suggests the need for exploration. When their interpretations are clearly in the service of resistance they are analyzed.

(6) When Mrs. Strong asked Mr. Mann, "You think I'm jealous?," I might have said, "What do you think?" or "Is it possible that you could be?" But if she denied it, I would not have pressed her further.

(7) When Mrs. Strong described the symptoms she was having at the moment (in response to their barrage) she said, "My head feels like it is full of something it's not supposed to be." I would have picked up her statement because her resentment and her attitude toward it were so close to the surface. I might have said, "I have an idea you are very uncomfortable right now because you are fighting off feelings you don't want to have anything to do with." In other words, I would have dealt with the defense first, because that was the way she was experiencing it. Whether her symptoms were psychological or not would have been too intellectual a matter for her, and they were, at any rate, part of the resistance. One cannot barge through this. It must be analyzed gradually.

(8) I would try to get her to articulate what she seemed to be experiencing, which I think was: "I have exposed myself and see how shamefully you treat me. I am getting worse rather than bet-

ter by exposing myself." She might well have expressed her affect more directly as a result of my last comment [7], but if not I might try to deal with the resistance by saying, "I wonder what your body is saying that your mind can't accept?" I have found this often works well.

(9) Mrs. Strong presented me with another opportunity when she said, "My eyes have just gotten worse." To this I might have replied, "We seem to be making you worse today." Again my manner would have to reflect understanding, not accusation.

(10) I would try to get Dr. Logan, and the others, to express their feelings of exasperation with her more directly and openly. If this did not yield results I might take the initiative by simply asking him if anything was bothering him.

This session clearly reveals a number of group processes, among them the enormous pressure to conform to group standards (subscribing to psychogenic causes of illness). More active intervention would interfere with group processes as soon as these served the purpose of resistance rather than therapy. Lakin says, "In the absence of overt therapist commitment the group members preempted therapist-like roles in application of the group standards." If these roles seemed to be an expression of resistance, analytic intervention would serve to make members drop them and speak for themselves.

Lakin and Dobbs were not at all inactive, however, in following the group events in terms of process analysis. Their summary shows that they had their fingers consistently on the pulse of intragroup relationships. It occurs to me that a general principle for therapeutic intervention might be established in connection with this process analysis, namely, that whenever one of the group processes interferes with valid communication, or with what the therapists consider a good therapeutic group atmosphere, the leader might bring it to their attention for exploration. Such a principle would be comparable to the analytic process of dealing with resistance. Not only would the role of the group dynamic therapist be more clearly defined but we would have a basis for comparison with analytic group therapy.

For example, the group pressure on the deviant continued to the point of making her a scapegoat. She in turn behaved in such a way as to prolong this reaction. If either side of such interaction is explored with the group, forward therapeutic movement can be resumed and tedious repetitions avoided. Group dynamic and analytic group therapists would agree that such intervention should not occur before the participants had experienced fully the emotional impact of the interaction.

Unfortunately this abbreviated attempt to compare methods does not give us the benefit of the continued interchange between author and discussant which would make it truly meaningful. However, it does indicate the way toward more fruitful discussions among different schools of thought or individual attitudes. At the twentieth annual congress of the American Group Psychotherapy Association a program was set up for just such a purpose. A clinical case recording was played and critically examined by representatives of several schools. It seemed to me that for the first time their customary defensiveness was replaced by reciprocal interest and respect, and I believe the experience proved to be productive and stimulating for everyone.

The therapist's verbal inactivity during the group session stimulates the development of the group processes and throws them into high relief. For this reason the method is an excellent one for research on group phenomena. The analytic therapist must also know when to be inactive so that the group members have a chance to carry the ball. In the beginning he has to take the lead more often. But they soon grasp the meaning of the mutual self-examination, and he can be more passive.

XVIII Group Analytic Psychotherapy

Group analytic psychotherapy combines the principles of analytic and group dynamic group psychotherapy. It is best illustrated by the work of its originators, S. H. Foulkes, W. R. Bion, and H. Ezriel. Faced with the problem of applying their therapeutic skills to groups of soldiers during World War Two, these psychoanalysts felt that it was not feasible to use the orthodox analytic technique of eliciting the libidinal regressive transference in this situation. They sought an approach which would be more appropriate to group treatment. Having been greatly impressed by the evolution of gestalt psychology during their lifetime, they decided to incorporate Kurt Lewin's extension of it into their theoretical formulations and to cull out from it their new technical procedures. Lewinian theory not only provided a plausible alternative for dealing with groups, but also left the way open for continuing to use their psychoanalytic knowledge and some of their old techniques, such as making conscious the latent content, structure, and process. They also retained certain psychoanalytic attitudes such as listening impartially, giving no advice, and withholding opinions. But they believe that it is the group dynamics which constitute the chief therapeutic agency, and which therefore provide the significant new dimension in group psychotherapy. Accordingly their therapists are trained in group dynamics as well as in psychoanalysis.

This title is the one Foulkes uses. Since it does no violence to the method which originated with Bion at Tavistock, I use it for the sake of unity to cover both approaches.

They perceive the therapy group in terms of the three basic tenets of Lewinian field theory. (1) They treat the group as an entity (a system in tension), look for the latent meaning of its interaction, and consistently formulate their interventions in relation to it. (2) Its energy is considered to derive from the tensions created by the needs of the members (parts) in interaction (in their struggle for life space) and to give rise to the group processes. The latter are the chief agency for change and are therefore harnessed by the leader for therapeutic purposes. (3) By focusing chiefly on the immediate group events, they put the principle of contemporaneity into practice. They differ somewhat among themselves in the way they interpret these concepts and in the degree to which they combine them with psychoanalytic principles.

I shall not attempt to describe in detail the way each works, for that has been done adequately elsewhere (Foulkes, 1948; Bion, 1948-1951; Stock and Thelen, 1958; Foulkes and Anthony, 1957). But I shall try to identify each of these leaders by his particular way of transposing Lewin's main principles into the group therapy context in conjunction with psychoanalytic principles.

THE GROUP AS AN ENTITY

In recent years the term "group as a whole" has become a familiar if not always well-understood concept in the literature of group psychotherapy. Lewin's simple scientific statement that the group is different from (not more than) the sum of its parts implies nothing in the least esoteric, nor is it intended to suggest a dichotomy between group and individual psychology. Yet, to many, it appears to be an animistic concept suggestive of the old "group mind" notion. Certain group processes arise out of the interaction, such as the tendency to set standards and to put pressure on members to conform to these standards, to produce leadership among its members, to develop subgroups, scapegoating, and the like. These processes are bipolar. They may be centrifugal or centripetal in nature, moving the group toward cohesion or disruption. Group analytic therapists deal with both the overt and covert aspects of these group processes in terms of depth psychology. Each conscious, preconscious, or unconscious interaction is assessed in relation to the total network of the group communication.

Of the three, Bion (1948-1951) adheres most strictly, both in theory and in practice, to the concept of the group as an entity.[1] From the start, he was determined to view the group on its own terms, as a whole, and in depth, yet to avoid the bias of individual psychoanalysis. Beginning with the premise that the group is prior to the individual, both historically and psychologically, he found his explanatory principle in the "social unconscious." This combination of sociological, psychoanalytic, and gestalt concepts produced a colorful but rather esoteric, almost mystical formulation reminiscent of the "group mind." Nevertheless, his observations have a high degree of clinical pertinence.

Bion has little to say about the role of the individual, but in order to account for the way in which a single member relates to group needs, he proposes the concept of "valency," which he defines as a "capacity for instantaneous and involuntary combination of one individual with another for sharing and acting on a basic assumption" (see Chapter VI).

Ezriel, who started in one of Bion's groups and was his colleague at the Tavistock Clinic, also sees the group as an entity, but he gives much more attention to the role of the individual. According to him, it is the psychological structure which gives it unity and coherence. He traces the steps by which it arrives at this organization. Each member, he says, has fantasies derived from unresolved infantile conflicts which create tension and bring about a striving toward satisfaction through his interaction with the other group members (i.e., through transferential behavior). In the course of this process a common denominator of all the members' fantasies is arrived at. This determines the nature of the group structure and its unitary quality.

Foulkes defines his position in regard to the group qua group as follows: "All communications and relationships which are of central importance for the therapeutic process and the analyst's therapeutic activities are seen as a part of a total field of interaction, the group matrix." He concerns himself primarily with this matrix. In another passage he sums up his viewpoint: "The group is a system of relationships displaying a flexible pattern of configurations; and it is organized about some focal point or points which are in recip-

---

[1] For an excellent critical review of Bion's work, see Scheidlinger (1960).

rocal relationships to each other." He writes: "We look for the response of the group as a whole to the communication of the individual patient, just as we view the individual patient's communications as coming from the group through the mouthpiece of the speaker." Clearly he does not contribute to the creation of a dichotomy for, as he says, "both the individual and the group properties must be observed in relations to each other"(Foulkes and Anthony, 1957).

In his research on the group-determined processes, he and Anthony have added one which they call "resonance." It consists of complementary relationships which develop between group members, such as that between the dominant and the submissive, the exhibitionistic and the voyeuristic, the elated and the depressed, and the like.

THE GROUP AS A FORCE FIELD: DYNAMIC THEORY

According to psychological field theory, the therapy group is an organism whose tensions are derived from the interacting needs of its members. It maintains a constantly changing equilibrium. To bring about change in one member changes the total gestalt qualitatively and also its state of tension. The ebb and flow of tension within the system affects every member. Thus a powerful force field is created out of these interacting tensions of its members. The therapist's function consists primarily in the management of these forces.

It is in combining this theory with Freudian libido theory that problems arise. Neither Lewin nor Freud considered individual psychology as basically different from group psychology, but each accounted for dynamic change in both units by different concepts of energy. The two theories are not incompatible as we have seen, and it is altogether possible that Freudian libido theory may eventually be reformulated in Lewinian terms by the comparatively simple solution of substituting for instincts the concept of needs which set up tension and create drives toward action. But such a change has not yet been widely accepted and until it is, group dynamic therapists will be subject to appearing ambiguous in their attempts to combine system-in-tension hypotheses with those psychoanalytic concepts which are dependent on libido theory.

Foulkes does not restrict himself to one dynamic theory. He believes that "the rise and fall of the 'group tension' constitutes the central dynamic and therapeutic factor in the therapy group." He believes it is derived from both individual and group sources, and from the interaction between them. He writes (Foulkes and Anthony, 1957): "Individual tension derives from the individual's dependency-independency [libidinal] conflict and appears wherever people get together in their struggle for 'life space.' The struggle, in turn, brings about interaction. The degree of conflict determines the amount of involvement and hence the degree of tension. A moderate amount of tension is optimal for therapeutic progress."

Foulkes goes beyond analytic and Lewinian theory and draws on communications theory. He says, "There is a force toward communication in humans which provides the energy to drive therapy forward" (Foulkes and Anthony, 1957). One may assume that therapeutic change will occur by way of the ensuing communications network and its interpretation.

Bion also has a good deal to say about tension, but his theorizing is not as clearly conceptualized as that of Foulkes. His relationship with Lewinian theory is barely discernible. Bion uses sociological theory on the one hand, and goes back to nineteenth-century instinct theory on the other. He complicates matters theoretically by speaking of group instinctual forces. He declares that tension arises out of the "primitive social unconscious" (one is reminded of Jung's racial unconscious) in the form of the "basic assumptions." These social unconscious needs set up tensions which lead to action (Bion, 1955).

By redefining transference in Lewinian terms, Ezriel (1950) makes a convincing integration of psychoanalytic and Lewinian dynamic theory. Individuals, he assumes, have "object needs." Since the needs are not fully met in infancy, people try to actualize them in the present. Doing so brings about tensions which also have the property of bringing about action. In the group there is "an unconscious interaction on the level of its needs. The push and pull among the members is characterized by an unconsciously determined process of selection, rejection, and distortion of one another's remarks." It creates a state of unrest and tension, seeking balance. The transferences are tension-reducing mechanisms which temporarily ward off the awareness of needs but never quite satisfy them. The resultant group structure functions as a stabilizer by delimiting the tensions. The leader's interventions bring about closure and a consequent release of tension, and a new structure develops.

THE PRINCIPLE OF CONTEMPORANEITY

The group dynamics therapist focuses primarily on the immediate events which occur in the group. History is used little, if at all. The group situation is indeeed well suited to restricting therapeutic interventions to the here and now, for the constant interaction puts limits on the time for dwelling on the past, even for therapists who specialize in genetic material. But analytic group therapists would insist on the therapeutic value of making repeated interpretations connecting the past with the present.

Foulkes' application of the principle of contemporaneity to group therapy is closer to the psychoanalytic viewpoint than that of the others. Nor is he inconsistent with Lewin's real intent when he states that he will not limit himself to any single time dimension, even though the immediacy of the group situation creates the urgency of the present. He sees each individual member of the therapy group as bringing with him an extension of his entire life space into the past and into the future in exactly the same way that each brings an extension to the realm of irreality within himself. In short, he sets limits to the idea of a historic group therapy.

Bion is at once more radical and more contradictory about the time factor. He sees the basic assumptions as deep social instinctual forces which combine "instantaneously" as a given moment during the group process to find their leader. Ambiguously, he adds, "they exist before and after it." The instantaneous instinctive activity is "anchored in man's innermost core as a group animal." Thus he obscures the concept of contemporaneity by combining it with that of instinct and with the "social unconscious."

Ezriel reports that he analyzes only the "here and now" aspects of the transference because, as he sees it, the group members do not have a common past nor a common life outside the group. To an analytic group therapist it is inconceivable to segregate the here and now aspects of the transference from the there and then, for in it past and present are inextricably interwoven. That is the point of transference, and therapeutic progress results from separating them out. However, Ezriel recognizes that "the patient's reactions in the session are the idiom used by him to express his unconscious fantasies which carry past needs into the present field." It is not the theory which is in contest here, but its technical application which excludes "there and then" interpretations.

DIFFERENCES IN PSYCHOANALYTIC ORIENTATION

We have tried to take note of certain variations among these three group therapists in their application of group dynamics principles. Nevertheless, the differences in psychoanalytic orientation among them complicate the picture, and it is necessary to take note of them. Foulkes and his followers have an "orthodox" Freudian orientation. Bion and Ezriel have a Kleinian orientation. Since their actual therapeutic interventions often reflect their psychoanalytic thinking, they reveal these differences as much as, or even more than, their group dynamics position. The resulting crosscurrents must be taken into account in any attempt to clarify the theoretical issues.

Both Freudian and Kleinian psychoanalytic orientations employ the concepts of the tripartite mental structure and the psychosexual development of the individual. The orthodox Freudian school, however, generally puts more emphasis on libidinal factors and the oedipal period, while the Kleinians emphasize the earliest preoedipal aggressive and omnipotent fantasies and tend to focus on "paranoid anxiety" and the "depressive core" (Klein, 1932). This difference emerges quite clearly in Bion's concept (1955) of "psychotic group." Because the group regresses to this preoedipal level, Bion believes that group therapy can penetrate deeper than individual therapy. Actually, there is no reason why any therapist who interprets both oedipal and preoedipal material should not reach these early layers either in individual or in group analysis. In our experience, both the neurotic and the psychotic problems contain conflict derived from both periods of life.

DIFFERENCES IN THE USE OF TRANSFERENCE

The group analytic therapists differ among themselves also in the degree to which they utilize the psychoanalytic technique of transference analysis. In this respect Ezriel seems to be a good deal closer to the American group therapists than are either Foulkes or Bion, for he relates each individual's transference to the total group fantasy in terms of his defenses.

For Foulkes (1957) the therapeutic or "T" situation in the group contains a unique combination of factors, including transference or "t" situations. The patients must be confronted with transference, but equally with their "current, here and now, real relationships." Again, he says, "Transference phenomena do occur in the group but they are not of permanent importance for the therapeutic trend of the group and they may be aborted by the integrative developments within the group." Unlike the American analytic group therapists he says little of the multiple intragroup transferences. Instead he seems to translate such interaction into group dynamics terms such as dovetailing, subgrouping, resonance, and the like. He feels that the group does something different from individual analysis and is not in competition with it. In the group, he says, transference is analyzed horizontally in breadth, while in individual analysis it is analyzed vertically and in depth.

For Ezriel, on the other hand, the group therapeutic situation is *synonymous* with the transference situation. After redefining transference, he outlines three levels of transference relationships which take place in the group. He speaks of the first layer as the "required relationship" which seems to be equivalent to the transference of defense as defined by Anna Freud, and reflects the ego's compromise with reality. It wards off a more anxiety-producing kind of transference which he calls "the avoided relationship," and seems to refer to the underlying infantile drives which are the motivating factors derived from infantile family relationships. These would include all the feelings connected with the oedipal situation, and in turn prevent what must seem to the patient "The calamitous relationship" from breaking through. This seems to refer to the unconscious preoedipal drives, including the frightening "paranoid anxiety" of which Klein speaks. All three levels may be observed in turn and must be brought to consciousness during the group therapy process, but in terms of the present fantasies and the group situation without tracing them back to their origins (Ezriel, 1959).

Bion has very little to say about transference, probably because of his desire to keep away from established concepts in order to find what is unique to the group situation, and also because of his insistence on seeing the group as a unity. However, it would be plausible to interpret the basic assumptions behavior as oral, anal, and oedipal transference of the group as a whole to the leader as the parent figure.

THE ROLE OF THE THERAPIST

To call the therapist the leader is itself a semantic indication of a philosophy of therapy. If the group forces are seen as the chief therapeutic agency, then it follows that the leader's function is to manage those forces.

According to Bion, Foulkes, and Ezriel, because the therapist always intervenes with the whole group in mind, he addresses his comments to it. Even when he chooses to do this through an individual, it is only because that individual represents what is going on in the group qua group. However, in translating the group processes, he tends to do it in group dynamics terms, although he may translate these into depth psychological language. That is to say, he will interpret any group event to bring out its latent meaning, and according to psychoanalytic concepts.

Bion's approach, here again, is the most typically group dynamic. Functioning primarily in the role of observer of the processes from the very beginning, he does no structuring for his therapy group. He calls this leadership by default, and this policy encourages the emergence of the group processes. His observations have led him to conclude that in the first phase the whole group acts *as if* it were in search of a leader on whom it might lean. He therefore calls this phenomenon "the basic assumptions group." He believes that the leader, himself prone to such assumptions, must not allow himself to respond to the latent demand but must interpret its meaning to the group. This interpretation brings about a restructuring of the group and frees the group members to work on their given task. Two other basic assumptions phases follow. In the second, they are in search of a leader who will guide them in "fight and flight"; in the third, he will lead them in "pairing" for love and sexual union. He handles these phases similarly, in turn, with the result that the underlying group emotion, which distracted them from their task, is allayed, and they are free to become what he calls "the work group." These two levels of functioning seem to be roughly parallel to Freud's secondary and primary processes, and to Thelen's "work and emotionality levels."

Bion later noticed another level of interaction, on a still more primitive basis. The basic assumptions group may be regarded, he says, as a neurotic group which is working out problems of family relations. Its activity wards off the deep-seated narcissistic anxiety of what he calls the "psychotic group." The latter concept is related to Klein's "paranoid position," but he considers it a phenomenon of the "social unconscious." He views the basic assumptions group as attempting to ward off this deeper level, in which the primitive fear of others is paramount (Bion, 1955). In interpreting it to the group as a whole, the leader helps it resolve this stage too.

Ezriel is more active analytically than Bion and pays much more attention to the individual, although it is always in relation to the whole group. Regarding the role of the leader he states, "It is by showing the relation of the role which each group member takes up in dealing with the common group tension in the drama performed in that session by the group as a whole, that we can demonstrate to each member his particular defense." The analyst must know the roles into which the various members may be driven. Ezriel feels that the group can make such interpretations for itself only when it models itself upon the leader. Later, the members are able to share in this function. He also believes that the leader may make an interpretation either to an individual or to a group. Further, in terms of the immediate situation, the leader must give a rational explanation of the patient's or the group's behavior, and he must demonstrate the causes of the behavior instead of merely pointing to them. He also intervenes to uncover unconscious fantasies which are common to all. In doing so, he restructures the group and brings about a marked reduction of tension (Ezriel, 1950).

Foulkes conceives of the therapist's role as that of a leader who guides the group processes as a conductor might lead a symphony orchestra, remaining constantly aware of the group's rhythms, its changing intensities, and its emerging themes. His task is to create and maintain an atmosphere in which the communications (i.e., associations) may flow freely and both transferences and immediate group-determined relationships may be interpreted. He makes few interventions, and these always for the purpose of bringing to the foreground of the communications that particular behavior which best represents the meaning of the total latent interaction. Each member is, according to him, continuously involved in this ever-changing network of communication, but on his own level, at his own pace, and in his own manner. The leader must be aware of each member's variations within the matrix at any given moment. But the total group is the target of his interventions even though at times he may select a single member for comment because he seems, at the time, to be its most adequate "mouthpiece."

In a seminar at Chapel Hill, May 1959, which I was privileged to attend, Foulkes gave a number of examples to illustrate his theories. We questioned how one of his comments, made to a single member exploring the reason for her lateness, could be considered an illustration of "treating the group." His rationale was that all the members would sooner or later be reacting in this way, and therefore his comment could help the whole group to grasp the meaning of latent motivation and simultaneously help to establish the therapeutic group atmosphere. Other situations which occurred later in the same group revealed that he might interpret oral, anal, or genital material to an individual if he considered that this individual best represented preconscious processes significant for the whole group at that time. For instance, he made interpretations concerning anality to one man who seemed to be giving expression to the group's apparent preoccupation with compulsive reaction formations against anal-erotic drives. This patient was the "mouthpiece" of the group. While such interventions might appear to the observer to be purely individual, Foulkes makes them only when they illuminate the group matrix. This point may be hard to detect in a practical situation, but it represents a genuine difference in point of view. Like Ezriel, Foulkes believes that the individual may be reached through the group, and the group through the individual. He therefore holds that it is necessary to keep both sets of properties equally in mind.

As therapy proceeds, the conductor continues to keep a careful watch over the group forces and tries to keep the resulting tensions at that level of moderation which he considers optimal for therapy. He allows himself to become a transference figure and acts as the "translator" (a communications term) of the content, process, and behavior, which occur in the interaction. His translations may be into the language of psychoanalysis as well as into that of group dynamics (Foulkes, 1948; Foulkes and Anthony, 1957).

Foulkes considers that he has gone well beyond psychoanalysis in his conception of group analytic therapy. He also feels that his work and that of the Tavistock group are much closer to each other than they are to the American analytic group therapists. However, the work of Semrad[2] and his associates is an exception, since they too have been much influenced by the group dynamics movement.

---

[2] Because so much unpublished material was made available to me, I selected the work of Thelen, Stock, Bennis, Schutz, etc., as examples of the group dynamic point of view instead of the equally outstanding work of Semrad.

XIX Further Examples of Group
Psychotherapy Based on Group Dynamics

In contrast both to the analytic group therapists and those who consider the group processes themselves as the primary source of therapy, there are a number of group therapists, each very different from the others, who have developed a group therapeutic process which is founded on group dynamics views. The first is that of Moreno who was a pioneer in the field. His approach is highly original and does not fit into the usual definition of group therapy.

MORENO'S CONTRIBUTIONS

Moreno (1953, 1954, personal communication) built up an original and creative version of group dynamics therapy. He is generally antipsychoanalytic (he prefers to call himself suprapsychoanalytic) as to method although he accepts some of the better established concepts. His most important contribution to group dynamics research is his sociometric method; and to group therapy, psychodrama. According to a personal discussion with him, he first became aware of the necessity for studying the dynamics of the group while he was working with prostitutes in Vienna during the World War I era. Verbal discussion with them was not too effective and revealed the need for an action method, a way of using groups and

---

Drs. Moreno and Bach have read and approved the sections devoted to their views. Dr. Papanek read the section on Adlerian group psychotherapy.

a method of measuring social closeness and distance. By studying the answers to a series of questions relating to a variety of aspects of "who likes whom" (such as whom would you most like to sit next to, live with, etc.) he collected data from which he could learn a great deal about the dynamics of interaction. This method, called sociometry, also had practical sociological applications, for it was found that groups which were made up on the basis of such tests worked together better than the average. Moreover, the therapeutic value of interaction among the members of the group became increasingly apparent to him.

He had also recognized the therapeutic significance of acting out for these delinquent girls, whose problems stemmed from pre-verbal phases of life. Many things could be expressed by them only through an action method. Since there had been no words in the original situation, he felt that words alone were incapable of striking at the core of their problems. Instead of regarding acting out as resistance Moreno saw it as a vital, therapeutic instrument if it could be brought within the boundaries of a controlled situation. This was the necessity which inspired the creation of psychodrama.

The basic principles of psychodrama as a therapeutic method are spontaneity and creativity. These are to be understood not as abstractions, but as functions growing out of the immediate relationships in the dramatized emotional situation. According to Moreno, psychodrama is group psychotherapy in depth.[1] Emotional problems are acted out by selected members with the help of the therapist-director, and later discussed with the whole group. An actual theatre is used. A theatre in the round is of course preferable, but any room can be converted for the purpose. A group formation may make up the nucleus of the procedure, or an open group may be drawn together for the occasion, but in either case additional helpers, such as trained actors, hospital staff members, or capable volunteers, are often introduced to fill in the gaps in required characterizations or increase the size of the audience. Because of the importance of spontaneity there is first a "warming-up" process conducted by the director. During this period the group is encouraged to discuss subjects for acting out, select a member whose problem would seem to lend itself to the dramatic method,

[1] Many analytic group therapists, among them Slavson, question whether it is psychotherapy at all.

assign parts, and give suggestions to each actor for playing his role. It may happen that no decision to dramatize the problem takes place, and the warming-up may continue as the psychotherapy for the session. Usually, however, there comes a point at which the therapist senses a readiness or need for expression in action. The production is the climax of the session. As soon as it begins he fades into the background and becomes a passive participant, while the actors move to the stage, real or improvised, to play out the drama, and the remaining members, the audience, find themselves observing and even experiencing some of their own problems vicariously.

The warming-up process requires a good deal of activity and creativity in the setting up of the therapeutic situation. Moreno sees this as the "operational expression of spontaneity." He criticized Lewin for having neglected this important aspect in his researches. He considers psychodrama an action psychology, explaining that it is because of the close connection between motivation and action that warming up is essential for obtaining valid clinical material.

There are many levels of performing psychodrama, and one must be chosen which can best be suited to the demands of the situation. In the deepest problems the patient-actors may be completely free and spontaneously live out their fantasies and emotions. It is often found advisable to have a part played more than once by an alter ego, allowing the actor to see himself through another's interpretations, and role reversals are in some cases valuable in which two individuals attempt to act out the experiences of each other, even to fathom the unconscious of the other. There can never be a fixed plan as would be the case where the script had been prepared, and the emerging pattern of the dramatization can by its very nature never be predictable.

The production is allowed to continue until it has reached a point where the director feels intervention is indicated, and its value is likely to lie in increased insight for all members of the group even though no interpretation is made. Subsequent constructive reactions, including changes in attitudes by the member whose problem has been studied, is almost always reported.

After the play, the director again becomes active and engages the actors and the audience in a full discussion. He is once more spontaneously himself, and in order to elicit the patients' fullest responses he does not hesitate to bring out strong feelings of his own, whether they are antagonistic or sympathetic. He thus gives the members the opportunity to discuss their reactions and crystallize the insights they have achieved while acting or as silent participants. This includes understanding their identifications, their angers, their patterns of behavior, and so on.

He regards his conception of therapy as close to that of the existentialists. Indeed, his definition of the patient-therapist relationship as a "meeting" is in terms that are very similar in tone to Buber's description of the I/Thou relationship, and he claims to have introduced the concept of "encounter" to Buber. The role of the therapist is one of movement from active participation to silent observation. Although he denounces the unequal therapist-patient relationship of psychoanalysis and insists on equality, one gets the impression of the role of the director as a benign "Deus ex Machina." He once wrote: "The God has to step down and become an actor" (Moreno, 1953).

Psychodrama can be used for many purposes. It becomes psychodramatic group therapy (Corsini, 1957) when the audience is part of the drama and group discussion follows. Then, the members of the audience may become the actors or the alter egos. Moreno also feels that much time can be saved if the therapist knows a good deal about relationships between the individuals in his group through sociometric analysis of the membership. For the most part particular emotional problems may be solved by producing or reproducing the fantasies, emotions, and attitudes that go to make them.

The method can, however, be used for long-term therapy by setting up a long series of psychodramatic sessions dealing with a variety of problems. The focus of therapy changes to the group, and the group is the new subject.

The process of psychodrama may be used once, a few times, or, in a closed group, many times, until the conflicts are solved. There are over one hundred theaters of psychodrama in mental hospitals, universities, and educational institutions in the United States and other parts of the world. It has been extensively used for over twenty years at St. Elizabeth's Hospital, Washington, D.C. (Overholser and Enneis, 1960), where among other results it served to arouse to action patients who had been long suffering from the deep lethargy of "institutionalism."

Bach's Theragnosis[2]

Dr. George Bach, originally trained in Lewinian Group Dynamics, considers this the soundest base for conducting group therapy. In practice he was among the first in this country to combine group dynamics with psychoanalytic concepts and methods of therapy. After a bow to Freudian theory and techniques and a limited acceptance of the concepts of transference and resistance, he seems in practice to utilize chiefly the concepts and techniques of the "interpersonal schools." He also uses certain of Bion's concepts and those of communications theory, and whatever else he finds useful, including role playing, art, and projective techniques. He does not, however, consider himself an eclectic, but says that he "fuses" the various approaches. His own contribution to the method he calls theragnosis, which consists of combining diagnosis and therapeutic interpretations in one process in which the therapist and the patients participate. It is through this synthesis, he feels, that the members' distortions are gradually corrected by consensual validation. In communications terms it consists in mutual self-correction through information gathering and sifting. In a chapter entitled "Contact Psychology" (1954), Bach describes the whole operation as a mutual process of neurotic set-up operations which are gradually, through theragnosis, and the result of consensual validation, understood and modified. The degree of comprehension achieved depends upon how much they have learned about their own distortions and the way in which these have contributed to their difficulties in the "interhuman traffic." Perhaps one of his greatest contributions lies in the fact that he has shown how these various approaches can be used successfully in combination and in making a first approach toward translation from one theoretical "language" into others.

In Bach's view the group is a force field of great therapeutic potential, as the foregoing statements indicate. Transference is only one of the forms of interpersonal relationship which can be handled within it. He asserts that individual patterns are not al-

[2] Bach (1954), personal communication.

ways the product of deep personal motivation. They may also result from immediate group pressure, which changes the level of
both group and individual tensions. In the group field the individual derives therapeutic value not only from insight but through
change in the cognitive processes which determine the self-image.
In this respect he claims to go "beyond transference."

Moreover, the group situation offers several important technical
advantages. First it serves as an opportunity for the individual to
integrate three levels of experience—the intrapsychic, the interpersonal, and the group dynamic. Secondly, it offers a kind of projective screen which is so complex a pattern of interactions that no
one individual can cope with it entirely rationally. For this reason
his irrational and primitive tendencies will come to the fore and be
open to understanding, integration, or correction. On the level of
reality it also offers the patient a chance to take action, to give as
well as to receive. Finally, by the way they "move in the interpersonal traffic," the group members learn the degree to which they
themselves participate in bringing about the satisfaction or frustration of their needs.

According to Bach, the role of the therapist lies first in establishing a good "work culture" through careful attention to the group
processes. Keen attention to the part each patient plays in these
processes will then give the therapist and the members insight into
that member's "way of life" and add to the effectiveness of the
theragnosis. Analysis of the transference will play its role along
with these processes, but of primary importance will be the therapist's appreciation of the rise and fall of the tensions within the
total group, and his ability to make the patient aware of the meaning of the dynamics of the group as a whole. The therapist's role
might be described as a "type of culture-centered leadership whose
concern is equally divided between the progress of the individual
and the establishment of the group culture."

Bach uses the term "theragnosis" for the process of confronting
the patient with his contact maneuvers in the group and with the
psychotherapist. Such confrontation is simultaneously diagnostic
and also therapeutic. It stimulates self-correction and change. The
individual's attempt to make others respond to him in a way that
helps and validates his self-image Bach calls "set-up-operations."
One of the therapeutically most fruitful types of work therapy

groups can engage in is to sort out the previously unrecognized nature and style of these set-ups, which in turn can then be viewed as
stimulating in miniature what the patient unconsciously is living
for; what type of interpersonal gratifications he is seeking; how ef-
ficiently or ineffectually he is going about this; how much effort he
spends in this direction; whether it is constructive and really to his
interest. Bach is convinced that psychiatric problems are best
solved by direct training or "coaching" patients in communication.
The therapy group provides a much better setting for such training
and practice in forms of communication which stimulate self-actualization and prevent self-frustration.

ADLERIAN GROUP PSYCHOTHERAPY

This method holds a unique position in our field. Papanek (1956,
1959, 1961) stated in a personal communication to me that Adlerians feel they bridge the gap between the analytic and the group
dynamic approaches. They differ from the British analysts and
other therapists who combine the two approaches, in that they
have not had to try to straddle or to integrate two theoretical systems. Instead, their own thinking was from the beginning so structured as to be in harmony with Lewinian theory. Adler had put
the holistic aspect of Freud's approach onto the center of the stage.
For instance, his view of the family as a constellation or social system fits in perfectly with the Lewinian statement of the whole as a
unit with interdependent parts. As Papanek points out (1961),
Adler had also used the term "social interest" (Gemeinschaftsge-
fühl) thirty years before the group dynamicists once more gave it
prominence. To him it meant "a primary natural tendency to
strive for societal living." This stress on man's social nature is, of
course, quite consonant with Freud's view—in this case, transference. Adlerians make it focal and are, in that respect, closer to the
cultural schools and social psychology. They perceive and utilize
the group as a "cognitive matrix" which has the potential of making the members aware of their faulty apperception and therefore
enables them to change their self, and other, images. The Adlerian
concept of the cognitive matrix has a function similar to the Sullivanian concept of consensual validation and to communications
theory.

Papanek writes (1961), "The child uses his position within the family to form his subjective apperceptive scheme,[3] which is equivalent to the 'phenomenological field' of the Gestaltists." I assume she refers to the psychological phenomenology of Lewin, because she later states that their emphasis is not so much on the objective situation as on the child's subjective response to that situation.

"On these perceptions the child bases his life style, which is a unique, self-consistent and relatively constant behavioral pattern directed toward a partly unconscious goal." When Adler first stressed the importance of the ego he was reawakening an interest which Freud himself had shown in the early years, and one which in recent times the Freudian ego psychologists have significantly revitalized. The break with Freud was not so much a difference of opinion about the importance of the ego but of its role and the fact that Adler diminished the importance of the id and the unconscious to the vanishing point. As a result, modern Freudians have more in common with Adlerian psychology than had the older psychoanalysts. But Freudians continue to give great importance to the deeper unconscious id aspects as well as to the libidinal aspects of human relationships. The tripartite mental structure is a cornerstone. Nor would they accept as psychoanalytic any method that does not deal with transference and resistance. Yet the latter point is a matter of semantics, as is evident in Papanek's explanation of how the life style is the connecting link between the past and the present. The Adlerian therapist's interpretations, though different in content, do aim to analyze the relation between the patient's distortions and his childhood experiences in the family. It seems clear from Papanek's paper, however, that they reserve such analysis for occasions when the restorative milieu of the group is for some reason unable to bring about a restructuring of the life style.

They emphasize several points in this connection. The group should be cohesive, but flexible and resilient, and offer a maximum stimulation for interaction. It is the therapist's function to create these conditions, and to encourage frank and direct communication while keeping the group in a fundamentally friendly and helpful frame of mind. Under such conditions they believe the members will gain in self-esteem, become more social, be more giving

---

[3] This is reminiscent of Cooley's argument.

to others, and in the process help themselves restructure their "subjective apperceptive schemes" and find more realistic "life styles." Such achievements in turn will give them new social satisfactions. In order to accomplish this purpose the group must not stagnate (become structurally rigid) but remain in a progressive equilibrium. The therapist must see that this occurs, and that each member's role in the group is demonstrated to be contradictory to the group patterns, or to his own life style, so that he may actually experience not only the similarity but the difference between the historical family and the present group relationships. Papanek believes that the therapist's spontaneous, frank, and friendly interventions in the group are of greater significance in producing such dynamic change than interpretations and insight, although both are used freely in Adlerian group psychotherapy.

XX Family Therapy

The years during which this manuscript has been in preparation have witnessed the emergence of still another form of therapy, that with the family group. The family is viewed as a dynamic entity, a unitary system-in-tension, and is therefore treated as a whole. This means that the family is the patient while the member who has been designated as the patient is perceived instead in the role of a symptom of the family illness. Because this form of therapy has achieved rapid popularity and its practitioners are reporting appreciable success in the difficult areas of delinquency and schizophrenia, it must be included in any current survey of group methods, even though it is still in the stage of experimentation and research, and the final outcome depends upon continued systematic evaluation of the experiences and the development of therapeutic and technical formulations of those who are engaged in its practice. Meanwhile their reports on research and therapy are stimulating and challenging to all of us and more than welcome in the world of group psychotherapy.

The problem for which family therapy provides a new answer[1]

---

[1] The fact that Handlon and Parloff (1962) point out some new difficulties, such as the fact that the cognitive organization of the family brings about joint resistance to recognizing the pathological role of its individual members whereas traditional group therapy facilitates it, is no serious obstacle, for experience will no doubt provide solutions to that problem.

has long been familiar to psychotherapists of all schools. From the beginning psychoanalysis implied the close relationship between the problems of the children and those of the parents. But the psychoanalytic method depends upon the sacrosanct relationship between the individual patient and his doctor, so that traditionally psychoanalysts have preferred to have as little contact as possible with the relatives of their patients. They reason that in the course of treatment the patient will gain sufficient ego strength to deal with the members of his family and that in any event his ultimate goal is to find an independent life for himself. This does not hold, of course, for married couples, and the husband or wife was often advised to go into analysis with another therapist. In fact, there has been a growing tendency among analytic group therapists (and even some psychoanalysts) to work simultaneously or concurrently with marital couples on the premise that neurotic individuals unconsciously choose their marriage partners to complement their unconscious needs and so maintain a neurotic balance (Bergler, 1948). Groups composed of marital couples are now quite common (Leichter, 1962).

Analytic therapy with children must also follow another course, because it has frequently been found that the child who has been treated is unable to withstand the old family pressures when he returns home and so falls prey to them once more. At the Brooklyn and the New Rochelle Child Guidance Centers, in the late thirties and early forties, Durkin, Glatzer, and Hirsch (1944) tried to deal with the problem by working concomitantly with the child and his mother, either individually or in groups. We found these groups, in which we treated the mother as patients in their own right, reasonably effective. (Others reported work with guidance or counseling groups with mothers.) But our solution left a serious problem, for it was seldom that we found the father available for treatment during clinic hours.

The problem, then, is old. The significant new contribution of family therapy lies in the more succinct articulation of the problem in field theoretical terms and the more direct way of dealing with the family as a whole.

As so often occurs with timely new approaches, a number of researchers in several locales are now working in this way quite independently. Ackerman (1958), in New York, developed studies of neurotic families out of his interest in psychoanalysis and social work. Another form grew out of the anthropological and medical research in schizophrenia at Palo Alto, California, under the direction of Bateson.[2] Several groups of social psychologists, among them Handlon and Parloff, are working under the aegis of the National Institute of Mental Health in Bethesda, Maryland. Salvatore Minuchin, together with several social workers, is at present undertaking an investigation, studying and treating families of childreen at the Wiltwyck School in New York. Charles Fulweiler works with the families of delinquents in California. And there are numerous others.

Because the family therapy described by Jackson and Weakland at Palo Alto (1961) originates within a framework of communications theory (combined with interpersonal techniques), about which we have as yet had little to say, it is a good example to choose for more detailed consideration. It rests on two basic hypotheses concerning interaction in schizophrenic families. The first gives rise to the concept of psychological family homeostasis, which states that a family develops an intricate pathological system of communications (network of relationships) which plays a role in the etiology and maintenance of schizophrenia. Such families are called schizophregenic. Variations of this concept seem to have been developed concerning the families of delinquents and of neurotics and may well be applicable to normal families if the word pathological is omitted from the definition. In spite of the fact that these families begged for help, Jackson and Weakland found that in treatment they tenaciously maintained their dynamic steady state, and their therapists had to find the means of breaking through it.

The second basic concept on which their family therapy is based is that of the "double bind," which in its simplest form may be defined as the habitual sending and receiving of contradictory or in-

[2] Project for the Study of Schizophrenic Communication, directed by Gregory Bateson. Staff consist of Jay Haley and John H. Weakland, Research Associates, Don D. Jackson, consultant, William F. Fry, consultant. The research project is located at the Veterans Administration Hospital, Palo Alto, California, and is financed by grants from the Josiah Macy, Jr. Foundation and the Foundations' Fund for Research in Psychiatry.
For the theoretical background of communications theory, see Chapter V.

congruent messages on different levels (such as verbal and nonverbal). It includes the responses of the receiver and applies to multiple as well as dyadic communication. The important factors are that this communication occurs within vitally important relationships, such as those between child and parent, and that the receiver is unable either to comprehend what is happening, to respond effectively, or to leave the field. The receiver's predicament is further complicated by the fact that the sender conceals, masks, or denies the incongruity of the messages (Weakland, 1962). It might be imagined that as the child's ego strength develops, he will find a way of cutting through the messages, sending back equally perplexing ones or seeking outside relief in more direct communication with playmates, other families, and in school. But if he cannot, then he remains the victim of his situation and may develop bizarre behavior or withdrawal (schizophrenia) as responses which "get back" at the senders in a way which gives some relief but perpetuates the pathology.

While I have not had the good fortune to observe family therapy at first hand, I should like to describe a case in individual psychotherapy which I discovered and where I was forced by our analytic work to explore in the minutest detail such a family network in order to help my patient extricate himself from its insidious influence, and this will serve to illustrate some of the concrete problems to which it gives rise. It will also serve as a contrast to family therapy in which all members of the family would have taken part and the object would have been to change the system, rather than to immunize the patient.

The patient, Ned, whom we met in Chapter XIII, was a young man of twenty-seven, a borderline case who was still living with and completely dependent upon his family. As the picture of his family emerged in private sessions, he became aware that he had been cast in the role of the "sick" but gentle, cheerful, good boy, while his younger brother was the vigorous, independent one with the temper. Ned was angered because his parents always referred to them as "the boys," as if neither had an identity of his own except in his family role. As was to be expected he had an outsized identity problem. After a good deal of analytic work on his early family relationships and much careful ego building, he was ready to assert himself at home. Unfortunately, under the cricumstances the only break he was able to achieve in his pattern was in terms of negative behavior. It was his decision that he would no longer take the dog for her evening walk. This dog was a multiple symbol for him, representing his mother as a dependent little girl with whom as a child he had identified himself strongly.

At first I was doubtful about letting his decision pass without further exploration because walking the dog was one of the few ways in which he pulled his weight in the family. But as he talked I realized that he was right, since whatever change he instituted at this time was bound to be a negative one aimed at destroying his family-prescribed "character." His mother was at first stunned by his refusal, and then she made a great fuss, as we had anticipated. When this did not move him, she took to bed for a few days with an undiagnosed illness. He became exceedingly anxious, but stood firm. At this point his father stepped in and created the kind of scene which reactivated Ned's boyhood fear of his father as a "roaring lion." But we had talked over this possibility, too, and he had figured out ways of standing his ground. By the next session he reported that his brother had told his mother that Ned was drinking too much (he had actually taken a few extra drinks in his moments of panic) and raised doubts in her mind about his therapy. She called me, and since I had maintained a friendly working relationship with her over the telephone merely by expressing sympathy for her difficulties, I was able to tell her now that Ned was going through a stage of treatment which was unfortunate for her but essential to his getting well, and to assure her that I did not feel he would become an alcoholic. I also told her that his present attitude would probably be temporary but that there might be more difficult times to come in other matters. She might feel free to call me.

After a few such episodes Ned became strong enough to assert himself with me and asked me not to speak with his mother again. I agreed that I would tell her his decision the next time she called.

Thus, step by step he learned how to recognize the cues which were drawing him into the family system and to respond to them differently than he had before.

Jackson and Weakland make it clear that certain basic differences exist between their method and that of traditional psychoanalysis and analytic group therapy. They are interested not at all in the intrapsychic aspect of the individual personality. They focus rather on the phenomenological aspects of interaction within the family group as evidenced in their communications, and on the on-going events (transactions) occurring in the immediate situation, making no attempt to search out childhood experiences, fantasies, or unconscious motivation.

Their therapeutic techniques evolve out of this viewpoint and the situations which confront the therapists. These techniques are still in the process of development. The therapists find it sufficient to see the family for a one hour to an hour and a half session a week and are experimenting with many of the mechanics of treatment, such as how many of the family members to include, what to do about absences, and so on. If an individual session is requested, it is granted but the other family members are also invited to have similar sessions.

Since the family members center their concern on the schizo-phrenic patient, and the patient, although he goes along with them by acting helpless and hopeless, will act up at crucial moments to keep the sick interaction going, they feel that the therapist's first task must be to change the focus of treatment from the patient to the family as a whole. He may start by telling them that their pur-pose is to work together for better understanding among them-selves so that they can get more out of family life. Or he may make it clear to them that his function is to clarify certain patterns of communication which create blocks among them. At any rate he must set up the framework within which they will work together, and he must indicate his standards and expectations. He then fol-lows through by refusing to be drawn into special transactions with any one member, or, which is even more difficult, into the family network itself. They will put a good deal of pressure on him to do so. Interpretation of individual transference phenomena is con-sidered out of place.

A third technique is to take an active role in cutting through time-wasting maneuvers (resistance), such as the patient's bring-ing in unrelated material just as a crucial revelation is being ap-proached, or the parents' tendency to drop everything in order to follow up whatever their sick child shows an interest in, however irrelevant it may be.

The therapist's intervention in the family's communication is not so much in terms of interpreting for them the repetitious, self-reinforcing patterns he perceives, but in guiding their interaction by shifting its intent. He may do this by giving direct, explicit messages himself, by making explicit what is implied in the incongruous messages that are sent and received, or he may himself send therapeutically conceived dual messages which are calculated to make them shift or come to grips with the family system. The use of such incongruent therapeutic messages needs further investigation, according to Jackson, especially the utilization of such messages via assigning family members special tasks to carry out.

While it is perfectly clear that this approach differs from analytic group therapy in that it eschews childhood experience, fantasies, and unconscious motivation, certain of the new practices are not radically different from those that a therapist must use in any situation. For instance, he must set up the framework, i.e., the standards and expectations of how therapy will function. (See Chapter XIII and Durkin, 1954.) In every possible kind of therapeutic situation the therapist must also take measures to avoid yielding to the neurotic demands of his patient. Resistance to such demands is of course more difficult when the whole family is, so to speak, in league against this intention.

Jackson distinguishes between his active approach and what he considers the passive one of traditional psychoanalysis. Actually most analytic group therapists have also modified the method a good deal in applying it to the new situation. They are, for one thing, more active. This has been necessary in order to regulate the development of anxiety as the patients are seen less frequently (Durkin, 1954) and has been reinforced by the increasing proportion of borderline, orally regressed, and character problems among the patients who come to him for help. More active techniques are also required in order to cope with the deep-seated, tenacious defenses of those preverbal conflicts such as helplessness, hopelessness, masochism, and pseudodependency which have been erected. We have, in fact, come to realize that these measures are also helpful with the apparently large deposit of narcissistic problems remaining at the core of many garden variety neurotic problems.

Many analytic group therapists are therefore more in agreement with Jackson than he is aware of. As Glatzer (1962) says: "Very often the unresolved masochism of the therapist makes him submit to the oral dependency of his patients. His own unresolved need to suffer may make him misuse the psychoanalytic role of passivity and allow him, for instance, to let such a patient run on interminably with fruitless and repetitious complaints or permit taciturn patients to starve for the milk of common sense intervention."

A real difference between the family therapy approach and that of analytic group therapy lies in the area of transference. Jackson does not consider insight into transferential situations helpful. He believes that transference is limited to the particular situation of individual classical analysis and that it does not emerge in an interactive one with an active therapist.

For reasons already explained, I disagree; and therefore it is my impression that the two methods need not be basically incompatible in this respect. Certainly they have much to offer each other. Family therapy presents a new approach that is both stimulating and enriching to analytic group therapy. We stand to learn, for instance, a great deal about our patient's object (interpersonal) relationships by giving more attention to the subtleties of their communications, and a study of communications systems provides us with a multitude of fresh ideas. It would be folly not to take advantage of this new information.

Of greater significance is the fact that family therapy offers us different ways of dealing with the obstacles which relatives of patients put in the way of recovery, and suggests new ways of approaching difficult and thus far minimally effective therapeutic handling of delinquency and schizophrenia which may prove equally valuable in treating neurotics.

On the other hand family therapists might well find it to their advantage to adapt what we know about transference interpretations and modes of dealing with countertransference manifestations for use in family therapy.

In summary, it would seem that the new approach teaches us something about the etiological contribution of the family to the patient's emotional disorder, clearly demonstrates its function in maintaining it and their status quo, and has shown definite therapeutic results which may or may not turn out to be definitive in the long run (Handlon and Parloff, 1962). We await its development with interest and with the certainty that our horizons will be extended.

XXI Summary, and Horizons
in Group Psychotherapy

Even when the misunderstandings among schools of group psychotherapists and the consequent exaggeration of differences among
them have been minimized, certain of their basic group therapeutic principles remain irreconcilable. They cannot agree on what
constitutes emotional illness, nor on which are the decisive etiological factors of neurosis. Consequently their conceptions of what
processes and techniques function to alleviate the symptoms and
bring basic changes in their group patients continue to be at
variance.

Freudian analytic group therapists accept the fundamental assumptions of psychoanalysis including the principle of unconscious motivation; the psychic origin of character, symptoms, and
anxiety; the tripartite psychic structure; and the stages of psychosexual development. They also accept the basic psychoanalytic
method of analyzing transference and resistance as these occur in
the group interaction. Although they may differ widely in their
utilization of the less well established secondary, and therefore
expendable, theoretical concepts, they have, in general, gone along
with the major changes that have occurred in psychoanalysis. For
instance, the majority of analytic group therapists no longer deal
primarily with the id; they think of the libido in modern scientific
terms and they give due emphasis to ego and superego functions.

Group therapists of the interpersonal psychoanalytic schools have of course, given up libido theory and emphasize the impact of cultural conditions on etiology. They speak of interpersonal relations rather than of transference and, in general, adhere more closely to the phenomenological data than do Freudians when making their interpretations. They also tend to regard the patient-therapist relationship as being more fully reflexive and to utilize it accordingly. For this reason their approach is more closely akin both to the existential and to the group dynamic methods. It has, as a consequence, been combined with them more often than has the Freudian analytic group approach.

The group dynamic therapist views the problem of group therapy primarily from its social aspect (with modifications according to the therapeutic system which he has combined with group dynamic principles). He sees the individual first as a group member, then as a patient. He considers that a member's problems are anchored in his inability to get along with other people; that he consequently suffers from a feeling of not belonging, of isolation. Experience in a group under appropriate conditions is thought to provide the solution to his problems by helping him become aware of what patterns of behavior interfere with his social relations and by permitting him to learn new ways of getting along. The latter will presumably be transferred to his outside life. The total group and its dynamic processes are considered the primary source of therapy. The group leader's function is to utilize the group as a dynamic force field and to guide its processes so that the freest possible interaction may take place. The therapist makes the members aware of these processes but otherwise remains as unobtrusive as possible. Since very few group dynamicists attempt therapy without utilizing a recognized therapeutic system in conjunction with these principles, interventions are made according to the ideas of the system that is combined with them. Thus, Bach uses interpersonal psychoanalytic principles and any others he feels will be useful; Foulkes uses Freudian concepts and communication theory; Bion employs Kleinian ideas; and so on.

Existential group therapists vary a good deal among themselves as to how far they accept the Freudian body of knowledge and apply it interpretively. Those like Minkowski, who stem from phenomenological psychiatry, are at one extreme in this respect; others, like Medard Boss, originally Freudian, are at the other. Those from the Horney school, whose concept of self-actualization, for example, fits in very well with existentialist principles, fall somewhere between the two. In common they maintain that intrapsychic factors do not constitute the primary problems of the neurotic individual. They push their base line back to ontological factors. They assume that man's neurotic problems stem from the way in which he deals with the ultimate facts of existence. If he cannot withstand what they view as the tragicomedy of life; if he cannot face the unbearable truth of *la condition humaine* (Sartre) or man's "throwness," or bear the ever-present dread of "nonbeing"; if he cannot take his responsibility in spite of these, then he cannot achieve authentic being but must lead an inauthentic existence. He thereby incurs existential guilt and it is existential guilt which brings about his neurotic choices, self-deceptions, and, eventually, neurotic guilt and the whole gamut of neurotic problems.

Every therapeutic endeavor must therefore concern itself with bringing about authentic being in the patient. Being and becoming are crucial concepts which have to be grasped in this process. The role of the therapist is to help his patient as he helps himself to achieve this ideal. He believes that this may best be accomplished by a fully mutual interaction with the group members. He stresses the patient's right to make his own choices, however, even the choice of illness. His interpretative emphasis is nonteleologic rather than rational and aims primarily at helping the patient to "apprehend" in contradistinction to comprehending life in this way. Thus, the philosophical approach which psychoanalysis avoids becomes an integral part of existential group therapy.

The reader will not be surprised to hear that the author, although decidedly enriched as a result of her investigations of other methods, and certainly influenced by them, continues to prefer the psychoanalytic framework and its techniques as an approach to group psychotherapy. Granting a degree of emotional resistance to fundamental theoretical change, I am nevertheless convinced that, on a realistic basis alone, the psychoanalytic approach offers more than any other to the group therapist. It alone is sufficiently responsive to the intricacies and subtleties of human behavior and especially to the depth of its sources. Common sense is an important ingredient in the therapist-patient relationship, yet clinical experience

impresses me newly each day with the need to go beyond the phenomenological data and plumb the depths of motivation via hypotheses which involve a high degree of inference. Interpretations
which entirely bypass this necessity are prone to miss the crux of
the patient's pathogenic conflicts which then remain unresolved,
even though some of his defenses may be exchanged for better
ones. Let us peruse the simple example of an apparently warm
friendly comment made by one group member to another during
the early stages of treatment. Mrs. A says admiringly to Mrs. X,
who has regularly been snubbing her, "You look so nice. How do
you manage it—always to look as if you came out of a band box? I
think you're wonderful."

The naïve worker who is interested and eager to see his group
integrate may take the comment at face value, for A's practised social manner and the studied warmth of her voice cover well the
anxiety and hostility which lie below their surface. If so, she underlines this apparent evidence of good feeling, indicating approval
by look or comment and unwittingly discouraging the exploration
of less acceptable and more bothersome hidden feelings.

A therapist who knows A's history and is looking for nonverbal
cues will notice a slight tapping of the foot. Indeed, experienced
group members may well detect and explore this sign of her ambivalence. They may even recognize that her pursuant comments are
really associations and may provide the connecting link between
the seeming compliment and the unconscious feelings signalled
by the foot tapping. For A goes on to talk about her mother's
charm and good grooming and how as a child A could never quite
seem to live up to mamma's demands (which to the small child
may have appeared greatly exaggerated). To turn a deaf ear to
historical material would cut off an important avenue to understand her present predicament. But even this probing does not
reach the deepest layers of pathogenic conflict, for the hostility itself is a defense which wards off more painful fears and fantasies.
If the hostility is brought into the open and given apparent approval of the therapist and group members, it may be only temporarily relieved and actually reinforced as a mode of defense.

The analytic group therapist constructs still another working
hypothesis on this account. He may, for example, conclude that
A's frustration of her attempt to please her mother has been con-

verted into getting satisfaction from quite a different motive. Her sloppy appearance, he assumes, must have expressed both an unacknowledged reproach to her mother and a secret inner sign of victory over her. But the victory is empty and assures her only of the opposite of her conscious wish. It regularly brings about rejection in the present as it once brought rejection from her mother. But she pretends by this mechanism to become the active initiator rather than the passive victim. She has salvaged a feeling of control over a situation in which she feels threatened. Here in the group, as in the outside world, she continues to court rejection from significant people in her social environment (I note that she has remained in an environment which values good grooming). The layer of anger which she persistently tries to ward off, itself may be seen to ward off an even more painful layer, characterized by the feeling of being overwhelmingly rejected and impotent. Two basic needs are involved: (1) her libidinal need for love (which she has confused with approval), and (2) her need to retain her individuality. She seems to have resolved the problem by turning her need for love into a need for rejection and must now turn pain into pleasure. Also, by indulging in negative exhibitionism she expressed her anger toward her mother without having to acknowledge it openly and without succeeding in adding proof that her mother was rejecting her. This gave her the right to feel sorry for herself. By not yielding she also gained satisfaction out of seeming to control the situation, of seeming to assert herself. But chiefly she warded off the ever present infantile fantasy of being swallowed up by mother (and her current substitutes).

This way of conceptualizing her difficulties is of course highly inferential and should be treated as a working hypothesis which may be proved or disproved by the clinical material the patient produces in response to it. In the group this will not be in the form of free associations but appear in her interaction with the group members. But we are not here concerned with whether or not this particular hypothesis is correct, but rather with the proposition that human behavior occurs on multiple psychic levels and the belief that these must be opened up if deeply founded changes are to occur in our group patients.

In spite of the apparently irreconcilable principles of these conceptual frameworks there is in actual practice a good deal of overlapping as well as the planned combining of methods. For instance, all therapists set up group conditions which are conducive to free interchange of thoughts and feelings. They differ chiefly in the terms they use in promoting this goal. Both analytic and existential group therapists intervene fairly actively because they see the therapist as the chief source of therapeutic movement, and their interventions will often deal with psychoanalytic concepts. Since there are also fundamentally complementary elements among the methods, therapists with an eclectic turn of mind tend to utilize whatever seems to increase their therapeutic effectiveness regardless of its origin.

For instance, it was a natural extension of the usual analytic process for me to learn to analyze the transference of any member to the group as a whole, but from Stock's group dynamic approach I learned also to ask myself how the group as such was reacting to that transference, how it was reacting to me or to the situation we were in, and lastly what problem (focal conflict) it was coping with at any given time. Knowledge of the experiential-existential method serves as a beacon to remind me of the need to probe my own as well as the members irrationalities and so to become quickly aware of countertransference even though I continue to deal with it quite differently than they do.

Similarly I hope that the analytic method serves to remind the others of the necessity of penetrating several layers of feelings (defenses) and of the here-and now- cum-there-and-then quality of the transference. It could serve to remind the existentialists that catharsis is not enough and that precise conceptualization enables patients to articulate the connecting link between their unconscious motivation and their behavior, and that being able to accomplish this is an ego-strengthening experience.

All of us may be enriched by understanding concepts different from our own, for it will give us a new slant on the phenomena we are all observing. Moreover it will be refreshing to the patients if we couch our interpretations in different words. We should freely borrow from one another in this respect.

Whatever the future may bring as a result of mutual understanding and slow absorption, it is not likely that there will ever be an integration of several therapeutic methods. Nor would it be desirable. What we can expect is new theories which will create growth-promoting conflicts just as communications theory is doing today.

While inestimable advances have been in the making, in group psychology a certain mellowing of the old disparities between the original individual psychoanalytic schools from which much of group therapy derived, has taken place. The old insistence on the correctness of one's conceptual framework still persists, but we have made more headway in this respect than we have realized or admitted. For instance, no one who has read Farau's account of the evolution of Adlerian psychology (1962) can fail to recognize the Freudian "aggressive forces" behind the Adlerian "striving for superiority." Farau himself mentions the growing acceptance by individual psychology of the unconscious and of transference. Similarly, no one who understands recent developments in psychoanalytic ego psychology can any longer take very seriously the old criticism that the Freudians focus too exclusively on the libido. Similarly, increasing interest among psychoanalysts in the preoedipal phases of child development and problems surrounding omnipotence and authority takes the sting out of the old argument against the singleness of Freudian interest in the oedipus complex. The reformulation of Freudian group psychology which I suggested in Chapter V, if accepted, would bridge the gap between Freudian and Bionic theories of group psychology. It may be that before too long we shall be able to communicate with social scientists as group therapists rather than as Freudian, Adlerian, or Sullivanian group therapists.

Progress of this kind in group psychology need not mean that our clinical assumptions will undergo basic change. We shall probably continue to do therapy within our own frameworks while testing translations into a common language in a research context. In this instance, clinical methods will lag behind conceptualization or perhaps continue to remain independent.

There is progress toward cooperation in still another area. As each new branch of social science began to achieve its basic goals, its theorists began to look beyond the borders of their particular territory. Psychotherapy, social psychology, sociology, and medical psychology have taken such steps. Psychotherapy has expanded its boundaries to include the treatment of groups. Whereas the psychoanalyst once rigidly excluded family members and even refused to confer with them, now marital couples are being seen conjointly with increasing frequency and family therapy is becoming highly popular. Social psychiatry has broadened the framework in which hospital patients are cared for, so as to include their relationship with the community at large. On another front they have been studying intergroup relations. Group therapists are beginning to search for more appropriate and effective ways of applying their techniques to the mental hygiene field and ways of bringing increasingly constructive influence to bear on the larger societal problem of national and international life.

As a consequence of these interdisciplinary ventures in research, in theory building, and in practice, we are moving forward on all fronts. For instance, we are beginning to find ways of meeting the ever increasing demands on group therapy. There has been an insistent call, on the part of hospitals, community mental hygiene projects, schools, and even industry for information and training in group psychotherapy. The analytic position that only reconstructive methods which actually resolve the patient's pathogenic conflicts may be called group psychotherapy is being questioned. Certainly we must strive to maintain the highest possible standards and training requirements. But is it not perhaps time that, in response to existing conditions, we revise our definition to include any consistent form of group treatment administered for the purpose of decreasing the ill effect of emotional disturbance on the group members? The answer for the present seems to be that, in setting up standards and training requirements, we must also outline a series of levels on which group therapy may be conducted,—in terms of suitability to the needs of the patients and the skill of the available therapists. Our efforts can thereafter be turned to improving training facilities and upgrading the standards. Such a policy would be distinctly realistic and have the advantage of relieving the present imbalance of supply and demand in group therapy.

The patients of psychotic wards in mental hospitals for instance, are certainly not candidates for analytic group therapy, although they have been known to be helped by the mere fact of belonging, of engaging in human relationships in an accepting atmosphere. In a group project for unmarried mothers who were being cared for while waiting for their babies, the therapist was able to help them face and come to grips with some of their hidden feelings toward their parents, the putative fathers, and themselves. Coming into closer touch with themselves and learning to communicate more directly within a permissive atmosphere brought about striking changes in their attitudes in the relatively short period of their stay at the home. Some of them felt ready to deal with their problems, others became interested in joining analytic therapy groups. It seems to me that this work represents a certain minimal level of therapy and that it would be useful to work out a series of such levels in terms of their suitability to the needs of the group requiring help. If we are to insure the sound development of the many and diverse demands which are being made on group therapists and group dynamicists we must work together to define group therapy and decide the appropriate levels for various kinds of problems and the kind or degree of training that is necessary for each. Furthermore, the boundary between therapy and other related forms of group work in which therapeutic effect is incidental to education, training, and so on should be defined without involving meaningless status implications.

The implications of this for the mental hygiene movement, which until recently could claim but few substantial contributions from psychology, are considerable. This category of service has suffered from certain initial misconceptions, functional inflexibility and the lack of communication among those from whom competent leadership might be expected, i.e., psychiatrists, psychologists, sociologists, nurses, and so on. It is a field which will benefit from an interdisciplinary approach.

In its early history the mental hygiene movement was led astray by the assumption that those who know how to unravel emotional knots would without further study and training be able to prevent untoward complications from developing in child rearing and that by spreading psychoanalytic information we might hope to produce an emotionally healthy generation. But whatever has to do with the unconscious is not appropriate for public consumption. It requires highly skilled preparation and serving. The concepts of psychoanalysis have often been misunderstood or distorted by unanalyzed leaders or by their audiences. For instance, the advice often heard in the twenties and thirties that greater parental love would cure the children's ills did not take into account that love

doesn't come on order. It frequently served to increase the frustrated parents' guilt and anxiety and by the same token, to decrease
their effectiveness as upbringers. Permissiveness had been preached
as a replacement for punitive discipline, but neurotic parents in
their dilemma often found it easier to eliminate the discipline than
the punitiveness. And they tended to confuse permissiveness with
love and became too lax with the result that in many cases their
progeny became arrogantly insecure and joined the ranks of the
kool kats and the beatniks. During this period, also, thoughtful
group therapists hesitated to apply treatment techniques to those
who came for education. There is an ethical principle involved
which guards the right of the individual. Like the surgeon, the psychotherapist dares not invite people into his chamber of operations. Indeed, his psychic surgery is even more delicate, and only
those who ask for his help may be treated.

Now we are on the brink of change. Group psychotherapy has
provided the connecting link between working with the individual
and dealing with larger societal units, between intensive treatment
and a dynamic method of education. The technique of bringing
heretofore concealed personal feelings and patterns of interpersonal behavior into awareness has proved modifiable. Peck and his
colleagues, in their attempt to improve the competence of a variety
of nontherapeutic hospital groups, definitely demonstrated that
changes did occur in the functioning of these groups as a result of
the members' ability to acknowledge formerly unconscious information regarding events, feelings, ideas, or impulses. The Leadership Training Laboratories also proved the effectiveness of increasing the group's awareness of its own processes. Both used
modifications of the familiar group therapy technique in that they
increased group awareness without probing too deeply or too
extensively.

I had occasion to come to grips with these issues recently, as I sat
as participant-observer in a Mental Health Workshop on Adult Relations for the people in my community. I was trying to decide
whether or not I should accept the leadership of such a group;
whether my group therapy skills were suitable to or modifiable for
those conditions. My experience may help to clarify some of the
issues and specific problems that must be met in the process of developing new methods of mental health education.

The subscribers to the workshop who had expected instruction and guidance knew nothing about group process. They were vastly puzzled, anxious, and eventually irritated about the unstructured nature of the actual situation. They could not see why we did not teach them something concrete about adult relations. They stoutly evaded all our encouragement to express criticism of the leader whom they liked, but discovered by experience that they were free to express it with impunity toward the sponsors. Their group decision to notify the authorities that a much more specific topic for discussion should have been provided them may have proved ego strengthening. We had no way of measuring its effect. The group members were unable to articulate (as we did among ourselves) the value of their experience. They admitted to no value in being able to express their feelings nor in being part of a group. We knew much more had happened in the emotional realm than they were aware of because although they continued to downgrade the workshop, they missed few sessions and voluntarily prolonged most of them, staying to talk long after the leaders left.

What exactly was gained? How could we measure it? We shall have to outline specific goals, devise suitable techniques, and determine appropriate criteria for measuring results. Such work as that done by Peck and his colleagues has given us a start in the right direction, but all general rules must be tested in relation to the specific situation in which they are to be used. For instance, in our case we would have to find a way of discovering whether our groups actually do gain more competence from a structured discussion in which they come to their own conclusions, out of being left on their own until they mobilize enough independence to get angry with their leader and turn to the group to take over its assigned task, or a middle course that utilizes group process. Perhaps one of these methods is preferable for certain types of members, and a different kind for others.

Several other areas need study. What is the relationship between the number and length of the sessions and optimal increase in competence? How can one deal with the members' needs to turn the discussion group into a therapeutic one? Will a repeated series of such workshops enable us to choose from among the members those who may themselves be trained as community leaders in mental health and those who may be referred to therapy groups? All these questions and many more need further investigation.

If we accomplish these tasks we shall be able to make a health-producing wedge into the presumably normal world whose emotional quirks are constrictive though not crippling. We can also expect to reduce the waste of human potential by recognizing ahead of time those who need psychotherapy and, by increasing the number of those who get such help, reduce the high proportion of complete breakdowns which at present overcrowd our hospitals. This is a rational program in which psychotherapists, together with mental hygiene experts and community leaders, may share. With continued study and emerging discoveries we can hope to arrive at "viable hybrid techniques" derived from group therapy and group dynamics which avoid the danger of releasing too much anxiety. The field of public mental health is burgeoning with new possibilities.

In the course of the research and the expanded practical services made possible by this broader conception of our goals, still wider horizons become visible. Group therapists, social psychologists, psychiatrists, and representatives of a number of related professions may find their capacity for contributing to the solution of contemporary social problems appreciably magnified. For instance psychologists, instead of giving their relatively untutored opinion to those who are in charge of government on the advisability of testing atomic weapons and offering their value judgments on political policies, may find the means to contribute to national and even international problems in the area of their greatest skill, the management of human relationships.

Bibliography

Abel, T. (1964), Idiosyncratic and Cultural Variations of Oral-Oedipal Patterns. *J. Psychol.*, 57:377-390.

Abraham, K. (1927), Ch. XXIII, Contributions to the Theory of an Anal Character (1921); Ch. XXIV, The Influence of Oral Erotism on Character Formation (1924); Ch. XXV, Formation on the Genital Level of the Libido (1925); Ch. XXVI, A Short Study of the Development of the Libido, Viewed in the Light of Mental Disorders (1924). In *Selected Papers*. London: Hogarth Press.

Ach, N. (1910), in Lewin, K. (1951). Pp. 5, 27, 66, 68, 84.

Ackerman, N. W. (1958), *The Psychodynamics of Family Life; Diagnosis and Treatment of Family Relationships*. New York: Basic Books.

———— (1961), Symptom, Defense, and Growth in Group Process. *Int. J. Group Psychother.*, 11: 131-142.

Allport, F. H. (1924), *Social Psychology*. Boston: Houghton Mifflin.

Bach, G. R. (1954), *Intensive Group Psychotherapy*. New York: Ronald Press.

Bales, R. F. (1950), *Interaction Process Analysis; a Method for the Study of Small Groups*. Cambridge, Mass.: Addison-Wesley.

Bateson, G., Jackson, D. D., Haley, J., & Weakland, J. (1956), Toward a Theory of Schizophrenia. *Behav. Sci.* 1:251-264.

Bavelas, A. (1950), Communication Patterns in Task-Oriented Groups. *J. Acoustical Soc. Am., 22:* 725-730.

Benne, K. D. (1958), Comments in Training Groups. *Research Reports and Technical Notes, No. 21.* Boston: Boston University Press.

Bennis, W. G. (1960), A Critique of Group Therapy Research. *Int. J. Group Psychother., 10:* 63-77.

—— (1961), A Case Study in Research Formulation. *Int. J. Group Psychother., 11:* 272-283.

—— & Benne, K.D. (1958), Patterns and Vicissitudes in Training Groups. *Research Reports and Technical Notes, No. 21.* Boston: Boston University Press.

—— & Shepard, H. (1956), A Theory of Group Development. *Human Relations, 9:* 415-437.

Berger, M. M. (1958a), Problems of Anxiety in Group Psychotherapists. *Am. J. Psychother., 12:* 505-507.

—— (1958b), Nonverbal Communication in Group Psychotherapy. *Int. J. Group Psychother., 8:* 161-178.

—— (1960), The Recognition and Management of Emergencies in Group Psychotherapy. From unpublished paper read at A.G.P.A. Conference, January, 1960.

Bergler, E. (1948), *The Battle of the Conscience; a Psychiatric Study of the Inner Working of the Conscience.* Washington: Washington Institute of Medicine.

—— (1949), *The Basic Neurosis, Oral Regression, and Psychic Masochism.* New York: Grune & Stratton.

—— (1952), *The Superego, Unconscious Conscience; the Key to Theory and Therapy of Neurosis.* New York: Grune & Stratton.

Berkowitz, L. (1953), Sharing Leadership in Small, Dicision-Making Groups. *J. Abn. & Soc. Psychol., 48:* 231-238.

Berman, L. (1954), Psychoanalysis and the Group. *Am. J. Orthopsychiat., 11:* 133.

Berne, E. (1960), "Psychoanalytic" versus "Dynamic" Group Therapy. *Int. J. Group Psychother., 10:* 98-103.

Bion, W. R. (1948-1951), Experiences in Groups. *Human Relations, 1:* 314-320, 1948; *2:* 487-496, 1948; *3:* 13-22, 1949; *4:* 295-303, 1949; *5:* 3-14, 1950; *6:* 395-402, 1950; *7:* 221-227, 1951.

—— (1955), Group Dynamics; a Re-View. In: *New Directions*

in Psychoanalysis, eds. Melanie Klein et al. New York: Basic Books, pp. 440-447.

Bonner, H. (1959), *Group Dynamics; Principles and Application.* New York: Ronald Press.

Borgatta, E. F., Bales, R. F., & Hare, A. P. (1955), *Small Groups.* New York: Knopf.

Bradford, L. P. et al. (eds.) (1964), *T-Group Theory and Laboratory Method.* New York: Wiley.

Brown, J. F. (1937), Psychoanalysis, Topological Psychology, and Experimental Psychopathology. *Psychoanal. Quart.,* 6: 227-237.

———— (1940), *The Psychodynamics of Abnormal Behavior.* New York: McGraw-Hill.

Buber, M. (1923), *I and Thou.* Edinburgh, England: R. & R. Clark, 1937.

———— (1948), *Between Man and Man.* New York: Macmillan.

Burrow, T. (1928), The Basis of Group Analysis. *Brit. J. Med. Psychol., 8:* 198-206.

Bychowski, G. (1952), *The Psychotherapy of Psychosis.* New York: Grune & Stratton.

Cartwright, D. & Zander, A. (eds.) (1953), *Group Dynamics: Research and Theory.* Evanston, Ill.: Row Peterson.

———— & ———— (1960), *Ibid.* Second edition.

Cassirer, E. (1944), *An Essay on Man; an Introduction to a Philosophy of Human Culture.* New Haven: Yale University Press.

Cattell, R. B. (1948), Concepts and Methods in the Measurement of Group Syntality. *Psychoanal. Rev., 55*:48-63.

Cherry, C. (1961), *On Human Communication.* New York: Science Editions.

Corsini, R. J. (1957), *Methods of Group Psychotherapy.* New York: Blakiston.

Deutsch, M. (1949), The Effects of Competition on the Group Process. *Human Relations, 2:* 129-152, 199-223.

Dreikurs, R. (1957), Group Psychotherapy from the Point of View of Adlerian Psychology. *Int. J. Group Psychother., 7*:363-375.

Durkin, H. E. (1948), The Theory and Practice of Group Psychotherapy. *Annals N.Y. Acad. Sci., 51*:867-928.

—— (1954), *Group Therapy for Mothers of Disturbed Children.* Springfield, Ill.: Charles C Thomas.

—— (1956), Mothers. In: *The Fields of Group Psychotherapy,* ed. S. R. Slavson. New York: International Universities Press, pp. 153-169.

—— (1957), Toward a Common Basis for Group Dynamics: Group and Therapeutic Processes in Group Psychotherapy. *Int. J. Group Psychother.,* 7:115-130.

—— Glatzer, H. T., & Hirsch, J. S. (1944), The Therapy of Mothers in Groups. *Am. J. Orthopsychiat., 14*:68-75.

Einstein, A. & Infeld, L. (1938), *The Evolution of Physics; the Growth of Ideas from Early Concepts to Relativity and Quanta.* New York: Simon & Schuster.

Eissler, R. S. et al. (eds.) (1945-1963), *The Psychoanalytic Study of the Child, Vols. I-XVIII.* New York: International Universities Press.

Erikson, E. H. (1950), *Childhood and Society.* New York: Norton.

—— (1959), Identity and the Life Cycle; Selected Papers. *Psychological Issues, Monog. 1.* New York: International Universities Press.

Ezriel, H. (1950), A Psychoanalytic Approach to Group Treatment. *Brit. J. Med. Psychol., 23*:59-74.

—— (1959), Role of Transference in Psychoanalysis and Other Approaches to Group Treatment. *Acta Psychother.,* 7 (Supp.) : 101-116.

Farau, A. (1962), Fifty Years of Individual Psychology. *Comprehensive Psychiat., 3*:242-254.

Fenichel, O. (1945), *The Psychoanalytic Theory of Neurosis.* New York: Norton.

Ferenczi, S. (1916), Stages in the Development of the Sense of Reality. *Contributions to Psychoanalysis, 1.* Boston: Badger.

—— (1926), *Further Contributions to the Theory and Techniques of Psychoanalysis.* London: L. & V. Woolf and Institute of Psycho-Analysis (Second edition, London: Hogarth Press, 1950).

—— (1950), *Sex in Psychoanalysis; Contributions to Psychoanalysis.* New York: Brunner.

Festinger, L. (1949), The Analysis of Sociograms Using Matrix Algebra. *Human Relations, 2*:153-158.

———— Schacter, S., & Back, K. (1950), *Social Pressures in Informal Groups*. New York: Harper.

Foulkes, S. H. (1948), *Introduction to Group Analytic Psychotherapy; Studies in the Social Integration of Individuals and Groups*. New York: Grune & Stratton, 1949.

———— & Anthony, E. J. (1957), *Group Psychotherapy; the Psychoanalytic Approach*. Baltimore: Penguin Books.

Fourezios, N., Hutt, M., & Guetzkow, H. (1950), Measurement of Self-Oriented Needs in Discussion Groups. *J. Abn. & Soc. Psychol., 45*:682-690.

Freud, A. (1936), *The Ego and the Mechanisms of Defense*. New York: International Universities Press, 1946.

Freud, S. (1908), Character and Anal Erotism. In: *Collected Papers, 2*. London: Hogarth Press, 1924, pp. 45-50.

———— (1910), The Future Prospects of Psycho-Analytic Therapy. In: *Collected Papers, 2*. London: Hogarth Press, 1924, pp.285-296.

———— (1914a), On the History of the Psycho-Analytic Movement. In: *Collected Papers, 1*. London: Hogarth Press, 1924, pp. 287-359.

———— (1914b), On Narcissism. In: *Collected Papers, 4*. London: Hogarth Press, 1925, pp. 30-59.

———— (1915), Instincts and Their Vicissitudes. In: *Collected Papers, 4*. London: Hogarth Press, 1925, pp. 60-83.

———— (1917), Mourning and Melancholia. In: *Collected Papers, 4*. London: Hogarth Press, 1925, pp. 152-170.

———— (1920), *Beyond the Pleasure Principle*. London: Hogarth Press, 1950.

———— (1921), *Group Psychology and the Analysis of the Ego*. London: Hogarth Press, 1940.

———— (1923), *The Ego and the Id*. London: Hogarth Press, 1927.

———— (1925), Negation. In: *Collected Papers, 5*. London: Hogarth Press, 1950, pp. 181-185.

———— (1926), *The Problem of Anxiety*. New York: Norton, 1936.

————(1931), Female Sexuality. In: *Collected Papers, 5*. London: Hogarth Press, 1950, pp. 252-272.

———— (1932), *New Introductory Lectures on Psycho-Analysis*. London: Hogarth Press, 1933.

Fried, E. (1961), Techniques of Psychotherapy Going Beyond Insight. *Int. J. Group Psychother.*, *11*:297-304.

Fries, M. (1935), *Guide to Film: Some Basic Differences in the Newborn.* New York: Film Rental Library.

Geller, J. J. (1954), Group Psychotherapy in a Community Psychiatric Clinic. *Int. J. Group Psychother.*, *4*:103-108.

——— (1962), Parataxic Distortions in the Initial Stages of Group Relationships. *Int. J. Group Psychother.*, *12*:27-34.

Glanzer, M. & Glaser R. (1959), Techniques for the Study of Group Structure and Behavior. *Psychol. Bull.*, *56*:317-332.

Glatzer, H. T. (1959a), Analysis of Masochism in Group Psychotherapy. *Int. J. Group Psychother.*, *9*:158-166.

——— (1959b), Some Clinical Aspects of Adult Therapy. *Am. J. Orthopsychiat.*, *29*:383-389.

——— (1962), Handling Narcissistic Problems in Group Psychotherapy. *Int. J. Group Psychother.*, *12*:448-455.

——— & Durkin, H. E. (1945), The Role of the Therapist in Group Relationship Therapy. *The Nervous Child*, *4*:243-251.

Glover, E. (1925), Notes on Oral Character Formation. *Int. J. Psycho-Anal.*, *6*:131-154.

——— (1955), *The Technique of Psycho-Analysis.* New York: International Universities Press.

——— (1956), *On the Early Development of Mind. Selected Papers on Psychoanalysis, 1.* New York: International Universities Press.

Goldfarb, W. (1944), The Effects of Early Institutional Care on Adolescent Personality: Rorschach Data. *Am. J. Orthopsychiat.*, *14*:441-447.

Goldman, G. D. (1957), Some Applications of Harry Stack Sullivan's Theories to Group Psychotherapy. *Int. J. Group Psychother.*, *7*:385-391.

Greenacre, P. (1952), *Trauma, Growth, and Personality.* New York: Norton.

Greenbaum, H. (1954), Group Psychotherapy with Alcoholics in Conjunction with Antabuse Treatment. *Int. J. Group Psychother.*, *4*:30-41.

Grinberg, L. et al. (1957), *Psycho-Analytische Gruppen-Therapie.* Buenos Aires: Spanish Edition Paidos.

Guetzkow, H. (1960), Differentiation of Roles in Task-Oriented Groups. In: *Group Dynamics: Research and Theory*, eds. D. Cartwright & A. Zander. Evanston, Ill.: Row Peterson, 1960, pp. 683-704.

Haley, J. (1959), The Family of the Schizophenic. *J. Nerv. & Ment. Diseases, 129*:257-374.

—— (1962), Whither Family Therapy. *Family Process, 1*:265-293.

Hall, C. S. & Lindzey, G. (1954), Psychoanalytic Theory and its Application in the Social Sciences. In: *Handbook of Social Psychology. Vol. I*, by G. Lindzey. Cambridge, Mass.: Addison-Wesley, pp. 143-180.

Handlon, J. H. & Parloff, M. B. (1962), The Treatment of Patient and Family as a Group: Is It Group Psychotherapy? *Int. J. Group Psychother., 12*:132-141.

Hartmann, H. (1958), *Ego Psychology and the Problem of Adaptation*. New York: International Universities Press.

—— & Kris, E. (1945), The Genetic Approach in Psychodynamics. In: *The Psychoanalytic Study of the Child, I*, eds. R. S. Eissler et al. New York: International Universities Press, pp. 11-30.

—— —— & Loewenstein, R. M. (1946), Comments on the Formation of Psychic Structure. In: *The Psychoanalytic Study of the Child, II*, eds. R. S. Eissler et al. New York: International Universities Press, pp. 11-38.

Heidegger, M. (1929), *Was Ist Metaphysik?* Frankfurt A. M.: V. Klostermann.

Heinemann, F. H. (1953), *Existentialism and the Modern Predicament*. London: A. & C. Black (Second edition, New York: Harper, 1954).

Hill, W. F. (ed.) (1961), *Collected Papers on Group Psychotherapy*. Provo, Utah: Utah State Hospital.

Hora, T. (1956), Beyond Counter-Transference. *Am. J. Psychother., 10*:18-23.

—— (1959a), Ontic Perspectives in Psychoanalysis. *Am. J. Psychoanal., 19*:134-141.

—— (1959b), Existential Group Psychotherapy. *Am. J. Psychother., 13*:83-92.

Illing, H. A. (1957) Jung's Theory of the Group as a Tool in Therapy. *Int. J. Group Psychother.*, 7:392-397.

Introduction to Contemporary Civilization, A Source Book (1954), Vol. I, Essays I and VII, Vol. II, Essays VII, VIII, and XIII. New York: Columbia University Press.

Jackson, D. (1957), The Question of Family Homeostasis. *Psychoanal. Quart., 31* (Supp. 90) :79-96.

—— & Weakland, J. H. (1961), Conjoint Family Therapy; Some Considerations on Theory, Technique, and Results. *Psychiatry, 24*:30-45.

Jackson, J. & Grotjahn, M. (1958), The Treatment of Oral Defenses by Combined Individual and Group Psychotherapy. *Int. J. Group Psychother., 8*:373-382.

Jaspers, K. (1941), *Rechenschaft und Ausblick: Reden und Aufsätze.* Munich: R. Piper.

Johnson, M. H. (1962), The Development of a Therapeutic Community on an Open Ward in a General Hospital. *Int. J. Group Psychother., 12*:99-106.

Johnson, P. E. (1959), *Interpersonal Psychology of Religion.* Boston: Boston University Press.

Kahn, D. L. & Katz, D. (1953), Leadership Practices in Relation to Group Productivity. In: *Group Dynamics: Research and Theory,* eds. D. Cartwright & A. Zander. Evanston, Ill.: Row Peterson, 1953.

Kaplan, S. R. & Roman, M. (1961), Characteristic Responses in Adult Therapy Groups to the Introduction of New Members: A Reflection on Group Processes. *Int. J. Group Psychother., 11*:372-381.

Kaufmann, W. A. (1950), *Nietzsche; Philosopher, Psychologist, Antichrist.* Princeton, N.J.: Princeton University Press.

—— (1956), *Existentialism from Dostoyevsky to Sartre.* New York: Meridian Books.

Klein, M. (1932), *The Psychoanalysis of Children.* London: L. & V. Woolf.

—— (1957), *Envy and Gratitude, a Study of Unconscious Sources.* New York: Basic Books.

—— (1961), *Narrative of Child Analysis; the Conduct of the Psychoanalysis of Children as Seen in the Treatment of a Ten-Year-old Boy.* London: Hogarth Press.

———— et al. (eds.) (1955), *New Directions in Psychoanalysis.* New York: Basic Books.

Koch, S. (1959), *Psychology: A Study of Science,* Vol. III. New York: McGraw-Hill.

Kubie, L. S. (1958), Some Theoretical Concepts Underlying the Relationships Between Individual and Group Psychotherapies. *Int. J. Group Psychother., 8*:3-19.

Lakin, M. & Dobbs, W. H. (1962), The Therapy Group Promotes an Hypothesis of Psychogenesis: A Study in Group Process. *Int. J. Group Psychother., 12*:64-74.

Lampl-de Groot, J. (1963), Symptom Formation and Character Formation. *Int. J. Psycho-Anal., 44*:1-22.

Leichter, E. (1962), Group Psychotherapy of Married Couples' Groups: Some Characteristic Treatment Dynamics. *Int. J. Group Psychother., 12*:154-163.

Lewin, K. (1935), *A Dynamic Theory of Personality.* New York: McGraw-Hill.

———— (1936), *The Principles of Topological Psychology.* New York: McGraw-Hill.

———— (1937), Psychoanalysis and Topological Psychology. *Bull. Menninger Clin., 1*:202.

———— (1943), Forces Behind Food Habits and Methods of Changes. *National Research Council, 108*:35.

———— (1951), *Field Theory in Social Science.* New York: Harper.

———— Lippitt, R., & White, R. K. (1939), Patterns of Aggression in Behavior in Experimentally Created Climates. *J. Soc. Psychol., 10*:271-299.

Lewy, E. (1961), Responsibility, Free Will, and Ego Psychology. *Int. J. Psycho-Anal., 42*:260-270.

Likert, R. (1932), A Technique for the Measurement of Attitudes. *Arch. Psych., 140*:1-55.

Lindzey, G. (1954), *Handbook of Social Psychology, Vols. I &II.* Cambridge, Mass.: Addison-Wesley.

Lippitt, R., Polansky, N., Redl, F., & Rosen, S. (1952), The Dynamics of Power. *Human Relations, 5*:37-64.

Mack-Brunswick, R. (1940), The Preoedipal Phase of the Libido Development. *Psychoanal. Quart., 9*:293-319.

Malone, T. P., Whitaker, C. A., Warkentin, J., & Felder, R. (1958), Rational and Non-Rational Psychotherapy; a Reply. *Am. J. Psychother., 15*:212-220.

Mann, J. (1953), Group Therapy with Adults. *Am. J. Orthopsy-chiat., 23*:332-337.

—— (1955), Some Theoretic Concepts of the Group Process. *Int. J. Group Psychother., 5*:235-241.

March, J. G. & Simon, H. C. (1958), *Organizations*. New York: Wiley.

Martin, E. A. & Hill, W. F. (1957), Toward a Theory of Group Development. *Int. J. Group Psychother., 7*:20-30.

May, R. et al. (eds.) (1958), *Existence: A New Dimension in Psychiatry and Psychology*. New York: Basic Books.

McDougall, W. (1921), *The Group Mind*. Cambridge, Mass.: Cambridge University Press.

Moreno, J. L. (1951), *Sociometry, Experimental Method and the Science of Society; an Approach to a New Political Orientation*. Beacon, N.Y.: Beacon House.

—— (1953), *Who Shall Survive?* Beacon, N.Y.: Beacon House.

—— (1954), Interpersonal Therapy, Group Psychotherapy and the Function of the Unconscious. *Group Psychother., 7*:191-204.

—— & Moreno, Z. T. (1960), An Objective Analysis of the Group Psychotherapy Movement. *Group Psychother., 13*:233-237.

Mullan, H. (1953), Conflict Avoidance in Group Psychotherapy. *Int. J. Group Psychother., 3*:243-253.

—— (1955a), Status Denial in Group Psychoanalysis. *J. Nerv. & Ment. Diseases, 122*:345-353.

—— (1955b), The Group Analyst's Creative Function. *Am. J. Psychother., 9*:320-334.

—— (1955c), Transference and Countertransference: New Horizons. *Int. J. Group Psychother., 5*:169-180.

—— (1956), The Nonteleological in Dreams in Group Psychotherapy. *J. Hillside Hosp., 5*:480-487.

—— (1957), The Group Patient as a Therapist. *Psychiatric Quarterly, Supp. Part 1*. Utica, N.Y.: State Hospital Press.

—— & Sangiuliano, I. A. (1958), Interpretation as Existence in Analysis. *Psychoanal. & Psychoanal. Rev., 45*:52-64.

Munroe, R. L. (1955), *Schools of Psychoanalytic Thought; an Exposition, Critique, and Attempt at Integration*. New York: Dryden Press.

Murphy, G. (1930), *An Historical Introduction to Modern Psychology*. London: Kegan Paul (Revised edition, New York: Harcourt, 1949).

Newcomb, T. M. (1943), *Personality and Social Change*. New York: Dryden Press.

Overholser, W. & Enneis, J. (1960), Twenty Years of Psychodrama at St. Elizabeth's Hospital. In: *Psychodrama and Group Psychotherapy, Monog. 36*. Beacon, N.Y.: Beacon House.

Papanek, H. (1956), Combined Group and Individual Therapy in the Light of Adlerian Psychology. *Int. J. Group Psychother.*, 6:136-146.

———— (1959), Emotion and Intellect in Psychotherapy. *Am. J. Psychother.*, 13:150-173.

———— (1961), The Adlerian Viewpoint in Group Psychoanalysis. Read at Association of Medical Group Psychoanalysts, June 3, 1961.

Parsons, T. & Bales, R. F. (1955), *Family Socialization; an Interaction Process*. Glencoe, Ill.: Free Press.

Peck, H. B. (1951), Group Psychotherapy and Mental Health. *Int. J. Group Psychother.*, 1:301-310.

———— (1961), Intergroup Patterns: a Mental Health Approach. *Int. J. Group Psychother.*, 11:387-397.

———— (1963), The Role of a Psychiatric Day Hospital: a Group Process Approach. *Am. J. Orthopsychiat.*, 33:482-493.

Preston, M. G. & Heintz, R. K. (1949), Effects of Participatory versus Supervisory Leadership on Group Judgment. *J. Abn & Soc. Psychol.*, 44:345.

Racker, H. (1957), The Meanings and Uses of Countertransference. *Psychoanal. Quart.*, 26:303.

Radke, M. & Klisurich, D. (1947), Experiments in Changing Food Habits. *J. Am. Dietetics Assn.*, 23: 403-409.

Rangell, L. (1954), Panel Report: Psychoanalysis and Dynamic Psychotherapy. *J. Am. Psychoanal. Assn.*, 2:152-166.

Redl, F. (1942), Group Emotion and Leadership. *Psychiatry, 5*: 573-596.

———— (1949), The Phenomenon of Contagion and "Shock Effect" in Group Therapy. In: *Searchlights on Delinquency*, ed. K. R. Eissler. New York: International Universities Press, pp. 315-328.

Reich, A. (1960), Pathologic Forms of Self-Esteem Regulation. In: *The Psychoanalytic Study of the Child, XV*, eds. R. S. Eissler et al. New York: International Universities Press, pp. 215-232.

Reich, W. (1933), *Character-Analysis: Principles and Techniques for Psychoanalysts in Practice and in Training*. New York: Orgone Institute Press, Second edition, 1945.

Renouvier, P. (1958), The Group Psychotherapy Movement and J. L. Moreno, Its Pioneer and Founder. *Group Psychother., 11*:69-85.

Roman, M. & Bauman, G. (1961), Interaction Testing: a Research Approach. *Int. J. Group Psychother., 11*:382-387.

Rose, S. (1957), Horney Concepts in Group Psychotherapy. *Int. J. Group Psychother., 7*:376-384.

Ross, I. C. & Harary, F. (1955), Identification of the Liaison Persons of an Organization Using the Structure Matrix. *Magt. Sci., 1*:251-258.

Ruesch, J. (1961), *Therapeutic Communication*. New York: Norton.

——— & Bateson, G. (1951), *Communication, the Social Matrix of Psychiatry*. New York: Norton.

Sager, C. (1960), Concurrent Individual and Group Analytic Psychotherapy. *Am. J. Orthopsychiat., 33*:225-241.

Sartre, J. P. (1948), *Existentialism and Human Emotions*. New York: Philosophical Library.

Schaffner, M. D. (1957), *Group Process*. New York: Josiah Macy, Jr. Foundation.

Scheidlinger, S. (1952a), *Psychoanalysis and Group Behavior; a Study of Freudian Group Psychology*. New York: Norton.

——— (1952b), Freudian Group Psychology and Group Psychotherapy. *Am. J. Orthopsychiat., 22*:710-717.

——— (1955), The Concept of Identification in Group Psychotherapy. *Am. J. Psychother., 9*:661-672.

——— (1960), Group Process in Group Psychotherapy, I & II. *Am. J. Psychother., 14*:104-120, 346-363.

Schilder, P. (1938), *Psychotherapy*. New York: Norton. Revised and enlarged edition by Lauretta Bender, 1951.

Schutz, W. C. (1958a), *FIRO: A Three-Dimensional Theory of Interpersonal Behavior*. New York: Rinehart.

———— (1958b), The Group Mind Revisited. Expansion of paper read at Eastern Psychological Association Meeting, Philadelphia.

———— (1961), The Ego as Leader. In: *Leadership and Interpersonal Behavior,* eds. L. Petrullo & B. M. Bass. New York: Holt, Rinehart & Winston, Chap. 4.

Schwartz, G. & Bishop, P. (1958), *Moments of Discovery,* Vol. I & II. New York: Basic Books.

Semrad, E. & Arsenian, J. (1951), The Use of Group Process Group Dynamics. *Am. J. Psychiat., 108*:358-363.

Shea, J. E. et al. (1958), Some Theoretical Concepts Underlying the Relationship Between Individual and Group Psychotherapies. *Int. J. Group Psychother., 8*:3-19.

Sherif, M. (1936), *The Psychology of Social Norms.* New York: Harper.

Slavson, S. R. (1953), Common Sources of Error and Confusion in Group Psychotherapy. *Int. J. Group Psychother., 3*:3-28.

———— (1956), *The Fields of Group Psychotherapy.* New York: International Universities Press.

———— (1960a), When is a "Therapy Group" not a Therapy Group? *Int. J. Group Psychother., 10*:3-21.

———— (1960b), Parallelisms in the Development of Group Psychotherapy. Presented at A.G.P.A. Conference, January, 1960.

Spitz, R. (1945), Hospitalism: an Inquiry into the Genesis of Psychiatric Conditions in Early Childhood. In: *The Psychoanalytic Study of the Child, I,* eds. R. S. Eissler et al. New York: International Universities Press, pp. 53-74.

———— (1959), *A Genetic Field Theory of Ego Formation.* New York: International Universities Press.

Stock, D. (1962), Interpersonal Concerns During the Early Sessions of Therapy Groups. *Int. J. Group Psychother., 12*: 14-26.

———— & Lieberman, M. (1960), *Psychological Issues in the Assessment of Total Group Phenomenon in Group Therapy.* Chicago: University of Chicago, Dept. of Psychiatry.

———— & Thelen, H. (1954), *Methods for Studying Work and Emotionality in Group Operations.* Chicago: University of Chicago Press.

——— & ——— (1958), *Emotional Dynamics and Group Culture*. Washington: National Training Publication.

——— & Whitman, R. M. (1958), The Deviant Member in Therapy Groups. *Human Relations, 11*:341.

Syz, H. (1961), Problems of Perspective Against the Background of Trigant Burrow's Group-Analytic Researches. *Int. J. Group Psychother., 11*:143-165.

Thelen, H. (1954), *Dynamics of Group at Work*. Chicago: University of Chicago Press.

——— et al. (1954), *Methods of Studying Group Operation*. Chicago: Human Dynamics Laboratory.

Thurstone, L. L. (1928), *The Measurement of Attitude*. Chicago: University of Chicago Press.

Weakland, J. (1962), Family Therapy as a Research Area. *Family Process, 1*:63.

Whitaker, C. A. & Malone, T. P. (1953), *The Roots of Psychotherapy*. New York: Blakiston.

——— & Warkentin, J., *Spontaneous Interaction in Group Psychotherapy*. Atlanta, Ga.: Atlanta Psychiatric Clinic.

White, L. D. (1956), *The State of the Social Sciences*. Chicago: University of Chicago Press.

Whitman, R. M., Lieberman, M. A., & Stock, D. (1960), The Relation Between Individual and Group Conflicts in Psychotherapy. *Int. J. Group Psychother., 10*:259-286.

Wolf, A. (1949-1950), The Psychoanalysis of Groups. *Am. J. Psychother., 3*:525-558; *4*:16-50.

——— & Schwartz, E. K. (1958), Irrational Trends in Psychotherapy. *Am. J. Psychother., 12*:300-315, 508-522, 744-766; *13*: 383-401, 1959.

——— & ——— (1960), The Mystique of Group Dynamics. In: *Topical Problems, Psychotherapy, Vol. II*. New York: Karger. pp. 119-154.

Name Index

Subject Index